Transnational Traditions

Transnational
TRADITIONS

▼ ▲ ▼

New Perspectives
on American Jewish History

Edited by Ava F. Kahn and Adam D. Mendelsohn

Wayne State University Press

Detroit

18 17 16 15 14   5 4 3 2 1

Library of Congress Control Number: 2014936561
ISBN 978-0-8143-3861-2 (paperback)
ISBN 978-0-8143-3862-9 (e-book)

Permission to excerpt or adapt certain passages from
Joan G. Roland, "Negotiating Identity: Being Indian and Jewish in America,"
Journal of Indo-Judaic Studies 13 (2013): 23–35
has been granted by Nathan Katz, editor.

Excerpts from Joan G. Roland, "Transformation of Indian Identity
among Bene Israel in Israel," in *Israel in the Nineties,* ed. Fredrick Lazin
and Gregory Mahler (Gainesville: University Press of Florida, 1996), 169–93,
reprinted with permission of the University Press of Florida.

Designed and typeset by Bryce Schimanski
Composed in Chapparal Pro and Bodonitown

CONTENTS

PART III
The Immigrant as Transnational

▼ ▲ ▼

PART IV
Creating New Homelands in Argentina, America, and Israel

▼ ▲ ▼

ACKNOWLEDGMENTS

No book can be completed without the considerable help of critical readers, obliging archivists, thoughtful colleagues, and supportive friends and family. First and foremost, we thank the contributors to this volume, without whom the publication would not exist. All worked diligently with us to produce this volume. Also important for a publication are encouraging editors. At Wayne State University Press, we thank production editor Kristin Harpster and editor-in-chief Kathryn Peterson Wildfong, who has remained patient and supportive throughout the publication process. Kathryn selected two thoughtful reviewers whose detailed feedback on an earlier version of the manuscript led to revisions and a much-improved publication. We thank them for their time and insight.

We are also indebted to archival and library staffs who helped us secure photographic images and research materials. We are particularly grateful to Philip Moses of the Australian Jewish Historical Society, Matthÿs van der Merwe of the Iziko Museums of South Africa, and Susan Snyder of the Bancroft Library of the University of California, Berkeley. It is always a pleasure to work with Kevin Proffitt, the Senior Archivist for Research and Collections at the Marcus Center of the American Jewish Archives. Dr. Gary P. Zola, Executive Director, and Eliza Ho, Associate Archivist at the Archives also helped us in securing images. We thank them. The leadership of Hadassah generously supplied unprecedented access to their archives when conducting the research for chapter 11. Their help and that of the American Jewish Historical Society where their records are housed is much appreciated.

Now for personal thank-yous. I benefited from colleagues who commented on conference papers presented at the Organization of American Historians and the Western Association of Jewish Studies. Also, heartfelt thanks to friends and colleagues who read versions of chapters: Ellen Eisenberg, Norm Frankel, Ruth Haber, and my husband, Mitchell Richman.

A.F.K.

This project, itself a long time in the making, coincided with the birth and first two years of my son's life. My thanks to my forbearing wife, and to Sam, who has made our lives so much fuller and funner.

A.D.M.

Transnational Traditions

INTRODUCTION

Simultaneously celebrated as a *goldene medina* (golden land) by Jews attracted to its many wonders and stigmatized as a *treyfe medina* (impure land) by those leery of its freedoms, America has long occupied an outsized position within the Jewish imagination. The success of Jews in the United States, and the tragic fate of many of their counterparts in Europe before and during the Holocaust, crystallized the idea in the minds of many American Jews that they dwelled in an exceptional land. While not particular to Jews and those who study them, such claims of exceptionalism have been difficult to displace. All too often, the trends and challenges encountered by American Jews have been held up as unique. American Jewish history has often been depicted as a subject that starts and stops at the US border. According to this telling, Jewish newcomers jettisoned their past connections upon reaching American soil. Historians of the United States in general felt little inclination to look beyond America's shores. Historians of American Jewry often have had particular reason to limit their purview. Eager to weave Jews into the American narrative, some may have been reluctant to look for American Jewish history abroad. Others may have been concerned that by harping on the ebb and flow of connections between Old World and New they would play into the hands of those suspicious of the loyalties and political proclivities of America Jews. Many may have been daunted by the linguistic, financial, and temporal demands of following immigrants back to their point of origin. Still others, perhaps conscious that American Jewish history is a comparatively new field, may have been satisfied that there was more than enough new territory to explore if they confined their focus exclusively to the United States.

This book reflects the efforts of contemporary historians to push back against the assumption that the experience of Jews in the United States can best be understood apart from the experiences of Jews elsewhere. Contributing authors to this volume seek to plug American Jewish history back into the wiring of Jewish life abroad. Rather than assume that American Jewry has been the passive recipient of ideas, identities, and trends carried to its shores—that influences flowed in one direction only—several of the chapters demonstrate how American Jews shaped elements of Jewish life in Europe and Israel. In identifying elements of the American Jewish experience that are transnational—that cross political boundaries—the contributors to this volume are aiding in a broader rethinking of American, and indeed modern, Jewish history.

For although Jews are the archetypal diasporic people, they have more often been studied by modern historians as citizens and subjects of single nation-states and empires—as American, Australian, Austro-Hungarian, Polish, Russian, or German Jews—than as a people whose traditions, identity, sense of solidarity, and commercial, social, and religious connections crossed borders, regions, and even oceans. This was not always the case. Heinrich Graetz, Simon Dubnow, and Salo Baron—the leading lights of earlier eras of historical writing about Jews—each composed multivolume surveys that identified unifying trends, themes, and processes that transcended political boundaries. Moshe Rosman, an eminent historian of modern Jewry, recently lamented that the soaring ambition of this earlier "transgeographical" approach has given way to a "national model of history-writing" focused on the narrower goal of seeking to understand how Jews influenced and were influenced by specific geographic contexts. If the "older histories discounted political geography," Rosman writes, "the newer ones privileged it." Rosman wondered whether the "political–geographical framework," for all of its advantages, has unintentionally blinded the "researcher to connections that may compose other contexts that might be more important and prompt a different overall view of the relations between Jews, non-Jews, and other Jews."[1]

Rosman's clarion call for a new transnational approach to writing about Jews in the modern world—a history that is sensitive to local context but also appreciates the interconnections, commonalities, and areas of overlap between communities—echoes that of scholars within several other fields of history. Among historians of America, Thomas Bender has become the loudest cheerleader for what he and others have described as "global history."[2] But he is far from alone: in 2009, the American Historical Association selected "globalizing historiography" as the theme of its conference. More and more scholars have begun to produce works that have fulfilled the broad ambition of eliding the national and the transnational. Unsurprisingly, some of the best work has been produced within fields that have maintained at least one eye focused abroad. In recent years, immigration historians have tightened their focus on the flow of migrants back to their point of origin, the continuing ties between immigrants and their homelands, and the complexities of immigrant identities.[3] A new crop of diplomatic historians have sought to situate "America in the world" by examining how the United States and its actions are understood from abroad.[4] And intellectual historians have traced how racial, legal, and political concepts moved backward and forward across oceans and borders, molding national identities and shaping thought and behavior.[5]

Historians of American Jewry have been somewhat slower to follow their lead but are well positioned to contribute to the broader dialogue. Consideration of Jews may well add a welcome level of complexity and nuance to discussion of transnational political identities (did Jews think of homeland in the same ways as other immigrants? How did their political affiliations and behaviors differ from that of other newcomers?), religious identities (to what extent do national contexts shape the contours of religious identification? Did Jewish institutions adapt to America in ways that were different from more hierarchical religious groups?), and economic networks (were Jewish commercial networks distinct? Have Jews related to capitalism in ways that are different from other ethnic groups in America?). As these potential avenues of inquiry suggest, transnational studies of America, and its Jews, will profit from asking comparative questions.

Not that historians of American Jewry have ignored this methodology entirely. The transnational approach has made its deepest inroads in the field of American Jewish history among those who study the colonial period. This largely reflects the growing interest in Atlantic history and the application of its methodology to Jewish settlement in the New World. While the majority of this work on Jews in the Atlantic world has examined the Dutch and Portuguese maritime empires, an increasing amount of research deals with the British Atlantic.[6] Some of this new scholarship applies the concept of Port Jews—perhaps the most innovative recent reinterpretation of the origins of Jewish modernity—to Jewish life in Charleston, Newport, Savannah, and New York.[7] North American and Caribbean Jewry have been placed into a larger matrix of social and religious interaction, intellectual cross-fertilization, and mercantile interdependence within the Atlantic world.[8] As in the broader field of Atlantic history, these studies have focused predominantly on the seventeenth and eighteenth centuries and almost uniformly terminate before 1825. Only recently has the Port Jewry paradigm been applied to a later epoch in American Jewish history.[9]

A handful of historians have productively applied comparative and transnational methodologies to analyze major themes in the nineteenth and twentieth centuries. Some earlier work looked for British and Caribbean influences on American developments. Bertram Korn, Jacob Rader Marcus, Maxwell Whiteman, and Stanley Chyet placed Jews who lived in America during the early national period into a context of contact and interaction with the Caribbean.[10] Jacob Neusner collated the contributions of a number of Anglo-Jewish immigrants to Jewish life in the United States in the nineteenth century. None followed his lead until relatively recently when Dianne Ashton, Michael Galchinsky, and Arthur Kiron began to trace the cultural bonds that linked Jews in Britain and America during the Victorian age.[11] Far more attention has been devoted to the cultural and religious baggage carried by central and Eastern European immigrants to America's shores. For a time several scholars engaged in a lively debate about the genesis of the Reform movement in the United States, which pitted those who argued for autochthonic origins against proponents of German influences.[12] More recently, a handful of historians of the "German" wave of European immigration to America have become far more attentive to the immigrants' origins and their continuing contacts with the *heimat*.[13] Others have profitably applied a comparative approach to the period of Eastern European mass migration—comparing, for example, the dense immigrant communities created in the Pletzl in Paris with the Lower East Side in New York City—and a handful have produced sophisticated studies using a transnational methodology.[14]

Although more modest in ambition than the agendas proposed by the likes of Bender and Rosman, the essays in this book contribute to their respective goals of producing transnational histories of America and its Jews. Our authors, leading scholars of American, Australian, Indian, Chinese, and Anglo-Jewry, reflect on episodes of continuity and contact between Jews in America and those elsewhere over the past two centuries. They employ transnational and comparative methodologies to place American Jewry into a broader context of cultural, mercantile, and social interchange with Jews in Europe, the Middle East, Asia, Australia, New Zealand, and South America. Together the essays challenge a historiographic tradition that has often examined Jewish communities in these regions as discrete units, ascribing developments primarily to local or national factors and deemphasizing the cross-currents that accelerated change here and abroad. Collectively these authors argue that the examination of patterns across national boundaries provides an essential context for understanding developments within American Jewry and the differences between Jewish life in America with that elsewhere. Unlike Graetz, Dubnow, and Baron, our contributors have identified areas of mutual influence and interaction between Jews in America and those elsewhere, rather than seeking overarching themes and unifying narratives.

Chosen because they inform and enrich our understanding of American and world Jewry, each of the chapters in this volume supplies a different perspective and approach to understanding the connections, real and imagined, between Jews in America and those abroad. Some chapters are comparative, contrasting the experience of particular subsets of Jews in two national contexts, while the majority are transnational in focus. This collection pushes the discussion of transnational and comparative American Jewish history forward by collectively posing several questions, not all of which have ready answers. How and why are certain ideas and concepts transmitted across borders? What does it mean to call someone a transnational? How is transnational behavior manifest? What is distinctive about American Jewry and the American Jewish experience? How has American Jewry influenced Jewry beyond its borders? How should one study Jewry in relationship to national identity?

In this volume we use the term "transnational" in two distinct but equally important ways. First, we use "transnational" as a descriptive term to explain cultural, religious, social, institutional, and economic linkages that spanned political borders and boundaries. Here we emphasize crosscutting connections between Jewish populations that have hitherto been treated by historians as separate. Second, we use it in its noun form as a distinct alternative to the term "migrant." Given the relatively low rate of return migration among Jewish immigrants to America, the latter term, when applied to this group, often implies dwindling connections to a now distant homeland and a transition to a new and dominant form of identity associated with the United States. Far from leaving their existing identities behind when entering and exiting America, many Jewish migrants acted as transnationals who carried multiple identities with them as cultural cargo wherever they went. At the same time, we follow Elliott Barkan's lead in recognizing that "immigrant experiences actually span a full spectrum of newcomer responses from disengagement from one's society of origin at one end to extensive, transnational engagement in homeland affairs at the other."[15] As several of the chapters in this volume illustrate, Jewish immigrant identities were dynamic, durable, overlapping, porous, and unpredictable. Instead of being diluted or disappearing, identities could be reimagined—given fresh meaning and life—in a new environment.

The chapters are grouped into four thematic sections. The first explores a set of new threads that connected Jews in the United States with those in the expanding settlement colonies of the British Empire in the mid–nineteenth century. As the chapters reveal, some of these connections were the product of changes within Jewish life; others were the consequence of broader historical events. The chapters in section two examine unfamiliar economic dimensions of Eastern European mass migration to the United States. As we will see, the act of immigrating created multidirectional economic opportunities. The third section discusses the transformations of immigrant identities in the United States and the complex manifestations that identity took. And the final chapters of this volume explore how context shaped the emergence of Jewish identities in America and abroad. Collectively these essays are intended to encourage further thought and research on the transnational connections between American Jews and those in the wider Jewish world. The chapters reveal how essential a sensitive understanding of context is. At the same time they reveal how broadening the context beyond America's shores can provide new perspectives on American Jewish history. This is not a project that will undermine the study of Jews in the United States, but will enrich it.

Notes

1. Moshe Rosman, "Jewish History across Borders," in *Rethinking European Jewish History*, ed. Jeremy Cohen and Moshe Rosman (Portland, OR: Oxford, 2009), 15–29.
2. Thomas Bender, ed., *Rethinking American History in a Global Age* (Berkeley: University of California Press, 2002); Thomas Bender, *A Nation among Nations: America's Place in World History* (New York: Hill and Wang, 2006).
3. See, e.g., James Belich, *Replenishing the Earth: The Settler Revolution and the Rise of the Anglo-World, 1783–1939* (New York: Oxford University Press, 2009); Madeline Hsu, Dreaming of Gold, Dreaming of Home: Transnationalism and Migration between the United States and South China (Stanford, CA: Stanford University Press, 2000); Eiichiro Azuma, Between Two Empires: Race, History, and Transnationalism in Japanese America (New York: Oxford University Press, 2005); Matthew Frye Jacobson, *Special Sorrows: The Diasporic Imagination of Irish, Polish, and Jewish Immigrants in the United States* (Cambridge, MA: Harvard University Press, 1995).
4. Andrew Zimmerman, *Alabama in Africa: Booker T. Washington, German Empire, and the Globalization of the New South* (Princeton, NJ: Princeton University Press, 2010);

Erez Manela, *The Wilsonian Moment: Self-Determination and the International Origins of Nationalist Anti-Colonialism* (New York: Oxford University Press, 2007).

5. Kariann Yokota, *Unbecoming British: How Revolutionary America Became a Postcolonial Nation* (New York: Oxford University Press, 2011); Christopher Tomlins, *Freedom Bound: Labor, Law and Civic Identity in Colonizing English America* (New York: Cambridge University Press, 2010).

6. See, e.g., Jonathan Israel's pathbreaking scholarship collected in *Diasporas within a Diaspora: Jews, Crypto-Jews and the World Maritime Empires (1540–1740)* (Leiden, Netherlands: Brill, 2002) as well as Francesca Trivellato, *The Familiarity of Strangers: The Sephardic Diaspora, Livorno, and Cross-Cultural Trade in the Early Modern Period* (New Haven, CT: Yale University Press, 2009); Paolo Bernardini and Norman Fiering, eds., *The Jews and the Expansion of Europe to the West, 1450–1800* (New York: Berghahn, 2001).

7. For the concept of Port Jewry, see Lois Dubin, *The Port Jews of Habsburg Trieste: Absolutist Politics and Enlightenment Culture* (Stanford, CA: Stanford University Press, 1999); David Sorkin, "The Port Jew: Notes toward a Social Type," *Journal of Jewish Studies* 50, no. 1 (1999): 87–97; David Cesarani, "Port Jews: Concepts, Cases and Questions," *Jewish Culture and History* 4 (winter 2001): 1–11 as well as the following journal issues devoted to Port Jewry: *Jewish Culture and History* 4 (2001); 7 (2004); and *Jewish History* 20 (June 2006).

8. See Eli Faber, *A Time for Planting; The First Migration, 1654–1820* (Baltimore: Johns Hopkins University Press, 1992); Jonathan Schorsch, *Jews and Blacks in the Early Modern World* (New York: Cambridge University Press, 2004); Holly Snyder, "A Sense of Place: Jews, Identity and Social Status in Colonial British America, 1654–1831" (PhD diss., Brandeis University, 2000).

9. Arthur Kiron, "An Atlantic Jewish Republic of Letters?" *Jewish History* 20 (June 2006): 171–211.

10. See Bertram Korn, *The Early Jews of New Orleans* (Waltham, MA: American Jewish Historical Society, 1969); Stanley Chyet, *Lopez of Newport* (Detroit: Wayne State University Press, 1970); Maxwell Whiteman, *Copper for America* (New Brunswick, NJ: Rutgers University Press, 1971). In addition to his scholarship, Marcus actively collected primary sources from the Caribbean for the American Jewish Archives.

11. Jacob Neusner, "The Role of English Jews in the Development of American Jewish Life, 1775–1850," *Yivo Annual of Jewish Social Science* 12 (1959): 131–56; Neusner, "Anglo-Jewry and the Development of American Jewish Life, 1775–1850," *The Jewish Historical Society of England-Transactions* 18 (1955): 231–42. See also Hyman Grinstein, *The Rise of the Jewish Community of New York, 1654–1860* (Philadelphia: The Jewish Publication Society, 1947); Israel Goldstein, *A Century of Judaism in New York: B'nai Jeshurun, 1825–1925* (New York: Congregation B'nai Jeshurun, 1930), 323–30. For more recent scholarship, see Arthur Kiron, "Golden Ages, Promised Lands: The Victorian Rabbinic Humanism of Sabato Morais" (PhD diss., Columbia University, 1999); Dianne Ashton, *Rebecca Gratz: Women and Judaism in Antebellum America* (Detroit: Wayne State University Press, 1997); Dianne Ashton, "Crossing Boundaries: The Career of Mary M. Cohen," *American Jewish History* 83 (1995): 153–76; Michael Galchinsky, *The Origin of the Modern Jewish Writer: Romance and Reform in Victorian England* (Detroit: Wayne State University Press, 1996); Michael Galchinsky, "Grace Aguilar's Correspondence," *Jewish Culture and History* 2 (1999): 88–110.

12. The skirmishing has diminished since Michael Meyer published *Response to Modernity: A History of the Reform Movement in Judaism* (New York: Oxford University Press, 1988), which balances indigenous influences against international trends.

13. See Avraham Barkai, *Branching Out: German-Jewish Immigration to the United States, 1820–1914* (New York: Holmes & Meier, 1994); Tobias Brinkmann, *Von der Gemeinde zur "Community": Jüdische Einwanderer in Chicago, 1840–1900* (Osnäbruck, Germany: Rasch Verlag, 2002); Hasia Diner, *A Time for Gathering: The Second Migration, 1820–1880* (Baltimore: Johns Hopkins University Press, 1992).

14. For comparative literature that deals with this later period, see several works comparing Jewish immigrant life in Paris and New York by Nancy L. Green; Lloyd Gartner, *American and British Jews in the Age of the Great Migration* (Portland, OR: Vallentine Mitchell, 2009); Selma Cantor Berrol, *East Side/East End: Eastern European Jews in London and New York, 1870–1920* (Westport, CT: Praeger, 1994); Linda Kuzmack, *Woman's Cause: The Jewish Woman's Movement in England and the United States, 1881–1933* (Columbus: Ohio State University Press, 1990); Andrew S. Reutlinger, "Reflections on the Anglo-American Jewish Experience: Immigrants, Workers, and Entrepreneurs in New York and London, 1870–1914," *American Jewish Historical Quarterly* 66 (1977): 473–84; Susan Tananbaum, "'Morally Depraved and Abnormally Criminal': Jews and Crime in London and New York, 1880–1940," in *Forging Modern Jewish Identities: Public Faces and Private Struggles*, ed. Michael Berkowitz, Susan Tananbaum, and Sam Bloom (Portland, OR: Vallentine Mitchell, 2003), 115–39. For a transnational approach, see Nancy Sinkoff, "Benjamin Franklin in Jewish Eastern Europe: Cultural Appropriation in the Age of the Enlightenment," *Journal of the History of Ideas* 61 (2000): 133–52; Sarah Abrevaya Stein, *Plumes: Ostrich Feathers, Jews, and a Lost World of Global Commerce* (New Haven, CT: Yale University Press, 2008); Eli Lederhendler, *Jewish Immigrants and American Capitalism, 1880–1920: From Caste to Class* (New York: Cambridge University Press, 2009); Tony Michels, *A Fire in Their Heart: Yiddish Socialists in New York* (Cambridge, MA: Harvard University Press, 2009); Rebecca Kobrin, *Jewish Bialystok and Its Diaspora* (Bloomington: Indiana University Press, 2010); David Slucki, *The International Jewish Labor Bund after 1945: Toward a Global History* (New York: Rutgers University Press, 2011).

15. Elliott Barkan, "America in the Hand, Homeland in the Heart: Transnational and Translocal Immigrant Experiences in the American West," *Western Historical Quarterly* 35, no. 3 (2004): 332.

PART I

An Anglophone Diaspora

Why begin with the Jewish Anglophone diaspora in a book about American Jewish history? The answer lies in the striking mobility of the mid–nineteenth century, a period in which American ports welcomed newcomers in unprecedented numbers and advances in sea travel intertwined lives across oceans. Men and women traveled freely (or in the case of some from Britain, as convicts) between England, Australia, New Zealand, Hawaii, and the United States. They sought new economic opportunities and enthusiastically seized the opportunities presented by long-distance travel. It was a time of rapid change, new ideas, optimism, and hunger for quick wealth. This section illustrates how commercial, religious, and family connections across the Anglophone Jewish world were influenced by and, in turn, influenced America.

Becoming a transnational in the mid–nineteenth century often involved sea travel. Faster and more reliable ships created new commercial markets, including new employment possibilities for rabbis and hazans. Transoceanic travel also facilitated the spread of ideas, carried in the heads and hearts of migrants, and in the books and newspapers they brought with them. The chapters in this section highlight a small (and overlapping) group of historical players, whose careers demonstrate how the spread of commercial networks and ideas often coincided and intertwined.

Some of the unexpected implications of travel between America and other Anglophone destinations are broached by Adam Mendelsohn in "The Sacrifices of the Isaacs." This chapter explores the emergence of an international marketplace for eloquent English-speaking Jewish ministers. Mendelsohn focuses on three brothers who led congregations on three continents: one at the center of Anglophone Jewish life in Britain, another in the United States, and a third in then remote Australia. Their careers displayed the parallel and intertwined development of religious leadership in the English-speaking world. Religious leaders in Britain's colonies and in the United States grappled with a shifting religious milieu that was complicated by their distance from the mainsprings of Jewish life. Mendelsohn explains how the convergence of cultural expectations created opportunities for rabbis to move between English-speaking countries. Congregations now expected their officiants to attract new members to their worship services—to keep Jews in the pews. Beyond the pulpit, Mendelsohn demonstrates that rabbis played a leading role in establishing a transnational Jewish press.

The extended reach of Anglophone Jewry connects chapters one and two. In much the same way that nineteenth-century rabbis traveled from colonial pulpit to colonial pulpit, some Anglophones, rabbinic and lay, traveled across the Pacific Rim. In "Roaming the Rim" Kahn explores how adventurers, merchants, and religious leaders, lured by gold rushes and other economic opportunities, circulated along the Pacific Rim from Dunedin, New Zealand to Victoria, British Columbia. In doing so, she challenges "the common understanding that Jewish communities on California's coast thrived solely because of the influx of Jews from the eastern United States and Europe." Kahn concludes that these Pacific Rim connections created new patterns of transmigration. These same themes are explored across a longer time period in chapter three "Creating Transnational Connections: Australia and California." Suzanne Rutland emphasizes the role played by Australian Jewish businessmen in developing California markets. In this chapter, Rutland focuses on two case studies, one from the nineteenth century and another from the twentieth, that reveal the importance of commercial links across the Rim and demonstrate how these connections have shifted over the past two centuries.

All three chapters demonstrate the value of considering the American Jewish experience in relationship to the broader Anglophone Jewish diaspora. Our understanding of Jewish life in Australia, Britain, and other parts of the English-speaking world gains in nuance, much as we gain a clearer appreciation of what is distinct and what familiar in American Jewish history.

1

THE SACRIFICES OF THE ISAACS

The Diffusion of New Models of Religious Leadership in the English-Speaking Jewish World

Adam D. Mendelsohn

To the eyes of many contemporary observers, the Jewish body politic in the United States and the British Empire appeared to be in crisis in the middle of the nineteenth century: bloated by immigration, plagued by low levels of synagogue affiliation and high rates of intermarriage, and struggling to adapt Jewish institutions to the free-wheeling circumstances of liberal societies.[1] American Jewry alone grew almost tenfold between 1840 and 1860. Although Anglo-Jewry grew more slowly, existing communal structures struggled to cope with a vast influx of transmigrants on their way to America.[2] In Australia and South Africa, Jewish settlers created a panoply of institutions from scratch, even as they coped with a significant gender imbalance and the difficulties begot of their distance from the mainsprings of Jewish life. Religious freedom presented a stern challenge to communal solidity in each of these contexts. As affiliation became elective and traditional powers of communal coercion decayed, synagogues scrambled to adapt. Congregations not only began to compete for members among themselves but also contended with rival confraternities that promised an alternative secular space for fellowship. A variety of Jewish leaders in the United States and the British Empire grappled with the implications of this new religious marketplace.

One key response, the radical reshaping of religious leadership during the middle decades of the nineteenth century, produced significant results. Synagogues from New Zealand to New York came to expect their hazans— very few of their officiants were trained and ordained rabbis—to provide a new carrot and shtick to lure Jews into the pews. Although this shift was intertwined with similar changes in Central Europe spurred by religious modernization, in America and the British Empire it took on a coloration shaded by its Anglophone context. This chapter explores the emergence of an international marketplace for Jewish ministers with particular skills who were in demand to fill pulpits across the English-speaking Jewish world. It takes as its case study three brothers whose careers chart the parallel and intertwined development of religious leadership on three continents. While their experiences point to commonalities in cultural and religious trends across political borders, they also reveal how local contexts had very real and very different implications for these three individuals. As the expectations attached to the role of religious leadership changed in the United States and British Empire, and a cohort of model ministers emerged, these and other hazans reshaped the rabbinate in the middle of the nineteenth century.

The New Model Minister

Prior to the 1840s, the responsibilities of hazans in the United States and the British Empire had largely been limited to leading prayer and performing a variety of duties that often included those of mohel—ritual circumciser—and *shochet*—kosher slaughterer. Drawing on innovations introduced in Central Europe, and influenced by the Christian milieu, Jewish innovators sought to transform the synagogue reader from a religious functionary who enjoyed limited authority and status into a "proper minister" who would supply "spiritual advice and guidance."[3] The new model minister was expected to perform the roles of preacher, pastor, and public figure. The keenest advocates of preaching on both sides of the Atlantic shared the conviction that pulpit instruction would address the ills that imperiled American and Anglo-Jewry. The introduction of regular vernacular sermons would restore "healthy religious sentiment" and "make religion lovely in the eyes of the multitude."[4] Ministerial responsibilities also shifted into the secular realm, reflecting the broad aspiration toward acceptance within the surrounding society. The model minister was expected to be the presentable and respectable public face of the community and its interlocutor with its Christian neighbors. The ideal hazan would be the counterpart and coequal of the Christian clergyman. The model minister was also obliged to assume extensive pastoral obligations, becoming actively involved in communal advocacy, fundraising, and administration. This privileging of preaching and public service transformed the role of the hitherto humble hazan.[5]

This change in understanding of the role of the hazan was interlinked with deeper changes within the Jewish community. Given the inadequacies of Jewish schooling in both England and America and the new expectation, tied to changing gender norms, that mothers should become the primary source of Jewish education for their children, the words of the hazan were accorded new significance. The introduction of the instructional sermon—the sermon for self-improvement—was intended to raise synagogue attendance and edify its audience.[6] Such a sermon would simultaneously sate the public appetite for popular education and introduce the audience—in many cases, the pews allotted to women in mid–nineteenth-century synagogues were full, but those allotted to men conspicuously empty—to the moral and theological tenets of Judaism. According to its proponents, the push for preaching would return "popular teaching" to its rightful place in the synagogue. Preaching also appealed to those who demanded that their religion adopt recognizable and respectable forms that would not inhibit Jewish acceptance into middle-class society. The sermon was restyled as a lecture and the preacher as a lecturer, "doctor," or "professor." This nomenclature served to elevate the importance of the preacher by drawing on the revered status of education in American and British society. The term "lecture" connoted educational and instructional content, suggested the seriousness and skills of the speaker, and implied the training and rigor of the academy.[7] Here Jewish innovators in America and the empire again drew heavily on the models of their Christian colleagues.[8]

The London *Jewish Chronicle,* for example, extolled the sermon as a "means of [producing] a powerful awakening of Jewish sentiment."[9] As this phrasing suggests, the success of evangelical preaching in galvanizing godliness provided a particularly alluring example. Britain and the United States were awash with revivalist preachers, and their message and methods had a demonstrable impact. Like their Christian counterparts, Jewish innovators argued that regular preaching in English was a necessary corrective for the deficiencies of religious education. The introduction of the vernacular sermon was also presented as the restoration of a practice that had biblical roots and that had fallen into disuse.[10] By contrast, the traditional *derashah* was denigrated as a sclerotic sermon, symptomatic of the primitive past.[11] But the success of the sermon depended on the speaker. The elevated educative role ascribed to the sermon required educated ministers of elevated status. In essence, Jewish communities from Australasia to America needed "enlightened men capable of being that to them which a learned ministry is to many gentile communities"[12]—hence the emergence of an informal and international ministerial marketplace where hazans with the requisite skills could seek employment in pulpits across the English-speaking Jewish world.

Yet very few of the men who ministered in synagogues in the United States and the British Empire prior to the 1840s were ordained or even formally trained. By promoting the professionalization of preaching, some hazans sought to alter the balance of power within the synagogue. The sermon would separate the hazan from the laity and act as a mark of professional distinction and differentiation. All could read the service, but only a specialist few could master the sermon. Isaac Leeser, the leading public proponent of traditional Judaism in America with a pulpit position, compared the "immense labor and research" required to write original sermons to "the quantity of literary labor which the best physician or the most erudite lawyer produces."[13] The plan to establish a college in London that would train hazans in both the Western classics and in traditional studies reflected this rethinking of the requirements of the rabbinate.[14] Over time as preaching, and not prayer, became the focal point of the service in many synagogues, the hazan came to occupy center stage.

Eloquent sermons, replete with the classical allusions and rhetorical style that pointed to a university education, provided an alternative source of legitimation for a rabbinate still grappling with the decline of its traditional role as arbiter of religious law (in free societies, fewer Jews cared to consult the Talmud in matters relating to their daily lives) and other challenges to its authority. If the *bet din*—the religious court—could be bypassed and Talmudic scholarship ignored, the stentorian hazan (and his steam-powered press) demanded the attention of a fickle flock. Proponents of preaching realized that its impact was limited to its immediate audience. The press could supplement the pulpit, spreading the preacher's message over vast distances. Again, the innovations of the Second Great Awakening were a source of inspiration. Just as the success of evangelical missionizing persuaded Jewish innovators to enhance the power of preaching, the industry and impact of evangelical publishers demonstrated the potential of the press. Evangelical movements grasped the implications of mass publishing, skillfully using it to communicate with their followers and to win new converts. Preachers and publishers marched in lockstep. Sermons were routinely reprinted in denominational newspapers as instructional and inspirational material. Printers also supplied a market of devoted readers who bought vast numbers of printed sermons.[15] Newspapers were regarded as an important adjunct to the sermon, and the press provided the means to preach to a dispersed Jewish population. The written word, and particularly the reprinted sermon, was seen to supply the education essential to revitalizing the Jewish community in the United States and the British Empire.

It was no coincidence that many of the pathbreaking preachers in America and the empire were also the pioneers of the English language Jewish press. Leeser (*Occident and American Jewish Advocate,* 1843), Samuel Myer Isaacs (*Jewish Messenger,* 1858), Isaac Mayer Wise (*American Israelite,* 1854), and Julius Eckman (*Weekly Gleaner,* 1857) all started their own newspapers.[16] Moses Nathan launched a monthly periodical, *First Fruits of the West,* in Kingston, Jamaica in 1844. In England, Morris Raphall started the *Hebrew Review and Magazine of Rabbinical Literature* (1834) and David Myer Isaacs edited the short-lived *Cup of Salvation* (1845). Jacob Franklin, founder of the *Voice of Jacob,* tried unsuccessfully to recruit Raphall as the newspaper's first editor.[17] These religious leaders, the majority of whom had been born in continental Europe, were receptive to the innovations of their Central European colleagues. They were certainly influenced by the example of Ludwig Philippson, who as a young preacher in 1837 started the *Allgemeine Zeitung des Judenthums,* and by the wave of Jewish newspapers founded following the Damascus affair.[18] All of these men recognized the potential of the press to reach and teach the dispersed Jewish communities of England and the United States. Moreover, the press provided a vehicle to advance their ambitions as educators, preachers, and self-publicists. The press would amplify their sermons across America and the British Empire and provide them with a huge new audience. The *Jewish Chronicle,* the *Voice of Jacob,* and the *Occident* routinely publicized, recorded, summarized, and critiqued sermons delivered by a variety of preachers.[19]

Hazans with saleable skills—foremost the ability to produce elegant pulpit oratory—benefited from the dramatic expansion of the Anglophone Jewish world. Those who could preach eloquently in English were a scarce commodity and were able to pursue the opportunities for personal and financial advancement that the English-speaking diaspora offered. Their reputations were carried across oceans and continents by the Jewish press that reprinted their sermons and sung their praises. Congregations in England competed with those in America, Australia, Canada, South Africa, and the Caribbean for a limited pool of hazans. The German congregation in Jamaica was careful to promise candidates for its vacant pulpit that the "dignity and emoluments of the post are equaled in very few home synagogues," pointing out the "many opportunities for a scholar to improve his income compatibly with his sacred functions."[20] American congregations poached a number of prominent preachers by offering salaries well above those of British synagogues.[21] Samuel Myer Isaacs moved from London to New York in 1839, swapping a low-status position for the pulpit of a leading New York congregation. Morris Raphall arranged a lecture tour to America in 1849, probably undertaken with an eye to finding alternative employment after his Birmingham congregation was forced to reduce his salary because of its own economic problems.[22]

The Brothers Isaacs

The careers of three brothers—Samuel, David, and Jacob Isaacs—neatly illustrates the diffusion of the new ministerial template across the Anglophone Jewish world as well as the potential mismatch between expectations and reality in the appointment and abilities of hazans. Although serving pulpits on different continents, these brothers were held to much the same standards in spite of the differences in duties, remuneration, and status they respectively enjoyed in each setting. In Liverpool and New York, David and Samuel Isaacs were regarded as exemplars of the new ministerial model. Jacob Isaacs, stranded in distant Sydney, was a victim of his siblings' success. When measured against a ministerial benchmark that had been bolstered by his brothers—Isaac Leeser singled out David and Samuel for particular praise for their homiletic skills—his services were seen as inadequate.[23] While they were themselves important agents of cultural transmission, Samuel, David, and Jacob Isaacs were bound by a common set of expectations and standards that had preceded them to their pulpits in Liverpool, New York, and Sydney.

Meyer Samuel Isaacs, the paterfamilias, was a successful merchant and speculator in Leeuwarden in Friesland at the turn of the nineteenth century. He had strong connections with England. His wife, Rebecca Samuels, came from an Anglo-Jewish family. As with many other Dutch Jewish merchants, Meyer Isaacs is likely to have traded with London. Certainly his business was badly affected by the British blockade of the ports of continental Europe during the Napoleonic Wars. Already deeply indebted by 1810, his financial position was ruined by the collapse of the value of his Dutch and French stocks after Napoleon's disastrous Russian offensive in 1812. Isaacs moved his family to London in 1814, following a stream of other Dutch Jewish merchants, traders, and poor immigrants who had already migrated in substantial numbers. Spitalfields, where the Isaacs family settled, was home to a Dutch Jewish enclave.[24] Meyer Isaacs became involved in Jewish education in London, opening a private Hebrew school in Spitalfields in 1818.[25] He was later appointed to the position of burial minister and Sabbath lecturer at the New Synagogue in London.[26]

Samuel

Meyer and Rebecca Isaacs had five sons (Samuel, Lewis, Jacob, David, and John) and one daughter (Rose). John became a successful businessman in New South Wales and Lewis apprenticed as a solicitor in London. Both John and Lewis were involved in Jewish communal life. Lewis became the house steward of the Hand-In-Hand Asylum for Jewish "decayed tradesmen" established in 1840 in part to rival a similar missionary institution. John served as a committee member of the infant York Street Synagogue in Sydney.[27] Three of their brothers, Samuel, Jacob, and David, traded on their religious upbringings to pursue careers as hazans. Samuel, the oldest of the Isaacs children, was born in Leeuwarden in 1804. His secular education—and perfect unaccented English—proved far more important for his later career than the religious lessons he received at a synagogue school. Samuel worked first as a Hebrew teacher and later as a principal at the Jews' Hospital. He also occasionally conducted services, and perhaps delivered sermons, at a synagogue in Bristol (where his brother David also briefly served as hazan).[28]

Samuel Isaacs's tepid prospects took a turn for the better in 1838, when he wrote to B'nai Jeshurun, an Ashkenazi congregation in New York, to apply for the newly created position of preacher and hazan. On the recommendation of an intermediary in London, the synagogue invited Isaacs to deliver a series of trial sermons to "judge his capabilities." The thirty-five-year-old Samuel married Jane Symons, twenty years his junior and probably his cousin, days before departing for New York.[29] After a honeymoon spent slowly crossing the Atlantic, Samuel arrived in September 1839. Clearly impressed with his preaching, B'nai Jeshurun appointed Samuel to the first pulpit position in the United States that required its incumbent to deliver regular sermons.[30] This predilection for preaching was probably linked to the Central European and English origins of many synagogue members, who may have become accustomed to hearing vernacular sermons in their homelands. Certainly the secessionists who splintered from B'nai Jeshurun in 1845 to form the rival Shaarey Tefila, taking Samuel with them, shared a common English orientation. (Four years later, B'nai Jeshurun recruited Morris Raphall, a prominent preacher from Birmingham who became America's first "celebrity rabbi," to fill Samuel's former pulpit.)[31]

During his stint at B'nai Jeshurun, Samuel delivered sermons at least once a month. By 1865, he preached every week. He rapidly developed a reputation as a powerful preacher; his orations reprinted in both the general and Jewish press. The *Occident* advertised his sermon schedule so that visitors to New York could hear him speak. Like Isaac Leeser, Samuel became a peripatetic preacher, invited to deliver sermons across the United States. By 1870 he had participated in the dedication ceremonies of more than forty-seven synagogues, a startling number that reveals the rapid growth of the American Jewish community. These occasions usually attracted large Christian audiences. Whist playing and Dickens reading, the urbane Samuel was at ease in both the secular and the religious realms. In effect, he became a presentable and respectable public face of American Judaism, able to impress status-conscious Jews and their Christian guests. He was sought after for other public events, speaking at school commencement exercises, institutional functions, charity evenings, and formal dinners. In 1845, he became the first Jewish minister to address the students of Yale University, and in 1865 he spoke at a mass funeral pageant for Abraham Lincoln in New York.[32]

Samuel also developed a reputation for outspokenness, lashing religious laxity and reform from the pulpit. To his mind, the American Jew needed to "adhere to every iota of his time hallowed creed" and not "permit one word of liturgy to be obliterated by the hand of innovation." Barely a year after his arrival from Britain, Samuel attempted to exclude members from B'nai Jeshurun who did not observe the Sabbath. Although unsuccessful, this effort demonstrated his willingness to embrace unpopular and exclusionary measures to defend tradition. He adopted a similarly stern position on conversion.[33] While approving Samuel's motivations, Isaac Leeser and others were critical of the tenor of his confrontational approach.[34]

Samuel had definite ideas about the appropriate status of the hazan, arguing forcefully for the prerogative of the minister in religious matters. He had little desire to be lorded over by the laity. Nor did he want to be confined to the role of a functionary expected "to chant a set number of tunes, to be a register of births, marriages, and deaths, to pay a number of visits to their respective members, to have a friendly chat with the female members, and to perform other trifling matters."[35] The minister should also command a professional salary. Samuel was certainly well compensated for his services.[36]

Yet with eight children, he had a large family to support. He supplemented his synagogue salary with special fees received for performing wedding ceremonies, emoluments for lending his imprimatur to local businesses and restaurants, and money generated by his Hebrew school. Samuel was entrepreneurial, selling books and religious articles from his home, including almanacs, prayer books, and Italian silk prayer shawls. He also acted as the agent for the Jewish-owned Jamaican *Weekly Gleaner, Jewish Chronicle, Hebrew Observer*, and the *Cup of Salvation* (edited by his brother David).[37]

In keeping with the expectations of the new ministerial template—combining the roles of preacher, pastor, and public figure—Samuel became deeply involved in New York and national Jewish communal life. Alongside other Jewish innovators in the United States and the British Empire, Samuel saw education as a panacea for a plethora of communal ills and, at the same time, the means to advance the social and political status of the community. He promoted a variety of educational initiatives aimed at both children and adults. Between 1842 and 1847, Samuel ran the New York Talmud Torah, a day school that taught secular and religious subjects. Together with Isaac Leeser, he proposed the creation of a training college for teachers and the rabbinate. He also joined Leeser and others in establishing the Jewish Publication Society. From 1857 until 1867, he edited the *Jewish Messenger*, a weekly newspaper that reached a national audience. In 1863 and 1864 he used his newspaper to push for the creation of the Hebrew Free School Association.[38] Samuel became involved in philanthropic and advocacy work (often alongside his son Myer Samuel), playing a pivotal role in the founding of the Board of Delegates of American Israelites, Jews' Hospital, the Hebrew Orphan Society, and the Jewish Home for the Aged.[39] He was also the early dynamo of the North American Relief Society for the Indigent Jew in Jerusalem, collecting money to be disbursed by Moses Montefiore and Hirsch Lehren.[40]

Samuel Isaacs made a triumphant return to England in 1851 (the trip paid for by his synagogue), visiting his family in Liverpool and London. The London Jewish press hailed his sermon at the New Synagogue, ruefully regretting that his "native talent," initially unappreciated in England, had first found favor in America.[41] He had been praised before as an example worthy of emulation in England. As early as 1842, the London *Jewish Chronicle* had paired Samuel with his brother David in Liverpool as "par nobile fratrum": exemplars of a new and exciting ministerial model. It was a "fortunate occurrence that two brothers should, so many thousand miles apart, be dispensing equal good in the same manner—the one to the Jews of New York, the other to those of Liverpool."[42] Although ministering on opposite sides of the Atlantic, both brothers were connected by a near-identical approach to religious leadership. Samuel's success as a preacher and public figure in America, and his brother's parallel experience in England, points to the extent of cultural integration in the two leading Jewish communities of the English-speaking world.

David

David Myer Isaacs was also born in Leeuwarden, six years after his brother Samuel. Little is known about his religious education beyond that he attended the Talmud classes of Aaron Levy, a dayan of the London Beth Din.[43] At age fourteen, David was employed to read to the blind wife of Chief Rabbi Solomon Hirschell, a position that probably reflected the influence of his well-connected father. He later supported himself as a private tutor to the children of leading London Jewish families. At age twenty-two, David was appointed lecturer to the synagogue in the seaport town of Bristol. For a young and ambitious minister, the small Bristol congregation was a stepping stone, a modest community from which ministers moved on after short tenures.[44] He announced his ambitions in an unsolicited letter of application to the Liverpool Synagogue in October 1834, describing how he had given "the most unqualified satisfaction" in his current post. David trumpeted his abilities as a preacher—"chiefly extemporaneous, the effusions of a mind deeply imbued with religious zeal remote from sophistry and superstition"—a major asset at a time when the Jewish community wanted its ministers to deliver sermons with the gravity and grace of an Anglican Bishop.[45]

Clearly impressed by his confident self-assessment, the Liverpool Synagogue hired David in 1835 to deliver sermons and serve as second reader to David Woolf Marks. The position he occupied was perhaps the "first regular pulpit for sermons in the vernacular erected in an English synagogue."[46] While others had preached in English before him, David has been credited with initiating the first sustained series of weekly sermons in England.[47] It was no accident that this innovation was initiated in Liverpool. A prospering port city, Liverpool had a Jewish population of approximately 2,300 in the mid-1840s.[48] The Jewish community was wealthy, buoyed by the industrial boom that made the city a hub in transatlantic trade. The city and its Jewish community had entrenched mercantile connections with the Caribbean, the colonies, and North America. The congregation had experimented with preaching before. A Mr. S. Bennaton, perhaps the first Englishman to preach formally in his native language, delivered sermons at the synagogue in 1824 and 1825; his brother Moses Nathan introduced the regular synagogue sermon to the West Indies, preaching in Kingston, Jamaica.[49] Possessing considerable oratorical abilities and a modern manner, David Myer Isaacs became the presentable figurehead of a community that sought to cement its status as a respectable part of Liverpool society.

David was a good fit for the successful and status-conscious elements within the community, gifted with a "forcible, somewhat impulsive and eloquent style of oratory, tinged with a peculiarly caustic humor."[50] His preaching was praised in the Jewish press, and his sermons were occasionally reprinted with a "large circulation."[51] His reputation also crossed the Atlantic: the *Occident,* published by Isaac Leeser in Philadelphia, commented that he was "well and favorably known by his lectures," and the Sydney *Voice of Jacob* reprinted an article praising his preaching.[52] David Isaacs's sermons in Manchester and Liverpool seem to have attracted enthusiastic audiences of Jews and Christians. He also became actively engaged in the public realm. Here again his activities conformed to the new model of ministering, serving as a pastor and public servant for the Jewish community. Like his brother in New York, David became an earnest advocate of Jewish education, acting as a board member, administrator, and occasional teacher for the Hebrew National School in Liverpool. He also encouraged adult education, founding the Literary Hebraic Society in 1844, starting a newspaper in the following year, and later teaching Hebrew at Queen's College. A skilled and tireless fundraiser, David collected money for both Jewish and general causes. Conspicuous Jewish generosity—support for the Lancashire Cotton Famine Fund, for example—would improve the image of the community in liberal and mercantile-minded Liverpool.[53]

David delivered occasional sermons and lectures in Manchester beginning in 1837. The speeches were funded by a group of Manchester grandees who hoped that popular education would revitalize religious life in the city. From 1838, David was paid an annual retainer to deliver fortnightly sermons.[54] These sermons were not universally well received. Abraham Franklin, a leading businessman and sponsor of the lectures, felt that the sermons focused too closely on "undisputed and well-known truth." His son, the augustly named Benjamin Franklin, a merchant based in Jamaica who was visiting Manchester in 1841, found Isaacs arrogant and "ungentlemanly," his sermons longwinded, "unconnected and egotistical," and his audiences small and indifferent.[55] The *Jewish Chronicle* felt that his sermons would be improved by "a little less redundancy of epithet and flower"—not an uncommon problem given the preferred Victorian mode of grandiloquent oratory—but hesitated to "deprecate what seemed so much to gratify others."[56] These sentiments do not seem to have found wide-spread support. Instead the Great Synagogue in Manchester made repeated efforts to recruit the Liverpudlian minister, finally succeeding in 1862.[57] Again he encountered a few detractors. Some Eastern European members of his new congregation were critical of the "English" character of the services and the centrality accorded to the sermon in the service.[58]

David Isaacs was an imposing figure, resembling his older brother Samuel in "voice, manner as well as physical build and genial social characteristic." Like his sibling, he developed a reputation for being "uncompromisingly Orthodox," outspoken, and sharp-tongued, never failing "to vigorously expose what he believed to be the shortcomings of his congregation." In 1845, he and Moses Samuel started the *Cup of Salvation,* a periodical that printed sermons, essays, and reviews relating to Judaism. (Isaac Leeser noted approvingly in Philadelphia that the "chief object of the editors seems to be the extension of strictly Orthodox principles among Israelites.") The short-lived publication was distributed in America by Samuel Isaacs and advertised in the *Occident.*[59] Although David Isaacs was "rigidly Orthodox," he was a proponent of the modernization of synagogue worship, suspending the sale of synagogue honors and shortening the Shabbat service.[60] He was also, according to a Reform minister who eulogized him, "a fairly tolerant man," accepting an invitation to preach in the Manchester Synagogue of the British Jews—an unusual step at a time when the traditional community was working to distance itself from religious reformers—and vacated his pulpit for his visiting Reform counterpart.[61]

For all his success as a preacher and public figure, David Myer Isaacs never achieved the financial success of his New York sibling. While the status of successful ministers in England compared favorably with that of their counterparts in America, their salaries did not.[62] This partly explains the decision of a number of English ministers, including Samuel Myer Isaacs, to seek employment across the Atlantic. David had sought to improve his financial position in 1841 by applying for the advertised post of preacher at the Great Synagogue in London but was turned down.[63] In 1849, the Liverpool Synagogue was forced to reduce his salary because of an economic depression precipitated by the political convulsions in Europe.[64] Lingering unhappiness over this treatment may have persuaded Isaacs to accept the pulpit of the breakaway New Liverpool Hebrew Congregation in 1851, a split similar to that of Shaarey Tefila and B'nai Jeshurun in New York. The move, however, did little to improve his long-term financial well-being.[65] This did not stop him from undertaking an expensive trip to New York in 1873 to be present at the celebration of his brother's seventieth birthday. According to the *Jewish Chronicle,* the visit was—like his brother's trip to London two decades earlier—"anticipated with great delight by the Jews of New York."[66] David died in 1879, leaving his wife and four daughters "entirely unprovided for." The Great Synagogue in Manchester appealed for contributions on their behalf in the pages of the *Jewish Chronicle.*[67]

Jacob

While David and Samuel were feted in England and America, the unheralded Jacob Isaacs served in humbler circumstances in New South Wales. Despite its inauspicious origins, by 1840 even the Australian Jewish community, at the edge of the British Empire, expected its religious leader to fit the mold of the new ministerial model. The rapid transformation of a marginal Jewish population in a peripheral penal settlement into a community that demanded the same sort of ministerial services that were supplied by Samuel and David Isaacs suggests the extent of integration within the English-speaking Jewish world at midcentury. Yet Jacob Isaacs's experience also reveals how these expectations, driven by exposure to information and influences from abroad, far exceeded local realities.

Convicts comprised the majority of the identifiable Jewish population that arrived between 1788 and 1830: 384 of the 463 Jews who settled in the Australia during this period were unwilling participants in chained migration. The first Jewish free settlers only arrived in 1821 but soon outnumbered the static Jewish convict population. A steady trickle of Jewish immigrants moved to New South Wales from England in the late 1820s and 1830s. By 1841, 856 Jews lived in the colony, of whom roughly 500 were immigrants near Sydney. This total included John Isaacs and his wife Rosa, who sailed for Australia from England in 1833. John opened a shop in George Street, the major commercial thoroughfare in Sydney. His involvement in retailing and petty trading was typical of these early immigrants.[68] Although isolated and provincial, the expanding Australian Jewish community was increasingly connected to the wider English-speaking Jewish world. In 1830, Aaron Levy, a dayan of the London Beth Din (and Talmud teacher to David Isaacs) was sent to New South Wales by Chief Rabbi Solomon Hirschell to secure a *get*—a bill of divorce—from a settler who had abandoned his young wife in England. While in Australia, Levy sold prayer books to individuals "who had no previous opportunity of possessing them" and a Torah scroll to the community by subscription.[69] The York Street Synagogue, consecrated in 1844, modeled its service, bylaws, and membership rules on those of the Great Synagogue in London.[70] John Isaacs, treasurer and longtime trustee of the Sydney Synagogue, purchased a Torah on the congregation's behalf from London.[71] John, a successful businessman, contributed £40 toward the building of the new synagogue, one of the largest individual donations.[72]

Jacob Isaacs arrived in Sydney in 1840. In his own words, "he had been induced to migrate to Sydney, because he had been informed that a person competent to undertake the situation of mohel, Schochet and Reader was required in Sydney."[73] The congregation had been without an officiating minister since 1838, and it is likely that his brother, a committee member, had advised him of the opportunities available in Australia. The advice was not necessarily sound. The Sydney Synagogue appears to have been in no rush to recruit Isaacs, delaying for two months after his initial overture before agreeing to his appointment. During this time, Jacob seems to have been employed by his brother. The committee then haggled over his salary, claiming that they could not "consistently with the present state of their funds engage him in these capacities at a salary sufficient to maintain him without him entering into business." Jacob rejected the initial offer of £100 per annum. He claimed to be "perfectly satisfied" with this sum, proposing to supplement it by teaching Hebrew and English but had been warned by his brother that the proposed pay would "not keep him and his family respectable," particularly given the "many duties involved which would take him very often and at no suitable time away from his business."[74] Jacob was only appointed after John and three other wealthy congregants agreed to pay half of his £208 salary.

Although officially given the title of "Reverend," Jacob was in effect a congregational functionary. In practice, his congregants referred to him as "Mister" or "Reader" but not as "Reverend."[75] Alongside his duties within the synagogue, primarily as *baal tefillah*—prayer leader—and his service as *shochet* and mohel, Isaacs was expected to perform marriages, funerals, and circumcisions for the rural Jewish communities of New South Wales.[76] He was caught uneasily in the low-status traditional position of a reader at a time when shifting expectations elevated the redefined role of the hazan—preacher, pastor, and public representative—to a level of higher regard and remuneration. The Sydney community differentiated between the functions performed by Isaacs and those of a "proper minister."[77] The apparent lack of initial enthusiasm for Isaacs's appointment may have been derived from the understanding that he did not conform to the profile of the model new minister. Unlike his brothers in New York and Liverpool, Jacob was not required to regularly deliver sermons. Unable or unwilling to deliver the silver-tongued sermons that underpinned his brothers' reputations, Jacob Isaacs preached rarely and was largely limited to "lectures" on the High Holy Days. He appears to have delivered his first sermon in 1846, more than six years after his installation, and seemingly did not supply the "spiritual advice and guidance" that the community desired.[78] In 1842, two years after Isaacs's installation, George Moss, the editor of the Sydney *Voice of Jacob* and a member of the synagogue committee, lamented that "Australasian Jews have hitherto not profited by the devotion of a Rabbi." The same issue pointedly reported on David Myer Isaacs's sermons in Liverpool, suggesting exactly what Moss had in mind.[79]

The Sydney Synagogue's ministerial aspirations accorded with fashion of the times but not necessarily with the realities of its remote location. New South Wales was a frontier colony at the edge of the empire. Shortly after his arrival, Isaacs had ministered to the convicted bushranger Edward Davis—"Teddy the Jewboy"—before his execution, a duty unfamiliar to the urbane metropolitan ministers that the synagogue hoped to attract.[80] Moreover, the community fell well short of the aspirations of Anglo-Jewry. Even the *Sydney Morning Herald* commented on the fact that Isaacs was the "only person formally dressed" at the consecration of the York Street Synagogue.[81] Nonetheless, the community believed that the introduction of regular sermons and religious education would elevate the "moral, social, and religious standing" of Australian Jews.[82] A number of letters written to the London Jewish press complained that there was "no flock so badly shepherded in this and most other parts" as that in Australia. The children were "growing up with about as much knowledge of their faith as the Aborigines, and the adults seem to want sadly some one to promote their spiritual welfare."[83]

For all his efforts, including a short-lived Hebrew school, Isaacs was never regarded as fully capable of fulfilling this function.[84] Yet his services were retained for sixteen years as the synagogue struggled to recruit a replacement. Its difficulties were not derived from a lack of effort. The congregation responded to the overtures of the newly appointed chief rabbi (figure 1.1) in 1846 by stating that its "first object" was "to obtain from England a reader who can lecture in English on Religious and moral subjects."[85] Even with the assistance of the chief rabbi, Nathan Marcus Adler, the synagogue had no success until a decade later. This delay was the cause of considerable frustration. Sydney was competing directly with other English-speaking communities for a limited number of suitable candidates. The congregation finally filled its pulpit in 1856. Hermann Hoelzel, formerly the hazan of the Hambro Synagogue in London, left his post in Hobart to serve as "minister and reader" of the Sydney congregation.[86] This change in fortunes probably reflected the gradual transformation of the status and success of the community after a long economic downturn in the 1840s. The discovery of gold in 1851 attracted substantial numbers of Jewish fortune seekers to Australia. The Australian Jewish population more than doubled in size over the course of the decade.[87]

Hoelzel's arrival in Sydney precipitated Jacob Isaacs's departure. According to a local correspondent writing in the London *Jewish Chronicle,* the new minister introduced "salutary reforms in the modes of performing Divine Worship," including preaching a weekly sermon. It was hoped somewhat optimistically that these steps would "render this congregation a pattern to all others, even in the principal towns of Europe and the other parts of the world."[88] The fit of optimism did not end there. The board of management appointed a second reader and mohel to relieve Hoelzel of his "arduous duties."[89] There was, however, no place for Jacob Isaacs. He did, though, leave on good terms, benefiting from the largesse of the prospering community. The congregation presented Isaacs with a gift of £200, liquidated his substantial debts of £322, paid his passage back to England, and guaranteed him a pension of £200 per annum.[90] His testimonial praised him for "affability of manner," a faint sentiment for a long-serving minister, suggesting that Isaacs's service was regarded as adequate but far from profound.[91] Whether intentionally or not, he did make one lasting contribution to the Sydney community. Shortly before his departure, Isaacs performed the marriage of Julia and Solomon Cohen. Julia's mother was subsequently discovered not to be Jewish, sparking an intracommunal conflict that led to a secession from the synagogue and the creation of a new rival congregation.[92]

Jacob Isaacs achieved little of the success of his illustrious brothers. While David and Samuel were seen as part of the vanguard of modern religious leadership, Jacob did not advance beyond the role of a synagogue functionary. He was never regarded as a "proper minister": he preached only rarely, remained relatively uninvolved in communal life, and did not achieve a public presence. To a large extent, Jacob was a victim of the circulation of information and ideas within the English-speaking Jewish world. Despite the paucity of suitable candidates, and its position on the periphery of the British Empire, by 1840 the Sydney Synagogue expected its appointee to fit the mold of the modern metropolitan minister. By contrast, Samuel benefited from

FIGURE 1.1. Colonial congregations looked to Nathan Marcus Adler, newly installed as chief rabbi of the British Empire, for assistance in securing hazans. This portrait made its way to several colonial congregations. In Sydney, George Moss reported that some of his "old fashioned friends were surprised at seeing the worthy Rabbi minus a beard, a fur cap, and a Polish peltz; not being prepared for the appearance of a modern ecclesiastic."

the mobility that the nascent English language diaspora afforded. Along with Morris Raphall and a legion of other able preachers, he crossed the Atlantic to advance his career. The same expectations that hindered Jacob worked to Samuel's advantage. Sophisticated and silver tongued, he achieved prominence as a preacher, public figure, and pastoral leader in America. Although David never achieved the financial success of his New York–based sibling, he shared his brother's reputation as the very model of the modern minister. Articulate and ambitious, Samuel and David Isaacs were hailed as "par nobile fratrum." Jacob, in exile in Australia, languished in obscurity. The same transnational trends in religious leadership that had been so kind to his two brothers left Jacob Isaacs a relative failure.

Ministers on the Move

The brothers Isaacs blazed a trail that was soon followed by others. Those who followed in their footsteps included Henry Abraham Henry, who left the Western Synagogue in London for Cincinnati in 1849, New York in 1853, and San Francisco in 1857; Sabato Morais, who spent five years at Bevis Marks in London before assuming the pulpit of Philadelphia's Mikve Israel in 1851; Arnold Fischel, who moved from England to become preacher at Shearith Israel in New York; Dattner Jacobson, who left Melbourne for an appointment at Gates of Prayer in New Orleans; Solomon Jacobs, who ministered in London, Kingston, Baltimore, Charleston, Philadelphia, and New Orleans; Raphael Benjamin, whose pulpit peregrinations took him from London to Melbourne, Cincinnati, and New York; and Emanuel M. Myers, who moved from London to the newly formed synagogue in the gold rush town of Ballarat, Australia, followed by stints in Launceston, Melbourne, Montreal, New York, and Waco, Texas (his brother Meyer H. Myers followed a similar circuit, ministering in Geelong in 1857, Saint Thomas in 1860, Kingston in 1862, Boston in 1865, and Kingston again in 1867).[93]

Some hazans followed a colonial circuit: Alexander Barnard Davis (Portsmouth, Brighton, Kingston, Sydney) and Isaac Pulver (Cheltenham, Cape Town, Melbourne, Hobart) gave up pulpits in provincial congregations for positions in a succession of frontier communities.[94] Hermann Hoelzel, the hazan of the Hambro Synagogue in London, left London for Hobart in 1853 and was later selected for similar service in Sydney. Abraham de Sola, son of the hazan of Bevis Marks, assumed a pulpit in Montreal in 1847.[95] Joel Rabinowitz swapped his job as second reader in Birmingham for the position of senior minister in Cape Town.[96] Perhaps the most unusual colonial trajectory was that of Isaac Zachariah, originally from Baghdad, who began his career as a private *shochet* for the Sassoon family in Bombay. Zachariah was drawn to Ballarat in Australia by the gold rush and from there to the boom town of Hokitika in New Zealand in 1867. Zachariah served as *shochet* and hazan in a synagogue built during the heady excitement of another bout of gold fever. Once the fever cooled in 1870, he and much of his congregation decamped for Christchurch, where he spent the rest of his career as hazan. Since his congregation demanded preaching, and he was at least initially illiterate in English, he wrote his sermons phonetically in Hebrew.[97]

These hazans carried considerable cultural baggage with them, further integrating and interconnecting the dispersed outposts of the Anglophone diaspora. Certainly the London *Jewish Chronicle* expected that colonial Jews would want their hazans to reproduce the recognizable sounds of the English prayer service in their synagogues. The newspaper advertised a volume of the music composed by the choirmaster of the Great Synagogue in London in the expectation that it would be

> adopted even more generally among the congregations of the Anglo-Jewish world. Music is the universal language. It appeals to all nationalities and to all tongues. But music becomes doubly impressive when interwoven with long association and experience. What melody can touch our heart with such force as the *Lecha Doudi* which we heard when we toddled by our fathers' side to "see Shabbos." . . . In the colonies, the founders of local synagogues have no doubt heard many of these in their youth, and their adoption would form a very desirable link between the generations and with the home country. Nothing can tend to make a Jew "at home" than if he heard *Yigdal* in the colonies to the setting of Mombach that he was familiar with in London.[98]

Whatever their musical preferences, a number of colonial congregations felt a particularly strong affinity with London. Nowhere was this more apparent than in Sydney. The consecration of the York Street Synagogue in 1844 was based on the identical order of service used for the new synagogue at Great Saint Helen's in London in 1838.[99] The synagogue derived the format of its service, organizational structure, and code of regulations directly from the Great Synagogue in London. The congregation was, however, forced to bow to local pressures, lamenting that "from circumstances every ceremony and rite cannot be so strictly complied as in the Mother Country."[100] The community expected that its ties with England would be reciprocal: it took for granted that metropolitan Jewry would assist in the outfitting of the new synagogue and library and supply many essential religious articles.[101]

As we saw in the case of David Isaacs, this desire to emulate the metropole raised undue expectations in many colonial congregations. The clamor to secure the services of a capable hazan and the publicity surrounding the peregrinations of polished preachers proved the undoing of some of their less talented counterparts. For all the freedoms and advantages that the international market for hazans provided, those who ventured to distant colonies often encountered a reality far removed from that of their celebrity colleagues. Jewish life in colonial settings presented several structural constraints on even the most ambitious and adroit religious leader. The congregations in Cape Town, Melbourne, and Sydney were lay led prior to appointing paid officiants and became accustomed to autonomy and flexibility in the application of Jewish law. Far from the religious authority of London, these communities initially adapted to local circumstances by relaxing the ban on intermarriage and cohabitation with non-Jewish women. They could not afford to do otherwise. In Cape Town, for example, Benjamin Norden, the leading light and major benefactor of the congregation, ensured that his sons, born of his Christian wife, were circumcised as Jews.[102] The Melbourne Hebrew Congregation also grappled with the issue of exempting some of its stalwarts from its rule barring intermarried men from holding synagogue office.[103] Accustomed to a long leash from London, these congregations and their strong-willed leaders chafed at the religious rigors demanded by their newly hired hazans. This, then, was the paradox for those peripatetic hazans who took advantage of the international marketplace for ministers that emerged in the mid–nineteenth century. While their skills were in demand across the English-speaking Jewish world from congregations as far from London and New York as those in Melbourne and Cape Town, their congregants quickly came to share the perspective of their coreligionists in England and America as what might be expected from a model minister. Far from finding greater authority in the farthest urban outposts of the British Empire, men like David Isaacs and others who followed him to these remote pulpits often discovered congregations and congregants emboldened by the autonomy and independence they had acquired because of their distance from the centers of Anglophone Jewish life, and every bit as demanding as their metropolitan peers.

Notes

1. On religious laxity in the United States, see Hyman Grinstein, "The American Synagogue and Laxity of Religious Observance, 1750–1850" (MA thesis, Columbia University, 1936). For a discussion of irreligion among Anglo-Jewry, see Vivian Lipman, *Social History of the Jews in England, 1850–1950* (London: Watts & Co., 1954), 19–23, 34–40, 65.

2. Lloyd Gartner estimates that more than a million Jewish immigrants spent some time in Britain on their way to America. Gartner, *The Jewish immigrant in England, 1870–1914* (London: Allen & Unwin, 1960), ix, 17, 35, 38. Vivian Lipman estimates a Jewish population of 60,000 in Britain in 1880 and roughly half that number in 1840. Lipman, "The Anglo-Jewish Community in Victorian Society" in *Studies in the Cultural Life of the Jews of England*, ed. Dov Noy and Issachar Ben-Ami (Jerusalem: Magnes Press, 1975): 151–59.

3. London *Jewish Chronicle* (hereafter *JC*), June 24, 1853; *Report of the Committee of the Sydney Synagogue* (Sydney, 1847).

4. *Occident and American Jewish Advocate* (hereafter *Occ*) 6, no. 4 (1848): 159.

5. For the transformation of the role of the rabbi, see Steven Singer, "The Anglo-Jewish Ministry in Early Victorian London," *Modern Judaism* 5, no. 3 (1985): 279–83.

6. On preaching in England, see Israel Finestein, *Anglo-Jewry in Changing Times* (Portland, OR: Vallentine Mitchell, 1999), 53–61, 65–70; Michael Goulston, "The Status of the Anglo-Jewish Rabbinate, 1840–1914," *Jewish Journal of Sociology* 10 (June 1968): 55–82; Morris Joseph, "About Preaching," *Jewish Quarterly Review* 3 (1891): 120–45. On the emergence of regular preaching in America in English, see Naomi Cohen, "Sermons and the Contemporary World: Two American Jewish Sources," in *Contemporary Jewry: Studies in Honor of Moshe Davis*, ed. Geoffrey Wigoder (Jerusalem: Institute of Contemporary Jewry, 1984), 23–44; Robert Friedenberg, *"Hear O Israel": The History of American Jewish Preaching, 1654–1970* (Tuscaloosa: University of Alabama Press, 1989), 19–84; Nathan Kaganoff, "The Traditional Jewish Sermon in the United States from Its Beginnings to the First World War" (PhD diss., American University, 1960), 1–99; Michael Meyer, "Christian Influence on Early German Reform Judaism," in *Studies in Jewish Bibliography, History and Literature in Honor of I. Edward Kiev*, ed. Charles Berlin (New York: Ktav, 1971): 293–96. On preaching in German in America, see Alexander Altmann, "The New Style of Preaching in Nineteenth-Century German Jewry," in *Studies in Nineteenth-Century Jewish Intellectual History*, ed. Alexander Altmann (Cambridge, MA: Harvard University Press, 1964): 65–116; Bernhard N. Cohn, "Early German Preaching in America," *Historia Judaica* 15, no. 2 (1953): 86–134; Adolf Kober, "Jewish Preaching and Preachers," *Historia Judaica* 7, no. 2 (1945): 103–34.

7. Isaac Leeser caustically remarked that in reality hazans in America were "a race of nondescripts who value themselves more for their title of Doctor of Philosophy or Master of Arts, or the fictitious Doctor of Divinity, which not one possesses by right" *Occ* 16 (September 1858): 304.

8. The sermon acquired similar status in many Protestant denominations and was considered the most important tool for providing religious instruction to adults. On revivalist preaching during the Second Great Awakening, see Louis Billington, "Revivalism and Popular Religion," in Eric Sigsworth, ed., *In Search of Victorian Values* (New York, 1988), 147–59; Robert Ellison, *The Victorian Pulpit: Spoken and Written Sermons in Nineteenth-Century Britain* (London, 1998), 11–56; Hatch, *Democratization of American Christianity*,

44, 67–122. For educational innovations, see Bradley, *Call to Seriousness*, 135–44; Hatch, *Democratization of American Christianity*, 49–122, 195; Noll, *Christianity in the United States and Canada*, 229–32.

9. *JC*, August 22, 1862.

10. See *JC*, April 15, 1842; May 6, 1842; July 15, 1881; Joseph, "About Preaching," 123.

11. *Occ* 2 (October 1844): 313–21; 6 (July 1848): 159–162; *JC* April 15, 1842; May 6, 1842; July 15, 1881. For similar attitudes toward the *derashah* in Germany, see Altmann, "New Style of Preaching," 77–78, 82; Kober, "Jewish Preaching," 103–4.

12. *Occ* 3, no. 5 (1845); for the identical sentiment, see also *JC*, May 22, 1842.

13. *Occ* 3, no. 12 (1846). Isaac Mayer Wise warned of the dangers of an improperly qualified preacher in the *Asmonean*, October 15, 1852.

14. See *JC*, January 7, 1842; January 14, 1842; February 11, 1842; April 8, 1842; April 15, 1842; May 22, 1842; *Voice of Jacob* (hereafter *VoJ*), December 10, 1841; April 29, 1842. For the debate over the formation of the seminary, see Singer, "Anglo-Jewish Ministry," 289–92.

15. See Ellison, *Victorian Pulpit*, 15, 46–47.

16. In addition, Wise started the German-language *Die Deborah*, and David Einhorn edited *Sinai*. For the Jewish press in America and England during this period, see Barkai, *Branching Out*, 107–8; David Cesarani, *The Jewish Chronicle and Anglo-Jewry, 1841–1991* (Cambridge: Cambridge University Press, 1994), 2–28; Hasia Diner, *A Time for Gathering: The Second Migration, 1820–1880* (Baltimore: Johns Hopkins University Press, 1992), 206–12.

17. Cesarani, *Jewish Chronicle*, 8–10.

18. Philippson also started the *Israelitisches Predigt-und Schulmagazin*, where he published many of his own sermons.

19. See *JC*, February 4 and May 6, 1842; *Occ* 3 (July 1845): 177–89; 4 (January 1847): 478–87.

20. *VoJ*, August 16, 1844.

21. For details of salaries paid to hazans in New York in the late 1850s, see Grinstein, *Jewish Community of New York*, 546n43.

22. Finestein, *Anglo-Jewry in Changing Times*, 181–82, 194; *JC*, February 1, 1850; February 8, 1850.

23. *Occ* 2, no. 7 (1844).

24. *JC*, December 31, 1869; May 9, 1879; Robert Swierenga, "Samuel Myer Isaacs: The Dutch Rabbi of New York City," *American Jewish Archives* 44, no. 2 (1992): 607–8, 619; see also E. Yechiel Simon, "Samuel Myer Isaacs: a 19th Century Jewish Minister in New York City" (D.H.L. thesis, Yeshiva University, 1974), 3–4.

25. A Mr. M. Isaacs is recorded as having visited the school attached to the Jews' Hospital in 1817. The visitor, most likely Meyer, was shocked by the appearance of Barnet Solomons, one of the pupils, who was "walking in the boys' ground in rags and dirt. . . . [He was] in appearance like a common beggar in rags." Isaacs advised the headmaster that if "habituated to cleanliness from an early example, they would gradually emanate from their present system." Qtd. in Todd Endelman, *The Jews of Georgian England 1714–1830: Tradition and Change in a Liberal Society* (Ann Arbor: University of Michigan Press, 1999), 238.

26. *JC*, May 9, 1879; Bill Williams, *The Making of Manchester Jewry, 1740–1875* (Manchester, UK: Manchester University Press, 1976), 91.

27. *JC*, January 19, 1855; *Occ* 5, no. 4 (1847); Finestein, *Anglo-Jewry in Changing Times*, 34.

28. See Swierenga, "Samuel Myer Isaacs," 608; Simon, "Samuel Myer Isaacs," 25, 206.

29. Samuel Isaacs's grandfather was Jacob Symmons. The marriage may have fulfilled a contractual stipulation for the new post. Swierenga, "Samuel Myer Isaacs," 619; B'nai Jeshurun letterbooks qtd. in Simon, "Samuel Myer Isaacs," 7, 32.

30. See Grinstein, *Jewish Community of New York*, 88–89; Kaganoff, "Traditional Jewish Sermon," 49–50.

31. Isaac Leeser commented that the members of Shaarey Tefila were "mostly natives of Great Britain." The congregation later sent an address, under Samuel Isaacs's name, to Nathan Marcus Adler, congratulating him on his installation as chief rabbi in London. See *JC*, June 11, 1846.

32. *Occ* 1, no. 4 (1843); 3, no. 4 (July 1845); March 12, 1863; Myer S. Isaacs, Diary, SC-5452, American Jewish Archives; Grinstein, *Jewish Community of New York*, 88, 408; Simon, "Samuel Myer Isaacs," 2, 8, 23, 47, 65–66, 71; Friedenberg, *"Hear O Israel,"* 45; Jonathan D. Sarna, *American Judaism* (New Haven: Yale University Press, 2004), 122; Hasia Diner, *A Time for Gathering: The Second Migration, 1820–1880* (Baltimore: Johns Hopkins University Press, 1992), 166.

33. B'nai Jeshurun had itself been formed barely two decades earlier in protest against the perceived laxity of Shearith Israel. Initially B'nai Jeshurun refused to admit Jews who violated the Sabbath. *Asmonean*, October 25, 1850; *Asmonean*, November 22, 1850; Grinstein, *Jewish Community of New York*, 339–43, 366; Simon, "Samuel Myer Isaacs," 42, 169; Swierenga, "Samuel Myer Isaacs," 610–11.

34. *Occ* 1, no. 4 (1843); Leopold Mayer, "Recollections of Chicago in 1850–1851," in *A Documentary History of the Jews in the United States, 1654–1875*, by Morris Schappes (New York: Columbia University Press, 1950), 309; *JC*, July 25, 1851.

35. *Occ* 1, no. 12 (1844).

36. It helped that he ministered to a wealthy congregation. In 1839, his starting salary was $1,100, rising to $1,200 in 1845, $1,600 in 1847, and $2,000 in 1855. By the end of his career, Samuel Isaacs was paid $3,500 per annum. In 1853, Shaarey Tefila took out a life insurance policy for their hazan valued at $5,000. In 1873, the congregation presented him with a gift of $4,250 collected for his seventieth birthday. On his retirement, he received a pension of $2,500 per annum. *JC*, June 24, 1853; Simon, "Samuel Myer Isaacs," 25, 53.

37. *JC*, January 26, 1846; Diner, *A Time for Gathering*, 215; Simon, "Samuel Myer Isaacs," 10–14, 43, 52.

38. *Occ* 1, no. 10 (1844); 1, no. 12 (1844); 4, no. 12 (1847); Grinstein, *Jewish Community of New York*, 231–36; Simon, "Samuel Myer Isaacs," 54–56, 143–67.

39. See *JC*, June 7, 1878; Alan Silverstein, *Alternatives to Assimilation: the Response of Reform Judaism to American Culture, 1840–1930* (Hanover, NH: Brandeis University Press, 1994), 43–45; Lance Sussman, *Isaac Leeser and the Making of American Judaism* (Detroit: Wayne State University Press, 1995), 216.

40. See Adler to Samuel Isaacs, February 4, 1857, ACC/2805/1/1/4, London Metropolitan Archives (LMA); North American Relief Society for the Indigent Jew in Jerusalem, Palestine Records, I-14, P-22, American Jewish Historical Society, New York; Salo Baron and Jeannette Baron, "Palestinian Messengers in America, 1849–79: A Record of Four Journeys," *Jewish Social Studies* 5 (1937): 124, 131–32. In cooperation with Holland, see

Moshe Davis, *America and the Holy Land: With Eyes Toward Zion* (Westport, CN: Praeger, 1995), 97–99.

41. *JC*, January 3, 1851; February 21, 1851; March 28, 1851; November 23, 1866. This was not the first time that he had been so praised. For other examples, see *JC*, March 20, 1846; August 21, 1846; June 24, 1853.

42. *JC*, March 25, 1842.

43. Although David Myer Isaacs's obituary in the *Jewish Chronicle* states that the Talmud classes were run by Israel Levy, it is far more likely that the classes were taught by Israel's father Aaron (1795–1875).

44. See Geoffrey Alderman, *Modern British Jewry* (Oxford, UK: Clarendon Press, 1992), 23.

45. Qtd. in Williams, *Manchester Jewry*, 91–92; see Singer, "Anglo-Jewish Ministry," 280; Goulston, "Anglo-Jewish Rabbinate," 55–56.

46. *JC*, October 7, 1870.

47. Both he and the writer of his obituary advanced this claim. See JC, October 7, 1870; *JC*, May 9, 1879.

48. See *JC*, January 9, 1846.

49. Nathan was presumably an anglicized version of Bennaton (probably Ben-Nathan). See *JC*, October 7, 1870; Joseph, "About Preaching," 126–27.

50. *JC*, May 9, 1879; see also Philip Ettinger, *"Hope Place" in Liverpool Jewry* (Liverpool, UK: Hope Place Hebrew Congregation, 1930), 34.

51. *JC*, March 4, 1842; March 11, 1842; October 2, 1846; June 30, 1848; May 9, 1879; *VoJ*, February 2, 1844. See, e.g., David Isaacs, *Funeral Oration Delivered on the Occasion of the Burial of His Most Gracious Majesty, King William the Fourth by the Rev. D. M. Isaacs published by request of the wardens of the Seel-Street Synagogue* (1837)

52. *Occ* 3, no. 8 (1845); 1, no. 12 (1844); Sydney *VoJ*, May 27, 1842.

53. *JC*, December 17, 1841; February 11, 1842; January 9, 1846; May 9, 1879; Cyril Hershon, *To Make Them English* (Bristol, UK: Palavas Press, 1983), 8–13, 16; Williams, *Manchester Jewry*, 330; Ettinger, *"Hope Place,"* 34, 74.

54. *JC*, May 9, 1879; Williams, *Manchester Jewry*, 91–95.

55. Benjamin Franklin was one of the early subscribers to the *Occident*. His brother Lewis moved to San Francisco following the gold rush and delivered the first recorded sermon in the western United States on Yom Kippur in 1850. See *Occ*, Second List of Subscribers, 1844. For the Franklin quote, see Williams, *Manchester Jewry*, 36; Norton Stern, "The Franklin Brothers of San Diego," *Journal of San Diego History* 21, no. 3 (1975): 32–42.

56. *JC*, March 4, 1842; March 18, 1842.

57. See Williams, *Manchester Jewry*, 266–67.

58. *JC*, June 2, 1865; June 9, 1865; Williams, *Manchester Jewry*, 300.

59. *Jewish Messenger*, May 16, 1879; *JC*, May 9, 1879; *Occ* 3, no. 8 (1845).

60. *JC*, October 2, 1846.

61. *JC*, May 9, 1879.

62. For ministerial salaries in Liverpool, see Ettinger, *"Hope Place,"* 33.

63. Isaacs later denied having made this application. See *JC*, October 9, 1874; October 16, 1874.

64. *JC*, January 12, 1849.

65. Adler to the president and the wardens of the Old Hebrew Congregation Liverpool, August 26, 1851; David Isaacs to Adler, September 5, 1851, ACC/2805/01/01/001, LMA.

His obituaries hint that he may have also been a spendthrift. See *JC*, May 9, 1879; August 1, 1879.

66. *JC*, December 27, 1872.

67. *JC*, August 1, 1879.

68. *VoJ*, November 25, 1842; Alan Crown, "The Jewish Press, Community and Jewish Publishing in Australia," in *Noblesse Oblige: Essays in Honor of David Kessler OBE,* ed. Alan Crown (London, 1998), 38; Israel Porush, "From Bridge Street to York Street," *Australian Jewish Historical Society Journal* 2, no. 2 (1944): 222; Report of the Committee of the Sydney Synagogue, 1845: 4; John Levi, *The Forefathers: A Dictionary of Biography of the Jews on Australia 1788–1830* (Sydney: Australian Jewish Historical Society, 1976).

69. Report of the Committee of the Sydney Synagogue, 1845: 4; Cecil Roth, "Rabbi Aaron Levy's Mission to Australia," *Australian Jewish Historical Journal* 3, no. 1 (1949): 1–4; Report of the Committee of the Sydney Synagogue, 1845: 4.

70. For the origins of the York Street Synagogue, see Joseph Fowles, *Sydney in 1848* (Sydney: Ure Smith, 1962), 64–66; Percy Marks, "The First Synagogue in Australia," *Royal Australian Historical Society Journal and Proceedings* 11 (1926): 224–30; *Laws and Regulation of the New Synagogue* (Sydney, 1845); *Occ* 5, no. 11 (1848); Suzanne Rutland, *Edge of the Diaspora: Two Centuries of Jewish Settlement in Australia* (Sydney: Brandl & Schlesinger, 1997), 48–49.

71. *VoJ*, January 16, 1846.

72. Report of the Committee of the Sydney Synagogue, 1845: 10–12.

73. Qtd. in G. J. F. Bergman, "Jacob Isaacs Sydney Synagogue's Second Minister and His Family John Isaacs, and Myer David Isaacs (Playwright)," *Australian Jewish Historical Society* 9, no. 4 (1982): 239.

74. In 1845, Jacob was described as an "agent of George Street North." See M. H. Kellerman, "Contemporary References to the York Street Synagogue," *Australian Jewish Historical Society* 3, no. 5 (1951): 239, 241.

75. See Israel Porush, *The House of Israel* (Melbourne: Hawthorn Press, 1977), 7.

76. See Helen Bersten, "Jews in Rural New South Wales," *Australian Jewish Historical Journal* 13, no. 4 (1997): 602; Bergman, "Jacob Myer Isaacs," 240.

77. Report of the Committee of the Sydney Synagogue, 1847.

78. *JC*, June 24, 1853.

79. Sydney *VoJ*, May 27, 1842; June 24, 1842.

80. See George Bergman, "Edward Davis: Life and Death of an Australian Bushranger," *Australian Jewish Historical Society Journal* 4, no. 5 (1956): 205–40.

81. Qtd. in Bergman, "Jacob Myer Isaacs," 240.

82. Report of the Committee of the Sydney Synagogue, 1845: 6; Report of the Committee of the Sydney Synagogue, 1847.

83. *JC*, April 20, 1860; February 22, 1861.

84. Bergman, "Jacob Myer Isaacs," 241; see also *JC*, March 23, 1849.

85. *JC*, January 27, 1854; Porush, "The Chief Rabbinate and Early Australian Jewry," *Australian Jewish Historical Society Journal* 2, no. 8 (1948): 483, 487–88.

86. *JC*, March 27, 1857.

87. Rutland, *Edge of the Diaspora*, 50.

88. *JC*, October 24, 1856; March 27, 1857.

89. *JC*, March 27, 1857.

90. By comparison, in 1844 a Jamaican congregation offered a minimum salary of £200 for a reader and teacher. *VoJ*, August 16, 1844; *JC*, March 27, 1857; Sydney Synagogue, *Report of the Board of Management Sydney Synagogue for the Year AM 5616, 1855 and 1856* (Sydney, 1856).

91. *JC*, December 12, 1856.

92. Jacob and his daughter opened a "seminary for young ladies" in London. *JC*, April 18, 1862; October 18, 1867. Jacob died in London in December 1866. *JC*, January 5, 1866; Rutland, *Edge of the Diaspora*, 59–60; Bergman, "Jacob Myer Isaacs," 242.

93. On Morais, see Kiron, "Golden Ages, Promised Lands." On Fischel, see Jonathan Waxman, "Arnold Fischel: 'Unsung Hero' in American Israel," *American Jewish Historical Quarterly* 60 (1971): 325–43; Grinstein, *Jewish Community of New York*, 92, 98. On Jacobson's troubled career in Melbourne, see Joseph Aron and Judy Arndt, *The Enduring Remnant: The First 150 Years of the Melbourne Hebrew Congregation, 1841–1991* (Melbourne, Australia: University of Melbourne Press, 1992), 46–57. For Raphael Benjamin, see Aron and Arndt, *The Enduring Remnant*, 44–46; Jonathan Sarna and Karla Goldman, "From Synagogue-Community to Citadel of Reform: The History of K. K. Bene Israel (Rockdale Temple) in Cincinnati, Ohio," in *American Congregation: Portraits of Twelve Religious Communities*, ed. James Wind and James Lewis (Chicago: University of Chicago Press, 1994), 178–79. For Emanuel Myers's Australian career, see Aron and Arndt, *The Enduring Remnant*, 33–37; *JC*, August 26, 1853; Sampson Samuel to Emanuel Myers, Board of Deputies Letterbook ACC/3121/B1/2, LMA. For his American career, see *American Israelite*, November 24, 1892 and the materials in SC-8610, American Jewish Archives. For Myer H. Myers, see Robert Swierenga, *The Forerunners: Dutch Jewry in the North American Diaspora* (Detroit: Wayne State University Press, 1994), 169. On his tempestuous career in Saint Thomas, see Judah Cohen, *Through the Sands of Time: A History of the Jewish Community of St. Thomas, U.S. Virgin Islands* (Hanover, NH, 2004), 95–102; *JC*, September 11, 1857; September 19, 1862; October 31, 1862.

94. A striking number of the abovementioned hazans were Dutch in origin. On Dutch Jews in America, see Swierenga, *The Forerunners*. On frontier communities, see Sander Gilman's introduction to Milton Shain and Sander Gilman, eds., *Jewries at the Frontier: Accommodation, Identity, Conflict* (Urbana: University of Illinois Press, 1999).

95. For De Sola, see Gerald Tulchinsky, *Taking Root: The Origins of the Canadian Jewish Community* (Hanover, NH: Brandeis University Press, 1993), 40–49.

96. Finestein, *Anglo-Jewry in Changing Times*, 58–60.

97. *JC*, September 8, 1899; Lazarus Morris Goldman, *The History of the Jews in New Zealand* (Wellington, NZ: A.H. & A.W. Reed, 1958), 105–7, 110, 184.

98. *JC*, July 15, 1861.

99. Israel Porush, "From Bridge Street to York Street," *Australian Jewish Historical Society Journal* 2, no. 2 (1944): 62.

100. *Report of the Committee of the Sydney Synagogue, 1845*: 3; Sydney Synagogue, *Laws and Regulations of the New Synagogue* (Sydney, 1845); *Occ* 5, no. 11 (1848); see also Percy Marks, The First Synagogue in Australia (Sydney: D.S. Ford, 1925); Rutland, *Edge of the Diaspora*, 48–49.

101. *VoJ*, November 25, 1842.

102. Benjamin Norden had married a non-Jewish women while in Cape Town. Joseph and his siblings were converted to Judaism and were certified as such by Nathan Adler in

October 1851. Another son, Daniel Norden, not granted Adler's imprimatur, was circumcised in 1856 at age twenty-two. See the Minutes of the Cape Town Hebrew Congregation, December 28, 1851; January 4, 1852; May 11, 1856, Box 1, Volume 3, BC 849, Manuscripts and Archives, University of Cape Town.

103. For the discussion of exemptions, see Minutes of the Melbourne Hebrew Congregation, August 4, 1844; July 18, 1845; July 27, 1845; August 3, 1845; December 22, 1850; June 20, 1853, Series 75, Box 43, Melbourne Hebrew Congregation Archive.

2

ROAMING THE RIM

How Rabbis, Convicts, and Fortune Seekers
Shaped Pacific Coast Jewry

Ava F. Kahn

Jewish communities along the Pacific Rim—in Australia, New Zealand, California, Hawaii—prospered in the mid–nineteenth century in part because of interconnections that crossed an ocean. All benefited from the impact of gold rushes that drew miners, merchants, and even rabbis from far afield and then across the Rim. Port towns, unlike mining communities, attracted not only adventurous young men ready to explore the world but also families seeking new economic opportunities. Of course, in the case of Australia, not all came voluntarily. Some arrived there as convicts, transported as guests of the British government. After receiving pardons, they, too, joined the gold rushes.

News of burgeoning Rim communities spread quickly, as innovations in newspaper printing and shipping accelerated worldwide dissemination of news, knowledge, and, all too often, hyperbole. These technological developments in turn accelerated migration and travel.[1] Although each voyage brought dangers, including the very real danger of shipwreck, for some, perpetual wandering became a way of life.[2]

This chapter uses a transnational approach to examine the interplay between the growing Jewish communities along the Pacific Rim during the second half of the nineteenth century. American Jewish history is enriched when we study its transnational dimensions and understand the patterns created by movement across the porous borders of the nineteenth century. Stressing the connections between Pacific Rim Jewish communities, this chapter proposes that to fully understand the history of American Jewish communities along the West Coast, we must look across the Pacific. Doing so challenges the common understanding that Jewish communities on California's coast thrived solely because of the influx of Jews from the eastern United States and Europe.

Divided into three sections—fortune seekers, convicts, and roaming rabbis—this chapter focuses on the lives of Jews who traveled the Rim, especially those who crossed the Pacific between the Antipodes and the West Coast of the United States. Jewish migration to the California coast often involved many stops along the way and should be viewed as part of a series of step-migrations. Once a merchant or rabbi moved from his native land, it was likely that he would move again and even again. Some Jews became community founders in multiple locations, often performing similar services in two hemispheres, thousands of miles apart. Some founders gained experience with each move, at times seeking to replicate their prior communities in a new land.

Migrants from the Antipodes landed in the United States during the early part of the California Gold Rush, before most easterners could travel overland or around Cape Horn. Because they arrived first, they left a defining imprint on early Western Jewish communities. They influenced synagogue constitutions, established a preferred style of communal organization, volunteered on local committees, provided knowledgeable leadership, approved kosher meat and products for sale, and supplied their coreligionists with matzah on Passover. In turn, their communities, the earliest in California, influenced the later formation of Jewish communities in Hawaii and throughout the West.

Jewish communities first formed in Australia and New Zealand during the nineteenth century. United by language, interconnected by trade and shared ideas and customs, Jews in Australia and New Zealand belonged to a British colonial diaspora. Such networks not only aided business connections but also smoothed the way for transmigration.[3] In Australia, the Jewish population rose from fewer than 1,200 in 1841 to 5,500 by 1861. Historian Jonathan Sarna describes Anglophone Jewry in the mid–nineteenth century as the "largest and the most culturally creative Jewish diaspora in the world."[4] Historian Adam Mendelsohn views many of these Jewish wayfarers as transnational in mindset, enthusiastically supporting the Manifest Destiny of "imperial England, and the expanding American west."[5] By the mid-1850s, San Francisco's Jewish population alone would reach 3,000, double the size of Chicago's.[6] By the 1870s California's Jewish population would top those of Pennsylvania, Ohio, and Illinois, remaining second only to New York's.[7]

Most Jews who traveled across the Rim for business opportunities did so by choice; they were not pushed by the type of extreme prejudice that existed in parts of Europe. Jewish Anglophones traveled the Rim for wealth and adventure, not religious freedom. Often their life stories were different from those of the young and single Jewish merchants of more recent European origin whom they met in the American West. Although some of the men were single, many of those who traveled east from the Antipodes were married. In most cases, the men were older than the majority who came for the gold rushes. A considerable proportion had been born in Britain but were already on the Pacific Rim when they learned of the California Gold Rush. Products of step-migration, they arrived on America's Pacific shore with families, business experience, and organizational expertise. Many shared an Orthodox upbringing and had the education, means, and desire to continue Jewish practice in their new homes. Crucially for the survival of West Coast Jewry, they had time to donate to community building and the large families needed to sustain community life. Not only had they experienced migration before, but they were familiar with the challenges of founding Jewish communities far from historic Jewish centers.

Fortune Seekers

News of California's gold discoveries reached Australia and New Zealand just a few months after the first finds. By early 1849, the streets of Sydney were full of men wondering where California was and how they could get there.[8] Before the end of the year, adventurous Jews from Down Under had booked passage to San Francisco. A founder of San Francisco's Jewish community, Israel Solomon had, by the end of 1850, completed two trips from Sydney to California and was among the first to assess the opportunities and arrange a return trip to settle with his entire family.[9]

Indeed, Jews from the Antipodes were so influential in the establishment of the San Francisco Jewish community that on a visit to his native London in 1907, Rabbi Jacob Nieto, of San Francisco's Sherith Israel, told the *Jewish Chronicle* that "originally, our congregation, . . . was formed of English emigrants from Australia . . . led by Israel Solomon."[10] Since Sherith Israel's founding fathers also hailed from Poland, Posen—then Prussian territory—and included native-born Sephardim, the predominance of those from the Antipodes in Rabbi Nieto's memory is significant.

It is possible to see how Nieto reached his conclusion by examining the lives of the Solomons and the Keesings, two multinational families who helped transform Rim life. Both families' wealth, experience, and religious fervor established lasting roots for the San Francisco Jewish community.

As examined further in chapter three, Jews played an important role in the Pacific Rim shipping industry. The Solomons, shipping agents and exporters in Sydney, transported the cloth, salt, honey, hardware, timber, and whole homes that were needed to build the city of San Francisco and to supply its multiplying population with food and goods. Their vessels also transported some of the multitudes who flocked to California, transporting whole Australian families to populate the city.

The prelude to this transpacific story started in 1833, when John Solomon, aged fifty, his wife Sarah (Simcha), forty, their only child, Israel, twenty-four, and his new wife, also named Sarah, twenty-one, joined the increasing number of free Jewish settlers from Britain who arrived in Australia in the 1830s and 1840s.[11] John opened a wine and spirits shop as well as a shipping agency that advertised for passengers and freight travel to Hobart Town.[12] Israel and his wife started a family that would eventually include twelve children. To help support this growing family, he entered the import–export business with a store on George Street, the main commercial street near Sydney's port.[13] Away from his business, Israel Solomon became a stalwart of the York Street Synagogue, where Jacob Isaacs would serve as reader.[14] Founded in 1831, the congregation purchased land and moved into its first permanent synagogue building in 1844.[15] Israel served as a trustee of the synagogue, held a seat on its governing committee, and, along with his father, donated to its building fund.[16] The devotion of both men was further illustrated by their nonmonetary contributions to the synagogue. At the consecration of the new synagogue, John presented the congregation with the Ten Commandments hand painted on glass, while Israel contributed a mantel and roller for the Torah. Both gifts demonstrated publically their religious dedication and their wealth.[17]

Even though they were well entrenched in synagogue and business life, the family only remained in Australia for five more years. When word of the California Gold Rush reached Sydney in late 1848, Israel Solomon immediately sailed off to investigate the new possibilities. After a short time in San Francisco, he came back to Sydney on a ship that carried California gold dust as visible proof to convince Australians that the fabled gold finds were real.[18] Having seen the wealth with his own eyes, Solomon returned only to "get his family and any friends who wanted to become rich."[19] With his father and

George Moss (also a donor to the York Street Synagogue and the founder of several of Sydney's Jewish cultural and educational institutions, including its first Jewish newspaper), he became the shipping agent for the new Sunderland-built barque *William and Mary*.[20] While other Australian Jews also formed shipping companies to take advantage of California's new demand for goods and Australians' desire to get rich quickly, the Solomons used their experience as shipping agents to finance their family's migration. Under the heading "Gold Mines of California," Solomon announced in the press that his ship would soon be sailing for California, notifying "all parties disposed to quit the colony, in order to better their condition, that he must proceed to sea on or about the 15th February."[21] To stimulate travel, the shipping company advertised that it would accept payment for passage in four installments; the advertisement assured potential travelers that the ship was "lofty and roomy between decks . . . and [that] her berths [were] fitted up with due regard to comfort and privacy."[22] To offer further reassurance to nervous travelers, Solomon stated that his own family would be traveling on the ship as well and that he had firsthand knowledge of California life. In the words of his advertisement, "The provisions will be of the first order, the charterer and [Solomon's] family proceeding with the vessel will be a guarantee both as to quantity and quality. Mr. Solomon will be happy to afford passengers by this vessel all necessary information respecting San Francisco and the adjacent country."[23]

On February 27, 1850, Israel Solomon set sail for San Francisco for a second time, this time with his wife, their seven children, and more than forty other families, including 70 children, 114 men, and 7 women traveling on their own.[24] The ship was also heavily laden with goods to sell, including bales of wool, boots, shoes, rum, and twenty cases of champagne. More importantly, its hull contained construction materials for the new city: a boiler, wheelbarrow, tinware, and many bundles of timber, including enough to build a home for the Solomons.[25] According to family lore, Solomon "had his house [in Sydney] taken down in sections" so it could be reconstructed in San Francisco.[26]

Solomon's enthusiasm and buoyant expectations were not shared by everyone. As the *William and Mary* left Sydney's harbor the emigrants encountered an incoming ship from California carrying unhappy returnees who yelled at them, "Come back—you will repent it if you go on."[27] However, proceed they did, and after 104 days at sea the ship arrived in San Francisco on June 11, 1850. Many of those on board set off to the mines, while families built homes and became part of the "instant" city.[28]

For John and Israel Solomon, arriving in San Francisco during the Gold Rush meant having to build their homes and businesses from scratch, even as they sought to create a religious community for themselves. When they arrived in San Francisco, the Jewish population probably numbered no more than two hundred, but it would grow into the thousands by middecade.[29] Before 1849, there was no known Jewish observance in California. As a traditional Jew, Israel immediately joined with others to start building the city's first Jewish institutions. With the experience he gained in Sydney, he served on the community-wide committee (before the formation of two congregations) to contract with a baker to produce Passover matzah and joined with other newcomers in announcing that there was a *schochet* so that the community would have kosher meat.[30] Before Passover in 1851, when disagreements over minhag and kashrut caused negotiations for a single community synagogue to be abandoned, Israel Solomon and his father, John, joined others in founding Congregation Sherith Israel.[31] Appointed to the committee charged with drafting the congregation's constitution and bylaws, Israel helped put in place a constitution that reflected his British origins.[32] The constitution they developed stated explicitly that the congregation would observe traditional Jewish practices "according to the Customs and usages of Minhag Polin to be the same as far as practicable and without departing from form and Custom, now in use in the principle [sic] Congregations of the United States and England."[33] With this constitution the founders sought to link themselves to other congregations in the United States as well as those in the British Empire. Although Solomon was a member of Sydney's York Street Synagogue, which also followed English practices, there were differences between the congregations. York Street followed an Ashkenazi rather than a Polish minhag. However, both congregations legitimized their form of worship by linking themselves to British Jewry.[34]

Soon after Sherith Israel's founding, the congregation elected Israel Solomon as its president, a position he held for thirteen of the next fifteen years. Solomon's biographer described him as an Englishman and an "ardent Jew," who never neglected to be in the synagogue for daily services and set an example for the congregants.[35] Leading by example extended to his family as well. When six-year-old Mary Goldsmith climbed the stairs to Sherith Israel's women's gallery in 1852, only the Solomon daughters greeted her.[36] It is likely that the congregation stayed Orthodox as long as it did because of Solomon's influence. When in 1870 the congregation voted for family seating—a step

York Street ("Sydney") Synagogue, 1844.

FIGURE 2.1. The York Street Synagogue, 1844, as pictured in the 1845 Report of the Synagogue. Courtesy of the Australian Jewish Historical Society.

that contravened conventional Orthodox practice—his ballot was 1 of 21 negative votes out of a total 105 cast.[37]

Israel's father, John, also played a substantial role in sustaining Sherith Israel. With his considerable capital he contributed significantly to the congregation's physical well-being. When in July of 1852 the congregation considered leaving rented quarters and building a synagogue, John Solomon offered the congregation $1,500 at 2 percent interest to "buy land to erect a synagogue"; later that same month, he offered an additional $500 without interest for a year.[38] This arrangement was accepted, and to safeguard his investment, John Solomon served on the synagogue's first building committee.[39] Given the involvement of the Solomons in planning and financing the new synagogue, it should not be surprising that the new building bore a strong resemblance to Sydney's York Street Synagogue. Not only did the congregation's practice reflect the Solomons religiously, but its physical building reflected their history as well (Figures 2.1 and 2.2).[40]

Unlike many of their fellow congregants, who arrived in California with little money, neither John nor his son, Israel, had to leave competitive San

FIGURE 2.2 Congregation Sherith Israel, 1854. BANC MSS 2010/720. Courtesy of the Bancroft Library, University of California, Berkeley.

Francisco for the rural gold country to seek his livelihood. Small merchants who owned stores in gold country returned to San Francisco to purchase goods and socialize. They could be synagogue members but could not afford the time to play leading roles in synagogue life.[41] The Solomons supplied the stability the congregation needed for its survival. In return for this stability and financial support, the congregation rewarded them with leadership positions.

The Solomons were not the only influential immigrants from the Pacific Rim. Serving on Sherith Israel's building committee with John Solomon was Barnet Keesing, a fellow migrant from England by way of the Antipodes. The Keesing family tree had Ashkenazi roots in Amsterdam.[42] By 1816 Barnet's father, Henry, had immigrated to London and married Rosetta Kasner in the Great Synagogue, the ceremony performed by Chief Rabbi Solomon Hershel.[43] Influenced by Joel Samuel Polack (who would later make his way back to New Zealand before settling in San Francisco), who had just returned from New Zealand with positive reports of opportunity there, Henry sent his eldest son to investigate. Known as the pioneering member of the Keesing family—"the uncle that came first"—the twenty-year-old Barnet left London in 1838 for New Zealand to determine whether it could be a new home for the family, which included nine children.[44] Barnet found great success in New Zealand as a merchant selling lemonade and ginger beer in addition to imported goods.[45] By midcentury, much of the Keesing family had left England. Some immigrated to the eastern United States, while Barnet's parents and several of his siblings joined him in Auckland. Soon his father became a wealthy merchant, a landowner, and the first president of the newly founded Auckland Hebrew Congregation.[46]

With his family settled safely in New Zealand, Barnet continued his life of travel. In 1845 he visited Australia, where he married the British-born Hannah Solomon in a ceremony in Sydney. As was the case for many early Jewish settlers, Hannah's father had not chosen to immigrate to Australia but had been transported there as a convict in 1833. His family joined him later.[47] After their marriage in Sydney, Barnet and Hannah settled in Auckland, where they started a family.

Developments in California, however, changed their plans. In December of 1848, the excitement of the California Gold Rush reached New Zealand, and, again, the footloose family packed its bags and set off.[48] Sixteen-year-old John Keesing went first, soon followed by Barnet and Hannah.[49] Hannah gave birth to the third of her eleven children, Kate, as their ship entered the Golden Gate in the fall of 1849. A congregational history reports that both Hannah and Barnet Keesing were present at the first Yom Kippur service in San Francisco in 1849.[50] This would have made Hannah the first woman to attend a Jewish service in San Francisco. However, the date raises some questions. The ship arrived at port three days after Yom Kippur, but the family may have come ashore in a small boat before their ship was able to get the necessary winds to anchor closer to the shore. Ten months later, Hannah gave birth to her fourth child, a boy, whose bris was described on the pages of the *Daily Alta California*.[51] The bris took place at the Albion House Hotel, owned by the Keesings. The Albion, whose name may reflect the Keesing's British heritage, became a well-known place to live and board as well as a meeting place for the Jewish community. The

San Francisco branch of the Keesing family grew wealthy as Barnet progressed, like his father in New Zealand, from being a merchant—supplying the new community with clothes, groceries, and prefabricated Australian homes—to owning a real estate business with a motto that would come to sum up California perfectly: "If you have land, you have everything."[52]

Alongside the Solomons, Barnet Keesing served on early San Francisco communal committees that decided on the location to hold High Holiday service in 1850 and to raise funds for a synagogue building.[53] To further ensure that his family could follow Jewish practice, Keesing placed himself on committees to hire a *schochet* for kosher meat and a baker for Passover matzah.[54] He was elected trustee of Congregation Sherith Israel in 1855.[55]

Visits and letters passed news back and forth between friends and family members in Australia, New Zealand, and California, keeping all well informed and encouraging and easing chain migration.[56] Joel Samuel Polack, the adventurer and chronicler who had enticed the Keesing family to move to New Zealand, now joined the Keesings in San Francisco. In Auckland, Polack had signed Barnet's sister Hannah's ketubah in 1846. Both the Keesing and Polack families were originally from Holland by way of England, and they had a lot in common. A traveler in his youth, the London-born J. S. Polack worked for the British War Office in South Africa and Mauritius for four years before uniting in 1830 with his brother Abraham, who had been transported to Australia by the British government for stealing a watch. After his emancipation Abraham became a leader of Sydney's Jewish community, serving as congregation president in 1836 and being a major contributor to the York Street Synagogue with Israel Solomon.[57] Joel did not stay long in Sydney, soon moving on to New Zealand, where he became an authority on and advocate for the Maori people, writing and illustrating *New Zealand; Being a Narrative of Travels and Adventures during a Residence in that County between the Years 1831 and 1837* (1838) and *Manners and Customs of the New Zealanders* (1840). He acquired tracts of land and achieved success as a merchant and brewery owner. In 1837, he traveled to England to appear before the House of Lords in support of organized British colonization of New Zealand. During this time he met the Keesings. When Barnet Keesing first arrived in New Zealand, he rented property from Polack. Returning to New Zealand in 1842, Polack became successful in the warehouse and shipping business, participating in the burgeoning trade with California. Like several other Jews from the Antipodes, he made his first contacts with California through the shipping business. To cement the connection, Polack served as the US vice-consul in New Zealand before leaving permanently for California in 1850.[58] J. S. Polack spent his last thirty years in San Francisco, where he, like Barnet Keesing, became involved in land speculation.[59]

In the years that followed, families continued to make their way across the Pacific, further adding Jewish influence from the Antipodes.[60]

Convicts

If the tale of Joel Polack bespeaks a better remembered and more eagerly recounted type of Jewish migration, his brother Abraham's experience reflects that which was less eagerly recalled and recounted. The role played by Jewish convicts transported from England to Australia as early settlers in California is little known. After their emancipation, some, like other Australians, sought riches in California during the gold rush.[61] Between 1788 and 1852, approximately one thousand Jews were transported to Australia for their crimes.[62] In England, poverty was rampant within the Jewish community. Jews had escaped their restrictive lives on the European continent to a freer England; however, overcrowding, limited prospects, and their adherence to Jewish Sabbath laws made it difficult for many to find work and succeed. Like others sentenced to transportation for life, most Jewish convicts were young, working-class men, with an average age of twenty-five who had been arrested for nonviolent crimes such as stealing, picking pockets, and forging money. Women accounted for only 7 percent of Jews convicted and transported.[63] Once in Australia, these Jews, convicts and emancipists (a convict who had been given a conditional or absolute pardon) alike, became a part of the new, vital Jewish society in the Antipodes. Some heard the call of the California Gold Rush.

Serving as the president of Los Angeles's Common [City] Council in 1870, the first Jew to do so, John Jones did not fit the stereotype of Jewish immigrants in California.[64] Records of his birthplace cannot be verified. Born of Polish parents in the early 1800s either in Poland or in London, at approximately age thirty he was sentenced at the Old Bailey to life imprisonment and transported to Australia for stealing a breast pin, although he was probably a counterfeiter as well.[65] Jones arrived in Australia in October of 1836.[66] Seven years later, he received his certificate of freedom.[67] Identifying with Australia's Jewish community, Jones contributed to Sydney's York Street Synagogue.[68] He would continue to support the Jewish communities of San Francisco and Los Angeles.

When news arrived of the California Gold Rush, Jones boarded the British brig *Broad Axe* in Adelaide, arriving in San Francisco 116 days later on August 3, 1850.[69] He spent the next twenty-five years dividing his time between San Francisco and Los Angeles, where he became a successful whole-sale grocer, real estate developer, and exporter, locating his store in down-town Los Angeles, the business hub for Jewish merchants.[70] As recorded by early Los Angeles Jewish pioneer Harris Newmark, at least twice a year Jones closed his store for six weeks while he went to San Francisco to pur-chase goods.[71] This was a common practice for Jewish merchants throughout the region, for the purpose of their trips went beyond purchasing goods to include attending synagogue services, renewing friendships, and enjoying the more cosmopolitan city.[72] In the mid-1850s, Jones, then worth, according to Newmark, a substantial fifty thousand dollars, returned to San Francisco for several years. In 1857 he joined his fellow former Australians, serving as Israel Solomon's vice-president of Sherith Israel.[73] He married the Scottish-born Doria Deighton, a Christian, and became a father.[74]

However, Jones's San Francisco stay did not last. By 1863 John and Doria lived in Los Angeles in a large adobe house previously owned by the governor of California.[75] Once again he engaged in community life. In the 1870s, John served on the Los Angeles city council, while his wife, Doria, served as the first treasurer for the Ladies' Hebrew Benevolent Society, a most unusual role for a Christian woman.[76] Far from Jewish centers, intermarriage was often tolerated to an extent not found in cities with larger Jewish populations. The Ladies' Hebrew Benevolent Society, founded by the wives of the city's Jewish merchants, took care of the poor and the sick and prepared the dead for burial with "every honor and rite the Hebrew religion accords."[77] Since the society had only thirty-nine members at founding, they most likely would not reject the altruistic and wealthy Mrs. Jones.[78]

This couple—John Jones, convicted at the Old Bailey, and his Christian wife—helped lay the foundation for Jewish communities in both San Fran-cisco and Los Angeles. Jones died in 1876. When Doria died in 1908, her estate was worth a million dollars, most of it in real estate.[79] Other former Jewish convicts also played a part in California Jewish life, but none are known to have become as prominent as the Jones family.[80]

Roaming Rabbis

Rabbis, lay readers, and mohels (men who perform Jewish circumcisions) also exhibited wanderlust. In the same way that nineteenth-century rabbis traveled across the United States from east to west or, as Adam Mendelsohn illustrated, from colonial pulpit to colonial pulpit, some rabbis roamed the

Pacific Rim. During their travels they encouraged community organization, led services, and provided expertise as officiants at marriages, circumcisions, and funerals. Without these men, Jewish communities might have been slower to develop or attracted fewer permanent members. In these new communities, religious leaders provided community structure, while at the same time they represented the public face of Jews and Judaism.

Some men traveled the Rim with a sense of adventure, seeking to be a part of the next gold strike or booming economy. Others followed family members or friends to far-flung lands, while still others traveled with altruistic intentions, such as fundraising for synagogue and orphanage construction.

English-speaking hazans and rabbis benefited from what Mendelsohn describes as "an international ministerial marketplace."[81] In the expanding English-speaking diaspora, well-spoken clergy enhanced small Jewish communities, making them more attractive to settlers. Several affected the development of Jewish communities along the Pacific Rim. An example is Jacob Frankel, whose story is in many ways familiar to those who study American Jewry; however, it has an Australian and New Zealand twist. Analogous to rabbis from Europe who moved between pulpits in the United States, Frankel served as a lay reader for congregations in England, Australia, California, and New Zealand. He traveled what might be described as a "colonial circuit."[82] Although never a British colony, California was, as we have seen, a popular destination for many midcentury Anglo-Jewish step-migrants.

Born in Breslau in 1812, Frankel received a good Jewish and secular education until age thirteen, when he began a career in commerce. Employed by an uncle, Frankel learned salesmanship, traveling and trading merchandise throughout Saxony and beyond.[83] Much like San Francisco's first rabbi, Julius Eckman, he left his family as a young man and settled in England. There Frankel studied with the chief rabbi, Solomon Hirschell, living in his home and becoming his companion (possibly meeting the Keesing family, who also attended the Great Synagogue).[84] In 1835, he married Sarah Moss, who gave birth to three children before they emigrated to Australia. In Hobart, Frankel opened a store and helped found the Hobart Hebrew Congregation.[85] Unfortunately for Frankel, his wife died while on a visit to Sydney, and, soon after, his Hobart business failed. His dreams of a stable and prosperous life in Australia dashed, he looked to escape to the California Gold Rush.[86]

In San Francisco, Frankel's poor luck continued. He joined the merchant class only to see his store burned to the ground several times, fueled by the fires that regularly swept the city in the early 1850s. Although he did not succeed in business, Frankel found that his religious training became an asset to the young Jewish community. As he had done previously in Australia, Frankel volunteered to become a reader in San Francisco; according to Sherith Israel's minute book, his offer was "unanimously accepted" by its members.[87] The founders appointed him the same day they chose a committee to draft a constitution for the newly founded congregation. Sherith Israel's early meeting places, like the stores of the merchants who were its members, were repeatedly destroyed by fires, and its members could not afford to pay for a rabbi or hazan. Frankel, who was described as a "chazzan with a good voice,"[88] fit in perfectly with the members of the congregation, as it was primarily made up of Poles, Poseners, and English Jews, including the Solomons and the Keesings, who had also lived in London and the Antipodes. Frankel agreed with community founders who were disappointed with the level of observance in the city. He characterized some of the city's Jews as having money as their only aim: "Sabbath, holidays, weekdays," he complained, "were all alike to them."[89] This was not the case with his fellow Australians, like the Keesings and Solomons, who served as the guardians of Jewish law for the congregation.

Frankel stayed only a few years in San Francisco. In 1852, he received a letter from his adult daughter with the news that gold had been discovered in Australia and that, with "thousands of persons of all nations . . . arriving weekly," she wanted her father to come home.[90] Thus, for a second time, Frankel boarded a ship to cross the Pacific in search of riches.[91] Before leaving San Francisco, Israel Solomon, Sherith Israel's president, presented Frankel with a medal made from precious California gold and inscribed in Hebrew and English, thanking him for his service to the young congregation.[92]

This return to Australia was not the end of Frankel's Pacific Rim travels. He settled in Melbourne, where he volunteered in the Bourke Street Synagogue.[93] There he remarried and fathered five more children. Then, following a third gold rush, he sailed to the South Island of New Zealand, where he served as a reader for the Dunedin congregation.[94] In 1864, Frankel finally found a permanent home in Wellington, where he became a paid reader, the hazan, and the driving force for the building of a synagogue, soliciting donations from as far away as Australia.[95] When the synagogue was dedicated in 1870, the choir sang hymns to melodies composed by Frankel for the occasion.[96] In part due to the dedication and learning of Jacob Frankel, Jewish communities thrived in five Pacific Rim cities.

Others followed Frankel's example in leaving California for Australia when word of new rushes arrived. One such man, Abraham Abrahamsohn, had quite a tale to tell. Born in Prussia, he was a man of many trades, baker and mohel among them. In 1849, he left his wife and children to set sail for the United States. After a year and a half in the east, Abrahamsohn arrived in California in the spring of 1851. In the year he remained in California, he undertook work as a miner, merchant, tailor, baker of matzah, and mohel. It was as an experienced Passover baker and a mohel that he helped establish the necessary infrastructure for San Francisco's burgeoning Jewish community. He explained in his memoir,

> In Germany, I had practiced circumcision on Jewish boys, an honorable, holy profession, which is never paid for there. A Jew from Regensburg who lived in San Francisco, and had seen my certificate asked me to come to San Francisco [from Sacramento] for the circumcision of his son. I received $60 for this and $10 for travel expenses. After I came back to Sacramento City, I bought all that I would need and set myself up in business in San Francisco as a circumciser, charging $50 for each child. Through this religious profession I had access to the richest and most prominent families. Since the Jews in this city were competing with their elders in Egyptian lands in the matter of offspring, I had much to do and in about half a year had laid by a profit of 800 Dollars.[97]

With few mohels in California and many births, Abrahamsohn could demand to be well compensated for his work. As Abrahamsohn's chronicle demonstrates, Jewish family life grew in 1850s San Francisco; clearly, the stereotype of young wild bachelors did not fit all. Unlike many American men who came west by themselves, Jews who established families in the west out of necessity sought out men with knowledge of Jewish practices for weddings, circumcisions, and their children's education as well as holiday observance.

Abrahamsohn invested his profits in a restaurant, which burned to the ground in one of the city's many fires. To add to his misfortune, he was a gambler, and his remaining money disappeared in the city's many gambling houses. Luckily for Abrahamsohn, he could always fall back on baking when his purse was depleted by gambling. When Passover approached, Mark Isaacs, the owner of a kosher bakery, hired him to bake Passover goods and matzah. Abrahamsohn recalled, "I went to see the Jewish baker Eisacks [Isaacs] who wanted help and for a daily wage of $8 and living expenses from six o'clock in the morning to 6 at night, I shoved Mazzen in the oven to bake."[98] The fact that there was such a demand for matzah again points to California's significant Jewish population, already near a thousand, and to the adherence of some of its members to Jewish practice.[99] Because of Abrahamsohn and others, Jewish life survived in the chaotic West. However, Abrahamsohn, the avid gambler, hoping not to lose more in California's gaming houses, left in 1852 to pursue the Australian gold rushes. There he succeeded, mining gold worth $2,000, but gave up this pursuit to sell baked goods to the miners, a much more reliable source of income.[100] Missing his family, Abrahamsohn returned to his home in Germany a year later, where he wrote his memoir. In his brief time in California and Australia, his abilities helped provide some of the necessities for traditional Jewish life on the Rim.

In the latter half of the nineteenth century, after the rushes had ended, roaming rabbis continued to sustain Western Jewish communities. When Rabbi Meyer Samuel Levy's mother died in London in the 1890s, the *San Francisco Call* reported that five of her children lived in the United States, four in London, and one in Australia.[101] Of the six who joined the British Jewish diaspora, two ventured to the Pacific Rim.[102] Rabbi M. S. Levy, as he was known, traveled widely, truly a roaming rabbi. Born in London in 1852, the son of a rabbi, he attended the Jews' Free School, married the English-born Annie Teacher, and then began a life of travel: Melbourne, San Jose, Oakland, San Francisco, and Honolulu.[103] Levy emigrated to Melbourne in the 1870s, where he taught Hebrew and prepared students for bar mitzvah at the nondenominational St. Kilda Collegiate College for two years before coming to California.[104]

Traditional in practice, but amenable to some reforms, Levy contributed a great deal to the development of the Jewish community in California. His activism and support of early Zionism marked his California tenure. He served Congregation Bickur Cholim in San Jose for eight years. As a native English speaker and an educator, it is not surprising that Levy found a welcome at the young California congregation. Their first permanent rabbi, he promoted religious education for children as well as adults. Like Samuel Isaacs in New York, Levy needed to supplement his income. He did so by offering English and bookkeeping classes, which he taught in his home.[105] Fulfilling the expectations of his congregation to be a civic leader, Levy became a celebrated orator, addressing Jewish and non-Jewish groups in the community.[106]

When in 1881 Levy moved from San Jose to Oakland to become the first rabbi of the First Hebrew Congregation, he attracted students who would carry on his legacy. Two of the students in the Sabbath school exceeded expectations. One student, Rudolph Coffee, would one day replace Levy as rabbi of the Oakland congregation. Coffee's cousin and fellow student Judah L. Magnes, influenced by Levy's Zionism and community activism, not only became the first rabbi born in the American West but also organized New York's communal organization, the Kehilla, and then helped found the Hebrew University in Jerusalem, becoming its first chancellor and president.[107] Magnes, who would become a renowned orator, gave his first speech in Levy's Sabbath school at age seven.[108] Beyond future rabbinical students, Levy's Sabbath school included a young Gertrude Stein, whose father was a close friend. Ray Frank served as one of the school's teachers. Later known as the first woman rabbi, she undertook some rabbinic studies and lectured widely in western congregations on biblical and Jewish topics.

When the Oakland congregation moved closer to Reform Judaism, Levy crossed the bay to San Francisco, where he served the traditional Beth Israel from 1890 until his death in 1916. In San Francisco he championed prison reform and challenged Mark Twain's hostile stereotypes of Jewish character.[109] Although never taking another pulpit, this much traveled rabbi also became a catalyst for the congregation in Honolulu, where his son lived.

Linked by family and business ties and proximity to each other and isolated from the eastern United States, Portland, Honolulu, and the Canadian city of Victoria became satellites of the San Francisco Jewish community. Levy traveled to these Pacific Rim cities to fundraise, perform religious rites, and seek adventure. When Oakland's First Hebrew Congregation required funds to rebuild after a fire in 1885, Levy set out on a very successful fundraising trip to Portland and Victoria, British Columbia.[110] When his son Herman joined Hawaii's merchant class in the mid-1890s, Rabbi Levy visited and lectured to general and Jewish audiences in Honolulu, where he became the Jewish community's unofficial advisor. Honolulu Jewry and the San Francisco Jewish community maintained permanent connections. Hawaiian merchants ordered their stock from San Francisco, and members of California families often went to the Islands to try to succeed in the less competitive Honolulu.[111] Trade treaties and eventual annexation in 1898 created an attractive economy that enticed Jews from the mainland. In 1899 Levy received an invitation to speak at Hawaii's Fourth of July celebration.[112] Since this was the first celebration after annexation of the Hawaiian Islands by the United States, Levy's speech received much attention.[113] The patriotic speech was printed on the front page of the newspaper alongside a large drawing of the speaker, with the title "Rev. M. S. Levy (The well-known Rabbi of San Francisco, orator of the day)."[114] Reading this speech without knowing Levy's biography, it would be easy to assume that he was a native-born patriot rather than a British-born rabbi and a multi–step-immigrant. In the aftermath of the American victory in the Spanish–American War, Levy declared Anglo-Saxon superiority, believing that Hawaiians would adopt the English tongue and that "one common purpose," that of the United States, would unite the world. In this talk, Levy stressed American ideals, Manifest Destiny, and his hope that Hawaii would shortly gain statehood. He proclaimed to his audience, "May you deserve the blessings of the American Constitution and all its privileges by your loyal adherence to the flag of our nation, and may the spirit of civil liberty, equality, fraternity, and brotherhood be the lever raising you to a higher and a nobler manhood,"[115] implying that Hawaiians needed to be raised above their current cultural and linguistic standing to be worthy of full citizenship. At the conclusion of the speech the gathered crowd broke into "storms of applauses."[116] Although part of a mutlinational family, after twenty-five years in the United States, Levy fully identified as a white American. His Jewish aspirations were saved for Jewish audiences.

Facing the Jewish community, he issued a call for a "permanent synagogue," a suggestion that spurred the community to action.[117] After Levy returned to San Francisco, a group of Honolulu Jews wrote him requesting copies of constitutions and bylaws from the city's congregations and benevolent societies to use as templates for their own organizations.[118] Thus the British-born, Rim-traveling Levy influenced Jewish communities in Australia, California, and Hawaii. The culmination of his life of travel came when he visited Palestine in 1913, a fulfillment of his Zionist dreams.[119]

Even after Rabbi Levy's sojourn in Honolulu ended, the Jewish community continued to received nourishment from his enthusiasm. His Oakland protégé, Rudolph I. Coffee, arrived in the Islands for an extended visit in 1902. The twenty-four-year-old rabbinical student, then enrolled at the Jewish Theological Seminary in New York, supplied much needed rabbinical support. He dedicated Hawaii's first Jewish cemetery, conducted the first funeral in the cemetery, and performed the wedding ceremony between his aunt, formerly of Oakland, and a longtime resident of the Islands.[120] Coffee wrote the first widely disseminated article on the history of Hawaii's Jewish community; published in the *American Israelite,* it became the source for much of the future writing about Jewish life on the Islands.[121]

The work of transnationals Frankel, Abrahamsohn, and Levy left lasting impressions on West Coast Jewry. Rabbis, lay readers, and mohels linked Rim communities together for financial support, religious knowledge, and clerical visits. They depended on each other. The Pacific Rim network they created, helped start and helped maintain communities over several generations. These men were not limited by their distance from eastern centers but rather looked to the cities of the Pacific Rim to connect with the Jewish world.

Conclusion

Looking west rather than east unsettles the way American Jewish history is traditionally oriented. The travels of Jacob Frankel and Israel Solomon, for example, demonstrate how California Jewry in part was shaped by men who had also played founding roles in Jewish life in Australia. News of California's gold discoveries reached the major cities of the Pacific Rim just a few months after the first finds. If Solomon, Keesing, Frankel, and other Antipodal transnationals had not already been on the Pacific Rim, it is unlikely that they would have arrived in gold rush California in time to substantially influence community life. They were in the right place at the right time to take advantage of the new riches and opportunities. Because they arrived early, they could help define what it meant to be a Jew in San Francisco and its satellite communities along the Rim. They influenced Sherith Israel's constitution, volunteered as synagogue readers, provided kosher and holiday food, and had a lasting impact on the community by making sure that the congregation's first rabbi was London born. Their choice, Henry A. Henry, followed the Isaacs brothers' transnational trail.[122] Most Pacific Rim migrants were older and wealthier than the men who came directly from Europe or the eastern United States. They shared the English language and an Orthodox upbringing and had the education, means, and desire to continue Jewish practice. Most important, for survival of West Coast Jewry, they believed in community building.

Another understudied dimension of early American Jewish life on the West Coast is the role played by former Australian convicts and their families. While the total number of Jews transported to Australia for their crimes who sought a new life in California was probably small, three of the Jewish families discussed here had at least one member who fit that category. They and their children participated along with free Australian Jews in crafting Jewish communities on all sides of the Pacific Rim.[123]

Current research on Jewish transmigrants from the Pacific Rim in the western United States leaves many questions unanswered. Future research may discover the relationship between Jews and gentiles from Antipodes in the United States, connections between earlier and later migrant families, and the interplay of Rim religious leadership.

Examining the lives of Pacific Rim Jews through a global lens broadens our understanding of American Jewish history. Porous borders simplified step-migration. Economic opportunities allowed new patterns of Jewish transmigration to emerge. As Suzanne Rutland discusses in chapter three, business and family relations persisted between Australasia and California well after the gold rushes ended. In the Keesing family alone there were several Pacific Rim marriages. Barnet's son Tom married a New Zealand cousin, while Kate, Barnet's daughter, also returned to the Antipodes to marry.

Several of the earliest links in this Pacific Rim chain remain alive until this day. Almost 150 years after Barnet Keesing first set foot in New Zealand, the extended family of more than three hundred gathered in Auckland for a reunion, with cousins coming from New Zealand, Australia, California, and beyond.[124]

Notes

This chapter benefited greatly from the help of Australians Suzanne Rutland, Liz James, Howard Freeman, Philip Moses, and Merle Langley and Americans Ellen Eisenberg, Victoria Fisch, Jeremy Frankel, and Mitchell Richman. I thank them all. Ruth Haber read several drafts of this chapter; her fortitude is appreciated.

1. Comparison of Jewish emigration to California and Australia is discussed by Rudolf Glanz in his final chapter "California—Australia the Parallelism of Jewish Emigration," in *The Jews of California from the Discovery of Gold until 1880* (New York: Southern California Jewish Historical Society, 1960), 161–64. In this chapter Glanz cites articles in the European Jewish press and notes the importance of Jews from Australia in San Francisco Jewish life. For an example from England, see "Jewish Female Emigration," *Jewish Chronicle* (London), January 14, 1853.

2. The experience of Isaac Lazarus Lincoln is an example. Lincoln, a mohel, left Melbourne with his family for the California Gold Rush. The family arrived safely in Honolulu; however, all but their son John, who remained in Hawaii, died on their way to California. Anthony Jospeh, "Lincoln, the Descendants of Nathan Ben Elijah and Australia: A New Appraisal," *Australian Jewish Historical Society Journal* 13, no. 4 (1997): 646.

3. Adam Mendelsohn, "Tongue Ties: The Emergence of the Anglophone Jewish Diaspora in the Mid-Nineteenth Century," *American Jewish History* 93, no. 2 (2007): 178–79, 184.

4. Jonathan Sarna as qtd. in Mendelsohn, "Tongue Ties," 178–79.

5. Mendelsohn, "Tongue Ties," 185.

6. Jacob Rader Marcus, *To Count a People: American Jewish Population Data, 1585–1984* (Lanham, MD: University Press of America, 1990), 28, 57.

7. Moses Rischin and John Livingston, eds., *Jews of the American West* (Detroit: Wayne State University Press, 1991), 35.

8. Jay Monaghan, *Australians and the Gold Rush: California and Down Under 1849–1854* (Berkeley: University of California Press, 1966), 1.

9. Ibid., 102.

10. "San Francisco Jewry," *Jewish Chronicle of London*, July 14, 1907, 18.

11. "John Solomon," in John S. Levy, *These Are the Names: Jewish Lives in Australia, 1788–1850*, by Levy (Carlton, Australia: Miegunyah Press, 2006), 734. For more about this period of Jewish migration to Australia, see Suzanne D. Rutland, *Edge of the Diaspora: Two Centuries of Jewish Settlement in Australia* (New York: Holmes & Meier, 1997), 25–49.

12. Levy, "John Solomon," 734.

13. "Israel Solomon," in Levy, *These Are the Names*, 733.

14. On Jacob Isaacs, see chapter one.

15. Rutland, *Edge of the Diaspora*, 29.

16. "Report of the Committee of the York Street (Sydney) Synagogue 1845–5605." Australian Jewish Historical Society Reprint, 1944, 13.

17. Ibid., 16.

18. Monaghan, *Australians and the Gold Rush*, 102. *The Sydney Morning Herald*, October 3, 1849, 2, accessed January 18, 2013, http://nla.gov.au/nla.news-page1513265.

19. Monaghan, *Australians and the Gold Rush*, 102.

20. Rutland, *Edge of the Diaspora*, 48.

21. "Advertising," *The Sydney Morning Herald*, December 1849, 1, accessed January 18, 2013, http://nla.gov.au/nla.news-article12914561; *The Shipping Gazette and Sydney General Trade List*, February 23, 1850 noted that the ship was loading for California.

22. Monaghan, *Australians and the Gold Rush*, 102; "Advertising," *The Sydney Morning Herald*, December 21, 1849, 1, accessed January 18, 2013, http://nla.gov.au/nla.news-article12914561.

23. "Advertising." *The Sydney Morning Herald*, December 21, 1849, 1, accessed January 18, 2013, http://nla.gov.au/nla.news-article12914561.

24. *The Shipping Gazette and Sydney General Trade List*, March 2, 1850, 62.

25. Ibid., 63.

26. Ida Fisher Raas, "Where We Came from & How We Got Here," May 1950, 6. This is likely, for others did the same. See the 1850s issues of *The Shipping Gazette and Sydney General Trade List*. There was a rapidly growing prefabricated home industry in Australia.

27. Monaghan, *Australians and the Gold Rush*, 116.

28. Charles Bateson, *Gold Fleet for California: Forty-Niners from Australia and New Zealand* (East Lansing: Michigan State University Press, 1963), 157.

29. Marcus, *To Count a People*, 28.

30. William Kramer and Norton B. Stern, "A Search for the First Synagogue," *Western States Jewish Historical Quarterly* 7, no. 1 (1974): 8, 12.

31. Sherith Israel and Emanu-El were founded within a week of each other.

32. "Minute Book" Congregation Sherith Israel, April 13, 1851. Magnes Collection, Bancroft Library, University of California, Berkeley; Ava F. Kahn, *Jewish Voices of the California Gold Rush: A Documentary History, 1849–1880* (Detroit: Wayne State University Press, 2002), 156.

33. "Minute Book" Congregation Sherith Israel, April 13, 1851. Also see "Sherith Israel Constitution, 1851," as qtd. in Kahn, *Jewish Voices*, 155–56.

34. In practice, both congregations probably followed similar minhagim, as at the time London's congregations were influenced by both styles. In San Francisco, they needed to differentiate themselves from Congregation Emanu-El, which was made up primarily of Germans. Where Sherith Israel had a mixture of men from England, Posen, and Poland as well as American Sephardim, Sydney's congregation was more homogenous.
35. "Israel Solomon," *Western Jewry: An Account of the Achievements of the Jews and Judaism in California*, ed. A. W. Voorsanger (San Francisco: Emanu-El, 1916), 149.
36. Mary Goldsmith Prag, "Early Days," in Kahn, *Jewish Voices*, 165.
37. Kahn, *Jewish Voices*, 161. Mixed seating had been discussed since 1864.
38. "Minute Book" Congregation Sherith Israel, July 11, 1852; July 18, 1852. Magnes Collection, Bancroft Library, University of California, Berkeley.
39. "Minute Book" Congregation Sherith Israel, July 18, 1852. Magnes Collection, Bancroft Library, University of California, Berkeley.
40. Other authors have assumed that Sherith Israel's architecture was influenced primarily by churches or the buildings of other ethnic groups. See, e.g., David Kaufman, "Early Synagogue Architecture," in *California Jews*, ed. Ava F. Kahn and Marc Dollinger (Lebanon, NH: Brandeis University Press, 2003), 42–43.
41. E.g., Michael Goldwater opened a store in Arizona while his wife and family remained in San Francisco. Upon retirement he served as vice-president of Sherith Israel. Ava F. Kahn and Ellen Eisenberg, "Western Reality: Jewish Diversity during the 'German' Period," *American Jewish History* 92, no. 4 (2004): 455–79 (published in 2007).
42. Agnew and Agnew, *A Colonial Cousinhood* (Auckland, New Zealand: A. & R. Agnew, March 1986), 4.
43. Ibid., 5; Claire Reynolds, "A Bird's Eye View of the Keesings—A Jewish Family of Early Auckland," in *Identity and Involvement: Auckland Jewry, Past and Present*, ed. Ann Gluckman (Palmerston North, New Zealand: Dunmore Press, 1990), 124.
44. The date is approximate, Barnet was in New Zealand in 1839. Agnew and Agnew, *A Colonial Cousinhood*, 5; Reynolds, "A Bird's Eye View," 124. For more about Joel Samuel Polack see page 13.
45. Barnet Keesing made a trip back to England in 1847–1848 to purchase goods. Agnew and Agnew, *A Colonial Cousinhood*, 9.
46. Agnew and Agnew, *A Colonial Cousinhood*, 7. For more about Henry Keesing and the Keesing family in New Zealand, see www.teara.govt.nz/en/biographies/1k5/1; Goldman, *Jews in New Zealand*.
47. Agnew and Agnew, *A Colonial Cousinhood*, 10.
48. Ibid., 9.
49. John Keesing returned to New Zealand a year later with a bag of gold. Agnew and Agnew, *A Colonial Cousinhood*, 26.
50. The record in *The Chronicles of Emanu-El* may refer to 1850, not 1849, as it also lists Israel Solomon as present, and he left San Francisco for Sydney in July of 1849. http://archive.org/stream/chroniclesofemanoocong#page/15/mode/1up/search/solomon; *The Chronicles of Emanu-El* (San Francisco, 1900), 16; Monaghan, *Australians and the Gold Rush*, 102.
51. *Daily Alta California*, San Francisco, June 14, 1850, 2.
52. Norton Stern, "Circumcision in San Francisco—1850," *Western States Jewish Historical Quarterly* 4, no. 1 (1971): 51.

53. Kramer and Stern, "Search for the First Synagogue," 5, 10.

54. Ibid., 12.

55. "List of Officers of the Congregation Sherith Israel 1851–1871" (San Francisco: Sherith Israel, 1871), 5.

56. Letters described the lives of friends and relatives in California. E.g., see Letter from John Webster to Dr. Hocken, February 21, 1894. Hocken Collection, ms-0084/013, University of Otago, Dunedin, New Zealand. Barnet and Hannah returned to New Zealand for a visit, as did one of their sons. A nephew visited the Keesings in San Francisco.

57. For more about Abraham Polack, see Rutland, *Edge of the Diaspora*, 17, 26, 28. "Report of the Committee of the York Street (Sydney) Synagogue 1845–5605." Australian Jewish Historical Society Reprint, 1944, 13.

58. For more about Joel Samuel Polack in New Zealand, see "Joel Samuel Polack," in Goldman, *Jews in New Zealand*, 33–39; Sir Leslie, Stephen, ed. *Dictionary of National Biography, 1921–1922* (London: Oxford University Press, 1921–1922).

59. There was controversy about his ownership of Yerba Buena Island in the San Francisco Bay. See "In the Matter of Yerba Buena Island: Memorial of Joel S. Polack of San Francisco to the Senate and House of Representatives of the United States of America in Congress Assembled" (San Francisco: Francis & Valentine, Commercial Printing Office, 1870); Letter from John Webster to Dr. Hocken, February 21, 1894. Hocken Collection, ms-0084/013, University of Otago, Dunedin, New Zealand.

60. Many Australian and New Zealand Jewish families have a branch that went to the United States in the 1900s; on the list are the Bergman family, who fled to Delores Park after the 1906 earthquake and fire. Photograph available from author and Harvey Cohen, Australia Jewish Historical Society.

61. For Australians in the California Gold Rush, see Monaghan, *Australians and the Gold Rush*.

62. Rutland, *Edge of the Diaspora*, 8. For more on this fascinating subject, see J. S. Levi and G. F. Bergman, *Australian Genesis: Jewish Convicts and Settlers 1788–1850* (London: Robert Hale, 1974).

63. Rutland, *Edge of the Diaspora*, 9.

64. Los Angeles Public Library, Chronological Record of Los Angeles City Officials, 1850–1938: Alphabetical index indicating name, office and term of service (Los Angeles: Municipal Reference Library, 1938), http://jgsla.org/index.php?s=john+jones; William M. Kramer, "They Have Killed Our Man but Not Our Cause," *Western States Jewish Historical Quarterly* 2, no. 4 (1970): 209–10.

65. "Jones, John," in Levy, *These Are the Names*, 360 records London as his birthplace, whereas Warsaw is credited on his Los Angeles tombstone. Levy lists only one Jewish John Jones, free or convict, in his exhaustive chronicle. Therefore, it is likely that this is the same John Jones.

66. Ibid., 360.

67. Ibid., 360. In 1841 he received a ticket to leave his assigned employment and in April 20, 1844 his certificate of freedom.

68. Ibid., 360.

69. Louis Rasmussen, San Francisco Ship Passenger Lists (Baltimore: Genealogical Publishing, 1978), www.maritimeheritage.org/inport/1850.htm. He later named his daughter Caroline Adelaide.

70. Harris Newmark, *Sixty Years in Southern California 1853–1913*, ed. Maurice H. Newmark and Marco R. Newmark, 4th ed. (Los Angeles: Zeitlin & Ver Brugge, 1970), 65–66.

71. Ibid., 65. As he later became an officer of Sherith Israel, it is likely that he planned his visits to San Francisco during Jewish holidays.

72. For a discussion of Western Jewish regionalism, see Ellen Eisenberg, Ava F. Kahn, and William Toll, *Jews of the Pacific Coast: Reinventing Community on America's Edge* (Seattle: University of Washington Press, 2009).

73. "List of Officers of the Congregation Sherith Israel," 5. John Jones is still listed as a member of the congregation in 1870; however, he only served as an officer for one term. It is likely that after 1858 he returned to Los Angeles but retained his membership in Sherith Israel. It is also possible that after his marriage to a non-Jewish woman he would have had to leave office. Neither Jones nor his wife was buried in a Jewish cemetery. In Sydney there had been difficulty between free Jews and emancipists in the early 1830s, but the matter was resolved and a united congregation formed. See Rutland, *Edge of the Diaspora*, 25–26.

74. Newmark, *Sixty Years in Southern California 1853–1913*, 65.

75. Ibid., 66. A daughter was born in 1863 in Los Angeles.

76. Ibid., 409.

77. Virginia Katz, "The Ladies' Hebrew Benevolent Society of Los Angeles in 1892," *Western States Jewish Historical Quarterly* 10, no. 2 (1978): 157–58. They also sent funds to the victims of the Chicago fire. In addition John Jones made a hundred-dollar contribution. Norton B. Stern, "Los Angeles and the Chicago Fire," *Western States Jewish Historical Quarterly* 6, no. 4 (1974): 263–66.

78. Katz, "The Ladies' Hebrew Benevolent Society of Los Angeles in 1892," *Ibid.* 10, no. 2 (1978): 158.

79. "Simple Funeral Services Will Mark Last Rites," *Los Angeles Herald*, March 26, 1908; "Pioneer Woman Dies at Country Home," *Los Angeles Herald*, March 25, 1908. It does not appear that she had a Jewish funeral.

80. One interesting story is that of a Jewish emancipist who left his family, traveled to San Francisco in 1850, and married a woman from a British Jewish family, giving his children the same names as those of the children he had abandoned in Australia. See www.ottolangui.com. Accessed April 7, 2014.

81. Mendelsohn, "Tongue Ties," 199.

82. Ibid., 200.

83. Jacob Frankel, "The Life of Jacob Frankel," *Australian Journal of Jewish History* 3, no. 3 (1996): 396.

84. Ibid., 399. Henry and Rosetta Keesing, Barnet's parents, were married by Chief Rabbi Herschel at the Great Synagogue in 1816.

85. Ibid., 403; Stephen Levine, ed., *A Standard for the People: The 150th Anniversary of the Wellington Hebrew Congregation 1843–1993* (Christchurch, New Zealand: Hazard, 1995), 59.

86. Frankel, "The Life of Jacob Frankel," 404.

87. "Minute Book" Congregation Sherith Israel, San Francisco. April 13, 1851. Magnes Collection, Bancroft Library, University of California, Berkeley.

88. Levine, *A Standard for the People*, 59.

89. Frankel, "The Life of Jacob Frankel," 405.

90. Ibid., 406.

91. The gold find was significant; one-third of the world's gold came from Australia between 1851 and 1861; accessed April 22, 2009, www.skwirk.com.au/p-c_s-17_u-453_t-1222_c-4673/sa/sose/gold-and-mining/discovering-gold/australian-gold-rush-timeline.

92. Frankel, "The Life of Jacob Frankel," 406. This medal is still treasured by the Frankel family.

93. Levine, *A Standard for the People*, 59.

94. Goldmark, *Jews of New Zealand*, 94.

95. Ibid., 122–23; Levine, *A Standard for the People*, 61.

96. Goldmark, *Jews of New Zealand*, 123.

97. Kahn, *Jewish Voices*, 79.

98. Ibid., 80. *Mark Isaacs Advertised Matzah and Board over Passover in 1851*. See Alexander Iser, California Hebrew and English Almanac for the Year 5612 (San Francisco: Albion, 1851).

99. By 1851, San Francisco had two large congregations and several benevolent societies. Kahn, *Jewish Voices*, 80.

100. "Interesting Account of the Travels of Abraham Abrahamsohn—Part III," *Western States Jewish Historical Quarterly* 2, no. 1 (1969): 59–60.

101. "Rabbi Levy's Mother Dead," *San Francisco Call* 83, no. 108 (March 18, 1898), accessed June 18, 2014, http://cdnc.ucr.edu/cgi-bin/cdnc?a=d&d=SFC18980318.2.155.

102. J. Leonard Levy, unlike his more traditional older brother, M. S. Levy, became a leader in the Reform movement, serving congregations in Sacramento, Philadelphia, and Pittsburgh. Editors, "A Rabbi Says 'No,'" *Western States Jewish Historical Quarterly* 5, no. 4 (1973): 270.

103. Stephen D. Kinsey, "Jewish Community of San Jose, California," *Western States Jewish Historical Quarterly* 7, no. 1 (1974): 78.

104. Aron and Arndt, *The Enduring Remnant*, 289.

105. Kinsey, "Jewish Community of San Jose," 78, 80.

106. Ibid., 82.

107. For more about Judah L. Magnes and the West, see William M. Brinner and Moses Rischin, *Like All the Nations? The Life and Legacy of Judah L. Magnes* (Albany: State University of New York Press, 1987).

108. Fred Rosenbaum, *Free to Choose: The Making of a Jewish Community in the American West* (Berkeley, CA: Judah L. Magnes Memorial Museum, 1976), 12; Magnes's age is given as eight in Fred Rosenbaum, "San Francisco-Oakland: The Native Son," in Brinner and Rischin, *Like All the Nations?*, 23.

109. Rosenbaum, *Free to Choose*, 10.

110. Rosenbaum, *Free to Choose*, 10. With his "persuasive eloquence," Levy raised $500.00 from the Portland community alone. William M. Kramer, "The Emergence of Oakland Jewry—Part III," *Western States Historical Quarterly* 10, no. 4 (1978): 367.

111. Most Jewish merchants and their families in Hawaii came by way of San Francisco. In fact, a Honolulu store proclaimed its origin: "The San Francisco Clothing Emporium." Kirk Cashmere, [no title page] Manuscript, Jewish history of Hawaii [129 pages], Archives of Temple Emanu-El, Honolulu, Hawaii. [possibly a senior thesis, Brandeis University], 16.

112. Ibid., 70.

113. Hawaii was annexed in 1898; it achieved territorial status in 1900 and statehood in 1959.

114. *Pacific Commercial Advertiser*, July 5, 1899, 1.

115. Ibid., 1.

116. Ibid., 1.

117. Kirk Cashmere, "Honolulu's First Congregation," *Hawaii Jewish News*, December 1980, 11.

118. Levy also sent the community a Sefer Torah for use in the community's High Holiday services, led in part by his son, Herman. Again, in 1901, Levy visited Honolulu. Previous weddings had been conducted by men who had received dispensations from Rabbi Aron J. Messing of San Francisco. Kirk Cashmere, Manuscript [title unknown], 71, 53, 74.

119. Kramer, "Emergence of Oakland Jewry," 354.

120. Cashmere, Manuscript [title unknown], 77–80.

121. Rudolph I. Coffee, "Jews and Judaism in the Hawaiian Islands," *American Israelite*, October 23, 1902, 1, 5. The article recorded both his praise of some members for their support of Jewish institutions including the newly dedicated cemetery and his critique of others for their refusal to identify with the Jewish community.

122. Henry A. Henry served Sherith Israel from 1857 to 1869. Born in London in 1806, he attended the Jews' Free School; emigrating to the United States in 1849, he served three eastern congregations before arriving in California.

123. For an interesting discussion of Jewish convict and free settlers in Australia, see J. S. Levy and G. F. Bergman, *Australian Genesis: Jewish Convicts and Settlers 1788–1850* (London: Rober Hale, 1974) especially see pages 208–10 for information about free and convict members of the Polack family.

124. Agnew and Agnew, *A Colonial Cousinhood*; Odeda Rosenthal, *Not Strictly Kosher: Pioneer Jews in New Zealand* (Wainscott, NY: Starchand Press, 1988), 203.

3

CREATING TRANSNATIONAL CONNECTIONS

Australia and California

Suzanne D. Rutland

Europeans first learned of Australia, the last continent to be discovered, in 1770 after Captain James Cook's voyage of exploration. The British government established a penal colony there in 1788. A dozen Jewish convicts were transported on the "First Fleet"—the seven convict ships sent to Botany Bay to lay the foundations of what developed into the city of Sydney. Thus, Australia was the first modern nation where Jews have been present from its very beginning. While Jews have always been a tiny minority, never constituting more than 0.5 percent of the population, they have played a significant role in Australia's economic and commercial development, initially as shopkeepers but later through developing trading networks and transnational connections with other regions that bordered the Pacific, including California. Indeed, American Jewry's shift westward had unexpected and important consequences for the Jewish communities of the Pacific Rim. The West Coast of the United States is Australian Jewry's largest neighboring community, and the two communities share commonalities in terms of their culture, high proportion of immigrants, and multicultural traditions.[1] For those who traveled westward from Australia by ship, San Francisco was the end of the sea journey. In recent years these connections have been strengthened, because the

West Coast is only separated from eastern Australia by a single air flight and is a transit location on the way to the East. In this chapter these connections will be explored, including a discussion of the stories of Moses Joseph in the nineteenth century and Frank Lowy, "Mr. Westfield," in the twentieth and twenty-first centuries. These two different case studies represent the shifts that have occurred in the Jewish trading and business networks across the Pacific Rim over the past two centuries.

Early Pacific Rim Connections: Moses Joseph

Among the Jewish convicts who arrived between 1788 and 1840 were a number who became shipbuilders and shipowners, building significant trading networks in the Pacific, including Moses Joseph. I became curious about Moses Joseph, the Jewish merchant and entrepreneur who first arrived in Sydney in chains, when I was appointed to a lectureship in the Department of Hebrew and Semitic Studies in 1997. At the time, my office was located in the Main Quadrangle, the oldest part of the University of Sydney, built in the 1850s. Every day I would pass a beautiful stained-glass window, with the name "Moses Joseph" and the word "*Yerushalayim*" (Jerusalem) written in Hebrew letters in the middle of a specifically designed coat of arms (Figure 3.1). The

FIGURE 3.1. Stained-glass window donated by Moses Joseph in 1857 to the newly founded University of Sydney. Courtesy of the Sydney Jewish Museum.

coats of arms in the other stained-glass windows obviously came from members of the British upper classes with long pedigrees, and my curiosity was raised about Moses Joseph. Who was he? What was his family story? How was he in the position to fund this elaborate window, which highlighted his Jewish ancestry and the centrality of Jerusalem?

As I delved into this topic, I found that Moses Joseph was a convicted felon, a peddler who stole a watch or some other jewelry from another trader. He was sentenced to transportation for life and sent to the colony of New South Wales, arriving in 1827 on the ship the *Albion*.[2] As Justice Howard Nathan, a descendant of the family, wrote, "He arrived in Sydney Town on 20 May 1827, well rested, fit, literate and vigorous: just the assets needed to help him on his way to wealth and respectability. Moreover, he had left a girl behind, who was prepared to follow him to the ends of the earth."[3] He was immediately assisted by fellow Jews, being assigned to the firm of Cooper & Levey, which was founded by another Jewish emancipist (a convict who had been given a conditional or absolute pardon): Solomon Levey. Levey had managed to achieve his freedom and create "one of the great mercantile houses of New South Wales" within eleven years of his arrival in chains.[4] During this period, it was common for Jews to intervene and take Jewish assigned servants/convicts into their care. It did not always work out well, but at least Australian Jewish emancipists and free settlers felt an obligation to try to assist their coreligionists. Moses Joseph was an example of this phenomenon: his being assigned to Cooper & Levey was not by chance.[5]

The fact that Moses Joseph was literate, unlike the vast majority of convicts, provided him with opportunities due to his value to both his employers and the government. While still a convict he wrote to Rosetta Nathan, the girl he had left behind, his first cousin, asking her to come to New South Wales to marry him. One might wonder why a young Jewish girl would be prepared to travel halfway around the world to marry a convicted felon, and even more why her family would have permitted her to undertake such a trip. However, her own father, Nathan Lyon Nathan (alias Nathaniel Newton), had been convicted of larceny in the Old Bailey in 1799 at the age of sixteen and had been sentenced to transportation to New South Wales. After serving his seven-year sentence, he applied in 1807 to return to London, where he married in 1808 and had nine children. All of his children migrated to Australian colonies or New Zealand as free settlers, attracted by the economic opportunities and influenced by their family members already established in Australasia through the process of chain migration.[6]

Rosetta arrived in Sydney in 1832, and she and Moses Joseph petitioned Governor Burke to marry:

> That the Petitioner [i.e., Moses] was for some time before he left England acquainted with and attached to your Excellency's other Petitioner Rosetta Nathan a reputable and virtuous young woman who lately arrived in this colony by the ship *Margaret* evidencing thereby the continuance of her attachment and determination to share the fate and misfortunes of Petitioner Moses Joseph.

> That your Petitioners are of the Jewish persuasion and with your Excellency's sanction are about to be married according to the rights and ceremonies of that religion.

> Your Petitioners therefore most humbly pray your Excellency to be pleased to sanction . . . and humbly implore that your Petitioner Moses Joseph may have extended to him the merciful indulgence of a Ticker of Leave or Exemption.[7]

Their request was met with a positive response and they were married in February 1832 by Philip Cohen, who had been authorized by the British chief rabbi to conduct Jewish marriages. Thus theirs was one of the first traditional Jewish marriages in Australasia. Two months later, Moses Joseph was granted a "certificate of exemption," which permitted him to be employed by his wife, Rosetta. They opened a tobacco shop, which prospered, and by 1839 he received a conditional pardon. The two then bought a property on George Street, the main thoroughfare in Sydney at the time, and in 1841 replaced the weatherboard building with a three-story shop, which they named "Commercial House." In the 1840s, Joseph acquired the leasehold of 50,000 acres around Bombala, in southern New South Wales, and became a wool buyer of significance. Israel, one of his brothers, had arrived in Australia in 1833 as a free settler, probably attracted by family connections and economic opportunities. Together in 1847 they patented the canning of preserved meat; so they were the founders of the food-processing industry in Australia.[8] They constructed meatworks in Camperdown, but this enterprise was soon overtaken by competition from another firm established by the Dangar family in Newcastle.[9]

Rosetta and Moses Joseph's commercial enterprise in New South Wales was to provide the basis of the trading empire, which they developed with a fleet of fourteen ships. The pride and joy of this fleet was the *Rosetta Joseph*, built in 1847 and named after Moses's beloved wife. The barque was built at the river town of Taree in northern New South Wales, located near forests of cedar, which was light and easy to work with and floated well. The barque was fitted out for both passengers and cargo. After its maiden voyage to Auckland, New Zealand, his brother Hyam Joseph advertised the return voyage, stating, "The fine new colonial clipper-built barque, ROSETTA JOSEPH 300 tons, coppered and copper-fastened. Capt Patrick. This vessel offers an excellent opportunity to parties proceeding to the above port, her cabins having been fitted with every requisite that can conduce to the comfort and accommodation of passengers."[10]

The experience of Rosetta and Moses Joseph and members of the Nathan dynasty as shipowners was not unique. There were about 60–65 Jewish shipowners in this period. The ships they owned ranged from eleven to fifty-one tons, with the larger vessels being capable of sea travel.[11] Solomon Levey, whose firm had assisted Joseph, was the first Jew to own ships. In the period from 1820 to 1828, he had an interest in around ten ships. The emancipist brothers Judah and Joseph Solomon cornered the grain market in Van Diemen's Land. Another emancipist pair of brothers, Vaiben and Emanuel Solomon, had an interest in six ships and dominated trade between New South Wales and South Australia. The extensive Cohen network begun by the deportation of Henry Cohen to Port Macquarie, together with Lionel Samson in Perth and the Levi/Phillipson family in Adelaide, developed links between the colonies of South Australia and Western Australia. Isaac Simmons, who arrived around the same time as Joseph, had interests in at least fifteen ships. However, historian John Levi claims, "None were so spectacular, and long lasting, as the dynasty established by Lyon Henry Nathan's children."[12] Many of these pioneering Jews were proud of their Jewish heritage, often naming their ships with clearly sounding Jewish names, with Isaac Simmons even naming one of his brigs *Jewess*.

Although gold had been sighted in New South Wales earlier, it took the "Californian gold rush before Australians could understand the rich possibilities of an economy based on gold."[13] Edward Hargraves, the first Australian to discover gold in New South Wales in 1851, had just returned from the Californian goldfields. But the California Gold Rush affected Australia well before the discovery of gold in New South Wales and Victoria. When the news of the Californian Gold Rush reached the Sydney press at the end of December 1848, Moses Joseph, following the example of his coreligionists, saw the commercial opportunities, realizing that the sea voyage from Sydney to San Francisco Bay was shorter than the long journey from New York or Boston around Cape Horn. In 1850, he decided to stock the *Rosetta Joseph* with goods required on the goldfields: picks, wheelbarrows, and other household goods. Captain Patrick again skippered the barque, which enjoyed an uneventful voyage of eighty days to California. After the merchandise was safely unloaded, the barque left San Francisco on October 15, 1850 with thirty-two passengers on board. Unfortunately, its return journey proved disastrous, as the ship foundered on the Elizabeth reef, 250 kilometers north of Lord Howe Island and 700 kilometers from Australia. Gold dust was jettisoned to lighten the long boat.[14] Captain Patrick realized that the boat could not be rescued, and the crew with all the passengers were loaded onto the small boats on board. After two days trying to reach Lord Howe Island, Patrick discovered that they were actually traveling backward and decided to make for Australian shores. Nine days and eight nights later, Port Macquarie on the New South Wales coast was sighted. All the survivors of the shipwreck landed safely ashore, exhausted and bedraggled but unharmed. As Justice Nathan commented, "This is one of the unknown stories of heroism and seamanship which mark so much of Australian history."[15] Moses Joseph did not suffer financially from this disaster since he was covered by insurance, but he seems to have forgone the idea of further trading with California.

Moses Joseph's life is a "rags-to-riches" story. By 1852 he had become the largest licensed gold buyer in New South Wales, sending more than 1,000 ounces to London in a single year.[16] He used his commercial success to build Sydney's Jewish community. Joseph served on the committee that bought land on York Street in Sydney in 1841 for the purpose of building the first synagogue in Australia, which was opened in 1844. He was president of the Sydney congregation for five years and he also worked to establish the first Jewish school in Sydney, the Sydney Hebrew Academy, in 1846. In 1848 he was granted an absolute pardon and he and Rosetta returned to London around 1870, where he also donated funds for the Jews' School in Stepney and other Jewish primary schools. He died in 1889 and Rosetta two years later in 1891. Not only had he broken away from poverty to achieve wealth and distinction for himself and his family, but he also worked hard to build Judaism in one of the newest centers at the "edge of the diaspora." His vision also included developing links between two centers in the New World, venturing across the Pacific Rim to do so. The foundering of the *Rosetta Joseph* highlighted the dangers of such enterprises at the time.

Other Jewish merchants in the colony of New South Wales were involved with the trade between the two gold rush centers and were among the first to act shortly after the announcement of the discovery of gold in late December 1848, when California was considered "one of the least known and most inaccessible ports of the world."[17] The firm Montefiore, Graham & Co. immediately sent a consignment of goods to San Francisco on the *Plymouth,* the first ship to leave Sydney Harbour in January 1849.[18] The firm followed with the *Despatch,* a much larger schooner, with Frederick Barrow Montefiore on board. He was the younger brother of Jacob Barrow Montefiore, one of the eleven founding commissioners of the free colony of South Australia, and Jacob Levi Montefiore. Jacob Levi arrived in Sydney in 1839 and initially joined another brother, Joseph Barrow Montefiore, in his firm. He soon went into partnership with Moses Joseph and, in 1846, established a partnership with a Scotsman, Robert Graham.[19] In August 1849, the *Despatch,* with Frederick Montefiore on board, was the first ship to return to Sydney with positive news about Californian goldfields, stimulating further trade and transmigration. Other ships owned by the firm, including the *Courier de Tahiti,* continued to ply the sailing route between the two centers and by 1850 the Montefiores of Sydney had established a permanent commercial business house in San Francisco.[20]

Jewish free settler J. H. Levien also left Sydney in January 1849, traveling on his clipper barque, *Lindsays.* Levien took a supply "of cigars, candles, kegs of brandy, tins of lemon syrup, men's shirts, carriage harnesses, and haberdashery—in short, more surplus goods bought at reduced prices in Sydney."[21] He remained in San Francisco for a period. Historian Jay Monaghan noted, "Levien had an eye for bargains and a respect for property which would be notable when the vigilantes assumed control of San Francisco."[22] Since Australians were suspected of starting the devastating San Francisco fire of December 1849,[23] Levien was among a group of prosperous Australians who stood on the docks to prevent Australians they considered suspicious from landing in San Francisco.[24]

Other Australian Jews were involved in the Pacific Rim gold rush trade. Samuel Lyons, a successful businessman and auctioneer who had also arrived in chains, took advantage of the business opportunities by selling goods to miners planning to travel to California. Another Jewish partnership, L. & S. Samuel, sent freight to San Francisco in February 1851 and L. Samuel also participated in a meeting to discuss the problem of a labor shortage in Sydney created by the California Gold Rush.[25] As Ava F. Kahn has discussed,

Israel Solomon, founder of the Sherith Israel Congregation in San Francisco, migrated from Sydney with his large family to California in 1850, together with a shipload of goods. Both Israel and his father John would have had close connections with Moses Joseph through their shops in George Street, Sydney and the York Street Synagogue, of which Joseph was president and Israel Solomon trustee. These Jewish connections were important in Jewish trading networks. Marriage within families was common, with cousins marrying each other. In this period, they also tried to develop Jewish religious institutions and the beginnings of a more extended community structure with education and welfare facilities.

The gold rush period developed other links between the goldfields in California and Victoria through transmigration. Adventurers, including Jewish men, continued to seek their fortunes between the two centers. The gold rushes also produced new Jewish trading networks in the colonies, the most important of which was the Michaelis-Hallenstein dynasty, which extended from Victoria to New South Wales and New Zealand. Moritz Michaelis arrived in Victoria from Germany in 1853 and was later joined by his nephew Isaac Hallenstein, who learned the tanner's trade in Germany and on the Californian goldfields. Hallenstein saw a future in the leather industry in Victoria and established a tannery business. In 1864 he went into partnership with his uncle. When Moritz Michaelis died in 1902, he was one of the hundred wealthiest men in Victoria. He also played a key role in the establishment of the St Kilda Hebrew Congregation, the third synagogue in Melbourne. There are other examples of transmigration, including Jews from Victoria moving to South Africa during the diamond mine boom there in the late nineteenth century.

Thus, in the colonial period in Australia, some of the Jewish emancipists and free settlers moved from being shopkeepers and auctioneers to creating trading networks and being involved in shipbuilding. However, by the end of the nineteenth century, many of these early families had assimilated, due to the small numbers of the Jewish community and the low ratio of females to males. In addition, British society was more stratified, so that Jews were poorly equipped to deal with the freer and more open society of the Australian colonies, where the emancipists could quickly become wealthy and rise up the social ladder. While they struggled to establish Jewish institutions in their new land, with synagogues being built in Sydney, Hobart, Launceston, Melbourne, and Adelaide by 1850, they lacked an infrastructure of Jewish education to act as a barrier to assimilation. Australian Jewry was not reinforced by East European migration, as occurred in other centers of the English-speaking world. In 1933, numbering only 23,000, Australian Jewry was an isolated and assimilated community. All this was to change with the advent of Nazism.

Expanding Pacific Rim Connections: Frank Lowy

Between 1933 and 1961, approximately 35,000 Jewish refugees and survivors arrived in Australia, with the most substantial migration being between 1946 and 1954. This was a watershed period for Australian Jewry, with the newcomers contributing to both the revival of Australian Jewry and postwar economic development. The key role played by this wave of Jewish migrants in Australia's financial growth can be seen in the fact that by the 1980s a quarter of those named in the annual *Business Review Weekly* listing of the 200 wealthiest Australian citizens, known colloquially as the "rich list," were Jewish entrepreneurs, most of whom had arrived either before or after World War II.[26] Yet, Jews only constituted 0.5 percent of Australia's population.

Among those who have been consistently listed in the rich list was another young Jewish man who, like Moses Joseph, arrived on Australian shores with nothing except his own wits, energy, and determination to succeed. Slovakian-born Frank Lowy had survived the Holocaust and, after moving to Israel and fighting in the Israeli 1948 War of Independence, decided to join his family in Sydney in 1952. His sister Edith had decided to migrate to Sydney with her husband after his relatives had offered to sponsor their migration to Australia.[27] His mother decided to follow them with his younger brother rather than migrate to Israel because of the difficult economic conditions in the Jewish state. His biographer Jill Margo noted, "His time in Israel empowered him in a way that would not have been possible in war-ravaged Europe. It gave him a fresh perspective. Rather than forcing him to live defensively, the country schooled him to fight fiercely for what could be his. Instead of depriving him and hurting him, in its rugged way, it fed and nurtured him. In place of the distrust that had grown in him during the Holocaust, it showed him the value in trust."[28] Flying to Australia in 1952, Lowy was about to begin his journey on a third continent, from Europe, to the Middle East, to Australia. Later, he added a fourth continent with his American business enterprises. These manifold experiences were to create a truly transnational experience.

Lowy's property company Westfield Holdings,[29] which was to develop large shopping centers across the Pacific Rim, began in 1957 with a business partnership between Lowy and Hungarian-born John Saunders, who had changed his name from Jeno Schwarz. They met when Saunders was running a delicatessen shop at Town Hall railway station in the center of Sydney and Lowy was delivering small goods to him. They started Westfield with a small shopping center opposite Blacktown station on the outer perimeter of Sydney's western suburbs in 1958.[30]

The concept of developing shopping centers at suburban perimeters emerged in postwar America. Viennese Jewish prewar refugee architect Victor Gruen played a key role in the development of the concept. By the late 1950s there were already 940 shopping centers in the United States, this number increasing to 17,520 during the next two decades.[31] However, in the late 1950s, the concept of a shopping center was still very new in Australia. When planning their shopping center in Blacktown, Lowy and Saunders, aware of the American concept, decided that instead of building a row of shops, they would "create a retail conglomerate in the form of a shopping centre," with twelve shops, a small supermarket, and a small department store around an open square.[32] John Saunders visited the United States to survey shopping centers, where he met developers and financiers. He also noted the key role played by cars and the provision of parking facilities.[33] Thus, at the same time that Victor Gruen was developing his concept of integrated shopping centers in the United States,[34] two young Hungarian Jewish Holocaust survivors of Hitler's Europe were developing a similar concept with Westfield on Sydney's periphery.

The 1950s and 1960s was a period of rapid growth in Australia due to the postwar realization that Australia needed to build its population through attracting migrants not only from Britain but also from the European continent. The Liberal Party government, in power from 1949 to 1972, also sought to develop Australia's infrastructure and to foster industrialization, trade, and tourism. Postwar Australia also moved from being in the United Kingdom's constellation to a new focus on the United States, the new superpower in the Asia–Pacific region, with popular culture being significantly influenced by American developments, although normally with a time lag.[35]

While the challenges of absorbing so many immigrants tended to result in a stop–start economy in the 1950s, on the whole jobs were available, and the Saunders/Lowy partnership benefited from these economic developments. The Blacktown complex, which opened in June 1959, was a great success and they were offered other projects and opportunities. Their next large project was in Hornsby, which was on Sydney's northern periphery. In order to learn more about building shopping centers, and also motels, Lowy set off in February 1960 on his first business trip to the United States with Westfield's consultant architect, Emery Nemes. Given that California was close to Australia, with a similar climate, they decided to focus their study there, driving from San Francisco to Los Angeles and investigating carefully on their way. As Margo, Lowy's biographer wrote, "Carrying a camera and notebook, they would record the layout of a center and try to get a feel for the place. After collecting pamphlets from the information booth they would sometimes knock on the centre manager's door, introduce themselves, and be shown around."³⁶ To raise funds for their projects, the Lowy/Saunders partnership floated a public company, called Westfield Development Corporation Ltd., in September 1960, and by the end of its first year the company was showing a substantial profit. The two men had learned much from their visits to the United States and understood that "correctly positioned and designed shopping centres can be the modern equivalents of a village square or the marketplace."³⁷ Their vision of a center combining modern consumerism with community activities matched Gruen's belief that commercial success would be assisted by the center's social functions. In his writing and speeches, Gruen constantly stressed that "market places . . . are also centers of community and cultural activity."³⁸ His company was located in Los Angeles, so it is not surprising that Lowy absorbed this message during his 1960 Californian visit.

From their small beginnings, the firm grew. In 1987, the partnership dissolved and Lowy went on to develop Westfield into an international company, again creating links with California. This was largely a new development since the earlier contacts and commercial links established between the West Coast and Australia had ended relatively quickly, in significant measure because of the vagaries of sea travel in the nineteenth century. After the wreck of the *Rosetta Joseph,* for example, Moses Joseph did not attempt to send any further materials to the Californian goldfields. With the end of the gold rush there, together with improvements in land travel from the East to the West Coast and later the opening of the Panama Canal, there was less advantage for Australian Jewish traders to maintain their links. However, in the post–Second World War Jewish entrepreneurs again began to look beyond Australian shores. The creation of the European common market encouraged them to focus on North and South America.

Until 1945, much of Australia's trade (largely wheat and wool) had supplied the needs of the United Kingdom, but once Britain joined the common market, Australia no longer benefited from advantageous tariffs. For example, Victor Smorgon, whose father Norman escaped from Communism in Russia with two brothers and arrived in Melbourne in 1927, established a meat-processing business in the 1930s. During the war years the business was granted an export license, and Norman Smorgon requested permission to travel to Chicago so that he could learn from the American meat-packing companies. Travel was restricted because of the war, and Norman was warned of the dangers. His response was that "the Pacific held few fears for a man who had lived through the Russian Civil War."[39] After visiting New York and relatives in Canada, he traveled by train to San Francisco and then traveled home on a cargo vessel. In 1948, Victor Smorgon undertook a trip to the United States to explore markets, and after being in Chicago, where he learned of a frozen food convention, he returned via California, visiting the fruit-growing areas there.[40] In 1950 the Smorgons began to export to the United States, starting with processed rabbit meat and then adding canned fruit products. From there his company has diversified and moved into steel production and export.[41]

Another entrepreneur, Isi Leibler, who arrived from Antwerp with his parents in 1938 when he was a three-year-old, developed a network of travel agencies, Jetset Travel, creating the largest travel organization across the Pacific Rim in the 1960s and 1970s. These are just a few other examples of the expansion of Australian Jewish business networks across the Pacific Rim in the postwar period.

Saunders and Lowy first entered the American shopping mall market in 1977, when they acquired a shopping center in Trumbull, Connecticut. This purchase was to lay the foundations for what was to become the Westfield empire, with its center in Los Angeles. Frank sent his son David to manage the first Westfield complex and as Frank Lowy forged ahead in the United States, "he left John behind, literally and figuratively," contributing to the end of the partnership in 1987.[42] In 1980, David Lowy located an American executive, Richard Green, who had significant experience with the shopping center business, particularly in Los Angeles, and he recommended that his father Frank meet Green. Describing this first meeting, Margo wrote:

> Green knew nothing of Frank's status in Australia or his background. . . . Although he found the father and son charming, he had to know if they were Jewish and made a remark designed to test this. As he was leaving Green spontaneously invited Frank and David to drive out with him and meet his family. . . . Green wouldn't have known,

but showing himself in the context of his family had been greatly to his advantage. In him Frank saw not only a man who knew about the shopping center industry but also one who was genuinely committed to his family—a quality he prized as highly as business ability. That afternoon, Frank decided to employ him.[43]

Coming from the same background, influenced by Jewish family values, clearly influenced Lowy to employ Green. These reactions typified much of the Jewish business stories. Jewish family and ethnic connections were significant in the development of business and trade in colonial Australia.

During that visit they saw the first property to be developed by Westfield in California, located in West Los Angeles between Beverly Hills and Santa Monica, and Frank decided to purchase it. He developed Westside Pavilion, which proved a success, making his company much more visible in the United States. In 1989, the Lowy family decided to expand their presence in America and Frank sent his middle son, Peter, to Los Angeles to achieve this aim.

This, however, was at the time when the 1989 depression was beginning to bite, so initially the company was not in the position to expand its operations. In February 1994, Frank closed a deal with CenterMark, which enabled him to upgrade his activities in the United States, making him one of the world's top shopping center operators. CenterMark was located in St. Louis, but within a year Peter had moved the full operation into Westfield's Los Angeles headquarters.[44] By this stage, Westfield Holdings had twenty-four centers in Australia and twenty-six in the United States. The Westfield signs have become a familiar sign throughout California. Peter Lowy also became active in the Los Angeles Jewish community, served as president of the University of Judaism, and was responsible for its merger with the Brandeis-Bardin Institute, after which it was renamed American Jewish University in 2007. Currently he is chairman of the *Jewish Journal of Greater Los Angeles*.[45]

The Holocaust survivor who had arrived in the Sydney of the 1950s with nothing except a determination to succeed has become one of the wealthiest men in the world, ranking among the top 500. In this way, Lowy became one of a small group of developers in the United States to participate in the expansion of shopping malls in the 1970s and 1980s, by which time 45 percent of all retail sales were taking place there.[46] These malls became more than retail centers, offering cultural and entertainment facilities. They tended to have a "striking sameness across the country in design and tenant composition,"[47] which was true of the different Westfield complexes.

As with Moses Joseph, Lowy did not restrict his success to enjoying his family and fortune. He has also generously supported institutions both Jewish and non-Jewish in Australia. He has been a major benefactor in the development of Jewish schools, with ongoing generous support to the largest Jewish day school in Sydney, Moriah College. He has also donated funds to the University of New South Wales, where his sons completed their university studies, and has established a major think tank, the Lowy Institute, to express his gratitude to Australia for allowing him to live in freedom and prosperity.[48]

Commonalities among These Stories

The successes of Moses Joseph in Sydney in the nineteenth century and Frank Lowy in the twentieth century had a number of features in common. Both Joseph and Lowy arrived with nothing—one in chains and the other as a Holocaust survivor—yet managed to emerge as two of the richest men of their time. In so doing, they created trading networks, which stretched from New South Wales in Australia to California, forming the basis of transnational commercial enterprises.

Numeracy and literacy were important elements in business success.[49] The fact that Moses Joseph was literate was a key factor in his success, and he was also keen to foster learning both within the Jewish and general communities of Sydney. As with Lowy and Saunders, most European Jewish survivors who arrived after 1945 in Australia brought few material possessions. They did, however, bring new industrial skills, and most reacted to the challenges of a new land with hard work, drive, and enterprise. The postwar Australian economy, with increased immigration and industrialization and growth of infrastructure, as discussed earlier, provided them with many business opportunities, which they maximized. In this period, the Liberal Party government provided subsidies to encourage the growth of local industry, and this applied to the clothing trade, a traditional area of Jewish business activity. As with many other immigrant groups, they encouraged their children to achieve academic success, resulting in higher educational standards for the Jewish community than for the general Australian population.

Partnerships, networking, and helping one another, whether through family or friends, was a major factor. As discussed above, when Joseph arrived in Sydney he was assigned to the firm of a successful Jewish emancipist, Cooper & Levey. Later he bought out members of his own family as well as his wife's family, the Nathans, and together they established a trading network that stretched from Australia to New Zealand and even faraway California, if only for a short period. This was true also of the Lowy/Saunders partnership in which, for thirty years from 1957 to 1987 Frank Lowy and John Saunders worked closely together building up their business empire. This networking allowed a pooling of resources and talent, facilitated problem solving, and enabled sharing of responsibilities.

The common ethnic heritage was also important, as partners could communicate easily. It is of interest to note that, in most of the successful partnerships, the two men came from the same national as well as religious background. In the nineteenth century, the Anglo-Jewish connection was important. When Richard Green met Frank and David Lowy for the first time in Los Angeles, he wanted to know if they were Jewish and asked an appropriate question. On the other hand, Frank Lowy valued Green's focus on family, which is so much a part of the Jewish cultural and religious tradition. Political scientist Peter Medding stressed that ethnic group networks provide important social support and reinforcement for members.[50] This was certainly the case for the various Jewish business partnerships. Australian Jewish entrepreneurship has been individual or family oriented and has almost never manifested itself in the context of large, national corporations.[51]

Imagination was another central ingredient, as "new products must be conceived, new ways of doing things conjured up, and ways around problems found."[52] Jews have tended to be innovators. The first steamboat to arrive in Australia in 1830 was the *Sophia Jane*; ten years later it was owned by Abraham and Saul Lyons, raising the question of to what extent Jews were being innovative in switching to steam power in the early colonial period.[53] Moses Joseph and his brother initiated canned meat into Australia in the 1840s. This innovation and ingenuity is also highlighted by the Holocaust experience in which, in the struggle for survival, it was often the young Jews who had the physical strength and ingenuity to stay alive. The number of Holocaust survivors, including Saunders and Lowy, who have made it to the top is a testimony to the human spirit and an ability to fight for life and security.

The ability and willingness to take risks is also important in terms of entrepreneurial skills and the building of transnational business enterprises. When Lowy and Saunders decided to purchase their first shop in Blacktown, neither had any capital; yet they were prepared to take the risks involved in this first investment. The Jewish trading heritage was one factor in this risk taking, but it was also due to the impact of the Holocaust. For those who had lost everything in the past, it was easier to take the risks to fulfill their business dreams and ambitious. Similarly, Moses Joseph was prepared to take risks in his trading enterprises, and sending the pride of his fleet to San Francisco is indicative of risk taking.

It is interesting to note that in each case discussed in this chapter, the successful businessmen started as shopkeepers, middlemen in a consumer economy. On the whole Jews on the goldfields were not miners. This pattern of Jews as the middlemen goes back to the role they played in urban centers in medieval times, when they were often forced into usury and money lending, due to their exclusion in Christian Europe from being members of guilds and the prohibition on their owning land. The connections between Jews across the Pacific Rim also fit into the Jewish history of trade. During medieval times, Jews were able to move more easily between the Christian and Muslim worlds than either Christians or Muslims and from the ninth century on they developed trading routes that spread from France to China. There were a number of reasons Jews were successful as traders. They were a literate people, they usually spoke a number of languages, and there were Jewish communities that were spread along the various trading routes, since Jewish communities were scattered across national and regional boundaries,[54] so that local Jews assisted the itinerant Jewish traders. Thus, as Jerry Muller argues, Jews were connected with trade and money in the medieval period, well before the commercial revolution of the seventeenth century, and this association had "ongoing effects," helping to explain the "disproportionate Jewish success under conditions of modern capitalism."[55]

The traditional Jewish background in shopkeeping and being the middlemen also enabled Saunders and Lowy to take advantage of the growing consumerism of the postwar period in Australia and later in the United States. Jeffrey Hardwick argued, "Gruen ushered in a new era of consumerism in America."[56] The Westfield partners first learned from that culture of consumerism, introducing American shopping center concepts into Australia, and later moved into the American consumer market. Other Australian Jews developed both large department chains and shopping centers, although not on the same transnational scale as Westfield.

Immigrant entrepreneurship played an important role in Jewish trading success. In her book *The New Boy Network*, Ruth Ostrow outlined the stories of those businessmen who took over corporate Australia in the postwar period. She noted that at least half of them were immigrants who arrived in Australia from "concentration camps or from war torn countries and pulled themselves up from nothing to the top rungs of business."[57] Research has shown that most immigrant ethnic groups tend to respond to the challenge of re-creating their lives in a new country, although they tend to concentrate in different areas of business activity, depending on their home culture.

There are a number of reasons Jews have contributed to Australian business and material culture, as seen in the cases discussed here. Most important was the willingness to work hard, "often seven days a week and sixteen hours a day to get somewhere,"[58] usually with the assistance of their wives. This was true of the Lowy/Saunders partnership. When he opened the Royal Coaches Exhibition at Indooroopilly, Shoppingtown, Prince Charles asked Saunders what the secret of his success was. Saunders responded that it was "about hard work and the challenges involved in overcoming difficulties."[59]

Thus, these many factors resulted in similar patterns of trading and Jewish communal development, which led to links between the eastern coast of Australia and California across the Pacific Rim, further extending the transnational nature of the Jewish experience and reflecting Australian Jews' interest in the United States as a place of economic opportunity and experimentation. The specific stories of Joseph and Lowy illustrate the role that Jews have played in Australia's commercial development, including building trading and business links across the Pacific Rim. Both men arrived with nothing, and due to hard work, determination, intellect, and ability were about to rise rapidly up the economic ladder, being listed among the wealthiest men in Australia within a relatively short period of time. Both men also identified strongly with their Jewish heritage and were substantial benefactors in the development of Jewish institutions in Sydney and, in Lowy's case, also in Los Angeles. Both men were innovative and saw opportunities in California, which they sought to maximize. However, in Joseph's story, these were short lived; in the case of Lowy they have been much more substantial and enduring. While Joseph decided to retire to London, Lowy has built his family dynasty in Australia and Los Angeles, fully leaving the Old World behind. Their stories illustrate the close association Jews have had with mercantilism and capitalism, thereby building transnational trading networks, which have been a feature of the Jewish experience since medieval times.

Notes

1. Twenty-seven percent of California's population are migrants, the highest proportion in the United States. Australia is also an immigrant country. Bryan Conyer, "Effecting Pluralism: Three Case Studies of Jewish Community Schools in Australia and the Western United States" (doctoral thesis, University of Sydney, 2012), 48.

2. John Levi, *These Are the Names: Jewish Lives in Australia, 1788–1850* (Melbourne, Australia: Melbourne University Press, 2006), 369.

3. Howard T. Nathan, "*Rosetta Joseph*: The Bell, Her Husband and His Money," *Australian Jewish Historical Society Journal (AJHSJ)* 17, no. 1 (2003): 10.

4. Levey arrived in chains in Sydney in 1815 and by 1826 owned property worth £30,000. John Levi and G. F. J. Bergman, *Australian Genesis: Jewish Convicts and Settlers, 1788–1860*, 2nd ed. (Melbourne, Australia: Melbourne University Press, 2006), 91.

5. Email comment by historian Rabbi Dr. John Levi, July 10, 2012.

6. Levi, *These Are the Names*, xvi.

7. As qtd. in Nathan, "*Rosetta Joseph*," 12.

8. Levi, *These Are the Names*, 364–65.

9. Australian Science and Technology Heritage Centre, *Technology in Australia, 1788–1988*, 78, accessed October 3, 2013, www.austehc.unimelb.edu.au/tia/078.html.

10. Qtd. in Nathan, "*Rosetta Joseph*," 15.

11. Peter Keeda, "Shipowners in the Nineteenth Century Australia" (MA essay, University of Sydney, 2010). Keeda went through a number of different sources to arrive at this figure and produced a table of all the possible Jewish shipowners in the colonial period.

12. John Levi, email correspondence, July 10, 2012.

13. Levi and Bergman, *Australian Genesis*, 316.

14. Dudley David Davis, *The Other Side of the Label* (Parts I and III), Monograph, State Library of New South Wales, 64.

15. Nathan, "*Rosetta Joseph*," 8. The *Rosetta Joseph* remained perched on the reef until 1858, when a salvage crew burned the timber in order to recover the metal in the boat. This included the ship's bell, which one of the salvagers probably took as a souvenir. This bell found its way onto another sailing ship, the *Holyhead*, which was shipwrecked at the entrance to Port Philip Bay, Melbourne on the Point Lonsdale Reef in February 1890. In 1968, a Melbourne scuba diver salvaged the bell and sold it to Moses Joseph's ancestor Justice Howard Nathan. Ironically, thieves managed to steal this bell from Justice Nathan's home, even though it had been firmly bolted into his fireplace. Hence, it has again disappeared from the pages of history.

16. Levi, *These Are the Names*, 371.

17. Jay Monaghan, *Australians and the Gold Rush: California and Down Under, 1849–1854* (Berkeley: University of California Press, 1966), 2.

18. The *Plymouth* departed on January 8, 1849. Ibid., 13.

19. Levi, *These Are the Names*, 540–42.

20. Monaghan, *Australians and the Gold Rush*, 124.

21. Ibid., 15.

22. Ibid.

23. Of the seventy suspects arrested after the fire, forty-five were from Sydney.

24. Monaghan, *Australians and the Gold Rush*, 154.

25. M. Z. Forbes, "The Jews of NSW and the Gold Rushes," *AJHSJ* 17, no 2 (1994), 286.

26. W. D. Rubinstein, *The Jews in Australia: A Thematic History*. Vol. 2: *1945 to the Present* (Melbourne, Australia: William Heinemann, 1991), 345–46.

27. Jill Margo, *Frank Lowy: Pushing the Limits* (Sydney, Australia: HarperCollins, 2000), 35.

28. Ibid., 52.

29. The company was initially formed as a private company in 1956 and was called Westfield Investments Pty Ltd. Lowy and Saunders chose this name because Australia was monocultural in the 1950s, so their foreign-sounding surnames were not suitable. They built their first shopping center at Bankstown, in the western suburbs of Sydney, and at the time were buying up and subdividing farmers' fields. Margo, *Frank Lowy*, 72.

30. Rudolph Brasch, *Australian Jews of Today and the Part They Have Played* (Sydney, Australia: Cassell Australia, 1977), 177.

31. Lizabeth Cohen, *A Consumers' Republic: The Politics of Mass Consumption in Postwar America* (New York: Knopf, 2003), 258.

32. Margo, *Frank Lowy*, 76.

33. Ibid., 77.

34. Viennese refugee Jewish architect Victor Gruen first developed his concept of a central shopping mall in an article published in 1943 in the *Architectural Forum* and over the following decade worked on different designs and concepts, with his first modern shopping center opening in Northland, Detroit in 1954. In 1956 he designed the first enclosed shopping center, Southdale, which opened in Edwina, Minneapolis. M. Jeffrey Hardwick, *Mall Maker: Victor Gruen, Architect of an American Dream* (Philadelphia: University of Pennsylvania Press, 2004), 124–31, 1142–47.

35. Philip Bell and Roger Bell, *Implicated: Americanising Australia*, rev ed. (Perth, Australia: API-Network, 2007).

36. Margo, *Frank Lowy*, 89.

37. Ibid., 91.

38. Hardwick, *Mall Maker*, 103. See also Cohen, *Consumers' Republic*, 262–63.

39. Rod Myer, *Living the Dream: The Story of Victor Smorgon* (Sydney, Australia: New Holland, 2000), 107.

40. Ibid., 27–28.

41. "Smorgon Steel Group Ltd. History," accessed July 10, 2012, www.fundinguniverse.com/company-histories/smorgon-steel-group-ltd-history.

42. Jill Margo: *Frank Lowy*, 138.

43. Ibid., 140–41.

44. Ibid., 181.

45. www.anderson.ucla.edu/media-relations/2013/peter-lowy.

46. John A. Dawson and J. Dennis Lord, eds., *Shopping Centre Development: Policies and Prospects* (London: Croom Helm, 1985), 211.

47. Ibid.

48. Accessed November 23, 2009, www.lowyinstitute.org.

49. Levi, *These Are the Names*, xiv.

50. Peter Y. Medding, "Introduction: Ethnic Minorities and Australian Society," in *Jews in Australian Society*, ed. Peter Y. Medding (Melbourne, Australia: MacMillan and Monash University, 1973), 3.

51. Rubinstein, in *Jews in Australia*, ed. Medding, 349.

52. P. D. Jack, "They Did It Their Way: It's Easy to Make Money: Just Do It." Money and Real Estate, 1. *Sydney Morning Herald*, September 26, 1984.

53. Keeda, "Shipowners."

54. Jerry Z. Muller, *Capitalism and the Jews* (Princeton: Princeton University Press, 2010), 2. See also Maristello Botticini and Zvi Eckstein, *The Chosen Few* (Tel Aviv: Tel Aviv University Press), 2012.

55. Muller, *Capitalism and the Jews*, 5.

56. Hardwick, *Mall Maker*, 4.

57. Ruth Ostrow, *The New Boy Network* (Melbourne, Australia: William Heinemann, 1987), 2.

58. Taped interview with George Bloomfield, Sydney, 1986.

59. Gabriel Kune, *Nothing Is Impossible: The John Saunders Story* (Melbourne, Australia: Scribe, 1999), 148.

PART II

From Europe to America and Back Again

The focus in section two shifts from the Pacific to the Atlantic. As we will see, connections between Europe and America were bidirectional, just as they were between Jews on the Pacific Rim. Much of the existing scholarship on Eastern European Jews in America has emphasized the experiences of migrants once they reached American shores. Some scholars believed that immigrants severed their connections with the Old World. The following chapters are revelatory in that they examine an unfamiliar dimension of Eastern European mass migration to the United States—how the act of immigrating created new economic opportunities on both sides of the Atlantic.

In the following chapters historians Eric L. Goldstein and Rebecca Kobrin explain how a familiarity with and continued connection to a place of origin could provide economic advantage to immigrants living in a new "hostland" as well the means to influence and shape cultural, social, and commercial developments in a distant homeland. While both chapters demonstrate the economic and human impact of such relationships, Goldstein's chapter also considers the effect of American Jewish ideas on Eastern European Jewry.

Rebecca Kobrin, in "Currents and Currency: Jewish Immigrant 'Bankers' and the Transnational Business of Mass Migration, 1873–1914," recovers a lost world where Jewish immigrant banks took the deposits of tens of thousands of immigrants and Jewish bankers bestrode the Lower East Side as moguls until crisis caused the banks and their owners to stumble spectacularly. She explains that the origins of these banks were "intricately tied to the business of mass migration" and that leading "bankers not only fueled but also left an indelible imprint on this largest population shift in modern Jewish history."

Eric L. Goldstein, in "A Taste of Freedom: American Yiddish Publications in Imperial Russia," challenges the common understanding that the Yiddish culture that developed in the United States was a "sideshow to the main act across the Atlantic Ocean." Instead he convincingly demonstrates that immigrant publishers and book vendors in America, beneficiaries of a land free of censorship and full of immigrants with disposable income, played an important role in developing a popular Yiddish literature that was exported in bulk to Russia. According to Goldstein, this American-produced mass literature served as a "crucial model for the development of a Yiddish mass culture in Eastern Europe" in the early years of the twentieth century.

Together these two chapters significantly expand our understanding of the passage of people and ideas across the Atlantic. European markets were expanded, not eliminated, when European Jews disembarked in New York Harbor. Jews in the United States, moreover, influenced and affected the flow of their coreligionists to the New World. And they shaped the reading habits and ideas of those who stayed in the Old World. By re-creating a lost world of transatlantic Jewish commerce, these chapters shatter several of our assumptions about the relationship between Europe and America and point the way for future scholarship to be as attuned to homelands as it is to hostlands.

4

CURRENTS AND CURRENCY

Jewish Immigrant "Bankers" and the Transnational Business of Mass Migration, 1873–1914

Rebecca Kobrin

Transfixed by the headlines in July 1914, all New Yorkers watched events unfold following the assassination of Archduke Ferdinand in Sarajevo. As conflict became more likely, European financiers and investors became paralyzed by the prospect of war and prompted the stock exchanges of Berlin, Budapest, Brussels, and Saint Petersburg to all suspend business at some point over the summer of 1914. In the "neutral" United States, American bankers remained confident that America and its financial capital in New York would continue to operate unscathed by the European crisis. But New York's East European immigrant Jewish community felt far from neutral.[1] Terrified by the idea of a European war, they were, as one *Forverts* (Jewish Daily Forward) editorial summed up, deeply concerned about "what . . . escalating political tensions [would] mean for the Jews."[2] Fearing the worst, thousands of East European immigrant Jews ran to withdraw their savings from their *bankn* [banks] to transmit back to Europe.

Overwhelmed by the sea of depositors rushing in to take out their money, several Jewish immigrant banks—a network of financial enterprises that kept immigrant Jews' money, sold them ship tickets, granted small loans, and processed currency exchanges for overseas transfer—were forced to suspend business. Soon New York State's banking superintendent closed the banks of A. Grochowski, the Deutsch Brothers, Adolf Mandel, M & L Jarmulowksy, and Max Kobre because they did not have enough funds in reserve to return their depositors' assets.[3] The Jarmulowsky bank alone had 15,000 depositors with more than $1,667,000 in deposits.[4] But that paled in comparison to the banks of Max Kobre (on the Lower East Side and in Brooklyn), which claimed more than 23,000 depositors who had placed $3,700,000 in them.[5]

The bank closings outraged thousands of Jewish immigrant depositors, and they began to riot. "A mob of 5,000" depositors "angered by their inability to draw their deposits," reported the New York Times, marched to city hall where they attacked the clerks. The riot necessitated the call up of reserve policemen as "clubs were swung and fists were struck out." In the end, nine men and women were arrested.[6] Since many of these institutions' assets were tied up in real estate that could not be quickly liquidated, the state crafted new banking legislation requiring greater regulation of immigrant banks that sold ship tickets. These new laws would doom the world of immigrant banking—a world that had made it possible for most Jews to come to the United States.

Few today recognize the names Grochowski, Deutsch, Mandel, Jarmulowksy, or Kobre. Many pass daily the landmark buildings that still loom over the tenements on the Lower East Side that once housed their "banks" and businesses through which they sold their ship tickets.[7] Few Jewish immigrants in early twentieth-century New York would have ever believed that men like Max Kobre or any member of the Jarmulowsky family would fail or that their failures would cause a riot on the streets of New York. In fact, the name Jarmulowsky, according to the popular Yiddish daily newspaper *Tageblat,* "was the guarantee of honesty" known to "every Jew in both the Old and New World" on account of his transnational business dealings, which "brought him into contact with thousands of immigrants" to whom he sold ship tickets.[8] Similarly, Max Kobre, as Aaron Domnitz recalled in his autobiography, "was like an older brother to all. . . . As with all men of wealth back in the Old Country, everyone deposited their money with him." Kobre, Domnitz summed up, "was the transnational broker who made migration possible; his bank was the 'clearing house' where we all exchanged news from the entire region."[9]

The coming pages look at the transnational businesses that flourished in and around Jewish immigrant banks in the decades leading up to 1914. The business practices of these transnational immigrant bankers enabled their enterprises to succeed phenomenally at the turn of the twentieth century. All were intricately tied to the business of mass migration or, more specifically, the transatlantic shipping industry that saw migrants as commodities. Through such practices as selling tickets on installment, using a transnational system of multilingual agents, and transferring money overseas, Jewish immigrant bankers earned great fortunes. Indeed, as the Holland American Line representative in New York complained at the beginning of the twentieth century, these Jewish immigrant businessmen cornered the market on prepaid tickets, selling thousands of transatlantic ship tickets through their banks.[10] Since their businesses ultimately failed and left few records, these banking businesses built on their transnational ties have been virtually erased from the annals of Jewish and American economic history, obscuring the transnational economic practices undergirding Jewish mass migration from Eastern Europe at the turn of the last century.

Economics, Transnationalism, and the Writing of Modern Jewish Immigration History

This chapter considers anew the saga of the mass dispersal of Jews from Eastern Europe by viewing it through a transnational economic lens. To be sure, this epoch in Jewish history is far from uncharted scholarly terrain.[11] Overall, the literature on East European Jewish migration, as Nancy Green and François Weil note, reflects the larger literature on migration and has been "resolutely a literature of *im*migration."[12] Framed almost entirely from the perspectives of the countries of arrival, we know much about East European Jewish immigrants' lives once they settled in New York, London, or Buenos Aires but little about how they got there or the transnational character of their movements (through Western Europe). As I argue elsewhere, few scholars conduct sustained transnational analysis of the paths taken by East European Jews,[13] obscuring how state formation, timing of migration, and economic development (in both region of origin and final settlement) shaped the experience of migration as well as the process of adaptation across time and space.[14]

In its transnational examination of Jews' pivotal role in the transatlantic business of migration, this chapter brings into sharp focus a critical question: how does the central narrative of mass Jewish immigration history appear different if we invite its commercial practices to center stage? To be sure, many scholars discuss the epic tale of Jewish mass migration to the United States. Their sagas often echo American nationalist mythology and Emma

Lazarus's powerful imagery. No one has yet asked how many of Emma Lazarus's "huddled masses yearning to breathe free" would not have been able to come to America but for the entrepreneurial spirit and ingenuity of transnational brokers like Sender Jarmulowsky and Max Kobre. As they sold tickets to hundreds of thousands of their coreligionists, these businessmen embedded East European migration in a larger system of distribution. Indeed, they saw migrants as a lucrative commodity to exploit through various commercial practices on both sides of the Atlantic. Their efforts not only fueled but also left an indelible imprint on this revolutionary population shift in modern Jewish history.

In the past decades, as transnationalism has become an increasingly important analytical category in American history, few have presented any sustained analysis of Jews. But Jews acted as the quintessential transnational migrants, to use the words of Nina Glick Schiller, as they "forged and sustained multi-stranded social relations link[ing] together their societies of origin and settlement."[15] A new vision of East European Jewish migration—that looks beyond the map of the United States—highlights that the process of Jewish immigration to the United States was never isolated or exceptional: Jews, like their newly adopted nation, have always been molded by foreign mentalities, international economic networks, transnational financial ties, and global business practices.

The Problem of the Immigrant Jewish "Banker" in the United States

Jewish bankers like Sender Jarmulowsky and Max Kobre exemplify the ways in which migration to the United States and American business practices were molded in the crucible of transnational economic concerns. Indeed, few contemporary historians comment on the transnational business practices of turn-of-the-century immigrant ship ticket brokers or immigrant bankers, but it was precisely these transnational ties and shifting loyalties that made them seem so suspect to early twentieth-century governmental authorities. In the numerous early twentieth-century conversations concerning immigrant restriction, nothing troubled US officials more deeply than the growing ranks of unqualified immigrant bankers who used their Old World ties to sell ship tickets and transfer money abroad.[16] Unlike traditional bankers, these immigrant businessmen usually operated out of other commercial enterprises, such as saloons, grocery stores, bakeries, or boarding houses.[17] Moreover, their banks were not chartered or regulated by any governmental authority. As the 1910 Senate Commission on Immigration bemoaned, this lack of regulation enabled these enterprises to use the deposits left with them for a myriad of speculative investments. Describing the methods by which immigrants become ensnared by immigrant bankers, the Senate Commission noted in 1910,

> Nothing is more natural than that the immigrant should take his savings to the agent [who brought him to America] and ask that the agent send them home for him. Having made the start, it is natural that he should continue to leave with the agent for safe-keeping his weekly or monthly surplus, so that he may accumulate a sufficient amount for another remittance or for the purpose of buying a steam-ship ticket to bring his family to this country or to return to Europe. It is not long before the agent has a nucleus for a banking business and his assumption of banking functions quickly follows.[18]

Few individuals better illustrated the ways in which ship ticket brokers became respected bankers in the United States than Sender Jarmulowsky. Born in 1841 in Grajewo, in the Lomza province of Russia–Poland, Jarmulowsky was orphaned at the age of three and then raised by the Rabbi of Werblow.[19] Impressed with his intellect, Jarmulowsky was sent to the Volozhin Yeshiva, where he received rabbinical ordination.[20] As was common in Lithuania, though penniless, Jarmulowsky's great intellect earned him a good match to Rebecca Markels, the daughter of a wealthy merchant.[21] While this match would enable Jarmulowsky to pursue his career in the rabbinate on a full-time basis, he opted instead to enter the business world.

Jarmulowsky and his new wife moved to Hamburg in 1868, where he opened a "passage and exchange" office through which he bought and sold steerage class tickets to the United States. Jarmulowsky pioneered a system that sold prepaid tickets and extended credit to prospective passengers.[22] His fortune was built on the fact that prepaid tickets were valid for a year, and Jarmulowky could purchase hundreds of tickets in bulk when prices were lower during the winter season, writing out the tickets to fictive people since name changes on tickets were processed at no extra charge. During the summer months, when prices increased, he sold these tickets to East European Jews with an extra profit margin. If prices dropped or tickets could

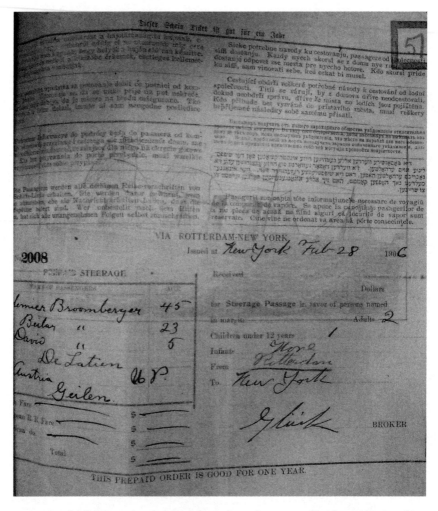

FIGURE 4.1. Sender Jarmulowsky's multilingual attachment to a Hamburg-American Line Ticket. Source: Folder IV BI, no. 14, Staatsarchiv Hamburg, Germany.

not be sold in time, his loss was limited to the 5 percent cancellation fee. Jarmulowsky also developed a new multilingual ticket that attracted prospective migrants from all over Eastern Europe to his office (Figure 4.1).

Although Sender Jarmulowsky was immensely successful he was denied residency in Hamburg (probably as a result of his birth in Eastern Europe) and ventured to America in 1873.[23] There he set up an office on the corner of Orchard and Canal Streets. Expanding his business by offering East European Jewish immigrants already in the United States a way to "pay out" in installments the cost of bringing their European relations to America, his business quickly flourished. As S. L. Blumenson recalled, "On the Square [Rutgers Square] stood the green, iron-grilled skyscraper which housed the Jarmulowsky bank, a name known in every town, village and hamlet across Europe. It was Jarmulowsky who provided the *shiffskarten,* the steamship tickets, to probably half the immigrants during the last two decades of the nineteenth century."[24]

As Blumenson's recollections evocatively capture, "bank" and "ship ticket salesman" were interchangeable terms in the Jewish immigrant world. Soon, by not only extending credit but also operating in the foreign currency markets and taking deposits, Sender Jarmulowsky was able to build the largest commercial bank on the Lower East Side, holding the deposits of more than 35,000 East European Jewish immigrants and sending millions of dollars back to the Old Country. His bank, however, did not earn its profits like other banks but was dependent on the revenue made from the sale of ship tickets.

Investigations from shipping companies along with court cases shed light on how Jarmulowsky made money off each ticket he sold on installment. Starting in the 1890s, as American officials complained to the shipping lines of the growing number of passengers arriving with debts as a result of buying their tickets on installment, the shipping companies set out to investigate those agents selling tickets for their lines, as they did not approve of such schemes. Through a group of detectives posing as migrants, several of the main shipping lines caught Jewish immigrant bankers such as Max Kobre, Louis Scharlach, Sender Jarmulowsky, the Markel Brothers, and others who all required a down payment of five to ten dollars followed by weekly installments of one dollar.[25] Infuriated, the shipping lines imposed fines on Jarmulowsky and all other ship ticket salesmen they found offering credit and selling tickets on installment.

Fines imposed by the shipping lines, however, did little to deter the agents from selling on installment as illustrated by an 1890 New York State supreme court case—*Michael Rosencranz v. Sender Jarmulowsky.* As one of Sender Jarmulowsky's clerks testified at an 1890 trial, Jarmulowsky made up to $16 profit per ticket. As the clerk described, during the winter season, Jarmulowksy purchased tickets for $8 and $9, and he sold them "for up to $24 (during other seasons)." Indeed, Rosencranz was suing Jarmulowsky because he had purchased tickets in New York for $10 to be sent to Sender Jarmulowsky's office in Hamburg for his wife and children. His wife was stranded in Hamburg, as the trial revealed, because six weeks earlier her husband had booked passage with another ship ticket salesman by the name of Wolff, whose business had failed, leaving his wife with no tickets to reach the United States. After receiving a letter from her husband that he had purchased tickets at a certain price for her and the rest of the family at the Jarmulowsky bank, she went there to claim her tickets. The Jarmulowsky branch office in Hamburg denied this purchase. At wits' end, she paid a higher price for the tickets after a clerk told her (as he testified in the trial), "Payment in full is always required. Because the price of tickets change sometimes and we want to satisfy [the purchaser] that if the prices are higher, we won't ask for more payment."[26] Rosencranz sued Jarmulowsky to return the extra money his wife had paid. Ultimately Rosencranz lost, but not because he did not sufficiently prove his case. Rather, the judge felt he could not adjudicate a business dispute that actually transpired in Germany. Indeed, the transnational character of Jarmulowsky's business dealings saved him from being penalized in New York City's civil court.

As the trial and shipping line investigations highlight, in the treacherous transnational business of mass migration, trust—that one would safely be transported to her destination and be charged fairly—was of paramount concern to the Jewish migrant. Indeed, Jarmulowsky's success hinged on his appreciation of these concerns, so he stressed his piety (reinforcing the impression that he would not cheat you) and always made sure people reached their destinations. As Louis Lipsky recalled about his mother's migration,

> The guardian who received my mother at the boat was Sendor [sic] Jarmulowsky. . . . His name stands high in the memory of our family. As far as we were concerned, he was the *Hachnosas Orchim* [spirit of hospitality] incarnate. He was known to thousands of Jewish families. He . . . remains in the memory of thousands of Jews as the man who freed them on the soil of the United States. I have met Jews from Pittsburgh, from Chicago, from Boston and other places, all of whom remember his name with warmth. He considered it his duty to receive personally the immigrants on arrival at Castle Garden. He provided them with a night's lodging, a good meal, and then dispatched them to their new homes, personally accompanying them to the railroad station to say goodbye.[27]

Similarly, Max Kobre's banks on the Lower East Side and in Brooklyn relied on his transnational ties with his in-laws in Europe and trust to create a lucrative business of ship ticket sales. Unlike Jarmulowsky, who opened his business when the sale of ship tickets was totally unregulated,

Max Kobre arrived in New York in 1891, several years before the continental shipping lines began to form treaties that clamped down on the prices agents could charge for their tickets. Kobre developed new ways to earn a profit. First, Kobre employed a wide range of newcomers who worked as peddlers to sell tickets to many different ethnic groups. As historian Torsten Feys points out, Kobre soon became infamous among representatives of the British and Dutch shipping lines for his practice of selling tickets on installments through these newly arrived peddlers.[28] Kobre also introduced new selling methods, such as cheaper cash orders, enabling him to further pierce the divided ethnic markets common in the sale of ship tickets. In fact, Kobre sold so many tickets that the Holland American Line secretly sent an agent to investigate his business practices in 1894. As Van den Toorn, the representative of the Holland–American Line in New York, reported, Kobre exemplified the corrupt business practices of Jewish agents whose selling on installments and through peddlers proved impossible to eradicate. The continental lines sent out Pinkerton detectives on a wide-range investigation catching Kobre and others in underselling their established rates. Although fined for his practices, Kobre and his business were up and running in less than a week.

When the North Atlantic Passenger Treaty made selling tickets less profitable, Kobre began to operate commercial banks that persuaded more than 23,000 depositors to leave funds with him. While he did run a bank on the Lower East Side, the mainstay of his business were enterprises he ran in the newer areas of Jewish immigrant settlement, particularly the Brownsville section of Brooklyn. The depositors in this new area of settlement were more Old World. Kobre's Jewish depositors in Brownsville had all been working hard and saving to get out of the neighborhood, the place that the writer Alfred Kazin observed, "all measured success by [one's] skill in getting away from it."[29]

Kobre's business in Brownsville shared several common features with many other immigrant banks. As historian Jared Day points out, immigrant bankers relied heavily on the loyalty of working-class immigrants as customers whom larger banks—which employed only English-speaking tellers—rarely tried to serve.[30] Max Kobre also provided "a wide range of ancillary services very specific to the immigrant community," most notably, business hours on Sunday (when all other banks were closed), the sale of ship tickets on installment, and the processing of small overseas money transfers.

In short, Max Kobre and Sender Jarmulowsky's ultimate successes were not related to any revolutionary or unique service they offered but rather that they acted like thousands of other immigrant bankers in the aftermath of the Civil War, who would accept small deposits and offer services—such as letter writing, money transfer of small amounts, and document translation—that mainstream American banks refused to provide. Mainstream American banks may have been a safer choice, as they were chartered, regulated, and constantly supervised by the state banking authority, but as Jared Day points out, they made foreign depositors feel "unwelcome," rarely employing translators and allowing their "staff [to] treat immigrants with impatience."[31] Jarmulowsky, on the other hand, and other Jewish immigrant bankers "fixed his bank hours to suit the convenience of his patrons"—with Sunday being his longest day of business, when every other bank in New York was closed. All these services were provided in Yiddish to ensure that little confusion occurred.[32]

By the turn of the twentieth century, Sender Jarmulowsky and Max Kobre had emerged as the symbols of the ability of East European Jews to transform themselves into respectable Americans through their participation in the business of mass migration.[33] Indeed, Jarmulowsky would soon abandon the Lower East Side and settle in one of the toniest neighborhoods in Manhattan. While his brownstone on East 93rd off Fifth Avenue had only six bedrooms, it was around the corner from Felix Warburg's mansion.[34] Max Kobre would purchase a brownstone in stylish Harlem. Despite the persistent image of tension between German Jewish elites and East European Jews in studies of this era, class apparently trumped ethnic background.[35] Sender Jarmulowsky would serve on boards with his new neighbors, most notably the Kehillah, the experiment of wealthier, Americanized Jews to establish a communal structure to unite all Jews in New York.[36] Sender Jarmulowsky's son Meyer would marry Fannie Lewisohn, daughter of the Hamburg merchant Leonard Lewisohn who founded in New York United Metals Selling Company, the largest copper dealer and purveyor of electric wires in the world.

The Jarmulowsky family was able to amass a great fortune by the end of the first decade of the twentieth century. America had been good to Sender Jarmulowsky, the orphan from Poland, and he became convinced he should construct a temple for the Lower East Side, albeit to banking not Judaism. There, newly arrived Jewish immigrants could worship their new American god. Hiring the esteemed architectural firm of Rouse & Goldstone in 1912, who had just completed the resplendent Langdon Hotel, the Jarmulowskys contracted to erect a twelve-story loft building on the same corner of Canal Street, where Sender Jarmulowsky had established himself thirty years earlier. Hoping this building would bring "uptown elegance and class to the Lower East Side," the Jarmulowskys purchased only the finest materials, with the lower section of the building composed of rusticated limestone. The bank stood apart from surrounding buildings by its sheer size and its giant, circular-roofed tempietto that rose fifty feet above the building to a dome, appearing as an altar from which all could worship capitalism. Inserted under the trading floor was a *beys midrash* (house of study) that enabled all who worked there to pray or study religious texts if they had a spare moment. The bank's façade and marble interior was discussed in detail on the pages of the *New York Architectural Digest*. Great excitement and a parade accompanied its grand opening on May 6, 1912.[37]

But Sender Jarmulowsky did not enjoy this new bank building for long, as he died less than a month later on June 2, 1912. As a revered philanthropist and celebrity of the Lower East Side, his obituary made the front page of all the major Yiddish newspapers.[38] Even the wealthier leaders of the Kehillah convened an emergency meeting of its executive board "to discuss the great loss to the Jews of New York" and how they could continue his "work for the unity of Jews" from all areas of New York.[39] He left his bank to his sons Meyer and Louis Jarmulowsky, and many were shocked that this supposed multimillionaire left an estate worth only approximately a half million dollars.[40] Many wondered where Sender Jarmulowsky's fortune had gone. The answer lay in Meyer Jarmulowsky's real estate dabbling. Purchasing thirty-seven properties with bank assets in East Harlem, the younger Jarmulowsky believed he would make even more money in East Harlem than with his previous investments, after hearing rumors concerning the construction of a new subway line along First Avenue.[41] But his lofty ambitions were thwarted by an event that transpired in Europe, in the distant city of Sarajevo. His customers' transnational economic ties to the family and friends across the Atlantic prompted them to run to claim all their hard-earned savings to send abroad.

Similarly, Max Kobre was caught totally unprepared by the response of his depositors to events in Europe. On September 17, 1914, Eugene Richards Lamb, the New York State banking superintendent, issued the following statement "concerning the affairs of Max Kobre":

The examination of the books, papers, and properties of Max Kobre's bank shows that according to the appraisals made by this

Department that the assets amount to $3,041,000. The admitted liabilities amount to $3,844,000.

These figures show an excess of liabilities over assets of $803,000.

The assets allowed by this Department are made up as follows: cash on hand, in banks, and securities, $609,000; bills discounted, $544,000; bonds and mortgages allowed at, $808,000; real estate owned, $1,646,000—less outstanding mortgages $858,000—net equities $1,019,000; other assets $51,000; total assets, $3,041,000.

This banker carried on a very extensive real estate business. At the time of the closing of the bank there were many outstanding building loans. The real estate owned by Max Kobre's bank consists of $1,050,000 improved property and of $822,000 unimproved property. These real estate parcels, which are all situated in New York City, are subject to mortgages of $858,000.

The unsatisfactory conditions of the affairs of the bank is due to unwise security and real estate speculation and to the apparent disregard of sound and safe banking methods in safeguarding the moneys of depositors. The superintendent of banks is seeking to locate additional assets and it is expected that other assets and properties which are now held by Mr. Kobre will be turned over for the benefit of the depositors.

This Department realizes that an immediate sale of the real estate and other assets could only be made at a tremendous sacrifice. Plans are under consideration to deferred payments. A definite announcement will be made as soon as the best method for handling this bank can be determined.[42]

Kobre was eventually indicted. But on June 5, 1916, the *New York Times* provocatively proclaimed, "Max Kobre Dead on Eve of Trial."[43] All were intrigued about the details of his death, since he had once threatened suicide during the two-year investigation of his bank failure and the closing of his private banks. During one of the many heated exchanges he had with assistant district attorney Leslie Tompkins, Kobre insisted that he would rather commit suicide than see his family lose their

Harlem home and all that he had worked hard to achieve in America. So when Kobre was found on his kitchen floor, "lying under an open jet of a gas stove," many were suspicious.[44] One police officer declared it suicide, only to be corrected shortly thereafter by the city coroner: Max Kobre died of heart disease, falling to the ground from a massive heart attack while heating himself some milk, to calm his nerves, so he could get some sleep before his trial. As the coroner summed up, "A man does not commit suicide standing up. . . . [The abrasions] found on Kobre's body indicated that the banker fell to the floor near the gas stove."[45]

But some still maintained it was a suicide. Indeed, the controversy that surrounded Max Kobre's death mirrored the conflicting attention his bank and its failure received in his lifetime. Indeed, Kobre's pre-1914 business trajectory was strikingly similar to that of Sender Jarmulowsky, as was the demise of his business empire. On June 18, 1917, Judge Augustus Hand presided over the bankruptcy hearing for Meyer and Harry Jarmulowsky. Seizing all buildings owned by the Jarmulowsky family, Hand set up a receivership, which he called the Loretta Corporation.[46] All anxiously awaited the auction of the Jarmulowsky properties, estimated to be worth $2 million in 1918. Although the auction room was filled with many bidders and some former depositors of the bank, the great interest did not turn into great profits; in the end only $371,850 was realized from the sale. Watching the claimants who held the government responsible, even though the Jarmulowsky bank was not chartered or checked by the New York State banking authority, Hand quickly realized the need for increased regulation of private banks along with new legislation to protect depositors and the state from corrupt bankers and their risky banking practices.

Over the next decade the decline of immigrant banking was spurred by increased legislative and regulatory action that aimed to make these institutions disappear. Progressive reformers joined forces with banking regulators to convince the government that these informal financial institutions were suspect and fraudulent. They mobilized public pressure and lobbied for new banking laws to suppress immigrant banks' capacities. As superintendent of banks Joseph Broderick declared in support of amendments to New York State banking laws in 1930, "The amendment will not only act as a deterrent to the formation of new bootleg banking concerns," referring to unregulated immigrant banks, "but will serve either to drive those in existence under the supervision of the Banking Department or out of business."[47]

Conclusion

What is the historical significance of transnational businesses operated by Sender Jarmulowsky and Max Kobre? First and foremost, the Kobre and Jarmulowsky families were far from exceptional: dozens of other East European Jewish immigrants inserted themselves into the American economy by conducting businesses that depended on connections on both sides of the Atlantic. The virtual erasure of these two men from the annals of history because of their failures has obscured the transnational ties shaping early twentieth-century American Jewish life and the larger world of American business. The narrative of East European Jewish migration has been shrouded for far too long by American nationalist mythology and Emma Lazarus's powerful imagery. But East European Jewish migration was embedded in a larger system of distribution in which migrants served as a lucrative commodity, a commodity expertly exploited by men like Sender Jarmulowksy and Max Kobre through various transnational business practices that both fueled and shaped this mass population shift. We cannot forget the role of their transnational entrepreneurial spirit when thinking about this pivotal epoch in American Jewish life.

Notes

1. Joseph Rappaport, "The American Yiddish Press and the European Conflict in 1914," *Jewish Social Studies* 19, nos. 3/4 (1957), 113–28.
2. *Forverts*, July 29, 1914, 3.
3. "Information RE: Private Bankers," P3/1542, Judah Leib Magnes papers, Central Archives for the History of the Jewish People, Jerusalem.
4. Ibid.
5. Ibid.
6. "5,000 Riot in Front of Closed Banks; Reserves Called to Disperse East Side Depositors Who Demand Their Money. March to See Whitman Police Forced to Use Clubs to Quell Angry Crowd," *New York Times*, August 30, 1914, 10.
7. New York City Landmarks Preservation Commission Report, "S. Jarmulowsky Bank Building, 54 Canal Street Borough of Manhattan," Designation List 419: LP-2363. October 13, 2009. See www.nyc.gov/html/lpc/downloads/pdf/reports/Jarmulowsky.pdf, accessed July 1, 2013.
8. Andrew Sorkin, *Too Big to Fail: The Inside Story of How Wall Street and Washington Fought to Save the Financial System* (New York: Penguin, 2009); "Reb Sender Yarmulowski," *Tageblat*, June 2, 1912, 1.
9. Autobiography of Aaron Domnitz (RG 128), 143. Aaron Domnitz, *My Future Is in America*, trans., Jocelyn Cohen and Daniel Soyer (New York: New York University Press, 2006), 143.

10. The Rotterdam Community Archives: The Holland-America Line Collection (hereafter G.A.R.-HAL), Folder 318.04: Passage Department, 221–26, Letters June 14, August 6, 23, September 5, and September 19, 1895.

11. A list of monographs focusing on East European Jewish immigration is too long to provide, but ever since Moses Rischin's pioneering *The Promised City: New York's Jews, 1870–1914* (Cambridge, MA: Harvard University Press, 1964), almost all scholarship on East European Jewish migration has approached its subjects from the vantage point of arrival and settlement. See Irving Howe's classic *World of Our Fathers*. Even migration studies dealing with places outside the United States focus on settlement and arrival. See, e.g., Lloyd Gartner, *The Jewish Immigrant in England, 1870–1914* (London: Allen & Unwin, 1960); Nancy Green, *The Pletzl of Paris: Jewish Immigrant Workers in the Belle Epoque* (New York: Holmes and Meier, 1986); Suzanne Rutland, *Edge of the Diaspora :Two Centuries of Jewish Settlements in Australia* (New York: Holmes and Meier, 1988); Victor Mirelman, *Jewish Buenos Aires, 1890–1930: In Search of an Identity* (Detroit: Wayne State University Press, 1990).

12. Nancy Green and François Weil, "Introduction," in *Citizenship and Those Who Leave: The Politics of Emigration and Expatriation*, ed. Nancy Green and François Weil (Chicago: University of Illinois Press, 2007), 1.

13. See Rebecca Kobrin, *Jewish Bialystok and Its Diaspora* (Bloomington: Indiana University Press, 2010). On this point, see Nancy Green, "The Comparative Method and Poststructural Structuralism—New Perspectives for Migration Studies," *Journal of American Ethnic History* 13, no. 4 (1994): 2–19 and her "L'Histoire comparative et le champ des etudes migratoires," *Annales: ESC* 45, no. 6 (1990): 1335–50. Max Weinreich's pioneering *Geshikhte fun der yidisher Shprakh: Bagrifn, Faktn, Metodn* (New York: Workmen's Circle, 1973) suggests just how useful such a transnational lens could be for the study of East European Jewry. Jonathan Frankel's pioneering study of Jewish socialism illustrated the intricate links between all migrant centers of Russian Jewish life and Russia, spanning New York, London, Paris, and South America; see Jonathan Frankel, *Prophecy and Politics* (New York: Cambridge University Press, 1981). The work of Sarah Stein also provides suggestive examples of how illuminating this methodology can be: see Sarah Abrevaya Stein, *Plumes: Ostrich Feathers, Jews, and a Lost World of Global Commerce* (New Haven, CT: Yale University Press, 2010) and her *Making Jews Modern: The Yiddish and Ladino Press in the Russian and Ottoman Empires* (Bloomington: Indiana University Press, 2004).

14. See Kobrin, *Jewish Bialystok*. Even though Nancy Green argued for such comparative work more than twenty-five years ago, few studies of Jewish migration prior to my book were written using a divergent model. See Green, "Comparative Method and Poststructural Structuralism," 2–19. Green did inspire exemplary work using the divergent comparative model concerning Italian and Irish immigration. This work illuminates that region of origin also played a fundamental role in shaping divergent immigrant experiences and influenced even the choice of destination country. See Donna Gabaccia, "Is Everywhere Nowhere? Nomads, Nations and the Immigrant Paradigm of United States History," *Journal of American History* 86, no. 3 (1999): 399. John Briggs, *An Italian Passage: Immigrants to Three American Cities, 1890–1930* (New Haven, CT: Yale University Press, 1978); Samuel L. Baily, *Immigrants in the Lands of Promise: Italians in Buenos Aires and New York City, 1870–1914* (Ithaca, NY: Cornell University Press, 1999); Donna

R. Gabaccia, *Italy's Many Diasporas* (Seattle: University of Washington Press, 2000); Donna R. Gabaccia and Fraser M. Ottanelli, eds. *Italian Workers of the World: Labor Migration and the Formation of Multiethnic States* (Urbana: University of Illinois Press, 2001); Malcolm Campbell, "The Other Immigrants: Comparing the Irish in Australia and the United States," *Journal of American Ethnic History* 14, no. 3 (1995): 3–22.

15. Nina Glick Schiller, Linda Basch, and Cristina Szanton Blanc, *Nations Unbound: Transnational Projects, Postcolonial Predicaments, and Deterritorialized Nation States* (New York: Gordon and Breach, 1994), 22.

16. Jeremiah W. Jenks and W. Jett Lauck, *The Immigration Problem: A Study of American Immigration Conditions and Needs* (New York: Funk and Wagnalls, 1911), xv, 96. This idea is further expanded in United States Senate, Reports of the Immigration Commission: Immigrant Banks, 61st Congress, 3rd Session, Vol. 37, Senate Doc. 753 (Washington, DC: 1911 [reprint, 1970]), 212–13.

17. Jared N. Day, "Credit, Capital and Community: Informal Banking in Immigrant Communities in the United States, 1880–1924," *Financial History Review* 9 (2002): 1, 65–78.

18. United States Senate, Reports of the Immigration Commission: Immigrant Banks, 61st Congress, 3rd Session, Vol. 37, Senate Doc. 753, 212–13. To be sure, this report is a rich primary source on the multiethnic character of turn-of-the-century immigrant banking but its limitations are nicely summed up by Oscar Handlin in his *Race and Nationality in American Life* (New York: Doubleday, 1957), 93.

19. "Yarmulowski gebrakht tsu kvure mit groys koved." *Morgn zhurnal*, June 4, 1912, 1.

20. On the high esteem all held for the Volozhin yeshiva, see Shaul Stampfer, *ha-Yeshivah ha-Litait be-hithavutah* (Jerusalem: Merkaz Zalman Shazar, 1995). A vivid portrait of life in this yeshiva and the high regard for its graduates can be found in Immanuel Etkes, *Yeshivot Lita: pirke zikhronot* (Jerusalem: Merkaz Zalman Shazar, 2004).

21. Glenn Dynner, *Men of Silk: The Hasidic Conquest of Poland* (New York: Oxford University Press, 2006), ch. 4; Shaul Stampfer, "Heder Study, Knowledge of Torah, and the Maintenance of Social Stratification in Traditional East European Jewish Society," *Studies in Jewish Education* 3 (1988): 271–89.

22. Torsten Feys, "Prepaid Tickets to Ride to the New World: The New York Continental Conference and Transatlantic Steerage Fares 1885–1895," 2–3 (unpublished manuscript). I would like to thank the author for sharing a manuscript of this article with me. Jarmulowsky, who worked in Germany, used methods developed in England earlier in the century. See N. Evans, "The Role of Foreign-Born Agents in the Development of Mass Migration through Britain, 1820–1923" in *Maritime Transport and Migration: The Connections between Maritime and Migration Networks*, ed. Torsten Feys, Lewis R. Fischer, Stephane Hoste, and S. Vanfraechem (Saint Johns, Canada: 2007). Pamela Nadell, "From Shtetl to Border: East European Jewish Emigrants and the 'Agents' System, 1868–1914," *Studies in the American Jewish Experience* 2 (1984).

23. On the difficulties East European Jews faced in Hamburg in this era concerning residency and status, see Rainer Liedtke, *Jewish Welfare in Hamburg and Manchester, 1850–1914* (New York: Oxford University Press, 1998), 142–63.

24. S. L. Blumenson, "Culture on Rutgers Square," *Commentary* 10 (1950): 66.

25. Van den Toorn was the representative of the Holland American line in New York City who launched the investigation. Van den Toorn reports that one woman was charged $59.50 for her passage and that of her child from Antwerp to New York, while the gross

rate charged by the lines amounted to &44.25. See G.A.R.-HAL, 318.04, Passage Department, 221–26, letter July 8, 1899. He notes that the same margin was used by Max Kobre; see G.A.R.-HAL, 318.03, Passage Department, 563, minute 122 October 22, 1896, 541 August 15, 1900. All these sources are qtd. in Torsten Feys, "A Business Approach to Trans-Atlantic Shipping: The Introduction of Steam-Shipping and its Impact on the European Exodus, 1840–1914" (PhD diss., University of Ghent, 2008), ch. 3.

26. *M. Rosencranz v. S. Jamelowsky* [sic], Fourth District Court, September 28, 1890, found in the Archives of the Supreme Court of the State of New York, Chambers Street, New York.

27. Louis Lipsky, *Memoirs in Profile* (Philadelphia, 1975), 12–13.

28. Feys, "Business Approach"; G.A.R.-HAL, 318.04, Passage Department, 221–26, Letter July 23, 1901.

29. Alfred Kazin, *A Walker in the City* (New York, 1951), 12.

30. Day, "Credit, capital and community," 67.

31. Ibid., 70.

32. Reports of the Immigration Commission: Immigrant Banks, 61st Congress, 3rd Session, Vol. 37, Senate Doc. 753, 214–18.

33. "Reb Sender Yarmulowski un zeyn tseyt," *Tageblat*, June 3, 1912.

34. Christopher Gray, "A Wave of Change for a Quiet Block," *New York Times*, February 25, 2007.

35. Rischin, *The Promised City*, 95–111; Zosa Szajkowski, "The 'Yahudi' and the Immigrant; a Reappraisal," *American Jewish Historical Quarterly* 63, no. 1 (1973): 13–44; Naomi Cohen, *Encounter with Emancipation: The German Jews in the United States, 1830–1914* (Philadelphia: JPS, 1984).

36. For a full discussion of this organization, see Arthur Goren, *New York Jews and the Quest for Community: The Kehillah Experiment, 1908–1922* (New York: Columbia University Press, 1970).

37. *Forverts*, May 4, 1912, 3.

38. "Sender Yarmulowski," *Foverts*, June 2, 1912, 1; Reb Sender Yarmulowski," *Tageblat*, June 2, 1912, 1; "Yarmulowski gebrakht tsu kvure mit groys koved," *Morgn zhurnal*, June 4, 1912, 1.

39. "Yarmulowski in eybige ruh," *Tageblat*, June 3, 1912, 1.

40. "Only $501,053 Left By Jarmulowsky: East Side Banker Had Been Reputed to be Multi-Millionaire," *New York Times*, August 14, 1912.

41. "First Avenue for Subway; Reasons Why East Side Line Should Be There," New York Times, November 19, 1904, 8; "For First Avenue Subway; East Side Improvement Association Treasurer Argues for It," New York Times, February 2, 1905, 8. Indeed, rumors of the construction of this subway line are still being debated. Michael Grynbaum, "Further Delays Possible for Second Avenue Subway," *New York Times*, July 22, 2009, A29.

42. Eugene Richards Lamb, "Statement Concerning the Affairs of Max Kobre," September 17, 1914, P3/1542, Judah Leib Magnes papers, Central Archives for the History of the Jewish People, Jerusalem.

43. "Max Kobre Dead on Eve of Trial: Under Indictment Two Years after His Three Private Banks Had Closed; Had Hinted at Suicide," *New York Times*, June 5, 1916, 2:7.

44. Ibid.

45. Ibid.

46. See the following cases: Jarmulowsky C.A.2 1919, Circuit Court of Appeals, Second Circuit, May 14, 1919; no. 161. *Robbing v. Bank of M. & L. Jarmulowsky*, 90 N. Y. Supp. 288.
47. Memorandum from Joseph Broderick to Mr. Samuel Rosenman, Counsel to the Governor, n.d., Legislative Bill Jacket 1930, ch. 678, Reel 5, New York Public Library—Science, Industry and Business Library, New York. I would like to thank Shira Poliak for pointing me to this source.

5

A TASTE OF FREEDOM

American Yiddish Publications in Imperial Russia

Eric L. Goldstein

Scholars have studied the history of Yiddish culture in both its Eastern European and American contexts, but seldom have they examined the relationship of these two centers of Yiddish to one another.[1] This gap seems to have resulted from the assumption that the Yiddish scene in the United States, as the product of an immigrant society focused squarely on Americanization, was never more than a sideshow to the main act across the Atlantic Ocean. For example, the renowned scholar Chone Shmeruk, in a study examining the role of his native Warsaw as a Yiddish literary center, argued that New York, the focus of Yiddish cultural activity in the United States, was "merely an offshoot" of the Eastern European hub.[2] Even Shmuel Niger, a writer, literary critic, and historian who lived and worked in the United States for more than three decades and paid an unusual degree of attention in his writings to the development of American Yiddish culture, concluded that before World War I, Yiddish New York was at best a "colony" of the Eastern European Yiddish empire.[3]

This chapter challenges these longstanding assumptions by examining the complex relationship between the markets for Yiddish print culture in the United States and in Imperial Russia at the end of the nineteenth and beginning of the twentieth century. While literary scholars like Shmeruk and Niger typically privileged works of high culture in making judgments about the relative importance of Yiddish cultural production in Eastern Europe and America, the evidence presented here refocuses our attention on the development of a popular literature for the Yiddish-speaking "masses," a process that was well underway in the United States almost two decades before it hit its stride in the *alte heym*.

In Russia, tsarist censorship and traditional authority structures retarded the development of Yiddish newspapers and other vernacular media before 1903, when the empire's first Yiddish daily, *Der fraynd* (The Friend), debuted in Saint Petersburg.[4] In the United States, however, newspapers, dime novels, works of popular science, and texts in Yiddish to help Americanize immigrants had already proliferated by the early 1890s among the large population of Eastern European Jewish immigrants as a result of America's free environment and consumerist ethic. Although this mass culture in Yiddish was the product of forces largely independent of the Eastern European milieu, it did influence the cultural life of the homeland owing to the fact that American Yiddish imprints of this era were regularly imported to Russia, where they became a highly sought after commodity. As the evidence presented here demonstrates, both Russian Jewish readers and cultural entrepreneurs were greatly interested in the popular Yiddish print culture emanating from the United States. In fact, so influential were these American imports that they ultimately served as a crucial model for the development of a Yiddish mass culture in Eastern Europe in the early years of the twentieth century, when censorship finally began to recede and economic development and urbanization began to make institutions like a daily press and commercial publishing houses possible.[5]

The First Center of a Yiddish Mass Culture

Although a mass culture in Yiddish reached its full flowering in America only in the 1890s, it had been developing slowly since the 1870s, when the first Yiddish newspapers were created for an American audience. A particularly important milestone in the growth of this press came in December 1875, when a pious Lithuanian Jew, Pesach Rubenstein, was charged by officials in New York with the murder of his cousin, Sarah Alexander, who was thought to have been carrying his child. The Rubenstein case became a subject of fascination in the general American press and also inspired a series of "true crime" pamphlets for a broad readership.[6] If non-Jewish readers were mesmerized by the case, however, even more captivated were the Yiddish-speaking Jews of New York, from whose ranks both the tragic victim and the despised murderer came. For Eastern European Jewish newcomers, coverage of the Rubenstein

case provided an introduction to the sensationalism of American popular culture, which could turn an immigrant tragedy into a titillating drama. Their
access to information about the trial, however, was more circumscribed than
that of the English-reading public. When Rubenstein was arrested, New York
had only one weekly Yiddish paper, the *Yidishe gazetn* (Jewish Gazette), which
in its second year of publication was still appearing irregularly and struggling
for survival. Not only did Rubenstein's trial help stabilize the fledgling periodical, but it also breathed new life into a moribund competitor, the *Yidishe
tsaytung* (Jewish Paper), and—according to one report—spurred the creation
of a third weekly paper as well.[7] By the winter of 1876, demand was so high for
news of the trial that publishers began for the first time to send young boys
out on the street to hawk the latest edition.[8]

The surge in Yiddish journalism caused by the Rubenstein case did not
persist long after the end of the trial. With relatively few Yiddish readers in
the years before the rise of mass immigration in the early 1880s, even weekly
Yiddish papers found it hard to sustain themselves. Not until 1885 did the
Yidishes tageblat (Jewish Daily News), the first successful Yiddish daily in New
York (and, in fact, in the world), make its debut. Still, the buzz caused by the
Rubenstein case did reveal something unprecedented about the public sphere
that was emerging among Jewish immigrants in America: cultural production
was driven increasingly by the demands and desires of the readers as opposed
to the agenda of the writers and publishers.

The growing power of a Yiddish-reading audience in the United States
marked a dramatic departure from trends in Eastern Europe, where elites
controlled public discourse among Jews and where the most robust publishing enterprises—including two major weekly newspapers and one daily—
remained in Hebrew throughout the nineteenth century, even though only a
small number of Jews could understand the language beyond the rudiments
of the prayer book.[9] In part, this situation was a result of the censorship laws
limiting Yiddish periodicals, which reflected tsarist officials' fears that newspapers in the spoken languages of minority groups might help galvanize mass
political movements in opposition to the government. Thus, although a few
Yiddish weeklies were published from time to time in neighboring Prussia
or Austro-Hungary and distributed within Russia, only two weekly Yiddish
newspapers, each lasting less than a decade, were published in the empire
before the easing of censorship in 1903.[10]

Popular novels were allowed by the Russian censors but not without significant controls on their contents. The most significant factor limiting the

spread of Yiddish popular fiction in book form, however, was not tsarist policy; it was the conservative and hierarchical nature of Russian Jewish cultural life. Russia's closed society and the lack of a highly developed commercial culture that might have yielded greater power to a popular reading audience meant that intellectual elites, especially rabbis and maskilim (proponents of the Jewish Enlightenment), held great sway over the publishing and distribution of Jewish works. Although rabbis and maskilim held goals that were often antagonistic to one another, both retained a sense of distance from and superiority to the "masses." This elitism was what propelled the dominance among both secular and religious writers of Hebrew over Yiddish as a vehicle for Jewish cultural expression during the nineteenth century. Although an increasing number of maskilim—among them Israel Aksenfeld, Shlomo Ettinger, Sholem Yankev Abramovitsh, and Yitskhok Yoel Linetski—began to write in Yiddish during this period, their works were mainly oriented to an educated audience and did not enjoy wide currency among the masses.[11]

A few truly popular authors like Ayzik Meyer Dik and Nokhem Meyer Shaykevitsh ("Shomer") did begin to reach thousands with their popular novels during the second half of the nineteenth century, but this type of Yiddish literature was generally viewed with suspicion and condescension by the intellectual establishment.[12] Even the publishers who brought out such works—like the Widow and Brothers Romm and the Matz Press, both in Vilna—accorded them an inferior status. Surviving accounts of these firms' publishing activities indicate that they viewed the sale of popular novels not as an end in itself but as a vehicle to help underwrite more esteemed projects—like Romm's famed Vilna Talmud (1886), which required significant overhead—or as a way to make up the shortfall from the sale of rabbinic and maskilic works, which were purchased by a relatively small circle of readers.[13]

Given the absence of a true market economy in which a mass culture in Yiddish might flourish, the social and intellectual authority vested in the intellectual elite meant that even popular writers themselves had to remain guarded in their efforts to cultivate a larger readership among the masses. The consequences of catering to the masses were made clear in 1888, when Shomer was put "on trial" as a literary hack by Sholem Aleichem in his pamphlet of that year, *Shomers mishpet* (The Judgment of Shomer). While Shomer's readers were probably not even aware of this critique, *Shomers mishpet* created a scandal among writers and intellectuals, forcing Shomer to leave Russia and take his family to New York in 1889. The popular writer never accepted the conclusions of his critics, which he continued to contest from abroad. Still, the ability of their invective to drive him into "exile" in America underscored the stigma felt by writers who were thought to have compromised their civilizing mission by courting the humblest of readers too directly.[14] In short, despite a thirst among the masses for Yiddish reading material in nineteenth-century Russia, there remained a strong aversion among literary producers to seeing popular taste as something that ought to be satisfied.

It is against this backdrop that we may appreciate the significance of the growing number of weekly and daily newspapers, monthly literary journals, and popular books that began to appear in Yiddish in the United States during the 1890s, rivaling the output of the largest Eastern European cultural centers. Few are aware of the fact, for example, that in 1900 there were six daily Yiddish papers in the United States—five in New York and one in Chicago—and none in the Russian Empire. Faced with a lack of venues for publication, even some of the "classic" Yiddish writers of Eastern Europe, despite their distaste for the popular cast of American Yiddish culture, had to turn to American periodicals in order to publish their work. During the 1890s, both before and after his abortive attempt to publish his sketches in small booklets called *Yontev bletlekh* (Holiday Pages), which were designed to circumvent the ban on Yiddish periodicals, Warsaw-based Yitskhok Leybush Peretz began to send stories and poems to two leading New York Yiddish newspapers: the socialist *Arbeter tsaytung* (Worker's Paper) and the Orthodox *Yidishes tageblat*.[15] During the late 1890s he also published poems in the independent monthly journal *Nayer gayst* (New Spirit), which was edited by his friend, the writer and theater critic Bernard Gorin.[16] Similarly, in 1894, Sholem Aleichem found an outlet for his feullitons in the *Filadelfier shtot tsaytung* (Philadelphia City Paper) as well as in *Di toyb* (The Dove), a Yiddish periodical published in Pittsburgh.[17]

While a robust journalism remained the most distinctive feature of the new American center, there was also a lively industry of book publishing—or rather, booklet publishing, as most of the books were published in the early years in installments and only later collected in complete sets. These *heftn*, as they were called, first emerged in 1892, when the immigrant entrepreneur Sigmund Kantorowitz commissioned the writer Abner Tanenbaum to produce a Yiddish version of a German serial novel about the intrigues of the Russian royal court. Soon a number of other authors entered the scene, like Getsl Zelikovitsh, who wrote potboilers like *Madam yeytser-hore* (Madame "Evil Inclination"), and David Hermalin, who first introduced Arthur Conan Doyle's Sherlock Holmes to Yiddish readers. The installments of such works sold like hotcakes from the bookstores and soda water stands of the Lower East Side, launching a revolution in the reading of popular fiction in Yiddish.[18]

The speed with which newspapers took up the publishing of serialized fiction took some of the steam out of the trade in *heftn,* but American Yiddish book publishing remained strong nonetheless—stronger than most literary historians have realized. In the wake of Kantorowitz's first successful publishing venture, a number of other bookdealers—most of whom began their careers selling prayerbooks, *sforim* (rabbinic works), and religious articles—redirected their attention to the more lucrative business of secular Yiddish book publishing. In the years before the turn of the century, firms like Rosenbaum & Werbelowsky, Meyer Chinsky, Judah Meir Katzenelenbogen, and Jacob Druckerman, among others, annually issued dozens of new Yiddish books and pamphlets, including not only original fiction but also translations of world literature, popular scientific works, dictionaries and language methods, and a host of other "how-to" guides to help immigrants adjust to their new surroundings. By 1898, journalist Abraham Cahan could call New York the "largest Yiddish book market in the world."[19]

Sending Yiddish Popular Literature Back to Russia

One might normally assume that foreign language cultural institutions (press, publishing, theater) established by European immigrants at the end of the nineteenth century were carryovers, at least in part, from similar institutions the immigrants knew in their former homes. But as we have seen, because of the marked difference between the open, market-oriented, and democratic culture of the United States and the closed, regulated culture of the Russian Empire, Yiddish literature for the "masses" took root and flourished in America earlier and in a more significant way than it did in the European homeland. In fact, because both economic and political conditions in the United States made the mass production of the printed word in Yiddish easier than it was in Russia, the Jewish immigrant community in America found itself by the 1890s in the unusual position of being able to provide Yiddish readers in Russia with new forms of cultural production that were as yet unavailable in the homeland.[20]

The earliest example of this flow of popular Yiddish literature from the United States to Russia occurred in radical circles. Among the most vigorous groups engaged in Yiddish cultural production in the United States during the 1890s were Jewish socialists, who became masters of the art of spreading radical propaganda among the Jewish working class. Radical literature from

America was smuggled into Russia beginning in 1886, when tsarist police confiscated copies of the socialist *Nyu Yorker folkstaytung* (New York People's Paper), edited by Abraham Braslavsky and Moses Mintz.[21] Memoirs of Jews active in radical movements recall that illegal copies of the works of American poets like David Edelshtat and Morris Rosenfeld were available in many of the clandestine reading rooms set up for workers in the Pale of Settlement. Because secular education and especially knowledge of science were considered central to radicalization, many of these libraries also featured copies of the socialist scientific journal *Di tsukunft*, which was one of the earliest sources providing Yiddish-speaking workers in Russia with articles on philosophy and political economy as well as on the natural and physical sciences. For similar reasons, radicals gravitated to the works of Abner Tanenbaum, who specialized in novels that wove bits of science into their plots and was particularly known for his popularizations of the works of Jules Verne, which he rendered in simple, idiomatic Yiddish.[22]

As Jewish socialists in New York developed a growing corpus of radical literature aimed at immigrants—everything from socialist parodies of Jewish liturgy and other antireligious propaganda to a whole range of popular scientific works—many of these titles were brought illegally to Russian cities to help in propaganda efforts there. By 1894, there was also an effort headed by the American radical Benjamin Feigenbaum and his colleagues to publish socialist pamphlets expressly for Russian Jews, which were smuggled into the country disguised with title pages from nineteenth-century rabbinic works in order to fool the border police. After 1897, when the Bund began to organize educational activities for Jewish workers, they initially relied to a large extent on the American literature that had been flowing illegally into Russia over the previous several years.[23]

Despite the importance of illegal socialist literature in carrying out propaganda efforts in Russia, however, it would be a mistake to assume that this was the only—or the largest—arena in which American Yiddish publications reached a Russian audience. By the mid-1890s, there was also a strong infusion of Yiddish publications into Russia that were produced by commercial publishing firms in New York and Chicago and sold openly by leading Russian Jewish booksellers.[24] These works filled a particularly important need in the Russian Yiddish book market during the transitional years at the end of the nineteenth and beginning of the twentieth century. During this period, increasing urbanization and rising literacy rates meant that the number of readers in the Russian Empire desiring secular works in Yiddish was growing rapidly. But because of the legal and financial burdens placed on publishers by onerous censorship restrictions and the comparatively conservative orientation of Jewish cultural producers who had not yet acclimated themselves to a consumer-driven market in literature, domestic literary production was not keeping pace with the demands of the expanding Yiddish-reading audience.

The failure of domestically produced Yiddish literature in the Russian Empire to satisfy the needs of common readers during the 1890s and early 1900s is ironic, considering that this period has traditionally been seen as a time of blossoming for Yiddish literature and culture in Eastern Europe. The publication of Sholem Aleichem's anthology *Di Yidishe folks-bibliothek* (Jewish People's Library, 1888–1889), for example, is generally hailed as a watershed in the history of Yiddish letters that paved the way for a number of other key works of both literature and literary criticism that helped legitimize Yiddish as a modern medium for artistic expression.[25] Yet as Sholem Aleichem's attack on Shomer demonstrated, the revolution he and his compatriots brought about was a highly conservative one, bent as much on suppressing the most popular forms of Yiddish literature as it was on broadening the reading audience for works they deemed to have greater merit. Before his departure for America in 1889, Shomer had outstripped every other Yiddish author in Russia more than five times over in the number of books he authored each year.[26] By contrast, the *Folks-bibliothek* and subsequent publications that are generally credited with laying the foundations of modern Yiddish literature—Mordechai Spektor's annual *Hoyzfraynd* (Home Companion, 1889–1890) and Peretz's *Yontev bletlekh,* among others—drew a relatively modest audience, embodying as they did a set of themes and a level of literary sophistication that were beyond the ken of most potential Yiddish readers. As official statistics on the publication of Yiddish books confirm, the inability of this group of more middle-brow authors to reach the large audience that Shomer had once served actually led the Yiddish book market in Russia to stagnate or even decline during the early to mid-1890s, rather than to grow in the way that the traditional narrative has suggested.[27]

This does not mean that the Russian Jewish scene of the 1890s and the first years of the twentieth century was bereft of authors who catered to popular tastes. After Shomer's departure for America, a handful of writers—most notably Ozer Bloyshteyn, Shimon Bekerman, Avrom Yitskhok Bukhbinder, and Yehoshue Budzohn—continued to write popular novels in Shomer's style.[28] But this group was never able to match the volume of popular literature that Shomer had previously produced, and they largely faded from the scene by the turn of the century, when only Bekerman was still active. Bukhbinder and Bloshteyn died in 1897 and 1898, respectively, and Budzohn had already retired from writing a few years earlier, in the mid-1890s. According to Zalman Reyzen, Budzohn had set aside his pen to enter business in Vilna partly owing to economic necessity but also because "of the attacks on the Shomer literature."[29] This detail, coupled with the fact that Bekerman continued throughout his career to sign his works "Sh. B." rather than revealing his full name, indicates that as late as the opening years of the twentieth century, popular writers of Yiddish were still unable to free themselves from the feeling that their legitimacy depended more on the opinions and approval of the intellectual elite than on the adoration of a mass readership.[30] As a result of these constraints, they were unable to adequately respond to the growing thirst for reading material that emerged as the horizons of Russian Jews were continually broadened by the social, demographic, and political upheavals of the period.

The obstacles that limited the blossoming of a homegrown popular Yiddish literature in Russia in the 1890s and early 1900s help explain why American Yiddish publications found such a ready audience in the empire during these years. The appeal of imported works, however, also had to do with their particular content and style. At first glance, the American imports consisted of literary genres that had long been available in Russia, including not only popular novels but also scientific and historical works, textbooks (lernbikhlekh), and collections of songs and poems. But advertisements in the Russian Hebrew newspapers (where Yiddish books were often advertised owing to the lack of a stable Yiddish press) make clear that the American imports were considered a market sensation that stood apart from domestically produced works in their ability to cater to the needs and interests of common readers.

Through their own experiences writing for a mass audience, American Yiddish authors had mastered the use of simple language and had perfected the art of popularization, making their works particularly well suited to those with limited reading experience. While domestically produced popular novels in Yiddish occasionally took their readers to far-off locations such as Africa, Turkey, and even America, overall these works focused on dramas of romance, matchmaking, and failed marriages, and they turned mainly to Jewish history, literature, and folklore for their source material.[31] By contrast, although they sometimes relied on traditional themes, American Yiddish writers regularly brought their readers modern stories of urban life, crime, and trials of the immigrant experience. They also focused their energies on popularizing for a mass reading audience the classic works of European literature, many of which had never before been placed within its reach. Just as they had done for immigrant readers in New York and Chicago, these American Yiddish publications spoke to the deepest desires of average, minimally educated Jews in the Russian Empire to connect with the wider world of possibilities beyond their familiar Jewish environment.[32] Finally, new books were published in America with greater frequency than they were in Russia, giving them a freshness that few domestically produced literary offerings could match.[33] Thus, in many ways during the last years of the nineteenth century and the opening years of the twentieth century, imported works from America satisfied the appetite of Russia's growing mass Yiddish readership more successfully than much of what was published domestically.

The forging of commercial ties that paved the way for selling American Yiddish publications abroad was initiated by the New York entrepreneur and bookseller Judah Meir Katzenelenbogen (see Figure 5.1), whose shop on Canal Street was a center of cultural activity on the Lower East Side. Katzenelenbogen was particularly well situated to launch such an enterprise because he had strong connections in the Eastern European Jewish book world. The Katzenelenbogens had been booksellers and publishers in the Lithuanian city of Vilna for decades, although they had never enjoyed the status of the Romms or the Matzes. By the 1890s, however, Judah Meir's brother Mordechai, who inherited the family's Vilna enterprise, was working hard to transform it into one of the city's most successful Jewish publishing houses and bookstores.[34] In pursuing this goal, he demonstrated a willingness to break from the convention of the larger firms that privileged works for the intellectual elite while treating popular works as a sideline. In forging a cooperative relationship by which Mordechai dispatched European books—mostly prayerbooks and religious texts—to his brother's New York store in exchange for the latest American novels and popular works, both Katzenelenbogens were able to advance their business interests in an unprecedented fashion.[35] They also helped catapult popular literature to a central position in the Russian Jewish book trade that it had previously not enjoyed.

The growing prominence of popular American works among the offerings of Mordechai Katzenelenbogen's bookstore was apparent by 1894, when he advertised for sale several Yiddish–English language methods written by the New York philologist and lexicographer Alexander Harkavy as well as American Yiddish novels such as *Velt banditen* (World Bandits) by Leon Zolotkoff and *Di yerushe*, a popularization of George Born's *The Inheritance*,

FIGURE 5.1. Judah Meir Katzenelenbogen, one of the leading Jewish booksellers and publishers on New York's Lower East Side, helped pioneer the importation of Yiddish books
to the Russian Empire beginning in the 1890s. Katzenelenbogen was one of the founding
partners of the Hebrew Publishing Company in 1901. Photo reproduced from *Minikes yontev bleter* (New York), October 1900.

by Moyshe Zeifert. The enthusiasm with which his customers received such
works is reflected in the dramatic growth of his American inventory in subsequent years. By 1899, the Vilna Katzenelenbogen was publishing large
advertisements in Eastern European Hebrew newspapers announcing what
he dubbed an *"Amerikaner birze"* (American stock exchange) of popular literature, through which he offered more than forty different American titles for
sale.[36] By the following year, his catalog had expanded to no fewer than sixty
American Yiddish works, most of which were sensational installment novels

sold in *heftn*.[37] In a profile of Judah Meir Katzenelenbogen published in a popular New York magazine he owned, the transatlantic enterprise he and his brother had created was billed as a major cultural accomplishment in the history of Yiddish literature. "These two brothers have abolished the spiritual border that has existed for so long between America and Russia," explained the article in *Minike's yontev bleter*. "When someone writes the history of Yiddish literature . . . in America, they will be unable to do so without giving a prominent place . . . to one who has used his capital and experience to develop the Jewish spirit and has produced such great results with his undertaking."[38]

In the wake of the Katzenelenbogen brothers' efforts, Russia became an increasingly important market for American Yiddish book publishers. After Judah Meir Katzenelenbogen joined with three other New York Yiddish and Hebrew publishers in 1901 to form the Hebrew Publishing Company, the new firm regularly supplied a number of European partners with its expanded catalog of titles.[39] Within a few years, the works of other firms joined those of the Hebrew Publishing Company on the shelves of Eastern European bookstores. The most significant of these was the radical-oriented publisher Alexander M. Evalenko, who began the International Library Publishing Company shortly after the turn of the century.[40]

All of this activity led to a significant presence of American books in the Eastern European book market from the mid- to late 1890s. Aside from Mordechai Katzenelenbogen, one of the earliest conduits for American books on the European side was the Warsaw bookdealer Yakov Lidsky. Born in 1868 in Slonim, Lidsky spent his youth in Moscow, where his father worked as a religious scribe and bookseller. After the expulsion of Jews from Moscow in 1891, Lidsky lived for a brief time in Minsk before emigrating to the United States, where he settled in Chicago and established a small Yiddish publishing house that specialized in popular literature and the publication of sheet music and penny songs for an immigrant audience.[41] In 1899, sensing that his American know-how could be applied to the much larger but largely untapped Eastern European market, he returned to Russia and opened the Progres (Progress) book concern in Warsaw.[42] We have no information on exactly who supplied Lidsky's inventory, but he clearly had a wide range of American contacts, billing himself as the "principal agent for all American and English publications."[43] For the first few years after his return to Europe, Lidsky concentrated exclusively on the sale of American books. In 1901, he even published a special catalog listing scores of American works available for sale (see Figure 5.2). His inventory represented the most complete offering of American Yiddish

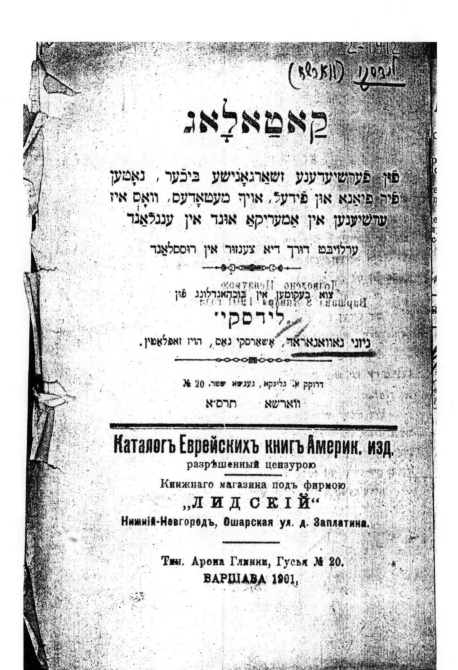

FIGURE 5.2. Having arrived in Warsaw from Chicago two years earlier, publisher and book-seller Yakov Lidsky issued this catalog of "various jargon books, notes for piano and fiddle, and [language] methods, which have recently appeared in America and England" in 1901. Almost all of the works listed inside were of American origin.

works in Eastern Europe, including not only novels but also popular scientific works, educational texts, theater pieces, and the sheet music in which he had specialized back in Chicago.[44]

Lidsky and Katzenelenbogen were the main booksellers specializing in the sale of American works, but they were clearly not the only ones selling Yiddish books from the United States. In 1898, the Warsaw book concern of L. Morgenshtern advertised the availability of several "new, highly interesting and scientific jargon books from America," including novels by the New York journalists Morris Hillquit and John Paley and a popularization of Jules Verne's *Twenty Thousand Leagues under the Sea* by Abner Tanenbaum.[45] The following year, entrepreneur Shlomo Zev Funk, the son of Vilna bookseller Yitskhok Funk, placed a large advertisement in *Ha-tsefira* headed "NEW FROM AMERICA" and listing thirty-one Yiddish installment novels offered for sale at his father's store (see Figure 5.3). In addition to the titles listed, the younger Funk assured his customers that "all old and new American stories not mentioned here are also available at the cheapest prices."[46] Because many potential readers of popular novels did not have the resources to buy complete sets of the installments, some of which numbered more than one hundred *heftn*, Funk's bookshop created a lending library from which "workers, servant girls, [and] house wives" could rent one *heft* per week for a modest fee and the advance of a small deposit.[47]

American Yiddish books were also sold by bookshops in more provincial locations outside the main cultural hubs of Warsaw and Vilna. In 1897, from the Polish textile-producing city of Łódź, L. Nüssel announced to "booksellers, librarians, and lovers of the jargon literature" that he had received from America "a transport of interesting books of the best Yiddish literature, written by the greatest and most excellent authors, such as Mr. A. Tanenbaum, and by the famous writer, Mr. N. M. Shaykevitsh."[48] American Yiddish books were sold even in the comparatively remote town of Rezhitsa in Vitebsk guberniya (now Rēzekne, Latvia), from where the bookseller Shereshevski advertised ten novels by Tanenbaum, including *Di Indianer first* (The Indian Chief) and *Goldgruben fun Kalifornien* (Gold Miners of California).[49]

While such advertisements for American Yiddish books were plentiful in the Eastern European Hebrew press of the period, it is nonetheless difficult to quantify exactly how many American imprints were reaching Russia during these years. One good source is the monthly journal published by the government's Committee on Foreign Censorship, which listed foreign books considered for approval by the censorship authorities for importation into the

נייעם פון אמעריקא.

דער פארלעגער שלמה זאב פונק אין ווילנא

האט יעטצט עבען ערהאלטען מיט דיא ערלויבניס פון צענזורע פאלג.ענדע
נייע האבסט אינטערעסאנטע אונד וויססענשאפטליכע ראמאנען, פערפאסט
פון דיא בעסטע מאלאנמפאללע שרייבער, וויא מאנענבוים, ראבינאוויץ,
שייקעוויץ, בן-פורת, אונד נאך אנדערע. הויפטלאגער אין בוכהאנדלונג
ביי ה' יצחק פונק ווילנא.

אומשולדיג געליטטען 55 בוינגען	דיא גיפט מישערין 59 ב'
דער וואמפיר, פארזעצונג פון אומשולדיג געליטטען 74 ב'	פראנציסקא, פארזעצונג פון גיפט מישערין 97 ב'
בלוטיגע גרעפין 92 ב'	איבער געלד אונד עהרע 60 ב'
ראקאמבאל אדער די געהיימניסספאלע ירושה 39 ב'	שווארצע הענר 27 ב'
טויז הערצין אדער דער געהיימער קלוב 25 ב'	נקמה פון א מאכטער 96 ב'
סער ווילליאם, פארזעצונג פון טויז הערצין 33 ב'	צווישען ליעבע אונד מיליאנען 26 ב'
די רויטע יארמילקעאדער דעם הענקערס זוהן 29 ב'	געוואלט אונד געפאנגען 40 ב'
געבילדעטער מערדער, פארזעצונג פון דיא רויטע יארמילקע 62 ב'	פערלארענע שיף 30 ב'
העלדין פון דער נאכט 30 ב'	אינדריאנער פירשט 25 ב'
ראוע פון שיקאגא 25 ב'	א רייזע ארום דער וועלט אין 80 טאג 19 ב'
דיא פערשווערונג אין אינגדיען אדער בלוטיגע געטטין קאליא 22 ב'	גאלד גרובען 40 ב'
קעטשין אונד קראנגען 31 ב'	שווארצע דיאמאנטען 10 ב'
א רייזע ארוים גרונד ים 26 ב'	פרויען הענדלער 95 ב'
איינגעמויערטע פרויא 17 ב'	גערויבטע קינד 156 ב'
	מאטרי פאריז 45 ב'
	שבט יהודה אין ריין זארגאן
	חומש רוסטי מאנרעלשטאס.

אויך אללע אלטע אונד נייע אמעריקאנער געשיבטען וועלכע שטעהען דא ניבט דערמאנט.
קאן מאן אויך ביי מיר בעקאממען צו דיא ביליגסטע פרייזען.
אויך בעקומט מען ביי מיר ביז 125 פערשיעדענע פראספעקטען בילדער.
אדרעססען:

Соломону Функу, Вильно, Стефановская д. Ш. Дразнина, или въ книж-
номъ магазинѣ Исаака Функа, Вильно.

FIGURE 3. Shlomo Zev Funk of Vilna was one of several Russian Jewish entrepreneurs who took up the lucrative trade in American Yiddish installment novels in the years around the turn of the twentieth century. He placed this advertisement in the Warsaw Hebrew newspaper *Ha-tsefira* on January 1, 1899.

empire. According to these lists, few American Yiddish books found their way to Russia before the mid-1890s, but in the ensuing years there was a sharp increase in the number of such titles coming before the censorship commit-tee. Between 1894 and 1899, the committee approved fifty American Yiddish works to be imported to the empire without any excisions and allowed seven additional titles with certain passages, deemed inappropriate by the censor, to be excised (such passages were covered over with a compound of black ink, glue, and bits of paper know euphemistically as "caviar").[50] In the same period, only fourteen American Yiddish titles were banned in their entirety from importation. During the early twentieth century the number of books imported varied according to economic and political conditions, but after the first Russian Revolution the climate for permitting American publications improved and, in 1907, a record seventy-five new titles were permitted. By the end of the imperial period, hundreds of American Yiddish titles had been legally imported into Russia.[51]

In addition to those books that were legally imported for sale, there is strong evidence that many of the Russian Jewish book concerns were selling American Yiddish works that had not received the required sanction of tsarist authorities. Despite the fact that Lidsky's catalog assured purchasers that all his American merchandise had been cleared by the censor in Russia, many of the titles he offered for sale do not appear on the lists of approved books maintained by the officials in Saint Petersburg. Interestingly, the catalog of American books indicates that they were for sale not from his Nalewki Street shop in Warsaw but from a shop in distant Nizhni Novgorod, outside the Pale of Settlement. Although Nizhni Novgorod was a center of the Russian book trade, and Lidski may have sold Yiddish books there during the famous annual trade fair, it seems more likely that the address was simply a ruse to throw off the police, allowing him to carry on an illegal trade in American books in Warsaw without being detected.[52] It is known that Lidsky was involved in smuggling socialist literature from the United States, a crime for which he spent time in a tsarist prison.[53] It stands to reason, therefore, that he brought in more mainstream, commercial literature illegally as well. In any event, it is probably safe to say that there was a much larger number of American Yiddish books available in Jewish bookstores in Imperial Russia than the records of official censorship approval indicate.

In addition to books imported legally and illegally, there were also a considerable number of American works that reached Russia in manuscript form and were published within the boundaries of the empire. Beginning in 1894, in partnership with the Romm Press and later branching out on his own, Mordechai Katzenelenbogen began to issue a series of new books by Shomer, the first of which was *Der Id un di grefin* (The Jew and the Countess), a "highly interesting and stirring novel of the Russian immigrants in America." Shomer, having fled the disapproval of his literary colleagues in Russia for the more hospitable cultural milieu of New York just a few years earlier, delighted in the warm reception his novels continued to enjoy among common readers in the Old Country. In fact, the novels Katzenelenbogen commissioned from Shomer were particularly appealing to Russian Jewish readers because they departed from traditional themes (including his own) and focused squarely on the struggles of Jewish immigrant life, about which Jews in Russia were intensely curious. Shomer's sense of vindication was apparent in the introduction to his second work for Katzenelenbogen, *Amerikaner gliken* (American Fortunes, 1895), in which he wryly chastised his European critics. "I thought that by leaving Russia I would have left you the field wide open to show off your talents," he wrote to the likes of Sholem Aleichem. "But . . . I now hear the complaints of the Russian booksellers: 'Woe! Send us new novels, [Shomer]. Our customers are tearing us apart, complaining that they have nothing to read, but we have nothing to give them.'"[54]

In soliciting manuscripts from American Yiddish authors, publishers such as Katzenelenbogen hoped to build on the success they had experienced with the sale of imported American works, but they also wished to cultivate and expand the audience for popular Yiddish literature in ways that imported works alone could not. Without a daily or stable weekly periodical press in Yiddish to break their teeth on, Jews in Russia were generally less accustomed to reading on a daily basis than were their counterparts in New York or Chicago. While they were drawn to the style and freshness of American publications, and while American Yiddish works were generally written in a simple, accessible Yiddish, Russian Jewish readers sometimes struggled with the fact that the imported works were published without vowel points, which many relied upon in making sense of a text.

Many Russian Jewish buyers—as mentioned earlier—also found the price of American *heftn* to be prohibitive. In America, customers usually bought the *heftn* individually for a small sum as they came off the press each week, and they were never aware of how many installments were to follow. In this way, publishers often made a handsome profit from the cumulative sale of the installments over the course of several months or even years, depending on how many *heftn* they issued. In Russia, although American *heftn* could be purchased either individually or in complete sets, they were generally imported only after the complete run was published, and advertisements made buyers aware of how many installments they would have to purchase in order to read the entire work. As a result, customers sometimes experienced sticker shock when they contemplated the purchase of a 270-installment work like Abner Tanenbaum's *Tsvishen menshen-freser* (Among Cannibals), which Katzenelenbogen originally advertised for 27.00 rubles, eventually lowering the price to 16.20. Even works with fewer *heftn*, like Harkavy's Yiddish version of *Don Quixote*, which was offered in 1900 in a complete set of thirty-seven

installments at the special sale price of 2.20, were still expensive for the average working-class Russian Jew.[55]

For these reasons, it made sense for Russian Jewish booksellers to aug-
ment the importation of American Yiddish works by publishing books written
by American authors but tailored to the specific needs of the Russian Yiddish-
reading audience. Published with vowel points, these editions were also kept
to a moderate length so that they could be divided into only four or five parts
and sold for a cost of no more than 1.50 for a complete set, bringing them more
easily into the reach of working-class customers.[56] While Mordechai Katzenelenbogen was a leader in this effort, competitors such as Yitzchok Funk also
published novels commissioned from the United States.[57] Lidsky, too, published
American manuscripts for his customers in Warsaw, but unlike his Vilna counterparts he focused more on textbooks than on novels. His first publication of
this sort was a popular science treatise on meteorites, shooting stars, and com-
ets titled *Shteyner vos falen fun himel* (Stones That Fall from Heaven), written by
the New York socialist journalist and editor Benjamin Feigenbaum in 1901.[58] All
told, no fewer than two dozen books by American Yiddish authors were published in Russia in the period between 1894 and 1907.[59]

Finally, also important to mention are the American Yiddish newspapers
that were imported legally into Russia in the late nineteenth and early twentieth centuries. It is unclear from the censorship records exactly who imported
these newspapers and for what purpose, but available evidence suggests that
they were sent over in single editions to individuals or libraries, rather than
to regular subscribers or for general sale by booksellers or newsagents. An
1892 advertisement for the New York *Yidishe gazetn* in the Jerusalem Hebrew
newspaper *Ha-tsevi*, listing subscription rates for various European countries, for example, explains that "an American newspaper cannot enter Russia."[60] Nonetheless, Jews in Russia who wished to occasionally obtain copies
of American Yiddish periodicals were apparently able to do so, a fact that is
especially significant given the strict limits officials placed on the publication
of domestic Yiddish periodicals before 1903. Already in the 1880s, copies of
the New York Orthodox Yiddish newspaper *Yidishes tageblat* were presented
to Russian censorship authorities for approval.[61]

Censors frequently banned certain issues of American Yiddish periodicals
or excised particularly offensive articles, but by the first decade of the twentieth
century, there were nonetheless a whole slew of these publications approved
for importation into Russia. Permitted titles ran the ideological gamut, including the Orthodox *Tageblat* and *Morgen dzhurnal* (Jewish Morning Journal); the

socialist *Forverts* (Jewish Daily Forward), *Folksadvokat* (People's Advocate), and *Der arbeter* (The Worker); the radical nationalist *Dos naye lebn* (The New Life), published by Khayim Zhitlovsky; and the vastly popular *Amerikaner* (American), whose appeal cut across political lines. Even more obscure newspapers like the Chicago *Yidishe arbeter velt* (Jewish Labor World) and the Pittsburgh *Folksfraynd* (People's Friend) passed successfully through the censor's office during these years.[62] By the First World War, then, there was an impressive array of Yiddish books and newspapers that had found their way to into the anxiously awaiting hands of Russian Jewish readers.

A Model for an Emerging Yiddish Mass Culture in Russia

While the numbers provided by the censorship records give us some indication of the importance of American publications in the Russian Yiddish book market at the turn of the century, it is hard to get a more precise measure of their overall impact given the lack of precise information on the total number of Yiddish books being published in Russia during these years. One reflection of the power they wielded is the condemnation they often received by some of the leading Yiddish authors and intelligentsia. In 1899, for example, writer and editor Gershom Bader, viewing Russian developments from just outside the Pale of Settlement in Galicia, decried the infusion of what he considered the worst sort of popular escapist fiction into the Eastern European market. He pointed to the way in which American publishers issued ridiculously long novels, sometimes sold in hundreds of installments, simply as a way to make more money. "No one among us can even get one of these books in hand," he wrote. "They are too long for one's memory and too expensive for one's wallet." Yet he had to admit that there were a significant number of buyers for these books, pointing to the fact that Katzenelenbogen, the Vilna bookseller, has "all the American *shmates* [rags] for sale."[63] Another self-appointed cultural guardian who lashed out against America was the "grandfather" of Yiddish literature, Sholem Yankev Abramovitsh (better known under the name of his literary persona, Mendele Moykher Sforim), who was outraged in 1909 when New York's Hebrew Publishing Company sold his collected works in Russia in unauthorized editions that were more complete and less expensive than anything he himself could afford to produce. In response, Abramovitsh led a campaign in the press that condemned American Yiddish publishing as a "plague from Canal Street" that threatened to destroy authentic Jewish culture and values.[64]

Abramovitsh's denunciation of American commercialism as a "plague," like Bader's characterization of American works as *shmates*, may have been an

honest assessment of the influence of American Yiddish culture on the Eastern European homeland, but it was also a defensive position concerning basic
changes occurring in the literary market in Eastern Europe. By the opening
years of the twentieth century, writers who had been used to thinking of
themselves as cultural guardians now had to face the reality that their authority would no longer go unchallenged as an emerging mass readership began
to participate more enthusiastically in the market for Yiddish books and to
demand works reflecting their own interests and tastes. While the expansion of this popular reading audience continued to be nurtured well past the
turn of the century by American imports and by the manuscripts American
authors sent to be published in Russia, these years also saw the blossoming of
a mass reading culture in Yiddish that relied much less on American sources
than it had in the 1890s.

Attempts by Russian Jewish entrepreneurs to develop their own versions
of popular American publications had begun almost since the first installment novels arrived from New York in the mid-1890s. During these initial
years, however, the social, political, and economic conditions were not yet
sufficiently favorable to support the launching of such homegrown efforts,
nor had Russian Jewish authors and cultural entrepreneurs had time to master the art of popularization and the business methods that were essential
for successfully reaching a popular audience. As a result, many of these early
efforts to create a domestic popular literature in Yiddish fell short of their
goals. In 1898, for example, just as the importation of American *heftn* was
at its height, the Warsaw entrepreneur Lazar Tsukerman, son of that city's
leading Jewish bookdealer, Abraham Tsukerman, announced the publication
of his own American-style installment novel, *Kapitan Dreyfus, der vershikter
afn Tayvils-inzel* (Captain Dreyfus, the Exile on Devil's Island), which was the
first Yiddish work of its kind published in Poland, if not in the entire Russian
Empire.[65] The novel's first installment began impressively with a press run
of 25,000 copies, although by the time the last of fifty-four installments was
issued, the press run had fallen to 8,000. While this was still an impressive
number, the decline illustrates that such a massive undertaking was more
difficult for a local businessman to sustain than Tsukerman had realized. As a
result, he never again attempted to publish an installment novel of this scale.
Although he did advertise a series of popular publications (novels and stories,
works of popular science and history, biographies, and translations) under
the name "Tsukerman's Folks-bibliothek" (Tsukerman's People's Library),
none of the titles he offered enjoyed anything close to the readership that

Kapitan Dreyfus had attained. His firm's Yiddish translation of Eugene Sue's French novel, *The Eternal Jew*, for example, was published in 1899 with a press run of only 1,000 copies.[66]

A similar process of trial and error was experience by the Jews in socialist circles who were attempting to develop domestically produced publications for Jewish workers that could replace the American pamphlets and journals like *Di tsukunft*, on which radicals had long relied to educate their adherents about science and political economy. In 1897, Warsaw publisher Avrom Hersh Kotik, working with the "Zhargonisher komitet" (Jargon Committee) of the Vilna Social Democrats, issued one of the first locally published collections of popular scientific booklets for Yiddish-speaking workers. Sold commercially as "Kotik's oysgaben" (Kotik's Editions), the series included translations of Russian and Polish works with titles such as *Vi hoben mentshen gelebt mit eynege toyzend yohr tsurik* (How Men Lived Several Thousand Years Ago) and *Vegn luft* (Concerning Air). But again, although the collection broke new ground in the effort to expand popular offerings in Yiddish, it failed to replicate the easy style and accessibility of similar American works. According to one report, "The language and the whole elaboration of the booklets were strongly unsuccessful."[67]

But if the development of indigenous Yiddish works for a mass audience proceeded in fits and starts during the 1890s, by the early years of the twentieth century the world of Yiddish print culture in Eastern Europe began to change dramatically. In 1903, permission was given for the first daily Yiddish newspaper in the Russian Empire—the Saint Petersburg *Fraynd*—to be issued, and in the years after a further relaxation of the press ban in 1905, other daily papers, mostly centered in Warsaw, began to appear. With the growth of Russia's first successful daily press in Yiddish, the stage had been set not only for an expanded readership but also for an increasing cadre of writers, editors, and publishers who learned how to effectively address the needs of a mass audience. In turn, a whole range of ancillary institutions—new publishing houses, libraries, and a range of popular weekly and monthly periodicals that were created to complement the daily press—emerged to create a rich, multifaceted reading culture that reflected for the first time the ability of the humblest readers to mobilize their power as consumers to direct the market for Yiddish print.[68]

Not that the intellectual elite yielded quietly to the growing supremacy of the mass audience. The staff of *Der fraynd*, for example, was drawn only reluctantly away from what historian Sarah Stein has described as its original "didactic, self-confident, and preachy" tone toward a popular style that readers found more pleasing.[69] As rival papers sprang up and competition emerged, however, the production of Yiddish print inevitably became more and more market driven and less easily controlled by the standards of the writers and editors. In 1909, *Der fraynd* moved from Saint Petersburg to Warsaw in order to identify itself more firmly with the new mass culture that emanated from the Polish city, but it ultimately folded, as a host of new rival publications proved more talented at serving the needs of the reading public. Although unsuccessful, the paper's move has been described by Stein as a landmark in the history of Yiddish culture, signifying the year by which "readers had become the engine of the Yiddish-reading public" in the empire.[70]

As this transformation toward the supremacy of the popular Yiddish-reading audience occurred in Russia, local cultural production grew to such an extent that the role played by works imported from America began to diminish, although they did remain an important factor in the reading culture of Russian Jews at least through World War I. A 1909 survey of the top-circulating books of the Jewish lending library in Bobruisk, for example, revealed that Abner Tanenbaum was still one of the most widely read Yiddish authors. Patrons checked out his books 1,552 times that year, more than twice as often as they requested books by any other Yiddish author with the exception of Sholem Aleichem, whose books circulated 2,220 times.[71] Ironically, the explosive growth of a mass audience for popular Yiddish literature during the early twentieth century had also brought a mass readership to Sholem Aleichem, who learned how to successfully navigate the market forces that he had earlier tried to suppress. Although he probably would not have acknowledged it, the rise of mass audience for low-brow popular fiction during the early twentieth century ultimately helped pave the way for a growing mass audience of middle-class readers who came to desire more middle-brow fare and could afford to devote greater resources to the purchase of books, helping him to become the best-selling Yiddish author of the period.[72] Statistics concerning print runs for 1909 ranked Sholem Aleichem as the leading author, with 66,500 copies of his books printed, but placed an American—Shomer—second, with a total print run of 28,000.[73] This second-place ranking is particular noteworthy when one considers that while Sholem Aleichem was still a productive author in 1909, Shomer had already been dead for four years.

While top-selling American authors like Tanenbaum and Shomer continued to loom large in the Russian Yiddish book market in the decade following the turn of the century, even more significant was the role American Yiddish print culture continued to play in providing models for the development of the indigenous institutions of Yiddish mass culture that were emerging in Russia during these years. In the publishing and bookselling world, the most palpable example of this was Lidsky's Warsaw publishing enterprise, which moved away from the sale and publication of American works as Lidsky was able to develop his own list of popular scientific titles as well as new fiction by authors such as Avrom Reyzen and Sholem Ash, which appealed to a broad audience. Lidsky also created a number of popular family magazines and almanacs very similar to the ones issued with great success by the Yiddish writer and editor Khonen Minikes in New York.[74] Initially, their pages were filled with articles and sketches by the same American authors who filled the pages of Minikes's publications: writers like Getsl Zelikovitsh, Morris Rosenfeld, Abner Tanenbaum, A. M. Sharkanski, and David Hermalin.[75] But here, too, Lidsky was eventually able to sever his reliance on American material and develop these publications into new platforms for an indigenous mass culture in Yiddish. Even in the choice of a business model, Lidsky took his lead from the American world of Yiddish publishing. In 1911, he formed with several partners what Zalmen Reyzen has called the first modern Yiddish publishing house in Eastern Europe—the Tsentral Farlag (Central Publishing House). Establishing this publishing house exactly ten years after the foundation of the Hebrew Publishing Company in New York, Lidsky in large part based the new company on the American firm by combining both the financial resources and the literary stock of a number of independent publishers to form one Yiddish publishing syndicate.[76]

The influence of American models on emerging Yiddish cultural institutions in Russia could also be seen in the world of journalism, which quickly surpassed book publishing as the most important dimension of Eastern European Yiddish culture during the first decade of the twentieth century. When Shaul Ginzberg, editor of the Saint Petersburg *Fraynd,* was launching his pioneer newspaper, for example, he logically looked to the writers of the American Yiddish press for help and advice. Not only did Ginzberg write to the famous Yiddish "sweatshop poet" Morris Rosenfeld and convince him to become a regular contributor, but he also sent inquiries to a whole host of other leading American writers, including Abraham Cahan, Philip Krantz, Leon Zolotkoff, Leon Kobrin, Morris Winchevsky, Benjamin Feigenbaum, and Getsl Zelikovitsh, hoping to get them involved.[77] Ginzberg even recruited the American Yiddish writer Khayim Aleksandrov (alias Khayim Miler) to be the editor of the newspaper's literary supplement, *Dos Lebn.*[78]

As happened in the book-publishing field, however, the local shapers of the Russian Yiddish press were quickly able to move away from reliance on American source material as they learned how to reach the mass audience on their own. The figure most responsible for building a readership for these newspapers was the editor Shmuel Yankev Yatskan, whose first journalistic undertaking, *Yidishes tageblat* (Jewish Daily News, 1906–1911), had the same name as New York's oldest Yiddish daily and was the first Eastern European newspaper in any language to sell for only one kopek, just as the New York *Tageblat* sold for one cent. While Yatskan seemed in many ways to be replicating the practices of the American Yiddish press, such innovations were now increasingly common in the broader Russian market for popular literature and were no longer simply the product of American Yiddish influence. By 1908, when he began to issue a second Warsaw daily, *Haynt* (Today), he proved himself a master of popularization in his own right. Yatskan built an entire industry of popular publications around *Haynt,* giving away popular booklets on science, history, and politics as premiums in order to attract subscribers. He also experimented with issuing sensational novels in installment booklets, but because he wanted to train his customers to read the daily press, he initiated the practice of publishing only the first several installments of a novel in *heftn.* In this way, after the readers were hooked, the *heftn* would stop and they would have to purchase the newspaper in order to continue to follow the story line. *Haynt* also published many novels and sketches by the rising class of "respectable" Yiddish authors, thereby contributing to the growth of multiple reading audiences.[79] Because of Yatskan's unprecedented willingness to prioritize the needs of the common reader, his paper succeeded in attracting an audience that dwarfed the readership of any previous Yiddish publication in Eastern Europe. As a result, *Haynt* became the longest running Yiddish daily in Warsaw, appearing continuously until 1939.

The Tables Turn

The phenomenal growth of mass cultural institutions after 1905 transformed the Yiddish literary scene in the Russian Empire in only a matter of years, ultimately altering the relationship between the American and Eastern European centers of Yiddish culture. A sign of the new power being exercised by Yiddish cultural entrepreneurs in Russia was the increasing ability to turn the tables and to market the products of the new commercial Yiddish publishing houses of the empire in the United States. As we have seen, previously Russian Yiddish authors like Abramovitsh had been frustrated at their inability to market their own works in Russia, while American firms regularly issued unauthorized editions and sold them successfully on both sides of the ocean. But with the growth of commercial Yiddish publishing houses in Russia, the entrepreneurs at the helm of these firms found ways of effectively combating American competition. Lidsky, while still head of the Progres publishing house in 1909, published several books simultaneously in Warsaw and New York for which he was able to acquire American copyright protection, perhaps because he had acquired US citizenship during his years in Chicago.[80] This move for the first time protected European authors and prevented American firms like the Hebrew Publishing Company from issuing their works without permission. After Lidsky joined with several other partners to form the Tsentral Farlag in 1911, the new company institutionalized this practice, going so far as to establish a branch in New York in order to copyright European works there and prevent American infringement on its expanding and increasingly lucrative market.[81] The following year, Tsentral took the additional step of formalizing a relationship with the New York bookseller Simon Druckerman (son of longtime Hebrew and Yiddish publisher and bookseller Jacob Druckerman), whom it named its exclusive agent in the United States.[82]

The traumas experienced in Russia and Poland during World War I temporarily stalled many Yiddish cultural endeavors there, while American Yiddish publishing efforts continued to operate robustly.[83] Following the war, however, the Eastern European center increasingly outpaced its American counterpart. First, the collapse of the Russian Empire in 1917 and the rise of several successor states that recognized Jews as a national minority group and gave to Yiddish an officially recognized and, in some cases, government-supported status, was a decided boon to the further growth of Yiddish cultural institutions. Meanwhile, the nativism that seized American political culture in the postwar years placed Yiddish-speaking Jews in the United States on the defensive. With the cutting off of immigration by the US Congress in 1924 and the continual acculturation of Jewish immigrants and their children to an English-speaking milieu, the audience for Yiddish publications began to recede dramatically. The first casualty was the once thriving Yiddish book market, which shrank to such an extent by 1930 that leading American Yiddish authors were forced to turn to firms in Vilna and Warsaw to publish their works. The publication of American Yiddish newspapers remained more robust during the interwar period than did the languishing Yiddish book industry. Because many American Jews continued to read the Yiddish papers as a supplement to their growing English repertoire and because of the sheer concentration of Jews in New York—in 1927 almost 30 percent of the city's nearly six million residents were Jewish—the city's Yiddish press enjoyed a larger annual circulation than its counterpart in Warsaw at least into the 1930s.[84] Overall, however, beginning in 1929 the circulation figures for New York's Yiddish papers began to fall, first by a few thousand each year and after 1931 by the tens of thousands.[85]

As the American audience for Yiddish continued to decline in the interwar period, the cultural institutions that had once been driven by the tastes and interests of a mass reading public gradually came under the influence of a small group of writers and intellectuals whose ideological commitment to Yiddish-ism significantly shaped the narrative of Yiddish literary and cultural history that they promoted in the surviving publications and in their scholarly works. Because their cultural nationalist worldview privileged works of high culture, they tended to downplay the influence of the most popular forms of literature that had once flourished among Yiddish-speaking Jews in America. While some of them did study and write about the origins of Yiddish literature and journal-ism in the United States, their hierarchical understanding of culture prevented them from recognizing the formative influence American Yiddish publications had exercised on the emergence and growth of a Yiddish mass culture in East-ern Europe. The bolstering of this group with a fresh wave of European Yid-dishist intellectuals who arrived in America as a result of the dislocations of the Second World War further cemented this narrative, which eventually helped shape many of the assumptions of modern scholarship on Yiddish culture.[86]

In underscoring the ideological nature of our received notions of Yid-dish culture, my purpose here is to suggest that we reassess the value of that huge body of work—the popular novels, translations, textbooks, and news-papers—that helped transform the lives and consciousness of Jewish immi-grants to America and gave common Jewish readers in Russia their first taste of the possibilities that awaited them as a mass market for Yiddish print cul-ture began to emerge at the end of the nineteenth and beginning of the twen-tieth century. Although these early American Yiddish publications may fall short of the aesthetic and literary standards of modern criticism, they ought to be recognized for the transformative impact they had on the lives of the average Jews who read them. Even more crucially, they deserve greater study as a primary example of the ways in which Jewish culture on both sides of the Atlantic was revolutionized by the democratic, free market cultural forms that may have first taken root in New York and Chicago but were ultimately no less consequential in Warsaw and Vilna.

Notes

1. The main exceptions to this trend are Tony Michels, "Exporting Yiddish Socialism: New York's Role in the Russian Jewish Workers' Movement," *Jewish Social Studies* 16, no. 1 (2009): 1–26 and Nina Warnke, "Going East: The Impact of American Yiddish Plays and Players on the Yiddish Stage in Czarist Russia, 1890–1914," *American Jewish History* 92, no. 1 (2004): 1–29. The Israeli scholar Hagit Cohen has also studied the interrelationship of American and Eastern European Yiddish cultural centers, focusing as I do on the book trade, but her conclusions do not significantly challenge the notion that Europe remained the "real" center of Yiddish culture during this period, a contention I critique below. See Cohen, "The USA-Eastern European Yiddish Book Trade and the Formation of an American Yiddish Cultural Center, 1890s–1930s," *Jews in Russia and Eastern Europe* 57, no. 2 (2006): 52–84 and the expanded Hebrew version, "Sakhar ha-sfarim ha-trans-Atlanti, u-tsmikhato she merkaz tarbut ha-Yidish be-Artsot ha-brit, 1890–1939," *Iyunim bitkumat Israel* 20 (2010): 437–66.

2. Chone Shmeruk, "Aspects of the History of Warsaw as a Yiddish Literary Centre," *Polin: A Journal of Polish-Jewish Studies* 3 (1988): 151.

3. Samuel Niger, "Yiddish Literature in the Past Two Hundred Years," in *Jewish People Past and Present* (New York: Jewish Encyclopedic Handbooks, 1952), 3: 199.

4. On the rise of the popular Yiddish press in Russia and the role of *Der fraynd* in particular, see Sarah Abrevaya Stein, *Making Jews Modern: The Yiddish and Ladino Press in the Russian and the Ottoman Empires* (Bloomington: Indiana University Press, 2006). On the censorship of Yiddish periodicals and books, see David Fishman, "The Politics of Yiddish," in *The Rise of Modern Yiddish Culture*, by Fishman (Pittsburgh: University of Pittsburgh Press, 2005), 18–32.

5. For a transnational study of print culture in the Anglo-American context, see Ann L. Ardis and Patrick Collier, eds., *Transatlantic Print Culture, 1880–1940: Emerging Media, Emerging Modernisms* (London: Palgrave Macmillan, 2008).

6. For an overview of the case and the publicity it generated, see Eddy Portnoy, "Who Is the Hebrew Girl Murderer of East New York?" *Guilt and Pleasure* 7 (spring 2008): 80–91.

7. The sole surviving copy of the *Yidishe tsaytung*, featuring coverage of the Rubenstein trial, is held by the archives of the Jewish Theological Seminary in New York. On the third newspaper, of which no copy remains and whose name we do not even know, see Alexander Harkavy, "Amol un haynt," *Der teater zhurnal un familien fraynd*, January 1, 1903, 6. Harkavy's reference to a newspaper started at the time of the Rubenstein trial cannot be a reference to the *Yidishe tsaytung*, because he specifically points out that the paper was printed, whereas the *Yidishe tsaytung* was lithographed.

8. See Samuel Stern, *Thrilling Mysteries of the Rubenstein Murder Never before Brought to Light* (New York: S. Stern and Cohn, 1876).

9. On this point, see Shaul Stampfer, "Literacy among Jews in Eastern Europe in the Modern Period," in *Families, Rabbis, and Education: Traditional Jewish Society in Nineteenth-Century Eastern Europe*, by Stampfer (Oxford: Littman Library of Jewish Civilization, 2010), 194.

10. Fishman, "Politics of Yiddish," 21–24.

11. See Alyssa Quint, "Yiddish Literature for the Masses? A Reconstruction of Who Read What in Jewish Eastern Europe," *AJS Review* 29, no. 1 (2005): 61–89.

12. David G. Roskies, "Ayzik-Meyer Dik and the Rise of Yiddish Popular Literature" (PhD diss., Brandeis University, 1974); Rose Shomer-Batshelis, *Unzer Foter Shomer* (New York: IKUF, 1950). On the emergence of popular literature among non-Jewish Russians, see Jeffrey Brooks, *When Russia Learned to Read: Literacy and Popular Literature, 1861–1917* (Princeton: Princeton University Press, 1985).

13. See Iris Parush, *Reading Jewish Women: Marginality and Modernization in Nineteenth-Century Eastern European Jewish Society* (Hanover, NH: University Press of New England/Brandies University Press, 2004), 145 and Ayzik Meyer Dik, "Opmakh mit Roms druker," *Fun noentn over* 1 (1937): 172–74. On this history of the Romm Press, see Shmuel Shraga Feigensohn, "Le-toldot defus Rom," in *Yahadut Lita*, ed. Natan Goren et al. (Tel Aviv: Am ha-sefer, 1959), 1: 268–302; Pinkhas Kon, "Al devar ha-defus shel Rom be-Vilna," *Kiryat sefer* 10 (1933–1934): 249–50; Kon, "Le-korot bet ha-defus shel Rom be-Vilna," *Kiryat sefer* 12 (1935–1936): 109–15; Khayim Liberman, "Al defus ha-almanah veha-ahim Rom," *Kiryat sefer* 34 (1959): 527–28. On the Matz Press, see David G. Roskies, *Yiddishlands: A Memoir* (Detroit: Wayne State University Press, 2008), 26–33.

14. See Justin Cammy, "Judging *The Judgment of Shomer*: Jewish Literature versus Jewish Reading," in *Arguing the Modern Jewish Canon: Essays on Jewish Literature and Culture in Honor of Ruth R. Wisse*, ed. Justin Cammy, Dara Horn, Alyssa Quint, and Rachel Rubinstein (Cambridge, MA: Center for Jewish Studies, Harvard University, 2008), 85–127 and Cammy's translation of Sholem Aleichem's original *Shomer's mishpet* (1888) in Cammy et al., *Modern Jewish Canon*, 129–85. For a more recent assessment of Shomer that views his work through the eyes of his readers, see Sophie Grace-Pollak, "Hashpa'ato shel Shomer al korei Yidish," *Khulyot* 10 (winter 2007): 69–79. The question of whether the books of Dik and Shomer were read primarily by women is a matter of debate, a full discussion of which is beyond the scope of this article. My own view is that men read popular novels in Yiddish as enthusiastically as women did, but because this practice challenged well-engrained gender expectations, the authors, consumers, and critics of these works all perpetuated the myth that Shomer and Dik were read primarily by women. For various opinions on this question, see Parush, *Reading Jewish Women*, 145–46, 150, 243–44; Quint, "Yiddish Literature," 84n68; Naomi Seidman, *A Marriage Made in Heaven: The Sexual Politics of Hebrew and Yiddish* (Berkeley: University of California Press, 1997), ch. 1.

15. N. B. Minkov, "Perets in Amerike," in *Literarishe vegn*, by Minkov (Mexico City: Tsvi Kesel, 1955), 6: 44–45; Nakhman Mayzel, ed., *Briv un redes fun Y. L. Perets* (New York: YKUF, 1944), 213–16.

16. *Nayer Gayst* 1 (June 1898): 493; (July 1898): 553. See also the announcement regarding Peretz's upcoming contributions at the end of the May 1898 issue (unpaginated).

17. Zalmen Reyzen, *Leksikon fun der yidisher literatur, prese un filologye* (Vilna: B. Kletskin, 1926–1929), 4: 628; Leon Kobrin, *Mayne fuftsik yor in Amerike* (Buenos Aires: Farlag Yidbukh, 1955), 1: 398; Maxwell Whiteman, "The Fiddlers Rejected: Jewish Immigrant Expression in Philadelphia," in *Jewish Life in Philadelphia, 1830–1945*, ed. Murray Friedman (Philadelphia: Ishi, 1983), 84.

18. For a survey of this literature, see Alyssa Quint and Eric Goldstein, "Pop 'Em in Yiddish: The Subterranean World of Yiddish Pulp Fiction," *Guilt and Pleasure* 7 (spring 2008): 110–13; Y. Khaykin, *Yidishe bleter in Amerike* (New York: self-published, 1941), 75–84;

and Eliyohu Shulman, *Geshikhte fun der Yidisher literatur in Amerike, 1870–1900* (New York: Farlag A. V. Biderman, 1943), ch. 4.

19. Abraham Cahan, "The Russian Jew in America," *Atlantic Monthly,* July 1898, 132. Hagit Cohen's contention that the majority of Yiddish books for sale in the United States during this period were European imports is a serious misreading of the sources. She bases this conclusion on the large number of European titles listed in American Jewish booksellers' catalogs but misses the fact that such catalogs provide no indication of what was actually being sold. Most of the European works listed in these catalogs were decades old; the fact that they were even still available for sale so long after their publication indicates that they were poor sellers, and as such, they likely continued to sit on the shelves unsold for many more years to come. Booksellers and publishers actively advertised in the Yiddish press, and presumably they advertised the works that they expected to sell most successfully. Therefore, advertisements are a much better indicator than catalogs of which books dominated the market, and a survey of these advertisements prove without a doubt that American publications dominated the Yiddish book market in the United States from at least the mid-1890s. See, e.g., the advertisements in *Yidishe gazetn,* June 5, 1896, 18; September 25, 1896, 3; November 27, 1896, 10; July 2, 1897, 19; February 3, 1899, 4; *Arbeter tsaytung,* November 1, 1895, 7; July 12, 1895, 7; April 10, 1896, 18; October 4, 1896, 6; April 25, 1897, 7.

20. This phenomenon was not totally unprecedented among other European groups, especially other minorities from the Russian Empire, for whom the emergence of vernacular popular culture had also been stunted by a ban on press and theater in their native languages. According to Darius Staliūnas, American Lithuanian periodicals were smuggled into Russian-occupied Lithuania during the years of the press ban and doubtlessly had an influence there. See Staliūnas, *Making Russians: Meaning and Practice of Russification in Lithuania and Belarus after 1863* (Amsterdam: Rodopi, 2007), 269.

21. See Eliyohu Tsherikover, "Fun di politsey-arkhiv in tsarishn Rusland: Di Rusishe tsenzur un di sotsyalistishe *Nyu-yorker yidishe folkstsaytung*," in *Di yidishe sotsyalistishe bavegung biz der grindung fun "Bund,"* ed. Eliyohu Tsherikover, Avrom Menes, Frants Kurski, and Avrom Rozin (Vilna: YIVO, 1939), 801–3.

22. Ezra Mendelsohn, *Class Struggle within the Pale: The Formative Years of the Jewish Workers' Movement in Tsarist Russia* (Cambridge: Cambridge University Press, 1970), 121; Sholem Levin, *Untererdishe kemfer* (New York: Sholem Levin bukh komitet, 1946), 107; L. Berman, *In loif fun yorn* (New York: Farlag "Unzer tsayt," 1945), 147.

23. Shakhna Epshtein, "Di tsukunft, der Bund, un di Idishe literatur," *Di tsukunft* 17 (January 1912): 66–72; Frants Kurski, *Gezamelte shriftn* (New York: Ferlag Der Veker, 1952), 250–59. The most comprehensive study of the importation of American Yiddish socialist literature into Russia is Michels, "Exporting Yiddish Socialism."

24. Most of the American Yiddish publishing firms were located in New York, although Yakov (Jacob) Lidsky, sometimes in partnership with Hyman L. Meites, did publish some Yiddish installment novels in Chicago in the 1890s, and at least one Yiddish novel was published in Cleveland, Ohio, during the same period. See Robert Singerman, comp., *Judaica Americana: A Bibliography of Publications to 1900* (New York: Greenwood, 1990), vol. 2, entries 4018, 4032, 4034, 4637, 4898, 5013, 5039, 5101, 5103, 5151, and 5448.

25. The classic account of the emergence of a modern Yiddish literary tradition is Dan Miron, *A Traveler Disguised: The Rise of Modern Yiddish Fiction in the Nineteenth Century* (New York: Schocken, 1973).

26. For a bibliography of Yiddish books published in Russia during the late 1880s, see Sholem Aleichem, *Di yudishe folks-bibliothek: A bukh fir literatur, kritik un vissenshaft* 1 (1888): 469–73; 2 (1889): 135–39.

27. This suggestion is based in part on a preliminary survey of the available volumes of *Spisok izdanii, vyshedshikh v Rossii* from this period. Also called *Spisok knig*, this source lists all books legally published in the empire in a given year and typically records the titles of "Jewish" books (regardless of language) in a separate section. A more formal survey of these lists needs to be undertaken in order to make more definitive conclusions and is planned as part of the larger work of which this chapter forms a part.

28. This group has been called variously the "imitators" or "disciples" of Shomer. See Leo Wiener, *The History of Yiddish Literature in the Nineteenth Century* (London: John C. Nimmo, 1899), 174; and Miron, *A Traveler Disguised*, 253.

29. See Reyzen, *Leksikon*, 1: 230–32 (Budzohn); 236–37 (Bukhbinder); 294–99 (Bloshteyn); and 342–44 (Bekerman).

30. Ibid.

31. Ibid.

32. See, e.g., the books advertised in *Ha-melits* (Saint Petersburg), February 2, 1896, 8.

33. On this point, see Yakov Lidsky's *Katalog fun fershiedene zshargonishe bikher, noten fir piano un fidel, oykh metodes, vos iz ershinen in Amerika und in England* (Warsaw: A. Glinko Printing, 1901), 4, which states that new books in America are published very frequently, and *Ha-melits*, May 1, 1896, 8.

34. On the Katzenelenbogen family's background and business activities in Vilna, see Khaykel Lunski, "Vilner bibliofiln, moykhrey-sforim un pakntreger," *Fun noentn over* 1 (1937): 295; Neil Rosenstein, *The Unbroken Chain* (New York: Shengold, 1976), 634–37.

35. In the opening years of the twentieth century, the Katzenelenbogen family's transnational cooperation in the Hebrew and Yiddish book trade expanded to South Africa, where two relatives of the Katzenelenbogen family ran Jewish bookstores: Jacob Kawarsky in Johannesburg and Moses Beinkinstadt in Cape Town. See Rosenstein, *The Unbroken Chain*, 634. On Beinkinstadt, who was particularly well known, see also Raie Rodwell, "The Jewish Bookshop in District Six," *Jewish Affairs* 28, no. 2 (1973): 33–35; Jonathan Boiskin, "Beinkinstadt's, 1903–1993," *Jewish Affairs* 48, no. 3 (1993): 39–42 and Veronica Belling, "The End of an Era: Beinkinstadt, Cape Town's Oldest Jewish Bookstore, Closes Down," *Jewish Affairs* 65, no. 2 (2010): 4–7.

36. *Ha-melits*, January 8, 1899, 6; *Ha-tsefirah* (Warsaw), January 9, 1899, 4.

37. *Ha-tsefira*, May 13, 1900, 4.

38. "Yehudah Meyer Katsenelenbogen," *Minikes yontev bleter*, October 1900, 2. The earliest issues of *Minikes yontev bleter*, many of which are not microfilmed, were accessed at the YIVO Institute for Jewish Research, Center for Jewish History, New York.

39. On the Hebrew Publishing Company, see Charles A. Madison, *Jewish Publishing in America: The Impact of Jewish Writing on American Culture* (New York: Sanhedrin, 1976), 77–79 and Israel Shenker, *Coat of Many Colors: Pages from Jewish Life* (New York: Doubleday, 1985), 245–48.

40. On Evalenko, see Robert A. Karlowich, *We Fall and Rise: Russian-Language Newspapers in New York City, 1889–1914* (Metuchen, NJ: Scarecrow, 1991), 51, 56, 179–85.

41. Reyzen, *Leksikon*, 2: 128–29; Bernard Yakubovits, "Asot ve-hefets sefarim harbeh: le-toldoteiha shel hotsa'at ha-sefarim 'Tsentral'—'Merkaz' be-Varshah (1911–1933)" (PhD diss., Tel Aviv University, 1997), 46–47. For a comprehensive listing of Lidsky's Chicago publications, see the index to Singerman, *Judaica Americana*, 2: 1169. In Chicago, Lidsky rendered his name variously as "Lidskin" or "Litzkin."

42. See Bal-Makhshoves (Isidor Eliashev), "Der nayer bikherferlag 'Progres,'" *Der Yud* (Crakow), July 11, 1901, 14–15.

43. See Lidsky's advertisement in the back matter of *Der nayer seder: a literarishe yontev blat* (Warsaw: J. Lidski, 1907). On Lidsky's background and career, see Reyzen, *Leksikon*, 2: 128–29; Avrom Reyzen, *Epizodn fun mayn lebn* (Vilna: B. Kletskin, 1929–1935), 2: 5–8, 12, 112–15; and the obituary in *Der moment* (Warsaw), June 3, 1921, 10.

44. *Katalog fun fershiedene zshargonishe bikher.*

45. *Ha-tsefirah*, July 11, 1898, 4.

46. Ibid., January 1, 1899, 5.

47. See A. Litvak, *Vos geven: etyudn un zikhroynes* (Vilna: B. Kletskin, 1925), 71.

48. *Ha-melits*, June 27, 1897, 8. See also Nüssel's advertisements in *Ha-melits* on August 13, 1897, 4; and in *Ha-tsefirah*, September 3, 1897, 7.

49. *Ha-melits*, January 25, 1897, 7.

50. For the practice of pasting over passages of foreign books with "caviar," see Mariana Tax Choldin, *A Fence around the Empire: Russian Censorship of Western Ideas under the Tsars* (Durham, NC: Duke University Press, 1995), 139–43.

51. *Alfavitnyi spisok sochineniiam, razsmotriennym inostrannoiu tsenzuroiu* (1894–1913). The original files of the Foreign Censorship Committee are located in *fond* (document collection) 779, Russian State Historical Archives (RGIA), Saint Petersburg. On the censorship of Jewish publications in Tsarist Russia, including those imported from abroad, see D. A. Elyashevich, *Pravitel'stvennaya politika i evreiskaya pechat v Rossii, 1797–1917* (Saint Petersburg, Russia: Mosti kulturi, 1999). For a general overview of the censorship of Western books by Russian authorities during the same period, see Choldin, *Fence around the Empire.*

52. See *Katalog fun fershiedene zshargonishe bikher*. On Nizhni Novgorod as a center of the Russian book trade, see Brooks, *When Russia Learned to Read*, 104–5.

53. On Lidsky's smuggling activity, see Reyzen, *Epizodn*, 2: 12 and *Der moment*, June 3, 1921, 10.

54. Introduction to Nokhem Meyer Shaykevitsh (Shomer), *Amerikanishe glikn* (Vilna: M. Katzenelenbogen, [1895] 1912), unpaginated. For the translation, I have relied on the quotation in Cammy, "Judging the *Judgment of Shomer*," 104.

55. For prices, see Katzenelenbogen's advertisements in *Ha-tsefira*, January 9, 1899, 4 and May 13, 1900, 4.

56. Ibid.

57. See, e.g., A[bner]. T[anenbaum]., *Di Amerikaner sheydim* (Vilna: Y. Funk, 1895). This book was also published the same year in Warsaw by Shuldberg Brothers.

58. Benjamin Feigenbaum, *Shteyner vos falen fun himel: a populere erklehrung vegen meteoriten, shternshnupfen un kometen* (Warsaw: Progres, 1901).

59. Works of this kind not mentioned earlier include Nokhem Meyer Shaykevitsh (Shomer), *Verkerte velt* (Vilna: M. Katzenelenbogen, 1897); *Di naye velt, oder der Idisher leben in Amerika* (Vilna: M. Katzenelenbogen, 1897); *Der Prezident* (Vilna: M. Katzenelenbogen, 1898); *Der zshentelman* (Vilna: M. Katzenelenbogen, 1899); *A punk Idishkeyt, oder der blut bilbul* (Vilna: M. Katzenelenbogen, 1899); Abner Tanenbaum, *Izabella, oder di geheymnisse fun Ishpanishen hoyf* (Vilna: M. Katzenelenbogen, 1895); *Ishpanishe kenigen* (Vilna: M. Katzenelenbogen, 1895); *Leyele, oder der letster zipts fun di iden in Shpanien* (Vilna: M. Katzenelenbogen, 1897); *Letster Yudisher korbn* (Vilna: M. Katzenelenbogen, 1898); *Der getoyfter id* (Vilna: M. Katzenelenbogen, 1902); *Sorele Arenshteyn* (Vilna: M. Katzenelenbogen, 1902); Sholem Lederer, *Der shrekhlikher ferbrekher* (Vilna: M. Katzenelenbogen, 1897); *Di tsigeyener* (Vilna: M. Katzenelenbogen, 1897); *Di gevezener tsigeyener* (Vilna: M. Katzenelenbogen, 1900); *Di Yudisher tsigeyenerin* (Vilna: M. Katzenelenbogen, 1900). The pioneering New York Yiddish socialist publicist Philip Krantz (né Jacob Rombro), who brought his American journalistic know-how to Vilna in 1906 to help establish a Yiddish worker's journal, *Di proletarishe velt*, also authored a number of Yiddish books published in Russia, including both socialist tracts and popular novels. See, e.g., *Di ayzerne maske, oder, di unglikhlikhe prints* (Vilna: n.p., 1894); *A shtrik arum haldz* (Vilna: M. Katzenelenbogen, 1901); *Di tsushterung fun Bastilye* (Warsaw: Kleyne folks bibliotek, 1906); *Klore diburim: tsu iden bikhlal un arbayter bifrat* (Vilna: Di proletarishe velt, 1907). On Krantz's time in Vilna, see Moshe Shtarkman, "Filip Krants un di 'Proletarishe velt,'" in *Zamlbukh lekoved dem tsvey hundert un fuftsikstn yoyvl fun der Yidisher prese, 1686–1936*, ed. Yakov Shatsky (New York: Amopteyl fun YIVO, 1937), 327–34. Other labor-oriented publications of this period by American Yiddish authors include Morris Rosenfeld, *Geklibene lieder* (Warsaw: Kleyne folks bibliotek, 1904) and Morris Winchevsky, David Edelshtat et al., *Di fraye harfe: a zamelbukh fun lieder* (Vilna: Di velt, 1907).

60. *Ha-tsevi*, July 8, 1892, 4.

61. See Elyashevich, *Pravitel'stvennaya*, 392.

62. Approvals for the importation of newspapers were not listed in the published *Alfavitny spisok* and must be gleaned from examining the original manuscript files of the Foreign Censorship Committee. See e.g., RGIA (fond 779, opus 4, file 305), 393, 438, 479, 680, 712, 755, 778; (file 306), 553, 731; (file 314), 622, 696; (file 316), 25, 118, 153, 241; (file 324), 235, 277, 354, 386. Tsarist authorities banned many articles in popular newspapers like *Forverts*, *Amerikaner*, and *Morgen dzhurnal* that were critical of the tsar, Christianity, and prevailing moral codes, but at the same time they permitted importation of an openly revolutionary publication like Zhitlovsky's *Dos naye lebn*. This pattern conforms to the trend observed by historian Marianna Tax Choldin, who describes how ineffective the censors were in deciding which literature ought to be excluded. "Single lines in obscure poems" were often banned by the Tsarist authorities, she writes, but Marx was "considered too abstract to be of danger." As a result, "the fence around the empire proved incapable of keeping out the really dangerous ideas." See Choldin, *Fence around the Empire*, 33.

63. Gershom Bader, "In unzer literatur," *Yidisher folkskalendar* 5 (1899–1900): 104–5.

64. See my unpublished paper, "Mendele Moykher Sforim's Dispute with America: Yiddish Cultural Politics in Transatlantic Perspective," Dina Abramowicz Memorial Lecture, YIVO Institute for Jewish Research, March 2004.

65. The novel, based on a German original, was popularized in Yiddish by Mayer Yakov Frid, but his name did not appear on the cover. For details of the publication, see Reyzen, *Leksikon*, 3: 194. See also the advertisements for *Kapitan Dreyfus* in *Ha-tsefira*, April 22, 1898, 5; April 24, 1898, 4; May 5, 1898, 4; September 8, 1898, 4; April 12, 1899, 7; and *Ha-melits*, June 24, 1898, 8.

66. *Spisok izdanii, vyshedshikh v Rossii* (1898): 408. The book was apparently cleared by the censor in December 1898 and published in 1899.

67. See the advertisement for *Kotik's oysgaben* in *Ha-tsefira*, December 31, 1897, 8; and Michels, "Exporting Yiddish Socialism," 6. The critique of the pamphlets is found in Reyzen, *Leksikon*, 3: 420.

68. For a survey of Russian Jewish reading culture during this period, see Jeffrey Veidlinger, *Jewish Public Culture in the Late Russian Empire* (Bloomington: Indiana University Press, 2009), chap. 3.

69. Stein, *Making Jews Modern*, 50.

70. Ibid., 51.

71. These statistics, originally compiled by librarian Avraham Kirzhnits, are cited in Veidlinger, *Jewish Public Culture*, 101.

72. More research needs to be done on the ways Sholem Aleichem reacted to the rise of a mass reading audience during the early twentieth century as well as on the class and educational background of the mass readership he garnered. On his ambivalent artistic identity and his desire to bridge the categories of popular and elite during the earlier phases of his career, see Cammy, "Judging the *Judgment of Shomer*."

73. Statistics are from *Knizhnaia letopis'* (1909), a government register of publication information that replaced *Spisok izdanii, vyshedshikh v Rossii* in 1907, cited in Veidlinger, *Jewish Public Culture*, 99.

74. Minikes was the editor of *Minikes yontev bleter*. On his career and an example of his literary production, see Mark Slobin, "From Vilna to Vaudeville: Minikes and Among the Indians (1895)," *Drama Review* 24, no. 4 (1980): 17–26.

75. See, e.g., *Der Esrog* (1905), in which more than 50 percent of the articles were by American writers like Zelikovitsh, Tanenbaum, Rosenfeld, Peter Wiernik, and Sharkanski. Similarly, about half the articles in *Der Shoyfer* (1905) were also by American authors, including Hermalin, Rosenfeld, Moshe Zeyfert, Yitskhok Reingold, Morris Winchevsky, and Tashrak (Israel Zevin). This practice was embraced by editors of many Eastern European publications. See, e.g., *May-blumen, a yontev-blat*, published in Vilna during the same period, which featured poetry by Rosenfeld and Sharkanski. Rosenfeld's work was often pirated by eastern European editors, like those of the Vilna newspaper *Di hofnung*, who culled some of his poems from the pages of the *Forverts* and reprinted them (see the issues of September 18/29, 1907, 2; October 4/November 17, 1907, 2). In 1911, Rosenfeld finally protested against such practices, arguing that Eastern Europe had "pirates who excel even more [at their crimes] than our [American] publishers" (*Der fraynd*, April 4, 1911, 3–4). See also Avrom Reyzen's recollections about reprinting the works of American authors, including Rosenfeld, in the publications he edited for Lidsky (*Epizodn fun mayn lebn*, 2: 182, 194–95).

76. Reyzen, *Leksikon*, 2: 128–29. On the shift toward secularization and toward Yiddish in the book trade in Eastern Europe, see Hagit Cohen, *Ba-hanuto shel mokher ha-sefarim: hanuyot sefarim Yehudiyot be-Mizrah Eropah ba-mahatsit ha-sheniyah shel ha-meah*

ha-tesha esre (Jerusalem: Magnes, 2005), ch. 3. On the modernization of the Russian literary market more broadly, see Beth Holmgren, *Rewriting Capitalism: Literature and the Market in Late Tsarist Russia and the Kingdom of Poland* (Pittsburgh: University of Pittsburgh Press, 1998).

77. Y. Lifshits, ed., *Moris Rozenfelds briv* (New York: YIVO Institute for Jewish Research, 1955), 106–7.

78. Stein, *Making Jews Modern*, 231. A parallel process occurred in the world of Yiddish theater in Russia, which looked to American impresarios and business models to establish itself in the post-1905 era. See Warnke, "Going East."

79. Moshe Grosman, "Vegn di sensatsionele romanen in 'Haynt' un zayer mekhaber," *Fun noentn over* 2 (1956): 53–67; Nathan Cohen, "The Yiddish Press and Yiddish Literature: A Fertile but Complex Relationship," *Modern Judaism* 28, no. 2 (2008): 153–55; and Cohen, "'An Ugly and Repulsive Idler' or a Talented and Seasoned Editor: S. Y. Yatzkan and the Beginnings of the Popular Yiddish Press in Warsaw," *Jews in Russia and Eastern Europe* 54–55 (2005): 28–53.

80. Among these were L. Shapiro's *Novelen*; Peretz Hirschbein's *Yoyel*; Yitskhok Meyer Vaysenberg's *Kine un tayve un andere dertsaylungen*; and Sholem Aleichem, *Menakhem Mendel*. All of them were published in 1909 by the Progres publishing house in Warsaw and copyrighted in New York or Washington, DC, under the name J. Lidski.

81. See *Katalog fun der feraynigter bukhhandlung "Tsentral"* (New York: Tsentral, 1913), a copy of which is in the Asian and African Department of the National Library of Russia in Saint Petersburg. The catalog lists a New York office of the firm at 169 E. Broadway.

82. See the copy of the contract between Tsentral and Druckerman, reproduced in Yakubovits, "Asot ve-hefets sefarim harbeh," 240–46.

83. Veidlinger, *Jewish Public Culture*, 283–91; Nathan Goldberg, "Decline of the Yiddish Press," *Chicago Jewish Forum* 3 (fall 1944): 17.

84. For the Jewish population of New York in 1927, see Jacob Rader Marcus, *To Count a People: American Jewish Population Data, 1585–1984* (Lanham, MD: University Press of America, 1990), 152. In 1927, New York's Yiddish press still had a circulation of 417,900, while as late as 1932–1933, the combined circulation of Warsaw's Yiddish newspapers was only 170,000. See Goldberg, "Yiddish Press," 17, and Antony Polonsky, "Warsaw," in *YIVO Encyclopedia of Jews in Eastern Europe*, ed. Gershon D. Hundert (New York: YIVO Institute for Jewish Research, 2008), 2: 2000.

85. Goldberg, "Yiddish Press," 17. For a more comprehensive discussion of the decline of Yiddish culture in the United States during the 1920s and 1930s, see Eric L. Goldstein, "The Struggle over Yiddish in Postimmigrant America," in *1929: Mapping the Jewish World*, ed. Hasia R. Diner and Gennady Estraikh (New York: New York University Press, 2013), 139–54.

86. Several studies have been written recently on the history of Yiddish scholarship in Eastern Europe, but so far little work has been done on the history and outlook of scholars and critics working in Yiddish in New York during the interwar and post— World War II period. The institutional hubs for this group included organizations such as the *Amerikanisher opteyl* (American Branch, known as *"Amopteyl"*) of the YIVO Institute for Jewish Research, founded in 1925 by Jacob Shatsky; the *Yidisher kultur gezelshaft* (Yiddish Cultural Organization), founded in 1934; and the *Tsentrale Yidishe kultur-organizatsye* (known in English as CYCO), founded in 1938; among others. Some

of the representative works on the development of Yiddish scholarship in Eastern Europe include Cecile Kuznits, "The Origins of Yiddish Scholarship and the YIVO Institute for Jewish Research" (PhD diss., Stanford University, 2000); Barry Trachtenberg, *The Revolutionary Roots of Modern Yiddish* (Syracuse, NY: Syracuse University Press, 2008); Kenneth Moss, *Jewish Renaissance in the Russian Revolution* (Cambridge, MA: Harvard University Press, 2009); Kalman Weiser, *Jewish People, Yiddish Nation: Noah Prylucki and the Folkists in Poland* (Toronto, Canada: University of Toronto Press, 2011); and Itsik Nakhmen Gottesman, *Defining the Yiddish Nation: The Jewish Folklorists of Poland* (Detroit: Wayne State University Press, 2003).

PART III

The Immigrant as Transnational

Do ethnic or national origins determine identity? What weight should historians give to self-identification and what to ascribed identities? As this section demonstrates, transnational identities can be murky, multiple, and mutable. The following chapters focus on the manifestation of identity among transnationals by examining how they identified themselves, how others viewed them, and how, in certain circumstances, they manipulated their identities for their own benefit. Identities were rarely static. And instead of being diluted or disappearing, as some earlier scholars of Jewish immigration suggested, Old World attachments and identifications could be reconfigured in the United States.

The authors of the following chapters explore the subject of transnational identities using different foci. Tobias Brinkmann stresses the centrality of language and religion, Lara Rabinovitch emphasizes personal choice and public display, while Jonathan Goldstein examines how ideology and migration can reshape identity. All three demonstrate the importance of context, surroundings, and outside influences in forming and reforming identities. Beyond the differences in their approach to identity, they employ distinct methodological frameworks. Rabinovitch presents a microstudy that reveals the role individuals play in crafting their public self-representations; her subjects reinvented themselves through a conscious process of weaving together transnational identities. Goldstein and Brinkmann, by contrast, focus on the structural level, revealing how political and economic factors delimited how people related to nationalities.

Tobias Brinkmann shows how complex and contextual an identity could be. His chapter is a forceful response both to those who have argued that

Central European immigrants transplanted wholesale a cultural heritage they had carried with them to American shores and to those who have proposed that immigrants bore few permanent traces of their Germanic origins. Brinkmann counters, "Neither the assertion that the 'German Jews' in America formed a branch of German Jewry nor the hypothesis that Jewish immigrants from 'Germany' were not 'German' is accurate." Instead he proposes that "Germans" in America can be viewed as transnationals who shared some elements of their identity with non-Jewish German speakers as well as forming part of the broad spectrum of Jewish immigrants in the United States. If Brinkmann drafts a broad-stroke canvas of German Jewish identity in the United States, Lara Rabinovitch, in "The Gypsy in Them: Imagined Transnationalism amid New York City's Little Rumania," paints an intimate portrait that reveals in fascinating detail how a handful of Romanian Jewish immigrants "actively took on a Gypsy Jewish identity for decades in Lower Manhattan." Beyond serving "as a form of entertainment, intrigue, and notoriety" to their contemporaries and to ourselves, the "self-fashioned Gypsyness of these Jews . . . provides a rich glimpse into the historical dynamism of immigrant identity."

In "No American *Goldene Medina*," Jonathan Goldstein continues this exploration of transnational identity in a chapter that examines the experience of Jews who settled in Harbin, China and then migrated to the wider Jewish world. In Harbin, Russian Jews became Zionists but continued to view Harbin as central to their identity. Because of the unusual circumstance they encountered in Harbin, individuals within the small Jewish community that formed there in the first decades of the twentieth century played unusually prominent roles as cultural and intellectual intermediaries, with consequences for both Russian Jewry and the later lives of Jews who left Harbin. Goldstein shows us how this sense of connection to Harbin persisted after these "*Kharbintsy*" emigrated to the United States, Israel, Canada, Japan, Australia, and elsewhere. The chapter forces us to carefully consider the pathways followed by Jews leaving Russia. A stop that otherwise might be considered a temporary way station is instead revealed to have much broader consequences for those who immigrated onward. The chapter is also useful in decentering America. By its nature, a collection of essays on American Jews and transnationalism valorizes the United States as a refuge, as a haven, as a powerful source of identity, and as the center of immigrant networks. The network of *Kharbintsy* that Goldstein uncovers in such rich detail had offshoots in the United States but developed its strongest branches elsewhere.

He forces us to consider the practical and philosophical reasons for immigrating or not immigrating to the United States and the ramifications of national immigration policies.

At their heart these chapters question assumptions about identity that are based on origins alone. Collectively they show that identities were reformed and remade in different environments, sometimes in response to shifting ideological imperatives, sometimes to adapt to changes in status, and sometimes to tap new sources of value.

6

"GERMAN JEWS?"

Reassessing the History of Nineteenth-Century Jewish Immigrants in the United States

Tobias Brinkmann

The encounter between immigrant and native has been a defining theme in American Jewish history. Unlike most major immigrant groups, Jews have come to the United States (and colonial America) not from one relatively clearly defined territory but from multiple centers of the diaspora, continuously over a period of more than 350 years. Different social, cultural, and linguistic backgrounds; distinctive religious traditions; and different periods of settlement have shaped American Jewish life from the earliest days. The seemingly uniform Jewish immigration waves were surprisingly diverse, even if the number of immigrants was small, as in colonial America. Most of the more than two million Jews from Eastern Europe who settled in the United States between the 1870s and 1920s spoke different Yiddish dialects, but they originated in distinct regions such as Galicia and Lithuania, moved to America at different times, and had strikingly different social, cultural, and economic backgrounds. The differences and occasional conflicts between Jewish immigrants and their descendants in America were (and are), however, less pronounced than outside observers assume, and labels can be misleading. Most Sephardi Jews living in colonial America during the eighteenth century, for instance, were Ashkenazim from Central and Eastern Europe who adopted the Sephardi prayer rite as they joined existing communities.[1]

Historiography

Until recently most scholars in the field of American Jewish history paid only fleeting attention to the paths of migration before and after arrival, to return migration, to the backgrounds of Jewish immigrants, to relationships between Jewish and gentile migrants from the same villages and shtetlach (small market towns), and to the ties Jews retained with relatives and friends in their former home communities and with Jews from the same home region who moved to other destinations. Apart from Yiddish- and German-speaking immigrant scholars, few historians have made use of sources in languages other than English. For instance, only one of three detailed surveys about the nineteenth-century "German Jewish" immigration to the United States published in the 1980s and 1990s is actually based in part on German language sources and literature.[2] Recent studies by Rebecca Kobrin and Tony Michels demonstrate the merits of analyzing American Jewish history in a transnational setting. Both authors make extensive use of sources in Yiddish, the language spoken by almost all Jewish immigrants from Eastern Europe. Kobrin highlights the links Jewish immigrants in New York established with their former home community in Bialystok and with Jews from Bialystok in Chicago, Buenos Aires, Palestine, and Melbourne. Michels shows that the Atlantic passage was not a one-way street. American Jews (and their political agendas) also traveled in the other direction, making a significant impact on Jewish Socialist movements in Europe before World War I.[3]

The following essay takes a closer look at Jewish immigrants from Europe who arrived between the 1820s and 1880s. These immigrants are often described as "German Jews" by historians, even though Jewish immigrants themselves, other Jews, German-speaking immigrants, and native-born Americans rarely used the actual term before 1880. In general overviews of American Jewish history the German immigration was long depicted as the second major immigration, following the limited colonial immigration and preceding the huge immigration wave from Eastern Europe. In recent years the division between the three seemingly distinct immigrations has been questioned. Most of the eighteenth-century immigrants were Ashkenazim and the nineteenth-century Jewish migrations from Central and Eastern Europe overlapped, especially since many migrants originated in regions along the undefined border between Eastern and Central Europe, in regions such as the Prussian province of Posen, which was part of Poland until 1792. According to Hasia Diner, whose works cover American and American Jewish history, the German Jewish immigration cannot even be described as German, because many pre-1880 immigrants did not come from Germany but from Eastern Europe. The immigrants who did come from Germany itself, she contends, were rural Jews who supposedly spoke Yiddish rather than German and observed traditional Judaism, resembling their Eastern European coreligionists rather than their gentile German fellow emigrants. Avraham Barkai, a scholar whose publications deal mostly with German Jewish history (in Germany), makes exactly the opposite case, emphasizing the Germanness of American Jews who originated in Central Europe long after the arrival. He depicts them as a transplanted branch of German Jewry.[4]

Diner's and Barkai's conflicting positions raise questions about the origins and characteristics of the nineteenth-century Jewish immigration before the beginnings of the mass immigration from Eastern Europe after 1880. Where in Europe did the earlier migrants come from and how did they define themselves? Which German (if any) and Jewish cultural baggage did they take to America? The interpretations by Diner and Barkai hint at the limitations imposed by the still dominant nation–state paradigm in modern Jewish history. Scholars firmly rooted in one national field sometimes venture uneasily into another. An analysis looking at developments on both sides of the Atlantic makes it possible to determine the place of the German Jews in American Jewish history more precisely.

Locating Germany

Authors in American Jewish history frequently use terms such as Germany, Poland, Russia, Central Europe, and Eastern Europe uncritically. These terms are vague because they do not take shifting borders or contrasting cultural and political concepts into account. Before the first modern German nation–state was created in the wake of the Franco–Prussian War in 1871, Germany did not exist as a territory with clearly defined boundaries. The more precise term "German states" for mid–nineteenth-century Germany refers to the member states of the *Deutscher Bund* (German Federation). This loose body was established at the Congress of Vienna in 1815 and comprised most German speakers in Europe but also sizeable groups whose members did not consider themselves German at all, for instance Czech-speaking inhabitants of the Austrian province of Bohemia and Moravia. Prussia and the Habsburg monarchy were the largest and most influential members of the German Federation, but Prussia's eastern provinces such as Posen and the Hungarian part of the Habsburg monarchy—both with significant Jewish populations—were not part of the German Federation. At home and abroad, even after 1871, most German speakers identified themselves as subjects of states such as Bavaria, Baden, and Prussia (or even specific Prussian provinces), rather than as Germans. Indeed, the extensive scholarship on German-speaking immigrants in nineteenth-century America demonstrates that many German-speaking immigrants became German only as they became American. During the Civil War, to give one example, thousands of recently arrived immigrants in the North joined German and Irish units to defend the Union.[5]

For many German-speaking immigrants, religion or class were more meaningful when they publicly expressed their identity than Germanness. American Jews in particular understood Germany in cultural rather than political terms. In 1865 Chicago Reform rabbi Bernhard Felsenthal praised Germany as the center of modern Judaism: "We must not distance ourselves from German Judaism and its influences. As in medieval times the sun of Jewish *Wissenschaft* was shining on the Spanish sky, this sun is now shining on the German sky, sending out its light to all Jews and Jewish communities, who live among the modern cultured peoples. Germany has replaced Sefard." Felsenthal was referring not to the (or a) German nation or to a clearly defined

FIGURE 6.1. New Synagogue Berlin (1866) in 2013. Photo by the author.

territory but to an intellectual Germany that was linked with modern Judaism. A few years earlier, in 1859, he stressed that politically the German states were "miserable," not least because not a single government had emancipated its Jewish population.[6]

Imperial Germany, the first modern German nation–state, was founded in 1871. It excluded territories belonging to the Habsburg monarchy with sizeable groups of German speakers but included several national minorities, especially Poles, living in Prussia's eastern provinces. Thus in the United States, even after 1871, many immigrants from Imperial Germany did not identify themselves as Germans, while quite a few immigrants from states other than Germany, such as Switzerland and the Habsburg monarchy, considered themselves Germans. Moreover, the formal creation of a German nation–state initiated a lengthy process of nation building that was not completed when Imperial Germany collapsed at the end of the First World War. Catholics and Socialists were subject to government discrimination after 1871, and German officials tolerated and in some cases openly supported anti-Semitic discrimination, for instance in the Prussian army. In the United States, German-speaking Catholics, Socialists, and Jews frequently had a distant relationship to the German state and its leading representatives. And Germanness was a much-contested concept, not only in Imperial Germany but also in the United States. The wide spectrum of German identities, in a period of strong immigration of German speakers, partly explains why during the second half of the nineteenth century German American immigrant communities in larger cities were only loosely organized, if at all.[7]

How many Jews did immigrate to the United States between 1820 and 1880, and where in Europe did they originate? Apart from a few essays, detailed studies about Jewish emigration from the German states have not been conducted. And arriving immigrants were not asked about their religion. Therefore, estimates about the number of immigrants range widely, from 100,000 to over 200,000. A sizeable group hailed from Bavaria, Baden, Württemberg, Hesse, and adjacent territories, such as Alsace. The rural population in these territories spoke almost exclusively various German dialects; as non-Christians, Jews constituted a visible minority.[8] The other two major sending regions, the Prussian province of Posen and Bohemia, which belonged to the Habsburg monarchy, had much more diverse populations. Both provinces constituted borderlands, which were claimed by different national movements; Prussia had only annexed Posen in 1792. Until 1918, the official government language in both provinces was German, while the majority of the population in Posen spoke Polish and in Bohemia, Czech. Early on, Jewish communities in these provinces identified with the German-speaking minority populations and with the respective imperial government, in part because leading representatives of the emerging Polish and Czech national movements excluded Jews. Another factor was elementary education in German. In Posen the Prussian state established a school system that reached over 75 percent of Jewish children by the early 1830s but only a little more than 50 percent of the Christian (and overwhelmingly Polish-speaking) children. In Bohemia, too, Jewish children were educated in German language elementary schools. In both regions, especially in Posen but also in rural parts of Bohemia, the economic conditions were challenging, and large numbers of Jews (and gentiles) moved either to the United States or to nearby cities, such as Berlin and Breslau or Prague and Vienna.[9]

For Jews in *and* from Posen and Bohemia, German culture and language had an even higher symbolic significance than for Jews from areas where German speakers formed the majority of the population. By emphasizing their Germanness, Posen and Bohemian Jews in the United States began to distinguish themselves from their coreligionists hailing from regions farther east, such as Galicia, Lithuania, and Hungary. The emergence of the image of the traditional and uneducated *Ostjude* (eastern Jew) was closely linked with the rise of the image of the modern and *gebildet* (educated) German Jew, as will be discussed in the final part of this essay. In the United States, these images influenced intracommunal relations (and conflicts) between Jews from different parts of Europe. Jews from the Habsburg monarchy and the Russian Empire had already begun migrating to the United States in more sizeable numbers during the late 1860s. In contemporary sources they are often described as Russian or Polish Jews. Due to inadequate research it is not known how many Jews immigrated to the United States before the turn of the century.[10]

Bildung

Almost all Jewish immigrants from Central Europe came from small rural communities, as did their Christian fellow migrants. Indeed, the migrations of Jews and non-Jews to America and to European cities during the middle of the nineteenth century were related, even though Jews had a different economic profile. During the early phase of the economic transformation, soon after the end of the Napoleonic Wars, the collapse of the feudal order, strong population growth, and the mechanization of agricultural production forced a growing number of people to look for better economic opportunities elsewhere, not least in nearby cities—and in America. Jews had been forced into the protocapitalist margins of rural economies for centuries. They worked as itinerant peddlers, cattle dealers, and moneylenders. Although most barely made ends meet and their position in some areas became even more precarious during the Napoleonic Wars and in the early phase of industrialization, Jews were better positioned than most of their Christian neighbors. Familiarity with markets, tight kinship networks, and knowledge about changing tastes and fashions, for instance in the clothing sector, partly explain why Jewish entrepreneurs emerged as trailblazers of this transformation. Truly remarkable, however, is not the success of a few famous business founders but the rise of the overwhelming majority of Central European Jews, in one generation, from members of a marginalized rural population into the mostly urban *Bürgertum* (bourgeoisie).[11]

From an American perspective, the hypothesis that Jewish migrants from states such as Baden, but also Posen, grew up in a traditional Jewish milieu and became modern only in America seems compelling.[12] Several detailed studies, however, cast the social transformation of Jewish communities in the early nineteenth-century German states (including Posen) and in Habsburg Bohemia in a different light by focusing on the impact of Jewish emancipation. State bureaucracies understood Jewish emancipation as an educational policy, granted in stages, and tied to proof of Jewish "improvement." Most Jewish community leaders did not oppose this policy because emancipation was part of an ambitious reform project that was based on universal Enlightenment principles rather than exclusivist nationalist visions and did not entail (at least not explicitly) the expectation that Jews convert to Christianity. Most Jewish communities in the German states invested heavily in the primary education of boys and girls soon after 1800 to demonstrate that they accepted the challenge to become modern. The schools promoted Enlightenment ideals, especially *Bildung,* which describes a constant process of (self-)education, critical reflection, deep appreciation of the arts, and openness to new ideas. In early nineteenth-century Central Europe, *Bildung* emerged as the creed of the *Bürgertum*. Reversing Pierre Bourdieu's thesis of the conversion of economic into cultural capital, German historian Simone Lässig argues that the Jewish primary schools provided girls and boys at an early age with the cultural capital that they would later invest successfully in a rapidly transforming economy and society. Jews acquired a bourgeois mentality and forms of behavior when they were still members of the rural underclass. Jewish girls and boys did not just learn how to read, write, and speak in German, they were familiarized with Enlightenment concepts and a bourgeois value system. Even more important, they were ready to embrace change.[13]

Modern Judaism

Jewish openness to modernity was also rooted in religious change, which occurred in the German states in the decades after 1800 and led to the founding of the Jewish Reform movement. Reform developed as a Jewish response to the opening of the ghetto and the massive social and economic changes. Its proponents were strongly influenced by the Enlightenment and the *Bildung* concept. Instead of copying elements of Christian worship and liturgy, distancing oneself from Judaism and Jewish life, converting, or rigidly opposing any changes to the Jewish tradition, reformers wanted to define a viable platform for Judaism in the modern world. They questioned the tradition, especially the authority of the Talmud and the halakah (Jewish law), and rituals they considered as outdated and meaningless. Reform theologians interpreted Judaism in its specific historical context as a progressive religion. Judaism had changed its forms, but the underlying spirit had persisted—the belief in one God, a strong emphasis on ethical values, and the vision of universal peace. External changes were necessary if parts of the ritual did not express the spirit of Judaism in the present age.[14]

In the German states, reformers faced many obstacles. State authorities closed down early Reform synagogues. And reformers had to compromise with traditional Jews within the state-regulated local community, the so-called gemeinde.[15] Even though most Reform theologians lived in cities such as Berlin and Frankfurt, the message of Reform was not lost upon rural Jews. Soon after 1815 governments in different German states began to regulate the rabbinical training; all candidates had to graduate from a university before they could be ordained and serve a Gemeinde. Thus even traditional-minded rabbis in small Jewish communities had been exposed to new ideas, and a number of influential Reform rabbis served small Gemeinden. Samuel Adler spent more than a decade at the Gemeinde in Alzey, a small town in Rhenish Hesse near Worms, before accepting a position at Temple Emanu-El in New York in 1857. David Einhorn, who left Europe in 1855, was employed for several years as rabbi in Mecklenburg-Schwerin. Admittedly, it is difficult, if not impossible, to determine how many Jews had been exposed to Enlightenment ideas at a primary school and in the synagogue before they left for the United States. But after the dismantling of the ghetto around 1800, rural

Jewish communities cannot be described as static and traditional. Almost all younger migrants spoke Yiddish and were familiar with traditional Judaism, but young men and women also could speak, read, and write in German and had enjoyed a good school education. Many were familiar, at least superficially, with ideas espoused by the Reform movement.

In the United States, Reform flourished as more immigrants from the German states arrived. Indeed, the arrival of a growing number of Reform Jews during the 1840s and 1850s doomed early attempts by Cincinnati rabbi Isaac Mayer Wise to unite American Jews across the religious spectrum under the roof of a single denomination. On his journeys across the United States Wise also called on Jews to preserve the "synagogue community," which resembled the all-encompassing European Gemeinde. Recently immigrated Reform rabbis like Adler and Einhorn fiercely opposed such moves. They defended the independence of their Reform congregations, recognizing the advantages of religious pluralism and freedom in the United States, where no chief rabbi or government meddled in the affairs of a congregation.[16]

The first Reform theologians trained at (German) universities reached the United States during the 1850s. At this point many congregations had already begun to implement some external changes to the service, but they lacked a comprehensive theological justification for these reforms. The disagreements between university-trained Reform theologians, who called for thorough and radical changes, and more moderate American rabbis has been described in the scholarship as a conflict between Germans and Americans over the future of Reform in the United States. "German" represented modern Judaism, a consistent theology, and *Bildung*, while "American" stood for pragmatic reforms and integration on American terms, such as switching from Hebrew to English as the language of the service. Leading Germans such as David Einhorn and the abovementioned Chicago rabbi Bernhard Felsenthal have been depicted as members of a detached elite.[17] This characterization is suggestive on a first glance: Einhorn was a stubborn intellectual who never felt quite at home in America and did not hesitate to praise German culture. His demand to introduce German as the language of the service, however, seems sensible because it was still the native language of most immigrants in the 1850s and 1860s and was widely spoken on the street in cities such as Cincinnati and Saint Louis. A closer look at Einhorn's theology shows that it is too simplistic to characterize him and his supporters as elitist "Germanizers." Through his supporters Einhorn made a lasting impact on the American Reform movement, long after his death in 1879. The 1885 Pittsburgh Platform, the first programmatic manifesto of the American Reform movement, was based largely on his theology. Einhorn considered America as a spiritual wasteland, but he also praised religious pluralism and the neutrality of the state in the religious sphere. Indeed, Einhorn's calls for a "Germanization" of Judaism in the United States must be understood in their specific American context. The so-called radical reformers were calling for a thorough modernization of Judaism along the lines of German thought but firmly on the basis of American religious freedoms.[18] Felsenthal explicitly called on Jewish reformers in Chicago to separate from more traditional-minded Jews and form their own Reform congregation because they *could*—in sharp contrast to the state-regulated German Gemeinde.[19] After the experience of government interference and conflicts with traditional Jews in Europe, immigrant reformers cherished the religious pluralism they encountered in the United States. In the religious sphere too, Germanization and Americanization were part and parcel of the same process. Germanization did not represent an ethnic or national identity but was a symbol for modern Judaism. Felsenthal and Einhorn and more than a few of their congregants recognized the close relationship between the universal Enlightenment ideals expressed in the American Constitution and those in their vision of modern Judaism.

Since most affiliated Jews in the United States belonged to a Reform congregation on the eve of the Jewish mass immigration in 1881, the transatlantic dimension of Jewish Reform theology should not be discounted. Around 1880 several dozen American rabbis, especially at large urban congregations, had graduated from leading German universities. Most were immigrants from the German states, the Habsburg monarchy, and the Russian Empire; a few, like Emil G. Hirsch and Samuel Sale, had grown up in the United States. German research universities in Göttingen, Heidelberg, Leipzig, Berlin, and several others enjoyed a worldwide reputation for academic excellence. Hundreds of Americans embarking on academic careers went to German universities for their graduate education during the second half of the nineteenth century, among them a number of men seeking to become rabbis. Urban Reform congregations especially expected applicants for rabbinical positions to have a German university degree under their belt. The first rabbinical seminary in the United States, Hebrew Union College (Reform), was founded in 1875 in Cincinnati. This background explains why German rabbinical seminaries such as the Reform Hochschule des Judentums (founded in 1872) in Berlin, the neighboring Neo-Orthodox Rabbinerseminar (1873), and the Jüdisch-Theologisches Seminar (1854) in Breslau were obvious destinations

FIGURE 6.2. Building of the former Hochschule für die Wissenschaft des Judentums (1907), Berlin in 2013, Photo by the author.

for many aspiring rabbis until the early 1880s. The Breslau seminary mediated between Reform and Orthodoxy and was a forerunner of Conservative Judaism in America. Dozens of future American rabbis graduated from these three seminaries. Most were Europeans who later immigrated to the United States. A few students went from the United States to Germany for their rabbinical training. Several were sons of immigrant rabbis—such as Richard Gottheil, Morris Jastrow Jr., and Emil G. Hirsch—who helped to institute Semitic studies as an academic discipline in the United States after their return.[20]

German Americans

Jews from the German states and adjacent territories formed a tiny part of a huge movement of German speakers to North America during the nineteenth century. In the cities and regions where German-speaking immigrants clustered, especially in the Midwest, Jews established several important communities. Cincinnati, a city dominated by German speakers after 1840, was home to one of the largest Jewish communities outside of New York during the 1860s. Although well-known Jewish businessmen and rabbis played visible roles in German American communities, the scholarship on German Americans and American Jews ignored or played down these ties for many decades.[21]

Just as the nation–state paradigm imposes constraints upon scholars researching migrations across borders, the ethnic paradigm in American immigration historiography has obscured contacts and community building across ethnic lines. As Michael A. Meyer has emphasized, in mid–nineteenth-century America, German speakers generally welcomed Jewish immigrants into their secular *Vereine* (associations).[22] Especially in the Midwest Jewish immigrants co-founded and sometimes even led German American associations. The term "German American" betrays a wide spectrum of groups and individuals. Apart from a common language (spoken in different dialects), Germans in nineteenth-century America shared little; they ranged from various Protestant groups, Catholics, and Jews to freethinkers, Socialists, and anarchists. Earlier arrivals, who had established themselves socially and economically, looked down on recent "green" immigrants. After the 1870s, working-class immigrants frequently sympathized with socialism and even anarchism, much to the distress of socially established German Americans. Political differences, the constant arrival of new groups, and, above all, strong regional identities represented serious obstacles to community building. The enormous diversity of German-speaking immigrants in mid–nineteenth-century America actually made it easier for Jews to join German *Vereine,* especially if they supported important community projects, such as hospitals and mutual aid societies.

The most visible movers and shakers of German American communities during the second half of the nineteenth century were "forty-eighters," political exiles who had found refuge in the United States after the failed revolution of 1848/49. Most were liberals who had embraced the cause of Jewish emancipation before their departure. Although few in number, they were influential opinion leaders, not least as editors of German language newspapers and as elected officials on the local and state level. The forty-eighters shared an important experience with Jewish immigrants from the German states. The latter had literally emancipated themselves as they stepped on America's shores, while the forty-eighters found political asylum in the United States. Leading representatives of both groups repeatedly praised America as a land of freedom and vowed to fight for the abolition of slavery. These declarations were not hollow statements. During a critical phase in the Civil War, in the summer of 1862, the Jewish community of Chicago raised and fully equipped a company made up entirely of Jewish volunteers. The company joined a German regiment led by Friedrich Hecker, one of the most illustrious forty-eighters. In August 1862 Hecker came to Chicago to formally receive the flag of the company. Addressing the Jewish community at a celebration attended by most Chicago Jews, he drew a parallel between Jewish emancipation in the German states and the emancipation of black slaves in the South: "What I could do in my former home-country to defend the [civil] rights of Jews against intolerance and race-hatred is being repaid today [by you]. . . . Just as emancipation was inscribed on our flags then, . . . this flag will be the symbol of emancipation."[23]

During the 1870s and 1880s, as modern anti-Semitism took shape as an organized political movement in Imperial Germany, newspapers edited by American forty-eighters took a clear stand against anti-Jewish discrimination in Germany (and the United States). The papers also covered events in the respective Jewish communities. It would be a mistake, however, to describe Jewish congregations and associations as full-fledged members of German American communities as one author has suggested, even if the evidence for a close involvement between Jews and other Germans seems overwhelming.[24] My research on Chicago indicates a broad involvement of Jews in German associations between 1850 and the early twentieth century. In the early 1850s Jews were among the founders and leaders of the German Aid Society, the main mutual aid association caring for Germans in Chicago. They also joined Germans as founders of the Republican Party in Illinois. Leading Jews and Germans worked closely together during the Civil War and its aftermath in Chicago politics, successfully introducing German language instruction in Chicago's public schools. During the 1860s and early 1870s Jewish businessman Henry Greenebaum was regarded as the leader of the loosely organized German community. A large parade, which celebrated German unification in 1871, was organized in the office of prominent Jewish lawyer Julius Rosenthal and was led by Greenebaum. Yet a closer look at other parades during the 1860s proves that Jewish involvement with other German speakers had clearly defined limits and was primarily a matter of individual choice. While many Jews marched in the German cohort during public parades, along with German *Vereine* and Protestant congregations, no Jewish association or congregation participated. In 1867 Chicago Jews organized their own parade to celebrate the beginning of the construction of the first Jewish hospital in Chicago. Even though the main speech at the end of the parade was given in German, this was strictly a Jewish event. Chicago Jews participated in the cultural life of German Americans and collaborated with them politically, but they organized their own distinct community. While many Jews provided funds to the German Aid Society, Jewish associations cared for all distressed Jews. The United Hebrew Relief Association (UHRA), which was founded shortly after the German Aid Society in 1859, was the social platform of the Chicago Jewish community; most Jewish congregations and associations were corporate members. The emphasis Chicago Jews placed on their own community betrays the legacy of the partly autonomous Jewish community in early modern Europe.[25]

Social Status

In American or America-related sources published in Europe, the term "German Jews" can rarely be found before 1880. An early example is the report of a correspondent who wrote for the main Jewish weekly in the German states. He described Jewish life in New York in 1846 as a conflict between different "nations":

> It is easy to understand, that this mixture of many nations cannot come together. The Portuguese behaves like a nobleman among the Jews . . . and indeed, he is a gentleman. The Pole here is the dirtiest creature of all classes, and he is responsible for the derogatory use of the name "Jew." . . . The German represents the majority among the Jews, he is efficient and knows how to assimilate to the conditions here. . . . The German is proud towards the Pole and evades him, for this the latter despises him.[26]

The observer, who primarily addressed Jewish readers in the German states, was hardly unbiased. The "national" categorization may well have referred to different religious traditions separating the established Sephardim (Portuguese) from recent immigrants who prayed according to the

German or Polish rites. In the mid-1840s, most Poles originated in the Prussian province of Posen, rather than the Russian or Austrian part of the former Polish state. The quotation is an early example of the negative image of the *Ostjude* among German Jews. The *Ostjude* image, as Steven Aschheim has stressed, was the negative mirror image of the modern German Jew. As Jews in the German states (including Posen) and in Bohemia left the ghetto, they distanced themselves from their own traditional background and thus from Jews who supposedly refused to become modern and symbolized the Jewish past—and who were considered embarrassing. Eastern Europe—a not clearly defined area east of the German states—was home to the main center of the Jewish diaspora and to large numbers of traditional Jews. Modernizing Jews in the German states were concerned that immigrating Jews from the east would threaten their recently gained and precarious status as partly emancipated Jews.[27]

Jews originating from the undefined borderland between Germany and the east, especially from Posen, Bohemia, and parts of Hungary, were particularly vulnerable to inner-Jewish discrimination, if they moved to European cities such as Berlin or to the United States. Within Jewish communities experiencing immigration, however, these stereotypes were only loosely tied to religious beliefs or versatility with German culture. Rather, as the quotation above illustrates, the discrimination was linked to social standing and indeed class: the Germans were hard working and aspired to lift themselves up to the same level as the Portuguese "gentlemen"; the "dirty" Poles were at the bottom of the Jewish hierarchy. Complicated relations between established and newly arriving immigrants who belonged to the same group was of course not an exclusively Jewish experience.[28] In Chicago and other American cities, Jews from the south German states excluded Jews from Posen. The association of poverty, lack of education and refinement, and public embarrassment with Jews from the east was quite common. In 1864 the directors of the Chicago United Hebrew Relief Association complained about recently immigrated Jewish peddlers, who were a burden for the Jewish community and were blamed for bringing the established Jews into disrepute; in the English text these Jews were described with the German word "*Ostjuden*."[29]

Two other examples from Chicago highlight that in the United States "German Jews" was primarily an expression of social status and indeed power within Jewish communities. In 1880/81 several Jewish immigrants from the Russian part of Poland wanted to establish a lodge in the rapidly expanding order of the B'nai B'rith. The established lodge members in Chicago rejected the application on technical grounds, but several supporters tabled the issue for a meeting of the Midwest lodges in January 1881. Most observers agreed that the true motive was to exclude Jews from Eastern Europe. Rabbi Adolph Moses, a native of Russian Poland who served a Reform congregation in Louisville, called on German Jews (in a German language Jewish weekly) to embrace eastern Jews instead of rejecting them. "Who has the misfortune . . . to hail from one of the Eastern regions outside of the South German paradise, this person comes from—oh, what a terrible thought—von hinter Berlin [from beyond Berlin]! The horror country 'Vonhinterberlin' generates stereotypes and strife in the darkest fantasy of the South German Jew, much to our embarrassment." Jews from Silesia, known as "Hinterberliners" or "Pollacks" stood at the top of this eastern hierarchy of shame. Lower down were Jews from Posen: "Beware, unfortunate man, if the God of revenge had destined your birth in a city of the Duchy of Posen!" Jews from Russian Poland (like himself) were regarded as so low that they found themselves outside of this status pyramid.[30] According to Rabbi Henry Gersoni, like Moses a Russian-born reformer and editor of a German language weekly, the leading opponents of the B'nai B'rith lodge in Chicago were German Jews from Posen and Bohemia, who themselves had been discriminated against as eastern Jews in previous years. At the decisive meeting of the B'nai B'rith lodges from the Midwest in January 1881, the opponents described the applicants as "uneducated," "dirty," and "ugly." One shocked member asked the opponents whether they wanted to launch a Jewish "anti-Semitic movement in Chicago." Nevertheless, the majority of the B'nai B'rith delegates voted against the application. Only when the story made headlines in the general press and beyond Chicago did the national leadership of the B'nai B'rith override the decision of the Midwest lodges and accepted the application.[31] This conflict occurred on the eve of the Jewish mass immigration from the Russian Empire and the Habsburg monarchy. But the Jewish immigration from the two empires had already increased during the 1870s. Most established Jews worried that they would lose control within their communities, as newcomers would upset the existing balance of power. The exclusion of Jews from the east by established German Jews organized in the B'nai B'rith lodges in Chicago and the Midwest was only superficially related to religious orientations and German culture; it was primarily a question of power and influence within the Jewish community.

After 1900, the term "German" related primarily to social status, economic success, and assimilation in an inner-Jewish context, as the second intriguing example shows. In the 1920s a young Jewish graduate student, the sociologist Louis Wirth, conducted interviews among Jewish immigrants in the so-called ghetto neighborhood on Chicago's west side. Wirth himself had immigrated to the United States as a child from Imperial Germany. The interviewees, who overwhelmingly hailed from the Russian Empire and the Habsburg monarchy, described Jews who were leaving the dilapidated inner-city area for the more upscale Lawndale neighborhood as "*Deitchuks*" (Yiddish for "German"). Among ghetto residents Lawndale itself was widely known under the name "*Deutschland*" (Germany).[32] For these immigrants, class and social status had almost completely replaced the older cultural, religious, and spiritual meaning associated with the term "German Jews." The transformation of the term highlights again how closely, on an inner-Jewish level, Germanness was tied to the process of Americanization.

Conclusion

This essay has shown that Germany made a significant impact on American Jews during the nineteenth century. Apart from their American-born children, most mid–nineteenth-century American Jews had grown up in rural communities in the south German states and adjacent territories such as Alsace, in Posen and Bohemia. A very large number had attended German language elementary schools. Jewish immigrants from Central Europe had not just enjoyed a solid school education; many had been exposed to elements of the *Bildung* concept and to Reform Judaism before their departure. Moreover, Jews formed a small part of the large but diverse movement of German speakers to the United States during the nineteenth century, and they participated widely in the communal life of German Americans. This involvement, however, was a matter of individual choice. Jewish communities positioned themselves outside the umbrella of German America.

The term "German Jews" has several layers that need to be distinguished from each other. In an American Jewish context, the term does not primarily refer to Germany as a political or geographic entity but rather to German culture and to shifting (and contested) images of modernizing and economically highly mobile immigrants who had achieved social status. For many mid–nineteenth-century Jewish immigrants Germany was a symbol for an inclusive culture without boundaries, which was closely linked with Enlightenment ideals, with academic excellence, and above all, as the quote by Bernhard Felsenthal at the beginning of this essay illustrates, with modern Judaism. Before 1880 Jewish immigrants from the German states and adjacent territories such as Bohemia and Posen rarely described themselves publicly as German Jews. When the actual term "German Jews" was more widely used after 1880, its meaning had transformed. Instead of a specific cultural identity, Germanness primarily expressed social status, economic success, and assimilation—for established Jews but also, as Louis Wirth's interviews from the 1920s prove, for more recent immigrants who did not come from German-speaking regions at all.

The image of German Jews as the "other" Jews—as a detached and overly assimilated Jewish elite—stuck until the end of the twentieth century among descendants of Jews who came to America after 1880.[33] The lingering perception can be traced to the encounter or rather the lack of an encounter between newly arriving immigrants from Eastern Europe and members of a small Jewish establishment. By distinguishing themselves from Jews who were perceived as upper-class Americans rather than Jews, the new immigrants were coming to terms with their own adaptation to American society. Most of the post-1880 immigrants from Eastern Europe were less well educated than their predecessors, and they faced more obstacles to rise socially and economically. Socially established German Jews lived largely in gentile middle- and upper-class neighborhoods at a time when post-1880 immigrants and their descendants were settling in inner-city working-class slums widely known as Jewish ghettos: New York's Lower East Side, Chicago's West Side, and the North End in Boston. By the 1920s more than half of the immigrants and their descendants had moved into white-collar occupations and to lower middle-class neighborhoods such as Brownsville and parts of the Bronx in New York, North Lawndale in Chicago, and Boston's Upper Roxbury. Around 1930 over half of the inhabitants of these neighborhoods were Jewish.[34] The Great Depression hit Jewish immigrants and their American-born descendants hard and delayed their movement from a tight-knit Jewish milieu into the American mainstream and into the suburban middle class until the 1950s.[35]

This background partly explains why the ambiguous image of the overly assimilated German Jew persisted into the second half of the twentieth century. For immigrant Jews and their descendants the German Jew was a positive and negative role model. Economic success, social mobility, perceived exclusiveness, status, and acceptance by non-Jews corresponded with the vision of upwardly mobile Jews. Yet few Jews keen to leave urban Jewish neighborhoods in the late 1940s and 1950s regarded the loss of Jewishness they associated with German Jews as desirable. More research has to shed light on this process. It should be emphasized that the loaded image of

German Jews overshadows the actual experiences of established Jews after 1880. Even though many were socially established, only a small minority was rich. Middle-class American Jews faced increasing social exclusion by gentiles even before 1900 and struggled economically during the years of the Great Depression.[36]

Scholars writing about Jewish immigrants who moved to the United States between 1820 and 1880 and their descendants should handle the rather complex and indeed loaded term "German Jews" cautiously. Neither the assertion that the German Jews in America formed a branch of German Jewry nor the hypothesis that Jewish immigrants from Germany were not German is accurate. A significant number of American Jews had a close relationship to German culture, to the German language, to relatives in the German states, and to German Americans before 1880, and not all of these Jews came from German-speaking parts of Europe. But even proponents of German culture like David Einhorn considered themselves first and foremost American Jews. The processes of Americanization and Germanization were closely related, in the religious sphere, for Jews who participated in the life of German Americans, but also socially. The shifting meanings of the term "German Jews" in the United States leads back to the beginning of this essay. The exploration of the conceptual history of German Jews shines light on the complicated intercommunal relations between American(-izing) Jews of different cultural and social backgrounds in a period of constant immigration from different subcenters of the Jewish diaspora. It is a mistake to take the multifaceted images associated with the terms "German Jews" and "*Ostjuden*" at face value. Rather, as this essay has attempted to show, it is necessary to decipher the meanings associated with these images. Since American Jewish history has been shaped by continuous immigration, much can be gained by transcending the artificial constraints of the ethnic and nation–state paradigm in American Jewish history and taking a closer look at the backgrounds of Jewish immigrants, their relationships to non-Jewish immigrants from the same place of origin, and sources in languages other than English.

Notes

1. Eli Faber, *Time for Planting: The First Migration 1654–1820*. Vol. 1: *The Jewish People in America* (Baltimore: Johns Hopkins University Press, 1992), 58–66.
2. Avraham Barkai, *Branching Out: German-Jewish Immigration to the United States 1820–1914* (New York: Holmes & Meier, 1994); no use of German-language sources: Naomi Cohen, *Encounter with Emancipation: The German Jews in the United States 1830–1914* (Philadelphia: Jewish Publication Society, 1984); Hasia R. Diner, *A Time for Gathering:*

The Second Migration 1820–1880. Vol. 2: *The Jewish People in America* (Baltimore: Johns Hopkins University Press, 1992).

3. Tony Michels, *A Fire in Their Hearts: Yiddish Socialists in New York* (Cambridge, MA: Harvard University Press, 2005); Rebecca Kobrin, *Jewish Bialystok and Its Diaspora* (Bloomington: Indiana University Press, 2010).

4. Diner, *Time for Gathering*, 1–5, 232–33; Barkai, *Branching Out*, 223–28.

5. Lawrence Fuchs, *The American Kaleidoscope: Race, Ethnicity, and the Civic Culture* (Hanover, NH: University of New England Press, 1990), 22; Kathleen Neils Conzen, "Immigrant Religion and the Public Sphere: The German Catholic Milieu in America," in *German-American Immigration and Ethnicity in Comparative Perspective*, ed. Wolfgang Helbich and Walter Kamphoefner (Madison, WI: Max Kade Institute, 2004), 69–116; Bruce Levine, "Community Divided: German Immigrants, Social Class, and Political Conflict in Antebellum Cincinnati," in *Ethnic Diversity and Civic Identity: Patterns of Conflict and Cohesion in Cincinnati since 1820*, ed. Jonathan Sarna and Henry D. Shapiro (Urbana: University of Illinois Press, 1992), 46–93; on German speakers within the American labor movement, see especially *German Workers in Industrial Chicago, 1850–1910: A Comparative Perspective*, ed. John B. Jentz and Hartmut Keil (DeKalb: Northern Illinois University Press, 1983).

6. Bernhard Felsenthal, *Jüdisches Schulwesen in Amerika: Ein Vortrag gehalten am 13. Dezember 1865 in der "Ramah-Loge" zu Chicago von Bernhard Felsenthal Prediger der Zionsgemeinde daselbst* (Chicago: Albert Heunisch, 1866), 36; Bernhard Felsenthal, *Kol Kore Bamidbar: Ueber jüdische Reform—Ein Wort an die Freunde derselben* (Chicago: Chas. Heß, 1859), 25.

7. See the essays in Dirk Hoerder and Jörg Nagler, eds., *People in Transit—German Migrations in Comparative Perspective, 1820–1920* (Cambridge: Cambridge University Press, 1995).

8. Tobias Brinkmann, *Sundays at Sinai: A Jewish Congregation in Chicago* (Chicago: University of Chicago Press, 2012), 11–30.

9. Sophia Kemlein, *Die Posener Juden 1815–1848* (Hamburg, Germany: Dölling und Gallitz, 1997), 78–89; Hillel Kieval, *Languages of Community: The Jewish Experience in the Czech Lands* (Berkeley: University of California Press, 2000), 28; Bernhard Breslauer, *Die Abwanderung der Juden aus der Provinz Posen* (Berlin: Levy, 1909).

10. Adolph Moses, "Die nationalen Vorurtheile unter den Juden." *Zeitgeist* [Milwaukee], August 5, 1880.

11. Jacob Toury, *Soziale und politische Geschichte der Juden in Deutschland, 1848–1871* (Düsseldorf, Germany: Droste, 1977).

12. Diner, *Time for Gathering*, 6–35.

13. Simone Lässig, *Jüdische Wege ins Bürgertum: Kulturelles Kapital und sozialer Aufstieg im 19. Jahrhundert* (Gottingen, Germany: Vandenhoeck & Ruprecht, 2004); see also Kemlein, *Die Posener Juden*, 78–89; Kieval, *Languages of Community*, 28.

14. Michael A. Meyer, *Response to Modernity: A History of the Reform Movement in Judaism* (New York: Oxford University Press, 1988).

15. Ibid., 62–99; George L. Mosse, *German Jews beyond Judaism* (Bloomington: Indiana University Press, 1985), 3; see also David Sorkin, *The Transformation of German Jewry, 1780–1840* (New York: Oxford University Press, 1987).

16. Brinkmann, *Sundays at Sinai*, 38–42.

17. Diner, *Time for Gathering*, 233.

18. Meyer, *Response to Modernity*, 244–50, 268–70.

19. Brinkmann, *Sundays at Sinai*, 47–48; Felsenthal, *Kol Kore Bamidbar*, 14–15.

20. Brinkmann, *Sundays at Sinai*, 115–17.

21. An important exception is Stanley Nadel, "Jewish Race and German Soul in Nineteenth-Century America," *American Jewish History* 77 (1987): 6–26; idem, *Little Germany: Ethnicity, Religion and Class in New York City 1845–80* (Urbana: University of Illinois Press, 1990); see also Jonathan Sarna and Henry D. Shapiro, eds., *Ethnic Diversity and Civic Identity: Patterns of Conflict and Cohesion in Cincinnati since 1820* (Urbana: University of Illinois Press, 1992).

22. Michael A. Meyer, "German-Jewish Identity in Nineteenth-Century America," in *Toward Modernity: The European Jewish Model*, ed. Jacob Katz (New Brunswick, NJ: Transaction, 1987), 247–67.

23. *Illinois Staatszeitung* (Chicago), August 20, 1862; reprinted in *Sinai: Ein Organ für Erkenntniss und Veredlung des Judenthums* (Philadelphia), September 1862, 231.

24. Nadel, "Jewish Race and German Soul," 8–12, 18.

25. Tobias Brinkmann, "Charity on Parade—Chicago's Jews and the Construction of Ethnic and Civic 'Gemeinschaft' in the 1860s," in *Celebrating Ethnicity and Nation: American Festive Culture from the Revolution to the Early Twentieth Century*, ed. Jürgen Heideking and Geneviève Fabre (New York: Berghahn, 2001), 157–74.

26. *Allgemeine Zeitung des Judenthums* [Leipzig], July 27, 1846, 448.

27. Steven Aschheim, *Brothers and Strangers: The East European Jew in German and German Jewish Consciousness 1800–1923* (Madison: University of Wisconsin Press, 1982).

28. John Bodnar, *The Transplanted: A History of Immigrants in Urban America* (Bloomington: Indiana University Press, 1985), 118.

29. *5th Annual Report of the United Hebrew Relief Association* (Chicago, 1864).

30. Moses, "Die nationalen Vorurtheile." All translations are mine.

31. *Jewish Advance* (Chicago), January 7 and 14, 1881; *Zeitgeist* (Milwaukee), February 3, 1881.

32. Louis Wirth, *The Ghetto* (Chicago: University of Chicago Press, 1928), 246–48.

33. Diner, *Time for Gathering*, xv.

34. Beth Wenger, *New York Jews and the Great Depression: Uncertain Promise* (New Haven, CT: Yale University Press, 1996), 15, 88–102; Gerald S. Gamm, "In Search of Suburbs: Boston's Jewish Districts, 1843–1994," in *The Jews of Boston*, ed. Jonathan Sarna and Ellen Smith (Boston: Combined Jewish Philanthropies of Greater Boston, 1995), 129–64.

35. Eli Lederhendler, *New York Jews and the Decline of Urban Ethnicity, 1950–1970* (Syracuse, NY: Syracuse University Press, 2001).

36. Brinkmann, *Sundays at Sinai*, 268–81.

7

THE GYPSY IN THEM

Imagined Transnationalism amid
New York City's Little Rumania

Lara Rabinovitch

We often drove out at night on the other side of the Hudson to Nyack
to [a Gypsy] encampment near the river in order to sing and dance
to our hearts' content. I sat by their campfires and listened to the
stories of their old men and of the Daias, the old women, and told
stories in my turn. They brought back memories of my early child-
hood and with them fresh courage and a freer outlook upon life. The
whole Gypsydom in New York opened its heart to me, and I gave
myself to it in return.[1]

As described in this excerpt from his 1941 autobiography, Romanian Jewish
immigrant writer Konrad Bercovici (1882–1961) often noted his affinity for Gypsies and Gypsy culture. Within the Romanian Jewish enclave of early twentieth-
century New York City he was joined by two other prominent immigrant Jews
from Romania, restaurateur and cultural curator Romany Marie (1885–1961)
and restaurateur and musician Joseph Moskowitz (1879–1954). Unlike most
other Jews from Romania or immigrants from elsewhere, Bercovici, Romany
Marie, and Moskowitz self-identified as Gypsies in writing or through costume,
performance, and persona for decades in Lower Manhattan.[2]

In contrast to the negative stereotypes held by Jews and non-Jews in both Europe and North America about Gypsies, these hybrid Romanian Gypsy Jews embodied the romantic cultural associations with the collective folklore of the Gypsies, particularly of the Balkan or European variations of the nomadic group. Rather than generating the kind of discrimination actual Gypsies experienced, the self-fashioned Gypsyness of these Jews served as a form of entertainment, intrigue, and notoriety similar to the phenomenon Christine Stansell has identified in bohemian culture in Greenwich Village during the same period.[3] Though bound up with the Romanian origins of each, this borrowed hybrid persona transcends strict national and ethnic categorizations and therefore provides a rich glimpse into the historical dynamism of immigrant identity.

If "modern historiography is inextricably linked with the modern nation,"[4] as Thomas Bender explains in the opening words to his volume on global history, the phenomenon of the Gypsy Jew fits neatly into neither the history of nations nor a history that accounts for transnationalism. Owing both to the adopted aspect of this hybrid persona and to the doubly diasporic nature of Gypsy and Jewish cultures, Gypsy Jews claimed no one national identity and did not bridge nationalisms by interacting across a regional network. Instead they claimed an imagined *nationless* identity and thereby publicly took on what we may call an imagined supratransnationalism or embodied transculturalism, which thrived within the interstices of the immigrant context. The transfer between nationalisms, cultures, or borders occurred here not across a geographic or even social network but physically within the individual persona of the Gypsy Jew through internal processes of cultural adoption and ethnic borrowing. If we consider this history as "more hybrid in the articulation of cultural differences and identifications than can be represented in any hierarchical or binary structuring," as Homi Bhabha writes, we may envision this phenomenon as an internalized, imagined transnationalism literally embodied within the character of the Gypsy Jew.[5]

The phenomenon of the hybrid Gypsy Jew may have taken root in Romania or its environs, but the cultural trend of Jews embodying Gypsy identities in public emerged most strongly in the Romanian Jewish immigrant context of the United States—and particularly within Little Rumania, a once vibrant corner of New York's urban landscape. Forgotten on maps of New York City today and largely ignored in the history of the United States, Jewish or other, Little Rumania once served as the geocultural locus point of immigrant Jews from Romania, a distinctive migratory group among the greater East and

Central European Jewish migration at the turn of the twentieth century. Beginning in 1900, specifically, tens of thousands of Jews from the newly independent Romanian principalities of Moldavia and Wallachia arrived on America's shores. In the post–World War I period, more arrived from Greater Romania, which included the annexed borderlands regions of Bucovina, Bessarabia, and Transylvania. Most Romanian Jewish immigrants ultimately settled in New York City, and many found collective identification in Lower Manhattan, specifically in the loosely bordered area known throughout the city as "Little Rumania," famed for its restaurants and cafés.[6] Romanian Jewish immigrant Marcus Ravage perhaps best described Little Rumania in his 1917 autobiography, *An American in the Making: The Life Story of an Immigrant*:

> Even as far back as 1900 this Little Rumania was beginning to assume a character of its own. Already it had more restaurants than the Russian quarter—establishments with signs in English and Rumanian, and platters of liver paste, chopped eggplant, and other distinctive edibles in the windows. On Rivington Street and on Allen Street the Rumanian delicatessen-store was making its appearance, with its goose pastrama and kegs of ripe olives and tubs of salted vine-leaves, and the moon-shaped cashcaval cheese made of sheep's milk.[7]

This ethnic enclave physically belonged to the Lower East Side, yet for decades, as Ravage and others have noted, through its distinctively named "Romanian" restaurants, cafés, and nightclubs in particular, it stood apart from the other East or Central European Jewish, Italian, and other immigrant enclaves.

Who were these Romanian Jews? Geographically and politically, Romania at the end of the nineteenth century stood at the crossroads of the Austrian, Ottoman, and Russian empires. Jews from Romania came to the New World with a somewhat different background and history than the majority of immigrant Jews who had come from the Russian Pale of Settlement. With Romania as a suzerainty of the Ottoman Empire until the late nineteenth century, Jews from Romania brought different "baggage," including Turkish influences in music, tales of Dracula and the Arabian Nights, and spices and recipes unknown to their Polish and Russian counterparts. The latter was influenced by Turkish methods of curing and smoking meats as well as the fertile topography of the country, which produced, among a great variety of fruits and vegetables, grapes for a robust wine industry. In addition to these distinctive cultural and gastronomic traits, many Romanian Jews also grew up in Romania in proximity to their Gypsy neighbors, who had lived in the area for centuries.

Large numbers of Gypsy peoples and Romani peoples migrated to Europe from the Indian subcontinent and dispersed for unknown reasons beginning in the early medieval period. In particular they populated several Balkan regions and remained a large and persecuted minority for centuries in Moldavia and Wallachia (formally unified in 1861 as Romania). Much of this history remains enigmatic, as few written histories exist of the Romani peoples and they do not self-identify on censuses and other governmental registries. However, it seems that Europeans gave these migrants the name "Gypsy," which originates in the Greek word for Egyptian, out of the belief that they had emerged from Egypt.[8] Many ethnic minorities populated Romania in the early modern and modern periods, and Gypsies and Jews remained among the largest ethnic groups in the young country, with some indications of cultural exchange.

Konrad Bercovici: The Gypsy Jewish Scribe

The prominent Romaninan-Jewish writer Konrad Bercovici (b. 1882) migrated to New York City in the early years of the twentieth century as a young man and ultimately became a prolific fiction and nonfiction writer (Figure 7.1). He published almost two dozen books on New York City, immigrants, Romania, Jewish life, art, and Gypsies, and he was a regular contributor to *Harper's Magazine* on these and other topics. Throughout his writing Bercovici regularly called attention to Gypsy culture but in his autobiography *It's the Gypsy in Me* (1941) in particular, he cites the foundational influence of the Gypsy culture surrounding him as a child and young adult, owing to his culturally diverse surroundings in Galatz, the Greek-dominated Danubian port city in Moldavia.

Like other Romanians, Bercovici grew up with exposure to Gypsies, but he professed to have a particular attraction to their elaborate caravans, folklore, and music from a young age.[9] Bercovici claims that as a child he not only had a Gypsy wet nurse and nanny, "Mama Tinka," but also spent weeks at a time with her, camped with other Gypsies:

> We went from Gypsy camp to Gypsy camp, and I liked the Gypsy children better than the pupils at the school. They had seen the world and knew things. They could ride, swim, help shoe a horse, put up a tent, weave baskets, blow bellows, and play the violin, the reed flute, and the cymbalon. I learned riding, basket weaving, and enough of Calo, their language, to make myself understood and to understand them.[10]

Bercovici also writes of later having accompanied his merchant father on extended trips throughout the region where he served as interlocutor to the

FIGURE 7.1. Konrad Bercovici, undated. Courtesy of the Library of Congress.

Gypsy blacksmiths. He remembers camping with Gypsies whenever it rained during these travels.[11] Bercovici also devotes part of his memoirs to describing an episode from his teenage years when he ran away from home and joined "a band of Gypsy musicians."[12] While other Romanian Jewish children may have lived within reach of Gypsy camps or even interacted with Gypsies regularly, Bercovici's particular fascination and proximity to Gypsy culture, or at least his perhaps embellished recounting of his experiences, stands out as rather unusual.

As an adult in New York City Bercovici often described himself as serving as a kind of scribe and representative of the Gypsies of Lower Manhattan, owing to his affinity with the group and his ability to read and write their tongue as well as English and other languages: "I learned Calo all over again and how to play at their weddings. I learned to play the violin all over again, to play it Gypsy fashion, so as to play at their festivities and be part of them and spend nights in their company."[13] At some point he also camped and traveled with a Gypsy group, "Calos from my own country," throughout New Jersey and Pennsylvania to enjoy the "sound of the violin, of dancing feet, of the many nuances of the language," before returning to New York.[14]

Soon this Gypsy presence in Bercovici's life influenced his writing process and literary output. His stories on Gypsies appeared in publications such as *The Dial*,[15] *Pictorial Review,* and *Good Housekeeping.* The success these garnered inspired him to delve further into this Gypsyness:

> The magazines published [my] Gypsy stories and stories of Roumanian peasants as fast as they got them.

> In writing these stories I relived my younger days in the wooded marshes of the Danube, heard the shepherds' flutes and the Gypsies' fiddles, and would often get out of bed to fix a scene on paper and to describe what I had just seen and heard in my sleep.

> Those stories seem to write themselves. Physically I was in New York with my family and friends; spiritually I was roaming somewhere between the Carpathian Mountains and the Black Sea.[16]

After writing *On New Shores,* a lyrical history of immigrants in the United States, Bercovici felt an "awakened . . . nostalgia" for Gypsies and consequently wished to return to Romania: "I simply had to go back, back to where I had come from, had to listen to and play Gypsy music with Gypsies, and eat peasant food again, and talk peasant language with peasants in their own homes."[17] He explains, "Of all my literary projects, the Gypsy stories were paramount in my mind."[18] Within three years of Bercovici's return from his European sojourn, the Cosmopolitan Book Corporation published his semi-historical book *Gypsies: Their Life, Lore, and Legends* (1928).

Bercovici's cultural identification with Gypsies moved beyond literary influence to a self-fashioned public identity he embraced and used to his advantage. For example, by the late 1920s his Gypsy identity seems to have played a role in the development of his ultimately tormented relationship with Charlie Chaplin as, in Bercovici's telling, their link was forged through shared experience owing to Chaplin's Gypsy roots on his mother's side.[19] Although Bercovici claimed no actual Gypsy lineage, he actively nurtured his Gypsy identity: "The legend of my being a Gypsy was growing, and I didn't care to dispute it. I wore flamboyant cravats and vests and welcomed the excuse to wear them; everybody said I was a Gypsy."[20] Bercovici's Gypsy flair extended far off the page and his reputation followed him throughout his appearances, particularly when he frequented the Romanian restaurants of Lower Manhattan, which he described in many of his works.

Nourishing a Community: Romany Marie

Romany Marie's (b. 1885) eponymous tavern stood out among Bercovici's most favorite haunts. This popular restaurant and café was owned by another self-fashioned Gypsy Jew, who had arrived from Romania in 1901.[21] Known for her genial and generous personality, Romany Marie (née Marie Marchaud) donned traditional Romanian or Gypsy garb and cooked her famed dishes while reading patrons' fortunes in the dregs of Turkish coffee remaining in their cups. She reputedly also insisted on evaluating people by their shadows.[22]

Similar to Bercovici, Romany Marie cited her youth in Romania, where she gravitated to Gypsy camps, as foundational in the later development of this adopted identity in New York.[23] While she seems to have independently created her Gypsy identity, Romany Marie counted Bercovici as a close friend. Among the strongest evidence for the depth of their friendship is in the reports of her funeral, during which Bercovici eulogized her using the metaphor of a centipede to describe her impossible reach and influence.[24]

Romany Marie's tavern had many locations within Lower Manhattan over several years, including Washington Square Park, Sheridan Square, Saint Mark's Place, Minetta Street, and Christopher Street in Greenwich Village.

Stephen Graham, a noted British writer and frequent contributor to *Harper's Magazine* and the *New Yorker*, devoted a chapter of his 1927 book *New York Nights* to Romany Marie and her tavern, describing the proprietress as

> stout, swarthy, empearled, with crimson ribbon in her black hair and peasant art evident in her embroidered dress, . . . a Jewess bearing the protective colouring of a Rumanian.[25]

One flyer advertised Romany Marie, then at its long-serving Christopher Street location, as giving "an honest glimpse of 'Romantic Romania,' a place where coals glow on an open grate, where, instead of jazz, come soft languid, Gypsy airs of the old Carpathians."[26] According to another dining guide, the Balkan-influenced dishes she prepared helped create this atmosphere:

> Plachinta Cu Carna a concoction of specially prepared meat, baked between layers of thin, flaky dough; Plachinta Brinza, made with goat's milk, instead of meat; or Saarmala, which consists of cooked, chopped meat, rolled in boiled cabbage leaves, and covered over all with a sauce piquant. . . . And then for dessert, there is Baclava, a native honey-cake; or Pondishpan, a sort of sponge cake, oozing nuts and raisins.[27]

In large part owing to the exoticism of the food and the tavern more generally, several noted personalities of New York's creative class made frequent visits to Romany Marie's. Graham writes of spotting the famed northern explorer Vilhjalmur Stefansson at Romany Marie's, where he was a regular,[28] and Romany Marie listed among her notable guests the Prince of Wales, Pablo Picasso, and Eugene O'Neill, whom she claimed wrote some of his plays "sitting before my fire."[29]

More recent scholars have corroborated this image: "'Romany Marie,' writes Stansell, was "a Moldavian Jewish garment worker . . . [who] capitalized on this market by turning herself into a Gypsy and moving to the Village to start a terrifically successful 'exotic' tearoom."[30] Romany Marie also posed for several artists, including the painters John Sloan and Chuck Adams. Other artists she counted among her friends included Diego Rivera, Willem de Kooning, and Isamu Noguchi. She also maintained a close relationship with her neighbor in Greenwich Village, Buckminster Fuller, who at one point designed the interior of her tavern[31] as, in one observer's interpretation, "a fetching orgy in futurism."[32]

Romany Marie's embodied Gypsyness undoubtedly added to her and her tavern's allure. The underlying sexuality of her persona and the tavern's private and perhaps not entirely wholesome corners also undoubtedly stoked her notoriety. Although she cultivated a mysterious air surrounding her origins, she resisted associations with cultures besides Romanian and Gypsy, particularly when one local newspaper columnist referred to her tavern as an "Arab hangout."[33] As a self-Orientalized curio on display nightly, Romany Marie helped to fuel—even literally—the appetite of many of the city's cultural elite for several decades, particularly from the 1910s through the 1940s. Romany Marie closed her tavern in 1950, and when she died eleven years later the *Village Voice* announced the sad news on its cover.[34] The *New York Times* memorialized her as a "Village figure" in its obituary of her: "For six decades she played the role of Gypsy so convincingly that her tea-leaf readings and palmistry were sought by neophyte artists. She played the role with zest, wearing colorful Gypsy costumes, laden with pounds of jingling jewelry and maintaining a slight air of mystery that obscured her simple, sturdy . . . Rumanian ancestry."[35]

The success of Romany Marie's undoubtedly lay in large part with the figure of Romany Marie herself. But the booming Romanian restaurant culture that defined Little Rumania also mutually reinforced the popularity of her tavern, even when it was located a few blocks away in the more gentile Greenwich Village. For example, a population study that focused in part on Romanian Jewish immigrants conducted by the Educational Alliance of the Jewish Welfare Board in 1924 indicated,

> At first glance the Rumanian hardly differs from the Lithuanian, Russian[, or] Polish Jew. But in the years of mass immigration the Lithuanian and Russian Jews took to the needle trades. . . .
>
> The Rumanian Jews mostly engage in the food and clothing business, restaurants and wine cellars. They love their work, enjoy the earthiness and lustiness, and the fame of their restaurants is so great that New Yorkers from all boroughs visit them.[36]

Moses Rischin, the pioneering historian of Jewish immigrant New York, mapped the few blocks constituting Little Rumania[37] and wrote that Romanian Jews "tippled wine" and exercised a monopoly on the food and wine industries.[38] This characterization had continued from a generation prior, when noted Romanian Jewish journalist David M. Hermalin wrote, "The occupations of the Roumanian Jews in the United States do not differ materially from the occupations of others, with the exception of their wine-cellars, coffee-houses, and restaurants."[39] Similarly, in his pioneering 1924 study of immigrants across the city, *Around the World in New York*, Bercovici also described Little Rumania: "Encompassing the district from Delancey Street to Houston Street and First Street, and westward to Second Avenue, is the region of the Romanian Jews, distinguished from the others by the number of cafés and dancing-places."[40] This Romanian food culture created a fertile ground for Gypsy Jews—"authentic" bearers of a lost or faraway tradition, albeit invented—to emerge for public consumption.

Joseph Moskowitz and the Soundtrack of Little Rumania

The interplay of New York's Romanian restaurant culture and the notoriety of these Gypsy Jews found another prominent example with Romanian immigrant Joseph Moskowitz (b. 1879), particularly within his popular restaurant Moskowitz and Lupowitz, which first opened on Rivington Street in 1909 and soon after moved to the more grand Second Avenue,[41] a few blocks north of Houston Street. The restaurant stood out as one of the most successful and long-lasting Romanian Jewish restaurants, in part by serving far more than food. One Works Progress Administration (WPA) study characterized the famed locale as a "semicabaret" where "there is singing and music" and where "Rumanian fellow-countrymen flocked."[42]

In 1938 an advertisement in *The Butcher Worker*, a Yiddish–English publication of the American Federation of Labor, promoted the Romanian "native dishes" and the "Gypsy atmosphere" of the restaurant.[43] One travel writer to New York highlighted the role Moskowitz himself played in "running Little Rumania" and charming his patrons with his "legendary" music.[44] As early as 1908 the *New York Times* proclaimed Moskowitz "the world's champion czymbalist [*sic*]."[45] Celebrities of every stripe frequented the restaurant, including Molly Picon, Groucho Marx, Clifford Odets, and Charlie Chaplin.[46]

The success of the restaurant hinged on the atmosphere created in large part by the figure of "Moskowitz," another self-fashioned hybrid, a Gypsy Jew on display for the public eye. And while no evidence seems to exist of any direct contact between Moskowitz and Romany Marie (though they at least knew of each other, given the fame of each of their respective institutions), both appear frequently in Bercovici's writing, including in his pioneering study of immigrant New York, *Around the World in New York*, in which he notes, "At [the Romanian restaurant] Moskowitz's you can hear Rumanian music, haunting melodies, tripping dances, while you eat the highly spiced food waiting for Mr. Volstead's[47] amendment to be forgotten."[48]

Yet the most evocative depiction of Moskowitz appears in Michael Gold's semiautobiographical novel, *Jews Without Money* (1927). Even if in part embellished, it offers a vivid account of the cultural representations at play, both of Gold's own fashioning and of the restaurant itself:

> Moscowitz[49] runs a famous restaurant now on Second Avenue. In those years he kept a wine cellar on Rivington Street. It was popular among Roumanian immigrants, including my father and his friends. Moscowitz was, and is, a remarkable performer on the Roumanian gypsy cymbalon.
>
> I remember his place. It was a long narrow basement lit by gas-lamps hanging like white balloons. Between the lamps grew clusters of artificial grapes and autumn leaves. There were many mirrors, and on them a forgotten artist had painted scenes from a Roumanian life—shepherds and sheep, a peasant, a horse fair. . . .
>
> At one end of the room, under a big American flag, hung a chromo showing Roosevelt charging up San Juan Hill. At the other end hung a Jewish Zionist flag—blue and white bars and star of David. It draped a crayon portrait of Dr. Theodor Herzl, the Zionist leader, with his pale, proud face, black beard and burning eyes. To one side was an open charcoal fire, where lamb scallops and steaks grilled on a spit. Near this, on a small platform, Moscowitz sat with his cymbalon. Strings of red peppers dried in festoons on the wall behind him. A jug of wine stood at his elbow and after every song he poured himself a drink.
>
> A cymbalon is a kind of zither-harp and is played with little ebony hammers. It is unmistakably a Gypsy instrument, for the music it gives forth is soulful and wild. As Moscowitz played, his head moved lower and lower over the cymbalon. At the crescendo one could not see his face, only his bald head gleaming like a hand-mirror. Then, with a sudden upward flourish of his arms, the music ended. One saw his shy, lean face again, with its gray mustache. Every one cheered, applauded and whistled. Moscowitz drank off his wine, and smiling shyly, played an encore.

> A hundred Jews in a basement blue as sea-fog with tobacco smoke. The men wore their derby hats. Some were bearded, some loud, sporty and young, some brown as nuts. The women were fat and sweated happily, and smacked their children. . . . The waiters buzzed like crazy bees. A jug of the good red Roumanian wine decorated the oilcloth on every table. . . . Moscowitz played a sad and beautiful peasant ballad. A little blubber-faced man with a red beard beat his glass on the table, wept and sang. Others joined him. The whole room sang.[50]

Although Gold otherwise grimly portrays life on the Lower East Side, his depiction of "Moscowitz" effuses with exoticism, melodrama, and full cups of wine and plates of food. It lacks the otherwise harsh social commentary for which Gold is usually noted. Furthermore, other texts corroborate many of the elements of Gold's visuals, with the Gypsy Jew figure of Moskowitz stoking the appetites of his audience and their nostalgic reveries.

Concomitant with this food culture, music played a central role in evoking this Romanian Gypsy Jewish hybrid culture within the collective imagination. Moskowitz was famed for his cymbalon playing, even beyond the restaurant. A *Washington Post* obituary of Moskowitz referred to him as "the dean of American cimbalon players." According to this same obituary at least Moskowitz composed "over 100 gypsy dances . . . and gave an annual recital at Town Hall of New York City."[51] Not unlike other observers, WPA researchers noted that music played a starring role in many Romanian Jewish restaurants such as Moskowitz's:

> In the evening the spirit of Roumania fills the air and the folk songs are gaily sung. Occasionally someone plays the piano in a native manner. There may also be a Roumanian musician, who sings at weddings and visits many restaurants where he plays various native melodies accompanied by a fiddler. . . . Sometimes songstresses, who also participate in card games with the customers, are employed in the restaurants. Most of the entertainment, however, is derived from the singing musicians who roam from one restaurant to the other, receiving contributions from the proprietors or the guests. Arias are mostly sung in a chorus.[52]

Depictions such as these note the Gypsy-inflected music of restaurants such as Moskowitz, most notably conjured with the cymbalon and through specific melodies about or from Romania.[53]

Through music, food, and aesthetics, Romanian restaurants such as Romany Marie and Moskowitz and Lupowitz served as what one recent study described as "deterritorialized ethnosites."[54] Novelist Richard Price described this phenomenon as a "restaurant dressed as theater dressed as nostalgia."[55] The exaggeration or even kitschiness of Gypsyness within these Romanian culinary contexts in particular shares commonalities with the history of ethnic restaurants in America, most notably, Italian, Chinese, and Greek restaurants and ethnic enclaves of early twentieth-century New York City.[56] With its semipublic air of spectacle and consumption, the restaurant or tavern served as an ideal place to display and partake in such complex self-fashioning.[57] And Romanian restaurants served as particularly apt sites for the character of the Gypsy Jew to emerge, given both the close association between Romanian and Gypsy culture and the phenomenon identified by historian Donna Gabaccia as "the symbolic power of food."[58] Their doubly strange identity, both Gypsy and Jew, reinforced the sense of intrigue and enticement for both Jewish and non-Jewish audiences alike.

Set to the evocative sound of the cymbalon and over heaping plates of steaks and soups and other Romanian Jewish foods, the character of the Gypsy Jew could be consumed in a phenomenon of adopted nostalgia, whereby "eating reduces difference [and] . . . distance . . . [and] evokes cultural and geographical appropriation."[59] Unlike Moskowitz and Romany Marie, Bercovici used his pen and his public identity as his mode of cultural transmission. Yet his personification of Gypsyness still focused in part on Romanian food and restaurant culture, particularly in New York City. Graham even describes Moskowitz approaching him at his table in the restaurant and speaking "of his friend in the writing world, Konrad Bercovici."[60] Bercovici, Romany Marie, and Moskowitz, unwittingly or not, helped to create the ethnic landscape known as Little Rumania through their performative roles as Gypsy Jews either on paper or in person. And although the contours of each of their relationships with each other remain somewhat unknown, Bercovici, Moskowitz, and Romany Marie shared at least somewhat overlapping social circles bred largely within and through Little Rumania.

This overlap likely reinforced their individual self-fashioning as Gypsy Jews, even though all three seem to have arrived at their hybrid identities independently. Although each had separately taken a leap of imagination to Gypsyhood, all seem to have perceived their adopted personas as an outgrowth of their Romanian roots and ongoing public identification with Romanian Jewish cultural life in Lower Manhattan. Bercovici, Romany Marie, and Moskowitz each arrived in the United States in their youth, their formative years mainly spent in Romania in large part among the Jewish community. We know less of Moskowitz's early Gypsy orientation, but at least in the case of Bercovici and Romany Marie, the presence of nearby Gypsy camps left an indelible mark. Nevertheless, with the exception of Bercovici's own active relationship with the Gypsy community of Lower Manhattan, no other strong social or cultural overlap between Gypsy and Romanian Jewish cultures—besides the figure of the Gypsy Jew—is evidenced at the time in Lower Manhattan, or perhaps anywhere in the United States. In fact, these three hybrid Gypsy Jews were among the most notable and visible carriers of *any* Gypsy culture in the country.

A Doubly Nomadic Hybridity: The Gypsy Jew as the Transnation

Clearly the phenomenon of self-Orientalized Gypsy Jewish performers raises a number of questions. While the identity of each seems to have hinged on a public persona, their full-body cultural assimilation of Gypsyness seems to indicate at least some—if not complete—internalization of a borrowed ethnic identity (or identities). The archetypal narrative of immigrant reinvention may in part stand at the heart of their endeavors; however, by adopting Gypsyness these individuals took on and perpetuated a rather extraordinary set of cultural products.

Above all the question remains as to why take on, particularly in the public arena of the street or print or restaurant culture, another marginalized ethnic identity, not least of which another maligned wanderer? None of the notable Gypsy Jews described here seemed to have professed any negative associations created by their self-fashioned Gypsyness. To the contrary, they embellished their difference.[61] Does this phenomenon, therefore, fit the pattern of other immigrant Jews who visibly took on the character of even more historically discriminated against minorities such as African Americans and Native Americans? By dramatizing this difference through Gypsy performance—akin to Al Jolson performing in blackface and Eddie Cantor in redface[62]—did these individuals put their Americanness in relief?

Because "discovery establishes priority," in the words of scholar and critic Michael Rogin, Gypsy Jews in part fit into the greater immigrant American narrative of "racial cross-dressing," which "promoted identification with native peoples as a step in differentiation from them."[63] In the setting of the restaurant, where "We quite literally 'eat the other,'"[64] the character of the Gypsy Jew may have helped mitigate the particular immigrant Jewish insecurity—highlighted by the added layer of the Romanian background—of not quite passing for white.[65] Following Rogin's theory, "racial masquerade pointed to white privilege," particularly through the use of music, the stage, or, in this case, the public setting of the restaurant. In other words, performing as Gypsy Jews amid rising nativist sentiment ironically helped to establish the American identity of immigrant Jews, either on stage or among those who watched it in the audience.[66]

Unlike blackface and other ethnic cross-dressing, however, the most salient aspect of the Gypsy Jew character might lie in the exotic nature of this ethnic borrowing. The popularity of Bercovici, Romany Marie, and Moskowitz as figures of cultural consumption over several decades in the early twentieth century should also be attributed to a collective fascination with other peoples as an implicit form of establishing power, a historical trend most widely characterized as Orientalism (particularly in the case of colonial power dynamics).[67] The Gypsy Jewish performances established an ethnic or racial superiority over this far-flung exoticism from another minority attempting to assert its position on the American social landscape.

Yet in addition to the American identity put into relief by the exotic Gypsy Jew cross-dressing, the particular attributes of Gypsyness added a further layer of complexity. The double identity of the itinerant Jew and the rootless Gypsy may have reinforced each other to create a powerful symbolic converse to the chaos of the warring of modern nation–states throughout the first half of the twentieth century. Amid encroaching anxieties over modernity, Gypsies may have represented—for the entertainers and, more temporarily, the entertained—a return to an indigenous, nomadic, pastoral, premodern, and in this case in particular, prenationalized imagined and nostalgicized ideal. As Svetlana Boym has written, "Modern nostalgia is a mourning for the impossibility of mythical return, for the loss of an enchanted world."[68] As "authentic" bearers of a past not divided by catastrophic world war, Gypsies—and the Jews who performed as Gypsies—might, in this performative and embodied transnational context, have served as symbolic alternatives or even talismans to the perils of urban life and nation–states divided by conflict.

In other words, much lay behind the shadows Romany Marie interpreted. The self-fashioned flair for the exotic among the Gypsy Jews profiled here— Konrad Bercovici writing Gypsy stories and traversing town and countryside in cravat and cape; Romany Marie reading fortunes while serving as genial cook, proprietress, and muse; and Joseph Moskowitz somberly playing the cymbalon to boozy, rapt audiences—uncovers a rich element of New York

City's past, a complex chapter in the history of Jewish immigration to North America and an unusual case of imagined transnationalism.

Notes

1. Konrad Bercovici, *It's the Gypsy in Me: The Autobiography of Konrad Bercovici* (New York: Prentice-Hill, 1941), 83.
2. I use the term "Gypsy" to match my historical subjects' usage, although "Roma" or "Romani" is currently preferred by most.
3. As Stansell has argued, "The bohemians were terrific self-dramatizers and self-aggrandizers, adept at creating themselves as a cast of fascinating characters: not only exuberant artists but plucky New Women, idealistic New Men, brilliant immigrant Jews, smoldering revolutionaries, and farsighted workers, all vaunting their renovations of artistic endeavor, politics, and sociability." Although Stansell focuses on Greenwich Village as the epicenter of this activity, I would extend this understanding to Little Rumania, which overlapped with the area culturally and nearly geographically. Christine Stansell, *American Moderns: Bohemian New York and the Creation of a New Century* (New York: Macmillan, 2000), 3.
4. Thomas Bender, "Preface," in *Rethinking American History in a Global Age,* by Bender (Los Angeles: University of California Press, 2002), vii.
5. Homi Bhabha, "Dissemination: Time, Narrative and the Margins of the Modern Nation," in *The Location of Culture* by Bhabha (New York: Psychology Press, 2004), 200–201. Cases of imagined transnationalism or embodied transculturalism that challenge conventional transnationalism may be found with other hybrid identity phenomena, e.g., Durán-Almarza and Emilia María, "Ciguapas in New York: Transcultural Ethnicity and Transracialization in Dominican American Performance," *Journal of American Studies* 46, no. 1 (2012): 139–53 or the imagined transnationalism of Latino/a discussed in the volume Kevin Concannon, Francisco A. Lomelí, and Marc Priewe, eds., *Imagined Transnationalism: U.S. Latino/a Literature, Culture, and Identity* (New York: Palgrave Macmillan, 2009). Rebecca Kobrin also discusses the phenomenon of fluid or even imagined immigrant identifications amid changing national borders in "The Other Polonia: Yiddish Immigrant Writers in Buenos Aires and New York Respond to the New Polish State," in *Choosing Yiddish: New Frontiers of Language and Culture*, ed. Lara Rabinovitch, Shiri Goren, and Hannah S. Pressman (Detroit: Wayne State University Press, 2012), 103–21. Finally, Tara Zahra provides an illuminating conceptualization of "national indifference" as an alternative to national identification that also challenges conventional transnational historiography: Zahra, "Imagined Non-Communities: National Indifference as a Category of Analysis," *Slavic Review* 69, no. 1 (2012): 93–119. However, while these transnational studies focus on diaspora groups that challenge traditional notions of ethnic identification or nationalism, the rootlessness of Gypsy culture and the further borrowing of identity among Gypsy Jews in particular adds another dimension of complexity to define and historicize this form of cultural identification to a non-nation through adoption.
6. Jews comprised nearly 90 percent of the émigrés leaving Romania, the highest proportion of East European countries throughout the period of mass migration 1880–1924. See Joseph Kissman, "The Immigration of Rumanian Jews up to 1914," *YIVO Annual of*

Jewish Social Science II–III (1947–1948), 176–79. See also Samuel Joseph, *Jewish Immigration to the United States from 1881–1910* (New York: Columbia University Press, 1914). Thus the area known as Little Rumania was associated with Jews from Romania primarily, although frequented by all kinds of Jews and non-Jews alike. For more on the history of this migration, see Lara Rabinovitch, "'The Gravest Question': Romanian Jewish Migration to North America, 1900–1903" (PhD diss., New York University, 2012).

7. Marcus Ravage, *An American in the Making: The Life Story of an Immigrant* (New York: Harper & Brothers, 1917), 88–89.

8. For more on this history, see David Crowe, *A History of the Gypsies of Eastern Europe and Russia* (New York: St. Martin's, 1996).

9. In his memoirs, noted doctor and public health specialist Benzion Liber, whose sister Naomi was Konrad Bercovici's wife, also notes the impression Gypsies left on him as a child throughout his discussion of his Romanian upbringing: *A Doctor's Apprenticeship* (New York: Rational Living, 1956).

10. Bercovici, *Gypsy in Me*, 5.

11. Ibid., 10.

12. Ibid., 13.

13. Ibid., 83.

14. Ibid., 94–95.

15. The American transcendental journal published between 1840 and 1929.

16. Bercovici, *Gypsy in Me*, 197.

17. Ibid., 201.

18. Ibid., 121.

19. Ibid., 157. For their relationship, see, e.g., Konrad Bercovici, "A Day with Charlie Chaplin," *Harper's Magazine*, December 1928, 42–49. In 1947 Bercovici sued Chaplin for plagiarism, citing Chaplin's film *The Great Dictator* as having originally been Bercovici's idea expressed to Chaplin while visiting him on a California sojourn. See Ryan Bernard, "*Bercovici v. Chaplin*, 1947," in *Great American Trials: From 1637–2001*, ed. Edward Knappman, Stephen Christianson, and Lisa Paddock (Detroit: Visible Ink, 2003), 428.

20. Bercovici, *Gypsy in Me*, 133. Several other sources corroborate Bercovici's Gypsyness; e.g., a 1931 article on the writer noted that he is "often categorized as a gypsy." Michael Kraike, "Unique Jewish Persons," *Canadian Jewish Chronicle*, November 27, 1931, 5.

21. Robert Schulman, *Romany Marie: The Queen of Greenwich Village* (Louisville, KY: Butler Books, 2006), 38.

22. Ibid., 96.

23. Ibid., 27.

24. Mary Perot Nichols, "La Reine Est Morte—There Is No Other," *Village Voice*, March 2, 1961, 1, 6.

25. Stephen Graham, "At Romany Marie's," in *New York Nights*, by Graham (New York: George H. Doran Company, 1927), 81.

26. Copy of 1920 flyer as reproduced in Schulman, *Romany Marie*, 96–97 (photo insert).

27. Rian James, *Dining in New York* (New York: John Day Company, 1930), 195.

28. Graham, "At Romany Marie's," 79. In a history on the explorer, Gísli Pálsson notes that Stefansson dined illicitly with his lover, novelist Fannie Hurst, at Romany Marie's and that he later met his future wife, Evelyn Schwartz Baird, at the same restaurant.

Travelling Passions: The Hidden Life of Vilhjalmur Stefansson (Lebanon, NH: University of Manitoba Press, 2003), 192, 187.

29. Graham, "At Romany Marie's," 81. See also Schulman, *Romany Marie*. O'Neill also frequented Berkowitz's Roumanian Restaurant and Joe's Roumanian Tavern, at least as indicated in Series IV, Box 7, File, 237, "Group Portrait at Table at Berkowitz's Roumanian Restaurant (New York, N.Y.) (194–)," File 238, "Group Portrait at Table at Joe's Roumanian Tavern (New York, N.Y.) (194–)," Eugene O'Neill, Jr. Collection, Beinecke Rare Book and Manuscript Library, Yale University, New Haven, CT.

30. Christine Stansell, *American Moderns: Bohemian New York and the Creation of a New Century* (New York: Macmillan, 2000), 97–98.

31. Noted widely but recounted by Romany Marie to Robert Schulman and reproduced in *Romany Marie*, 105–15.

32. Rian James, *Dining in New York* (New York: John Day Company, 1930), 195.

33. "Ben Finkle, who was for years a columnist on the *Jewish Daily Forward* under the name Marshelik, said I had a gift for creating unexpected corners for privacy, and for making the places look like some sort of Arab hangout. Arab! Ach! My cooking was continental with an emphasis on the Romanian." Recounted to Robert Schulman and reproduced in *Romany Marie*, 63.

34. Nichols, "La Reine Est Morte," 1, 6.

35. "Marie Marchand, 'Village' Figure," *New York Times,* February 23, 1961. See http://query.nytimes.com/mem/archive/pdf?res=F00812FD3F5D1B728DDDAA0A94DA405B818A F1D3, accessed March 24, 2014.

36. "Jews of New York Population Composition: Rumanian Jews of New York," WPA Federal Writers' Project, N.Y.C. Unit, "Jews of New York," Box 3, Folder 98, Municipal Archives, New York City.

37. See Moses Rischin's map in *The Promised City: New York's Jews, 1870–1914* (Cambridge, MA: Harvard University Press), 77.

38. Rischin, *Promised City,* 88, 141. Rischin also noted, "After 1907 Levantines, last on the scene and even stranger than the rest, for they were alien to Yiddish, settled between Allen and Chrystie streets among the Rumanians with whom they seemed to have the closest affinity" (Ibid., 76).

39. D. M. Hermalin, "The Roumanian Jews in America," in *American Jewish Yearbook* (Philadelphia: Jewish Publication Society, 1901), 100.

40. Konrad Bercovici, *Around the World in New York* (New York: 1924), 88.

41. Louis Anzelowitz bought the restaurant soon after though Moskowitz remained the face of the business.

42. Untitled article, WPA Federal Writers' Project, N.Y.C. Unit, "Jews of New York: Restaurants/Food" Box 8, Folder 257. Municipal Archives, New York City.

43. Advertisement in *The Butcher Worker* (May 1938). New York City: YIVO Institute for Jewish Research, RG 117, Box 20, Folder unmarked.

44. Graham, "Moskowitz," in *New York Nights* by Graham, 155.

45. "Champion Cymbalist in Playing Here Now," *New York Times,* April 26, 1908, C4.

46. See New York, NY, Tamiment Library/Robert F. Wagner Labor Archives, Elmer Holmes Bobst Library, New York University Libraries, Sam Reiss Photographs—Part I: Negatives Photos.021, Subseries O: Moskowitz and Lupowitz Restaurant, Box 5.

47. A reference to Minnesota representative Andrew Volstead, who in 1919 as chairman of the House Judiciary Committee championed a bill prohibiting the manufacture and sale of alcoholic beverages, also known as the National Prohibition Act.

48. Bercovici, *Around the World*, 88. Bercovici also describes an experience similar to the many he describes in New York when he visits Paris and on a trip back to Romania, where he writes of a hotel three hours outside of Bucharest: "I ate and ate and drank and drank. I sent wine and more wine to the Gypsy musicians and sang with them. When a newspaperman came to talk to me, I asked him to join us, called for more wine, more food, and talked and talked. When another newspaperman came to our table, I called for still more wine and more food." Bercovici, *Gypsy in Me*, 248.

49. In actuality spelled with a "k" and known as "Moskowitz and Lupowitz" by at least the mid-1920s.

50. Michael Gold, *Jews without Money*, 3rd ed. (New York: PublicAffairs, [1930] 2004), 114–16.

51. "Joseph Moskowitz, 76, Dies; Noted Player of Gypsy Music," *Washington Post Times Herald*, June 19, 1954.

52. "The New York Roumanian Restaurants: Jewish Foods and Jewish Eating Places," WPA Federal Writers' Project, N.Y.C. Unit, "Jews of New York: Restaurants/Food" Box 8, Folder 257, Municipal Archives, New York City.

53. This type of southern European Balkan music, influenced by neo-Byzantine sonic qualities and peasant folkways, played a strong role in the development of klezmer. According to one ethnomusicologist, the region was "to klezmer almost as New Orleans was to American jazz." Hankus Netsky, "American Klezmer: A Brief History," in *American Klezmer: Its Roots and Offshoots*, ed. Mark Slobin (Berkeley: University of California Press, 2002), 13. For more on the history of klezmer and its Gypsy and Moldavian roots specifically, see Walter Zev Feldman, "Music: Traditional and Instrumental Music," in *YIVO Encyclopedia of Jews in Eastern Europe*, ed. Gershon Hundert (New York: YIVO Institute for Jewish Research, 2010), accessed March 5, 2014, www.yivoencyclopedia. org/article.aspx/Music/Traditional_and_Instrumental_Music.

54. I borrow this term from Laurier Turgeon and Madeleine Pastinelli, who argue that an "ethnosite" is a restaurant "in which the foreign is made familiar and the global miniaturized. They provide the opportunity to 'taste' difference and to 'eat' exotic cultures from faraway places without leaving home." "'Eat the World': Postcolonial Encounters in Quebec City's Ethnic Restaurants," *Journal of American Folklore* 115, no. 456 (2002): 247.

55. Richard Price, *Lush Life* (New York: Picador, 2008), 19.

56. See, e.g., Andrew Coe, *Chop Suey: A Cultural History of Chinese Food in the United States* (New York: Oxford University Press, 2009); Donna Gabaccia, "Inventing 'Little Italy,'" *Journal of the Gilded Age and Progressive Era* 6, no. 1 (2007): 7–41.

57. For more on the history of restaurants and specifically the understanding that they were "publicly private" places, see Rebecca Spang, *The Invention of the Restaurant: Paris and Modern Gastronomic Culture* (Cambridge, MA: Harvard University Press, 2000), 85–86.

58. "To understand changing American identities, we must explore also the symbolic power of food to reflect cultural or social affinities in moments of change or transformation."

Donna Gabaccia, *We Are What We Eat: Ethnic Foods and the Making of Americans* (Cambridge, MA: Harvard University Press, 1998), 9.

59. Turgeon and Pastinelli, "Eat the World," 247.

60. Graham, "Moskowitz," in *New York Nights* by Graham, 157.

61. At least in the case of Bercovici one incident seems to evidence his response to anti-Semitism: "Once he attended a party in Harlem to which colored society had been invited. Most of the negroes, unaware that he was Jewish, voiced anti-Semitic feelings unrestrainedly, but he said nothing just then. However, at the close of the party, when all were asked to inscribe their autographs in a journal, he calmly traced out his name in Hebraic letters!" Michael Kraike, "Unique Jewish Persons," *Canadian Jewish Chronicle,* November 27, 1931, 5.

62. Most famously seen in *The Jazz Singer* (1927) and *Whoopee!* (1930), respectively.

63. Michael Rogin, "Making America Home: Racial Masquerade and Ethnic Assimilation in the Transition to Talking Pictures," *The Journal of American History* 79, no. 3 (1992), 1052.

64. Gabaccia, *We Are What We Eat*, 9.

65. For more on Jewish identity and race, see Eric Goldstein, *The Price of Whiteness: Jews, Race, and American Identity* (Princeton, NJ: Princeton University Press, 2006).

66. Rogin, *Making America Home*, 1052–53.

67. Many scholars have approached this field first outlined by Edward Said, *Orientalism* (New York: Vintage, 1978); however, a salient example for further reading relating to this topic in particular may be found in Micaela di Leonardo, *Exotics at Home: Anthropologies, Others, American Modernity* (Chicago: University of Chicago Press, 1998).

68. Svetlana Boym, *The Future of Nostalgia* (New York: Basic Books, 2001), 8.

8

NO AMERICAN *GOLDENE MEDINA*

Harbin Jews between Russia, China, and Israel, 1899–2014

Jonathan Goldstein

For *Kharbintsy*, as the Jews of Harbin, China, liked to call themselves, the *"goldene medina"* of the United States was not an attractive alternative. Before the Russian Revolution, these enlightened entrepreneurs, steeped in the culture of the Russian haskalah, preferred to remain in a Russified environment, albeit one with civil rights and privileges unavailable within Russia proper. America was an uncivilized wild west compared to the world of Tolstoy and Chekhov, not to mention the Volozhin Yeshiva and religious Zionism. After the Russian Revolution, the *Kharbinsty* may have considered the United States as a destination, but American immigration restrictions of 1924 made that difficult. For those who sought to leave after World War II, McCarthyite restrictions on former Russian and Soviet residents made immigration to the United States next to impossible.

The handful of *Kharbinsty* who emigrated to the United States will be discussed in this chapter. However, its primary focus will be on the majority of *Kharbinsty*, who created a unique transnational identity as an alternative to immigration to the United States. Beginning in the late nineteenth century, *Kharbinsty* developed a transnationalism that mixed national, cultural, linguistic, political, and religious elements. The two main architects of this carefully crafted alternative to immigration to the United States were Dr. Abram Kaufman (1886–1971), long-term head of the Harbin Jewish hospital and leader of the secular "Harbin Jewish Spiritual Community," and Rabbi Aharon Moshe Kisilev (1866–1949), the community's long-serving religious leader.

After World War II 1,046 *Kharbintsy*, with their distinctive identity, emigrated to Israel. They retained fond memories of Harbin in a new place of residence. They have taken on Israeli citizenship, transforming themselves from Zionists to Israelis. Nevertheless, their unique combination of Israeli identity with positive remembrance of Harbin is reaffirmed by means of return visits to China; scholarships from their Tel Aviv–based immigrant organization, or Landesmannschaft, for Chinese students to study in Israel; historical seminars organized in Harbin; genealogies, necrologies, and publications in Russian, Hebrew, and English; and the maintenance of the Harbin Jewish cemetery, the largest in East Asia. Among the best-known *Kharbintsy* to reaffirm and celebrate this combined form of national identity are members of the family of former Israeli prime minister Ehud Olmert.

The Nature and Scale of the Harbin Jewish Community

The Chinese city of Harbin is alternatively spelled "Kharbin" in romanized Russian (hence a male resident refers to himself as a *Kharbinets*, a female as a *Kharbinka*, and both use the plural term *Kharbintsy*). "Haerbin" (in romanized Chinese) is located some 300 miles inland and some 240 miles south of the Russian border. It was constructed in 1898 on the site of a small Chinese village that was the hub of a 250,000-acre territorial concession that tsarist Russia leased for eighty years from the then-imperial Chinese government. Russia, in exchange, strengthened China by means of a secret defense pact against Japan. Russia's commercial objective was to build a railway across Manchuria, one of China's agriculturally, industrially, and minerally richest regions. This "Chinese Eastern Railway," abbreviated CER in English and KVZD in Russian, was administered as an independent enterprise by a company of the same name. An additional benefit of the CER and its adjacent railway zone (*polosa otchuzhdenia* in Russian) was that it provided a shortcut linking Irkutsk and Chita on the Trans-Siberian Railway with the Russian Pacific Ocean port of Vladivostok, thereby saving hundreds of miles of travel. The Russians enlarged the village of Harbin at the point where the railroad crossed Manchuria's largest river, the Songhua (Sungari), creating a transshipment point for rail-borne and river-borne freight. In 1898 China granted Russia additional permission to build a spur line linking Harbin with the Yellow Sea ports of Dalian and Port Arthur, also known as Dairen,

Dalny, and Lushun. Unlike Vladivostok, which was ice bound for six months of the year, these warm water ports were open year round. After Japan's victory over Russia in their war of 1904–1905, the Chrysanthemum Nation took possession of the southern spur line and renamed it "The Southern Manchurian Railway."

Notwithstanding this loss to the Japanese, Harbin grew as a Russian immigrant boomtown. By 1916 it had a residential Russian population of 34,200. By 1922, because of the vicissitudes of the Russian Revolution and subsequent civil war, Harbin's Russian refugee population grew to 120,000, out of a total urban population of 485,000. Some 35,000 expatriate Russians lived elsewhere in Manchuria. Although the 120,000 figure fell to 55,000 after 1932, as thousands sought refuge from Sino–Japanese hostilities in unoccupied Peiping (Beijing), Shanghai, Tientsin (Tianjin) as well as the Soviet Union itself, Harbin remained a major center of the Russian diaspora until the early 1960s. In addition to ethnic Russians, a mosaic of other East Asian nationalities gave Harbin a cosmopolitan flavor: Chinese (300,000) predominated, followed by Koreans (34,000) and Japanese (5,000 in 1922 rising to 15,000 after 1932).[2]

Even before the Russian Revolution, Harbin had significant pockets of emigrant Russian minorities: Armenians, Baltic Germans, Estonians, Georgians, Poles, Ukrainians, Tatars, and Jews. To facilitate the migration of minority laborers and entrepreneurs to the railway zone rather than to other attractive locations such as the United States, the CER administrators and their patrons in the finance ministry in Saint Petersburg took the unusual step of granting immigrants both residential permission and economic and political freedoms that were unavailable in Russia proper, especially for Jews. Immigrants arrived from the tsarist empire on tsarist passports and regarded themselves as Russians living in the CER zone—Russia's colony in Manchuria. The fundamental rights of these settlers remained even as Bolshevik and tsarist factions battled for control of Russia proper, with the Bolsheviks ultimately victorious. Tsarist passports then became null and void, rendering most Russians in Manchuria stateless. Many stateless Russians took out travel documents issued by the Nansen Committee for International Refugees. Others used identity papers of the "Far Eastern Republic," or DVR (Russian: *Dal'nevostochnaya Respublika*), an anti-Bolshevik regime that was established in Chita, Central Siberia, in the early 1920s and was absorbed by the Soviet Union shortly thereafter. Other stateless Russians took out Soviet citizenship in order to retain their CER civil service jobs, which were restricted to Chinese or Soviet citizens. A very small number took out Chinese citizenship.

Jews lived in the railway zone throughout these turbulent decades, which included two world wars (1914–1918 and 1939–1945); two major local wars (Russo–Japanese, 1904–1905 and Sino–Japanese, 1937–1945); the Chinese Revolution of 1911, which abolished Chinese imperial rule; two local conflicts (Sino–Soviet in 1929 and Sino–Japanese beginning in 1931); and two revolutions involving civil wars (Russian, 1917–1920 and Chinese, 1946–1949). During this period Harbin was under at least six different political authorities: tsarist Russia (1898–1917); the local Chinese warlord Zhang Zuolin (Chang Tsolin, 1917–1931); Japan (via its puppet regime of Manchukuo, under the restored Manchu emperor Henry Pu-yi, 1931–1945); the Soviet Red Army (1945–1947); contending Chinese nationalist and Communist forces (1947–1949); and the People's Republic of China since 1949. Despite this potpourri of ownerships and jurisdictions, the railway zone resembled the US Panama Canal Zone in terms of its basic function and peculiar internal rights and privileges. Both territories were commercially valuable shortcuts that saved enormous amounts of travel time. And both were under the peculiar jurisdictions of their respective colonial masters. Indeed, the Harbin railway zone may have served as a model for US president Theodore Roosevelt when he established the Panama Canal Zone early in the twentieth century.[3]

Russian Jews migrated to Harbin and the railway zone primarily as entrepreneurs. Unlike their kinfolk who immigrated to the United States, *Kharbintsy* did not see themselves as refugees. They exchanged goods with Jews and non-Jews in the United States, China, Central and Western Europe, the Levant, Japan, and Korea as well as with Mongols, native Siberian peoples, and other ethnic minorities. Under these fortuitous conditions the Jewish community grew from zero in 1898 to the first settler in 1899 to about 5,000 in 1919 (the time of the Olmert family's arrival) to a high point of perhaps 13,000 in 1931. By 1935, Harbin's Jewish community had declined to about 5,000. By 1982, in the wake of the Chinese Communist Revolution of 1949, the Jewish community had diminished to one elderly resident.[4]

Over and beyond economic opportunity, the civil rights available in Harbin enabled Jews to develop a cultural profile and transnational identity virtually nonexistent in imperial or Soviet Russia itself. Some Jewish émigrés to Harbin had the good fortune to have been among the small number of Russian Jews accepted into the colleges, universities, academies, and technical training schools of Russia proper. Russian policy shifted over time with respect to academic admissions, but for much of Russia's history, Jews were excluded from the country's institutions of higher education. In a rare example of Jewish matriculation from an Imperial Russian university, Raissa Menkes, mother of University of Southern California East Asianist Peter Berton, studied engineering at the Women's Higher Polytechnic in Saint Petersburg for two years. Far more common was the case of Russian-born Dr. Abram Kaufman, head of the Harbin Jewish hospital, and his first wife, both of whom had to travel to Switzerland to study medicine. This career pattern was also forced upon Chaim Weizmann, Selig Brodetsky, Alexander Gurvich, and many other Jews in Russia who were victimized by a repressive and restrictive quota system.

Still other *Kharbintsy* acquired a Western-style education in Harbin itself, where an enlightened railroad administration permitted elementary, high, and technical schools to be open to Jews. These institutions included the Russian language Commercial School (Kommercheskoe Uchilishche) and Oriental Institute (Orientalni Institut). Future Israeli Radio and *Haaretz* newspaper correspondent Moshe Medzinsky (1897–1983) studied for four years at the Commercial School. Gregory Grossman and his cousin Misha studied at Harbin's German secondary school, the Hindenburgschule. They were thrown out when Hitler came to power. Hebrew University's chief engineer Evsey Podolsky and Israel Railways acting general manager Leonfreid "Freddy" Heymann matriculated at Harbin Polytechnic Institute (Kharbinskyi Politekhnicheskii Institut), today's Harbin Institute of Technology. Harbin thus became one of the few places in the world where a significant number of Jews studied railroading along with many other technical subjects. Finally, the railway administration placed no obstacle in the way of Jews emigrating abroad for higher education, an activity that was difficult in Imperial Russia and next to impossible in the Soviet Union. Thus Harbin-born Nuissa Hanin, née Madorsky, matriculated in chemistry and pharmacy at the University of Bologna in 1938 and then returned to China (Tianjin).

Both Russian- and foreign-educated Jews brought their advanced training skills to Manchuria. Still other *Kharbintsy* received their university educations abroad and then made distinguished careers in the United States and elsewhere. Among the Harbin Jews whose skills ultimately benefited other societies were the civil engineer and earthquake specialist Boris Bresler and the aforementioned economist Gregory Grossman, both of whom were among the lucky few who were able to enter the United States. Both matriculated and later taught at the University of California at Berkeley. Harbin-born Evsei Domar was also fortunate enough to be admitted to the United States, where he became a world-renowned economist at the Massachusetts

Institute of Technology. *Kharbinets* Hayyim Tadmor, an Assyriologist, rose to become vice-president of the Israel Academy of Sciences and Humanities.[5]

For those Jews who chose to remain in or return to Harbin, the constant inflow and outflow of intellectuals created an environment with a broad range of political, economic, and religious thought. The railway zone served as a pressure release valve on the intellectual cauldron that was Russia proper, both imperial and Soviet. Significantly, Harbin had a minority of Karaites, who were not formally recognized as Jews in Israel until the mid–twentieth century. Among the best-known Karaites were the tobacco merchants Eli Aaronovitch (1874–1936) and Abraham Aaronovitch (1877–1953) Lopato, who were originally from Trakai (Troki), Lithuania. There were forty-one Karaite graves in Harbin's Foreign Catholic Union Cemetery before its demolition in the 1950s. Harbin's long-serving rabbi Aharon Moshe Kisilev embraced pre-Herzlian Zionism while a student at Rabbi Shmuel Mohilever's Volozhin Yeshiva. Kisilev's fellow students included the future Hebrew linguist Eliezer ben Yehuda, national poet Hayyim Nachman Bialik, and Ashkenazi Chief Rabbi of Palestine Avraham Yitzhak Kook ("Rav Kook"). In Harbin, Kisilev published Russian and Hebrew language tracts, which affirmed the compatibility of traditional Judaism with religious and ultimately General Zionism. Kisilev's innovative writings have been reprinted in the United States and incorporated into the curricula of many modern American Orthodox/Zionist yeshivot, or Jewish rabbinical seminaries.

Under Rabbi Kisilev's influence from 1913 to 1949, as well as that of Dr. Kaufman, *Kharbintsy* became overwhelmingly Zionistic, with most of the older generation embracing Theodor Herzl's (1860–1904) General Zionism. In the beginning, the rabbi and his allies had an uphill fight. Some *Kharbintsy* favored the moderate socialist, anti-Zionist politics of *Der Algemeyner Yidisher arbeter Bund in Lite, Poyln, un Rusland* (Yiddish: The General Union of Jewish Workers in Lithuania, Poland, and Russia, usually referred to as "the Bund"). Lazar Epstein (1886–1979), a leader of that group in Russian Poland, Kobe, Harbin, and later Tianjin, challenged General Zionism, as did the ultrareligious Agudat Israel. The Bundist-oriented, anti-Zionist Yiddish language newspaper *Der Vayter Mizrekh* (the Far East), edited by Meir Birman, competed with the Russian language General Zionist publication *Evreiskaia Zhizn'* (Jewish Life). There was also a clandestine, anti-Bundist and anti-Zionist Communist Party in which a few Jews were active. Arguably the most famous Third International Communist in Harbin was Lazar Epstein's son Israel, who also briefly immigrated to the United States but later returned to the People's Republic of China to become a

Maoist, distinguished journalist, and member of the National People's Consultative Congress, one of the highest honors a Chinese citizen can receive.[6]

Perhaps most significant for this book's focus on transnational identity, Harbin was the East Asian entry point for Vladimir Zev Jabotinsky's militant Zionist Revisionist movement Brit Trumpeldor (abbreviated as "Betar"), which counted among its adherents future Israeli Herut party leaders Judith Hasser, Eliyahu Lankin, Yana Liberman, and Mordechai (also called "Motti" or "Motya") Olmert, father of future Israeli Likud prime minister Ehud Olmert. From 1932 to 1942 Harbin Betar published its Russian language journal *Gadegel* (The Flag, referring to the blue and white Zionist flag). *Gadegel* challenged but never overtook the much larger circulation of its General Zionist rival *Evreiskaia Zhizn*. When Harbin Jews ultimately migrated en masse to Israel in 1949, it was Yana Liberman of Betar who organized this seaborne exodus. Harbin's two major Jewish sports organizations also reflected Zionist ideological rivalry: Betar for the Revisionists versus Maccabi for the General Zionists. Despite its breakaway status from mainstream Zionism, Betar would cooperate with other Jewish organizations at times of natural disaster, such as when flood waters breached the banks of the Sungari River. Betar also buried its ideological differences with other Jewish movements when it came to combating the virulent anti-Semitism present in Harbin's White Russian community, which also thrived in this relatively unrestricted political environment. Harbin Betar prided itself on its activism and energy. Israeli journalist and lexicographer Emmanuel Pratt, one of its earliest members, maintained unabashedly in 1988 that "until today, Chinese Betarim in Israel are considered the elite of the pure Betar movement"[7] (See Figure 8.1.)

An external witness to Harbin's vibrant transnational identity was the British Zionist fundraiser Israel Cohen. In his report about a 1920–1921 visit, Cohen compared the Manchurian city to Singapore and Manila, whose intellectuality he found utterly blasé. Harbin, on the other hand, manifested a

> vigorous Jewish consciousness ... [in] a struggle of parties, in which the Right, Centre, Left, and Extreme Left were always engaged. There were ceaseless public discussions, especially on Saturday night, between the rival adherents of Zionism pure and simple, Zionism without Orthodoxy, Orthodoxy without Zionism, Zionism with Socialism, Socialism without Zionism, Hebraism in Manchuria, and Yiddishism in Palestine.... I soon realized that there were ... hundreds of Jews in Harbin who were eager to go to Palestine.... There was no need for me to gain

FIGURE 8.1. The ship *Wooster Victory* with Jews from China en route to Israel, Cape Town harbor, January 16, 1949. Yana Liberman of Betar organized this exodus. John H. Marsh Collection, copyright Iziko Museums of South Africa.

converts: my task was confined to spreading information and obtaining donations from a relatively small group.[8]

The Olmert Family as a Case Study of Transnational Jewish Identity in Harbin

Prior to World War II a lucky few of the Harbin Jews immigrated to the United States. This was always a very limited immigration. A handful of *Kharbinsty* also managed to get into British-Mandate Palestine. Still others emigrated to Argentina, Australia, Brazil, Canada, Great Britain, Hong Kong, Japan, and the Soviet Union. In all these cases *Kharbintsy* became citizens of their new places of residence. Perhaps the best-known example of the transnational identity of emigrant *Kharbintsy* is the family of former Israeli prime minister Ehud Olmert. The evolution of the Olmert family's identity can be traced using the four-stage paradigm that historians Tony Kushner, Sarah Pearce, and Milton Shain have invoked for explaining the development of national identity in many parts of the world. Their scheme focuses first on "leavings," or what motivated Jews to abandon their ancestral homelands; second, "passages," or how the vicissitudes of travel to relatively unknown destinations shaped Jewish consciousness, thought, and behavior; third, "identity," the new cultural and intellectual characteristics that Jews adopted at their new destinations; and fourth, "return," or how Jews, in their new homelands, remembered and utilized ties to their ancestral homelands and assumed a form of transnational rather than purely national identity. I use this four-part analytical framework to explain the forging of the transnational identity of one Israeli family with strong Harbin roots.[9]

[1] "Leavings"

In 1919 Ehud Olmert's grandfather Iosif Mosifovitch was a middle-class merchant in the Russian Volga River port of Samara, a city that came to be known as "Kuybyshev" in the Soviet period. Iosif Olmert fled from one part of Russia to another to escape uncertainty and economic hardship. By word of mouth and from published reports, Iosif learned that in Harbin Jewish and non-Jewish Russians enjoyed an array of economic, political, and cultural freedoms unavailable in Russia proper. That year Iosif made the momentous decision to move himself, his wife, and children away from the chaos gripping their ancestral homeland. Despite the optimistic predictions of leaders of the emerging Soviet Union, for many Jews 1919 was a time of political uncertainty, social upheaval, famine, and virulent anti-Semitic pogroms that were byproducts of a fierce civil war raging between Red and White Russian factions. Unlike other Russian Jews who made their way to the United States, Iosif, in Samara, had little chance of escaping westward. Furthermore, he and his family had a strong devotion toward things Russian, an identity he feared would be lost in the American melting pot. Iosif therefore turned eastward, traveling across Russian-built railroads and jurisdictions that were precariously switching hands on a daily basis. Despite these upheavals in 1919, Iosif persevered, as he and his family still considered their nationality to be Russian. What must have become increasingly problematic for them was to which of several battling Russian factions did this family owe its allegiance?[10]

[2] "Passages"

The "push" of Samara and the "pull" of Harbin brought the Olmerts east. The sheer chaos and vicissitudes of travel from one place to another in turbulent postrevolutionary Russia helped crystalize the national and political ideas not only of Iosif and his wife, who became devoutly anti-Bolshevik, but also of Iosif's young son Motti, who had been born in Samara in January or May 1911. Motti was eight years old when his father made the momentous decision to relocate the family. By 1919 Iosif had reached Harbin but left his wife Michal and their children in Irkutsk, just north of the Chinese border. That year Iosif wrote his wife, urging her to take the children and head southeast to Harbin. In his autobiography Motti explains how this railroad trip contributed to his embryonic Zionist Jewish identity. He records,

> My mother immediately began preparations [for the trip—ed.] because many dangers were involved. Between Irkutsk and the Chinese border the Ataman Semyonov took over and they hated the Jews. [Here Motti is referring to the Japanese-backed White Russian warlord Ataman Grigorii Mikailovich Semyonov (1890–1946), commander of the Transbaikalian Cossacks. Jews also feared Siberian Ataman Ivan Pavlovich Kalmykov (1890–1926). In Urga (today's Ulan Bator, Mongolia) Jews of a small merchant community were murdered on sight or after torture by the White Russian troops of Freiherr Roman Nikolai Maximilian von Ungern-Sternberg (1885–1921), whom Semyonov had appointed as governor of the large area to the east and southeast of Lake Baikal known as Dauria. Sternberg displayed extreme cruelty to his own subordinates, thereby earning the nickname "Bloody Baron." He was also known as the "Mad Baron" because of his erratic behavior. The vicious anti-Semitism which Jews experienced as they crossed Siberia also thrived in White Russian enclaves throughout Manchuria and north China. It was particularly virulent among tens of thousands of White Russian émigrés in Harbin.—ed.] My mother warned us and stressed that we hide our national identity. In those days, because of my mother's warning, I was beginning to question what it meant to be Jewish. The question of identity is associated with other issues I found out about in Irkutsk from the Jews who were there. They were talking about a Jewish country of our own—Eretz Israel—where they were about to go. Those things were absorbed in my mind although I did not understand them and they were kept deep in my memory.[11]

[3] Forging "Identity" within a New Geographical Context

Amid this uncertainty and chaos, twenty hours after leaving Irkutsk Michal Olmert and her children reached Harbin and reunited with Iosif. Both anti-Bolshevik parents resumed their traditional lifestyles as shopkeepers. This was not the case for the younger generation, particularly Motti. Here he underwent an ideological epiphany.

By the time of the Olmerts' arrival in Harbin, Jewish identity had already been defined as a mixture of nationalism, culture, language, politics, and religion. Both Motti and his future wife Bella Vugman matriculated at Harbin's Russian-language Commercial School. Motti also studied Chinese at the Oriental Institute. According to Teddy Kaufman, who was slightly younger, Motti knew Chinese well enough to teach Russian to Chinese students in Chinese. It was in this Russified Sino-Judaic context that Motti's intellectual and political identity further evolved.[12]

Prior to the Olmerts' arrival, and under the influence of Rabbi Kisilev and Dr. Kaufman, the older generation within the Harbin Jewish community had overwhelmingly committed to General Zionism. By the mid-1920s many members of the younger generation, under the influence of the Bolshevik Revolution, tended to sympathize with the left wing of the Zionist movement. By 1928, both Motti Olmert and Bella Vugman leaned toward the leftist but anti-Soviet Zionist youth movement: Hashomer Hatzair. They had been influenced by Russian refugees David Laskov and his wife Zippora, who had already had a taste of Siberia. The Laskovs had been exiled by order of the Soviet government and, at great peril, crossed the Soviet–Chinese border. The Laskovs suggested to the older Jewish youth in Harbin that they join Hashomer Hatzair. A letter was sent westward to Hashomer headquarters, requesting formal recognition of a Harbin chapter. Even before a response was received back, the leftist Harbin Jewish youth began meeting under the banner of Hashomer Hatzair.

At that crucial moment, while communications were being exchanged across the Chinese Eastern and Trans-Siberian railroads, a politically astute businessman, Alexander Gurvich, arrived from Palestine. Gurvich had been born in Minsk in 1899 to a middle-class family that was very much part of the Russian haskalah, or Jewish Enlightenment. He attended high school in Saint Petersburg and, like other adherents of the Russian haskalah, was obliged by the Russian quota system to seek higher education in the west. In 1925 Gurvich matriculated in politics and economics at the University of Hamburg. There he embraced the right-wing ideology of Vladimir Zev Jabotinsky's Betar movement, the ideological precursor of Israeli political parties from Herut to Likud. Upon graduation from Hamburg, Gurvich immigrated to Palestine. According to Motti,

> Gurvich was our teacher. He came to us at a time of crisis in Zionist ideals, when many left Eretz Israel and returned to Europe. In those dark and overcast days, he acquainted us with Jabotinsky's theories

[which—ed.] meant the obligation first of all of moving to Eretz Israel. Gurvich had not only made aliyah [immigration to the Land of Israel—ed.] but was a *chalutz,* a pioneer, in the full sense of the word. He established factories, made employment for others, and went about developing trade and industry as well as the agricultural sector.[13]

Gurvich met regularly with the young Zionists in Harbin. According to Motti, "He tried to prove to the youth that joining Hashomer Hatzair had been a mistake . . . for based on their beliefs, they were closer to Betar than to Hashomer Hatzair. Within a short time, the older youth came to the conclusion that they belonged to the National Camp of Jabotinsky. They sent a letter to Betar headquarters in Riga which approved their joining." A minority of the Harbin Hashomer Hatzair refused to go along with the switch to Betar and instead joined the Communist Party youth movement Komsomol. That tiny faction migrated to Birobidjan in the Soviet Union and was never heard from again.[14]

Gurvich remained in Harbin until 1939. In 1930, under his influence, Motti left China for agricultural training in Holland preparatory for immigration to Palestine. His wife-to-be Bella Vugman left Harbin directly for Palestine on a phony marriage certificate to fellow Betarnik Eliayhu Lankin, who was already an official Palestinian resident. When Motti ultimately reached Palestine in 1933, the phony marriage to Lankin was dissolved, Motti married Bella, and they settled near Binyamina. They threw themselves into Revisionist politics and had four sons: Amram (Ami) in 1936, Yirmiyahu (Irmi) in 1943, Ehud (Udi) in 1945, and Yosef (Yossi) in 1950. Yossi was named for his grandfather Iosif who was buried in Harbin in 1941.

By 1930, the question of national identity was fixed in the minds of Motti Olmert and Bella Vugman. They would become Israelis, although at that time they held a variety of British-Palestinian and other identity documents, which they considered temporarily necessary but ultimately worthless. Aspects of their Chinese sojourn, on the other hand, would linger in their consciousnesses, transforming their Israeli national identity into something more, a mild form of transnational identity. It should be emphasized that even in this early stage in their ideological evolution immigration to the "*goldene medina*" of the United States was not even under consideration.[15]

[4] Return to and Memorialization of the Chinese Homeland

According to Kushner, Pearce, and Shain, a fourth stage in the formation of transnational identity involves memorialization of and even a return trip to one's ancestral homeland. This became a characteristic of many *Kharbinsty*, Jews and non-Jews alike. In Australia, in a democratized Russia, and many other locations of the far-flung Harbin diaspora, publications and networks of associations sprung up for non-Jewish former residents. Jewish and non-Jewish Australian alumni of Harbin's Polytechnic Institute meet regularly. They have published a newsletter for over thirty years. According to Australian former Harbin resident Mara Moustafine,

> Other publications have emerged, including *Russian Harbintsy* [sic] *in Australia*. Following the collapse of the Soviet Union, active Harbin associations sprang up quickly in a number of Russian cities, suggesting that informal networks existed long before. Now, periodicals with names like *In the Hills of Manchuria, Russians in China,* and *Harbin,* have a substantial following among *Harbintsy* [sic] around the world. Their pages are laden with histories of Russian institutions and life in China, personal reminiscences, searches for erstwhile friends, necrologies, and nostalgia.[16]

With respect specifically to Harbin's Jews, it was in Harbin where Motti Olmert and Bella Vugman assumed a Zionist national identity, a commitment to leave China for Palestine, and a determination to become Israeli. They nevertheless maintained their China ties and warm remembrances. Unlike some European Jews who retain only negative feelings toward their ancestral homelands, including many members of this author's family toward Poland, Amram fondly recalls chinoiserie, or artifacts manufactured in the West but in a Chinese style, prominently displayed in the Olmert house in Nahalat Jabotinsky, near Binyamina. Ehud maintains, "China is the country which hosted our parents. They studied in China. They spoke Chinese, and . . . Chinese culture is part of my heritage and memory as a young kid in the State of Israel. So China is not just another country for me."[17]

Perhaps the fullest expression of that remembrance and its central role in transnational identity has been the return visits to China by members of the Olmert family. These trips began in the 1940s and are ongoing as of 2014. The first member of the Olmert family to revisit was Motti in 1947. He wished to visit his mother Michal, who was still in China, and to assist her exodus to Eretz Israel. His second motive was subversive. He was traveling on behalf of the Irgun, the Jabontinsky-oriented underground movement in Palestine. Motti was under the direct orders of Irgun commander Menachem

Begin (1913–1992) and in communication with his old Betar guru Alexander Gurvich. Gurvich was at that time operating out of the United States as a vital agent in the worldwide Betar underground network. Motti's assignment was to raise funds for the arms ship christened *Altalena,* after Jabotinsky's pen name. *Altalena* was bringing weapons to the Irgun in Palestine to force the British out. In Shanghai and Tianjin Motti collected about $100,000, a considerable amount of money in 1947. This sum was about 40 percent of the cost of purchasing and supplying the vessel. In June 1948, *Altalena,* with several hundred Irgun fighters aboard, reached the shores of Palestine, albeit weeks after the departure of the British. Israeli prime minister and defense minister David Ben-Gurion was determined to bring all militias under the direct command of the Israel Defense Forces (ZAHAL). Despite Motti's best efforts, and under direct orders from Ben-Gurion, *Altalena* was sunk off the Tel Aviv beachfront after a pitched battle between Revisionists and units of ZAHAL. The official ZAHAL assault team was under the command of a young officer named Yitzhak Rabin, the future prime minister of Israel.[18]

The second family member to reestablish Chinese ties was Yossi. Because of Mao and Communism, return trips to China were next to impossible for Israeli passport holders between 1950 and the late 1980s. In the national election of 1977, the ideological heirs of Jabotinsky came to power in Israel, ushering in Menachem Begin as prime minister. At that same time China was opening to the West under the pragmatic leadership of Deng Xiaoping. In 1989 Yossi, as a representative of Prime Minister Yitzkak Shamir's successor Likud government, met in Israel with Chinese pilots, including the chief test pilot of the Chinese Air Force. This was a time when Israel was establishing its first military and diplomatic contacts with China. In 1991, again at the directive of the prime minister's office, Yossi helped China set up a Tel Aviv office for its official press agency, Xinhua. That office, and a branch of China's official state travel service, Luxingshe, performed intermediary duties until the establishment of formal diplomatic missions in January 1992. In June 1992, after Likud lost the national elections to Yitzhak Rabin's Labor Party, Yossi went to China on a private visit. There, he became the first family member to actually revisit Harbin.

The third family member to reestablish Chinese ties was Amram. He was a professional agronomist who had maintained the family farm near Binyamina even as a teenager when his father returned to China to raise funds for *Altalena.* In 1998 Amram, in his capacity as chief executive officer of Agridev-Agricultural Development Company, visited China at the invitation of the Chinese government. While there he learned that the grave of his grandfather

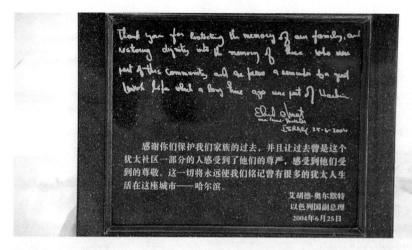

FIGURE 8.2. Inscriptions on obelisk at entryway to Harbin's Huangshan Jewish cemetery. The inscription reads, "Thank you for protecting the memory of our family, and restoring dignity into the memory of those who were part of this community and are a respect to a great Jewish life which a long time ago were part of Harbin. Ehud Olmert, vice–prime minister Israel 25-6-2004." The Chinese inscription says the same. Courtesy of Jonathan Goldstein.

Iosif was in dilapidated condition in Harbin's Huangshan Jewish cemetery, which, with over 700 graves, remains in 2014 the largest Jewish cemetery in East Asia. Amram returned to Israel and encouraged his brothers to help restore their grandfather's tombstone, the graves of some other relatives, and the graves of the grandparents of (Ret.) Israeli Brigadier General and right-wing parliamentarian Efraim "Effi" Eitam (Fine).

In 1998, Amram was appointed agricultural attache in Israel's Beijing Embassy. In that capacity he laid the groundwork for future appointments as professor of agronomy at Beijing's China Agricultural University and at Qingdao's Laiyang Agricultural University. He also helped Israel establish in China a dry lands research station, a project of the Ministry of Foreign Affairs' Foreign Assistance Program (MASHAV, headed at that time by Benjamin Abileah).[19]

When Ariel Sharon's Likud party returned to power in the national elections of 2001, Ehud became the fourth member of the family to renew ties with China. By 2004 Ehud had already served eleven years as the Likud mayor of Jerusalem and was a vice–prime minister in Sharon's national government. Ehud visited China in that capacity. Under Ehud and Amram's supervision the family purchased two new monuments for the Harbin Jewish cemetery and inaugurated the process for the cemetery's total rehabilitation. One monument is their grandfather's reengraved tombstone. The second is a triumphal obelisk at the entryway to the cemetery (Figure 8.2). It bears the following verbose but heartfelt inscription in Chinese and English: "Thank you for protecting the memory of our family, and restoring dignity into the memory of those who were part of this community and are a respect to a great Jewish life which a long time ago were part of Harbin. Ehud Olmert, vice–prime minister of Israel 25-6-2004."[20]

Another way in which the Olmerts have preserved the memory of their Chinese experience and made that remembrance part of their transnational identity is by participating in a series of historical seminars about the Jews of Harbin. These symposia have brought Israel-based *Kharbinsty* together with their worldwide brethren, especially the handful of their kinfolk who were lucky enough to escape to Australia, the United Kingdom, and the United States. Unlike the thriving Landesmannschaft of the Harbin Jews in Israel, the always-miniscule American branches, in San Francisco, Los Angeles, and New York, no longer meet on a regular basis and effectively have ceased to exist. The two all-inclusive Harbin symposia were cosponsored by the Communist Party of Harbin's Daoli (formerly Pristan) district, Israel's Beijing Embassy, and the Tel Aviv–based Israel-China Friendship Society and Igud Yotsei Sin (Society of Former Jewish Residents of China), headed by Dr. Kaufman's son Teddy. The first seminar, in which this author took part, was held from August 29 to September 2, 2004.[21] The second, in which Amram Olmert and his wife Regina participated, was held in June 2006. By that time Ehud Olmert had become prime minister of the State of Israel. In that capacity Ehud gave videotaped greetings in English to the gathering. Amram Olmert and Teddy Kaufman recited the Jewish prayer for the dead at the grave of Iosif Olmert in a ceremony covered by television, radio, and print media from Harbin, Beijing, and Shanghai.[22]

On January 8, 2007, Prime Minister Ehud Olmert visited China once again. His task this time was not to memorialize Harbin but to discuss the existential threat that Iran poses to Israel.[23] In a broader sense Prime Minister Olmert was rekindling his family ties to China, which were established during his father's perilous train journey from Irkutsk to Harbin eighty-eight years previously. That train trip into China initiated the rich, fluid, and complex process of the formation of the transnational identity of the Olmert family.

Conclusion: Harbin Jews' Transnational Identity

The city of Harbin meant different things to different people. For the Olmerts, the experience of living among Chinese was far greater than for some other Jews, who existed within a European bubble within China. Such isolation did not, of course, spare them life-threatening encounters with expatriate White

Russians, a trauma that became a motivating factor in the community's veer toward Zionism and ultimate immigration to Israel. On the subject of Jews' contacts with "Chinese" rather than "Russian" Harbin, the late University of Southern California *Kharbinets* Peter Berton, fondly known as "Zaika" (little rabbit) within the *Kharbintsy* community because of the large ears he had as a child, comments,

> Every Jewish family's experience was not like that of Motti [Motya] Olmert. The Olmerts were almost a unique case. You talk to me, Fred (Heymann), Teddy (Kaufman), Yossi Klein, and all I can think of, except Podolsky, none of us spoke any[thing] but street pidgin Chinese or had any Chinese friends. I had one Chinese friend. Most didn't at all. . . . Having Chinese trinkets does not make any of the Harbin Jews know anything about Chinese history or culture. I think that things may have been different in Tientsin or Shanghai. Otto Schnepp learned Shanghai dialect because the refugees lived in Hongkew among Chinese, and not in the International or French settlements. So I think you should make the case [for] nostalgia for Harbin as a foreign city and not as a Chinese city, because it was not. The neighboring Fujiajian was, and we very seldom or even rarely or never visited it. I can't remember going there. That was China in the 1930s to 40s, not Pristan [Daoli.], Novyi Gorod, Modyagou, or Nakhalovka where Jews or Russians or Poles, Germans, Tatars or Americans/British lived. [Only] the very rich Chinese lived amongst the foreigners.[24]

Isaac Shapiro, who lived in Harbin for five years, adds, "By choice, most Harbin Jews, who never encountered persecution or discrimination, lived through the twentieth century neither integrating nor assimilating with the broader Chinese community."[25]

Or were the Olmerts so unique? Whether they lived in splendid isolation or in close proximity to the native Chinese population, many *Kharbintsy* in addition to the Olmerts treasure memories of their former residence. Australian Mara Moustafine writes,

> For *Harbintsy* [sic], there was no single identity, but rather a range whose parameters included religion, tradition, political orientation, and accident. While living in China, the factor that united them all was their origins in the Russian empire. In emigration, the reverse proved to be true. However removed they may have been from the reality of

the China around them, for most *Harbintsy* their life in China became the defining element of their Russian identity. When I told a Chinese journalist that I considered Harbin my "homeland," my identification was not with some "lost world" of Russia, but with the multiethnic and pluralist mix of "Russian Harbin." What other place could have produced a child with direct roots to Byelorussian Jews, Tatar Muslims, and Orthodox Russians, and whose forbears also straddled both sides of the Soviet/White émigré political divide?[26]

The presence in Israel of transnational personalities with multicultural awareness and critical linguistic skills has helped the state create and solidify ties with contemporary China. This has become increasingly important for Israel, as the Middle Kingdom has become the world's second largest economy and a military powerhouse. The Harbin municipality has refurbished the city's New Synagogue and installed a Jewish history museum. It contains exhibits on three Jewish personalities with international stature: Albert Einstein, who visited China in the 1920s on a fundraising mission for the fledgling Hebrew University of Jerusalem, to which he donated his entire personal archive; Harbin's own Israel Epstein (see above); and Jacob Rosenfeld, a Jewish physician who served with Mao Zedong's Eight Route Army, moved to Israel, and is buried in Tel Aviv. Chinese ambassadors to Israel routinely visit Rosenfeld's grave.[27] In 2004, in yet another expression of the ties that bind former Harbin Jews to their ancestral homeland, Teddy Kaufman, president of both the Society of Former Jewish Residents of China and the Israel–China Friendship Society, published his Hebrew language memoir *Yahadut Harbin Asher B'Levi.* The book appeared in English two years later under the lachrymose title *The Jews of Harbin Live On in My Heart.*[28] In 2005 Teddy Kaufman and Heilongjiang Academy of Social Sciences professor Qu Wei published an anthology of papers from their 2004 joint conference titled, again emotionally, *The Homesick Feeling of Harbin Jews.*[29] In a modern Jewish history replete with instances of butchering, pogroms, and the Holocaust, expatriate *Kharbintsy* consciously and continuously reinforce their positive ties to their mother city. They are thereby able to sustain their distinct transnational identity as *Kharbintsy* who are also citizens of a reborn State of Israel.

Notes

1. Abram Kaufman's Kh.E.D.O. (Russian: *Kharbinskaia evreiskaia dukhovnaia obschina*) was sometimes also referred to as *Evreiskaia dukovnaia obschina Kharbina. Obschina* was not a civil or secular organization but more like a religious parish. It was formed in 1903 as the "Harbin Jewish Spiritual Committee" and kept birth, marriage, and death

records. The official stamp of the Jewish community used the Hebrew name at the center *Ha-vaad shel ha-kehillah ha-ivrit b'Kharbin* with Chinese translation above and Russian translation in smaller letters below.

For a running history of *Kharbintsy's* affirmations of mixed Russian, Chinese, and Jewish identity, see issues of the Igud Yotsei Sin *Bulletin*, published in Tel Aviv in Russian, Hebrew, and English since the 1950s, especially vol. 56, no. 399 (August–September 2009), 1–67, and Teddy [Theodore] Kaufman, *Yahadut Harbin Asher B'Levi* (Tel Aviv: Igud Yotzei Sin, 2004), translated as *The Jews of Harbin Live On in My Heart* (Tel Aviv: Association of Former Jewish Residents of China in Israel, 2006). See also *Israel–China Voice of Friendship*, the quarterly organ of the Igud's subsidiary, the Tel Aviv–based Israel–China Friendship Association, and Mara Moustafine's "The Harbin Connection: Russians from China," in *Beyond China: Migrating Identities*, ed. Shen Yuanfang and Penny Edwards (Canberra, Australia: Centre for the Study of the Southern Chinese Diaspora, Australian National University, 2002), 75–87. The Igud has included in its frequent celebrations such German immigrants as Max Weissler, whose family passed through Harbin en route from Berlin to Manila. The Igud also includes former Jewish residents of China with no Harbin association. A special section of the Igud *Bulletin* is devoted to news about Shanghai in general and that city's Baghdadi Jewish population in particular. Of total immigration from China to Israel between December 24, 1948, and September 1, 1951, of 5,277, *Kharbintsy* numbered 1,046, second only to Shanghai's 3,564.

For research assistance with this chapter, the author would like to thank first and foremost former Israeli prime minister Ehud Olmert, who read this full text in draft form and provided helpful corrections to it on February 15, 2007. For additional help the author would like to thank the former prime minister's foreign media advisor Miri Eisen and professors Dan Ben-Canaan of Heilongjiang University; Stephen Levine of the University of Montana; Irene Eber, Meron Medzini, Yitzhak Shichor, and Ben-ami Shillony of the Hebrew University of Jerusalem; Henrietta Mondry of the University of Canterbury, New Zealand; Suzanne Rutland of the University of Sydney; librarians Amira Stern of the Jabotinsky Institute, Tel Aviv; Rochelle Rubinstein of the Central Zionist Archives, Jerusalem; and Professor Emeritus William Small, librarian Mel Johnson, and computer technician Andrei Strukov, all of the University of Maine. The author greatly appreciates the assistance, hospitality, and friendship of the following interviewees: the late Peter Berton, Harbin, August 2004; the late Boris Bresler, Cambridge, Massachusetts, August 1992 and Tel Aviv, June 28, 1995; the late Leonfried Heymann, Harbin, August 2004 and Haifa, Israel, January 4, 2007; the late Harry Hurwitz, Jerusalem, December 25, 2005; the late Theodore Kaufman, Harbin, August 2004, and Tel Aviv, January 2, 2007 and December 27, 2011; Yaacov Liberman, Harbin, August 2004 and San Diego, California, December 15, 2006 and March 22, 2013; Amram Olmert, Tel Aviv, January 1, 2007; Yossi Olmert, via telephone from New York, December 10, 2006; and Teddy Piatsunovitch, Harbin August 31, 2004; Herzliya, Israel, January 1, 2007; and London, England, November 5, 2103. The University of West Georgia's Dean Randy Hendricks very generously provided the financial assistance and professional leave time at the Academia Sinica, Taipei, which made the research and writing of this chapter possible.

2. John Stephan, *The Russian Fascists* (New York: Harper & Row, 1978), 37–40.

3. In the mid-1920s Manchuria, referred to as Dongbei in Chinese, was the "property" of the local Chinese warlord Zhang Zuolin, whom the Japanese assassinated in 1928. In

1929 there was a skirmish between Chinese and Soviet forces near the border town of Manzhouli. Japan became a significant actor in Northern Manchuria after 1931. The Soviet Union sold the railway zone to Japan in March 1935. The vagaries of the Japanese occupation and Sino–Japanese hostilities, which had erupted four years earlier, prompted some additional 30,000 Russian families to return to the Soviet Union, over and beyond those who had fled in 1932–1935. Out of those 30,000 families, 48,133 individuals were promptly arrested as Japanese spies and 30,992 were shot. In the case of Jews specifically, the uncertainty of life under both the Soviets and the Japanese, plus a history of Japanese collusion in the 1933 kidnapping and murder of Harbin Jewish pianist Semion Kaspe, prompted more than half of Harbin's Jews to flee south to relative safety of Shanghai and Tianjin's international concessions. By the end of the 1930s, the overall Russian population of Harbin dropped to about 30,000. Following the end of World War II in 1945, the Soviet Union resumed control of the railway zone. In April 1946 it gradually ceded parts of Manchuria to the Chinese Communists. By 1954, the entire railway zone, including Port Arthur at its southern tip, was under direct People's Republic of China control. By then most remaining Russians had emigrated. To make life even more complicated for the handful of Russians who remained in Harbin into the 1960s, "exit visas," a peculiarity of Communist regimes in general, were under the control of the Soviet Union by means of its quasiofficial "Society of Soviet Citizens," headed by Lev Shickman in Beijing. See Moustafine, "Harbin Connection"; Boris Bresler, "Harbin's Jewish Community, 1898–1958: Politics, Prosperity, and Adversity," in *The Jews of China*, ed. Jonathan Goldstein. Vol. 1 (Armonk, NY: M. E. Sharpe, 1999–2000), 200–215; Zvia Shickman-Bowman, "The Construction of the Chinese Eastern Railway and the Origins of the Harbin Jewish Community, 1898–1931" in Goldstein, ed. *Jews* 1: 187–99; Israel Epstein, "On Being a Jew in China: A Personal Memoir," in Goldstein, ed. *Jews*, 2: 85–97; Yosef Tekoah, "My Developmental Years in China," in Goldstein, ed., *Jews*, 2: 98–109; Alexander Menquez, "Growing Up Jewish in Manchuria in the 1930s: Personal Vignettes" in Goldstein, ed., *Jews*, 2: 70–84; *Mantetsu Chosa Bu* [South Manchuria Railway Company, Research Department], *Zai-Man Yudaya Jin No Keizai-Teki Kako Oyobi Genzai* [The Economic Past and Present of Jews in Manchuria] [November 1940], *Yudaya Mondai Chosa Shiryo Dai 27 Shu* [No. 27 in the Jewish Problem Investigation Materials Series], marked "*Gokuhi*" [Top Secret], 20–21, 44–46, cited in Menquez, 70; Sam Ginsbourg, *My First Sixty Years in China* (Beijing: New World, 1982), 199; Isador A. Magid, "'I Was There': The Viewpoint of an Honorary Israeli Consul in Shanghai, 1949–1951," in *China and Israel, 1948–98: A Fifty Year Retrospective*, ed. Jonathan Goldstein (Westport, CT: Praeger, 1999), 41–45; Yaacov Liberman, *My China* (Jerusalem: Geffen, 199) 57, 95–97, 151–65; Joshua A. Fogel, "The Japanese and the Jews in Harbin, 1898–1930," in *New Frontiers: Imperialism's New Communities in East Asia, 1842–1953*, ed. Robert Bickers et al. (Manchester, UK: Manchester University Press, 2000), 88–108; David Wolff, *To the Harbin Station* (Stanford, CA: Stanford University Press, 1999); and Herman Dicker, *Wanderers and Settlers in the Far East* (New York: Twayne, 1962). According to Soren Clausen and Stig Thogerson's *The Making of a Chinese City: History and Historiography in Harbin* (Armonk, NY: M. E. Sharpe, 1995), 160, there were 450 Russians left in Harbin in 1964.

On the Japanese orchestration of the Kaspe kidnapping, murder, and exoneration of the murderers, see Marc Driscoll, *Absolute Erotic, Absolute Grotesque: The Living, Dead, and Undead in Japan's Imperialism 1895–1945* (Durham, NC: Duke University Press, 2010), 239–42; Amleto Vespa, *Secret Agent of Japan* (Boston: Little Brown, 1938), 32–36, 205–30; Isaac Shapiro, *Edokko: Growing Up a Foreigner in Wartime Japan* (New York: iUniverse, 2009), 11–12, 16; and Stephan, *Russian*, 80–90, 162, 166–67, 200, 335, 346.

4. Fogel, "The Japanese," 88–108; Bresler, "Harbin's," 200–215; Menquez, "Growing Up," 70–84; Wei Qu and Li Shuxiao, eds., *The Jews in Harbin* (Beijing: Social Sciences Academic Press, 2006), 158–59, 172–75.

5. Among the distinguished non-Jews who emigrated from Harbin were the historians Nicholas V. and Alexander V. Riasanovsky, both of whom matriculated at the University of Oregon. They were the sons of Valentin A. Riasanovsky, an authority on Chinese and Mongol law who had matriculated at the University of Saint Petersburg and taught at Harbin's Juridical Institute. Alexander became a historian at the University of Pennsylvania and Nicholas at the University of California at Berkeley. According to his 2011 obituary in the *American Historical Association Perspective*, Nicholas "may have been the best known historian of Russia of the last half-century." *American Historical Association Perspective* 49, no. 7 (2011): 46; Stephan, *Russian Fascists*, 50; Nuissia Hanin obituary, *Bulletin of the Igud Yotzei Sin* [Tel Aviv] 58, no. 406 (2011): 116; Email from Peter Berton to the author, December 15, 2011; Wei Qu and Li Shuxiao, eds. *The Jews in Harbin* (Beijing: Social Sciences Academic Press, [2003] 2006), 1, 228.

6. On the Epsteins, see Jonathan Goldstein, "Israel Epstein in China: A Case Study of Father/Son Conflict in Jewish Ideological Formation" in *At Home in Many Worlds: Reading, Writing and Translating from Chinese and Jewish Cultures. Essays in Honour of Irene Eber*, ed. Raoul David Findeisen, Gad C. Isay, Amira Katz-Goehr, Yuri Pines, and Lihi Yariv-Laor (Wiesbaden, Germany: Otto Harrassowitz, 2009), 295–311; Jonathan Goldstein, "The Lazar Epstein (1886–1979) Papers in YIVO: Their Usefulness to Scholars of Asian Jewish History," *Journal of East Asian Libraries* 156, no. 1 (2013): 1–10.

7. Emmanuel Pratt qtd. in Greer Fay Cashaman [sic], "Bringing Hebrew to the Chinese," *Jerusalem Post International Edition*, September 17, 1988: n.p. Reinforcing Pratt's observation, Peter Berton writes the author in an email of February 7, 2012 that in Harbin Betar was "the preeminent Jewish youth organization. . . . The others were of no competition in ideology or sports." Email from Peter Berton to the author, February 7, 2012; Interview by Jonathan Goldstein with Theodore Kaufman, Tel Aviv, January 2, 2002. For examples of the intellectual vibrancy of Harbin, see Aharon Moshe Kisilev, *Mishbere Yam: Sheelot U-Teshuvot Be-Arbaah Helke Shulkan Arukh* [The Waves of the Sea: Response to the Four Parts of "The Set Table"] (Harbin, China: Defus M. Levitin, 1925/1926); Kisilev, *Natsionalizm I Evreistvo: Stat'i, Lektsii, I Doklady* [Nationalism and the Jews: Articles, Lectures and Reports] (Harbin, China: Evreiskaia Zhizn', 1941); Kisilev, *Imre Shefer* ["Good Words" or "Beautiful Sayings"], a collection of sermons published posthumously in Tel Aviv by Bezalel-Levitsky with a 1951 introductory letter from Israel's Ashkenazi Chief Rabbi Isaac Herzog; *Evreiskaia Zhizn'* [Jewish Life], no. 47 (November 2, 1938): 14–16, 23–25; no. 48 (November 25, 1938): 7–10, 24–25; Violet Gilboa, comp., *China and the Jews* (Cambridge, MA: Harvard University Library, 1992), 40, 43; Shickman-Bowman, 196; *Passage through China: The Jewish Communities of Harbin, Tientsin, and Shanghai* [*Derekh Erets Sin: Ha-Kehillot Ha-Yehudiot Be-Harbin, Tiyeng'tsin Ve-Shanghai*] (Tel Aviv: Nahum Goldman Museum of the Jewish Diaspora, 1986) [exhibition catalog], vii–xii; Dicker, 21–60; Liberman, *My China*.

8. Israel Cohen, *A Jewish Pilgrimage* (London: Valentine Mitchell, 1956), 203–4.
9. This paradigm was first suggested to me at a panel on "Passages" at a conference on "Jewish Journeys," University of Cape Town, January 9, 2007. See "Program, Jewish Journeys, International Conference in association with the University of Southampton's Parkes Institute for the Study of Jewish/Non Jewish Relations, 8–10 January 2007, University of Cape Town."
10. Iosif Olmert tombstone, Huangshan Jewish Cemetery, Harbin, China. In 1897 Samara had a population of 90,000. Among them were 1,327 Jews. By 1917 the Jewish population had grown to approximately 3,000–5,000. Anna Spon, *Istoria evreiskoi . . . v Samare*, accessed March 11, 2014, www.ijc.ru/istoki37.html. According to Teddy Kaufman, who knew the family well, the Olmerts were also escaping anti-Semitism and Communism when they left Samara. Email from Theodore Kaufman (of Tel Aviv) to the author, February 1, 2007. In a March 24, 2006 speech to the US Congress, Prime Minister Ehud Olmert reported that his parents "escaped persecution" in Russia and "found sanctuary in Harbin." *The Washington Post*, May 24, 2006: n.p.
11. On Semyonov and other anti-Semitic warlords, see Epstein, "On Being," 90, and James Palmer, *The Bloody White Baron* (New York: Basic Books, 2009), especially 156–57 on the Urga pogrom. This should not be confused with the August 1945 massacre of Russians in Hailar. It was conducted by retreating Japanese troops on the eve of the arrival of the Soviet Red Army. Forty-two bodies of Soviet citizens were later unearthed in a mass grave. Moustafine, "Harbin Connection," 79, 85. Iosif's wife Michal, or Michele, died in 1965 and is buried in Binyamina Cemetery, Israel. Mordechai died in 1998 and is also buried in Binyamina. Mordechai Olmert, *Darki B'Derech Rabim* [My Way on the Way of Many Others] (Tel Aviv: Or-am, 1981), 12; Interviews of Yossi Olmert, via telephone from New York, December 10, 2006; Yaacov Liberman, San Diego, California, December 15, 2006 and March 22, 2013; Amram Olmert, Tel Aviv, January 1, 2007.
12. Motti adds, "There were two difficult years in front of us. My father was an administrator and didn't succeed in finding work that suited him. All the luxuries that we had became scarce. My mother opened a shop for milk and groceries. For the first time in our lives we were impoverished. I was then nine years old and with the beginning of studies in the 1920s I entered junior high school. My sister studied at the same school whereas my brother studied in a senior high school that was much more famous. The owner of this famous high school . . . was an administrator of the railway. Few Jewish students studied in it. Most of the teachers and students were ethnic Russians. On the other hand the high school where my sister and I studied was built shortly before and located in a Jewish area. A large part of the students were Jewish and even the building was owned by the Jewish community. In Harbin there was also a "Talmud Torah"—a Jewish elementary school—in which, besides general studies, Hebrew and religious studies were taught. In the city there were two synagogues, an old age home, and a huge library of the Jewish community. Community life was lively especially thanks to the hundreds of Zionists who left Russia and were on their way to Eretz Israel." Mordechai Olmert, *Darki*, 14–15; Interview, Theodore Kaufman, Tel Aviv, January 2, 2007.
13. David Laskov graduated from the Haifa Technion and served with distinction in the Engineering Corps of the Israel Defense Forces (ZAHAL). For some years he held the record as the longest serving active duty soldier in ZAHAL. A contemporary of Motti recalls, "Harbin was a place where the interests of Russia, China, and Japan all converged. This

gave the town a cosmopolitan character . . . where Russian was the language spoken by the Jewish population . . . a small island of Russian Jewry beyond its borders." Alexander Gurvich, qtd. in Joseph Chrust, *Alexander Gurvich [1899–1980] Portrait* (Tel Aviv: Jabotinsky Institute, 1986), 4; Ehud Olmert, Beijing, speaking to the Chinese news agency Xinhua, qtd. in *Jewish Telegraphic Agency Daily Briefing,* January 8, 2007, 1; Mordechai Olmert, *Darki,* 14–15; *Betar in China, 1929–1949* (Tel Aviv: Igud Yotzei Sin?, ca. 1974), 14.

14. Chrust, *Alexander,* 6. Veteran China Betar leader Yaacov Liberman claims that Revisionism was a powerful stimulus instilling Zionism in Harbin's Jews. Elaborating on the explanations of Berton and Pratt, Liberman maintains, "Throughout the years, while the fate of political Zionism sailed between the calm waters of the Balfour Declaration and the rough seas of the British White Paper, Betar in China led the Jewish communities in their complete identification with Jewish independence and Statehood. . . . The Jews of China were no longer identified solely by the method of worship. They were now seen on the various sport arenas, on street parades, assembly halls and public gatherings. The ghetto mentality was eradicated." Most importantly, "from the early thirties Betarim from China left comfortable homes and comparatively easy lives to join other Betar teams for *plugot avoda* duty in Palestine." Yaacov Liberman, "Achievements of Our China Betar," in *Betar in China,* 137; Email from Teddy Kaufman (of Tel Aviv) to the author, February 1, 2007. Photos of Motti Olmert in his Betar uniform in Harbin, ca. 1929–1930, appear in Wei Qu and Li Shuxiao, *The Jews in Harbin,* 127 and *Passage through China,* 47.

During the 1920s through the 1960s, "Birobidzhan" was usually spelled "Birobidjan," sometimes "Biro-Bidjan," and very rarely "Bira-Bidjan." Approximately 4,000 Jews remain there in 2014. See Robert Weinberg, *Stalin's Forgotten Zion: Birobidzhan and the Making of a Soviet Jewish Homeland: An Illustrated History, 1928–1996* (Berkeley: University of California Press, 1998); Wei Qu and Li Shuxiao, eds. *The Jews of Harbin* (Beijing, China: Social Sciences Academic Press, 2006), 229, 241, 243; and many publications by Canadian Yiddishist Henry Srebrnik and Israeli/Bar Ilan University Yiddishist and former Birobidzhan resident Ber Boris Kotlerman.

15. Mordechai Olmert, *Darki,* 26; Bressler, "Harbin's," 207–8; Chrust, *Alexander,* 3–6; Interviews of Theodore Kaufman, Tel Aviv, January 2, 2007; Yossi Olmert, via telephone from New York, December 6, 2006; Yaacov Liberman, San Diego, California, December 15, 2006; Amram Olmert, Tel Aviv, January 1, 2007.

In Harbin, Gurvich was editor/publisher of the Revisionist Russian-language weekly *Gadegel* (the Cyrillic rendition of the Hebrew *ha-degel,* literally meaning "the flag" and having specific reference to the blue and white Zionist flag). See complete issues of *Gadegel* for 1940 and 1941 in Jabotinsky Institute, Tel Aviv. Gurvich's acceptance into the Harbin Jewish community was greatly enhanced by his marriage to Raisa Zondovitch, who came from one of the city's wealthiest Jewish families. She had been sent to study agriculture in the Nahalal collective settlement in Palestine. Regarding the Komsomol youth organization, in Israel in 2007 there was a weekly Russian-language newspaper titled *Komsomolskaya PravDA!* The emphasis on the last syllable *DA!,* meaning "yes," mocked the entire Komsomol enterprise, its hypocrisy and bloody history.

16. Moustafine, "Harbin Connection," 80–81.

17. Ehud Olmert, Beijing, Xinhua, 1; Amram Olmert interview, January 1, 2007. It is unclear just how much Chinese Mordechai and Bella Olmert understood and spoke,

Teddy Kaufman's comment notwithstanding. As already noted, they matriculated in a Russian-speaking high school, the *Kommercheskaya Gymnasia*. Both they and their parents surely knew some street Chinese, which ethnic Russians and Jews used to communicate with the local Chinese population. Interview of Theodore Kaufman, Tel Aviv, January 2, 2007.

18. Chrust, *Alexander*, 21; Transcript of tape recording of Mordechai Olmert, ca. 1959, made by Jabotinsky Institute, Tel Aviv (in Hebrew); see also postal correspondence and four telegrams between Mordechai Olmert and Alexander Gurvich, in Russian and English, 1947–1948, Jabotinsky Institute, Tel Aviv.

19. Yossi Olmert interview, December 10, 2006; *Yediot Achronot* (of Tel Aviv), March 16, 2001, 5C.

20. Amram Olmert interview, January 1, 2007; Olmert monuments in Huangshan Jewish cemetery, Harbin; Wei and Li, *Jews* (2006), 1–2, 148–49, 227, 231.

21. Jonathan Goldstein, "Chinese Jews Return to Harbin, See a Bright Future," *China Research Center Newsletter* [Kennesaw, Georgia] 3 (October 2004): 2–3; accessed March 11, 2014, www.chinacenter.net/News/NewsOct04/News-10-04.html; Qu Wei and Teddy [Theodore] Kaufman, eds., *The Homesick Feeling of Harbin Jews* (Harbin, China: Heilongjiang Academy of Social Sciences, 2005).

22. Matanzas Ben Avraham, "International Forum on the History and Culture of the Jews of Harbin," *Bulletin of the Igud Yotsei Sin* [Tel Aviv] 52, no. 390 (2006): 28–31

23. Ehud Olmert, Beijing, Xinhua, 1; Wei and Li, *Jews* (2006), 1–2, 148–49, 227, 231; "PM Olmert's Speech at the Concert Celebrating 15 years of Israeli-Chinese Diplomatic Relations," Beijing, January 11, 2007, text issued by prime minister's office, accessed March 11, 2014, www.pmo.gov.il/PMOeng/Communication/PMSpeaks/speechesin110107.htm?Display Mod. According to Yitzhak Shichor, "Upon his return, Prime Minister Olmert ordered his aides to draft a plan for even deeper relations with China." For a full analysis of Olmert's January 2007 China trip, see Shichor, "Reconciliation: Israel's Prime Minister in Beijing," *The Jamestown Foundation China Brief* 7, no. 2 (2007): 12–14.

24. Ehud Olmert, Beijing, Xinhua, 1; Wei and Li, *Jews* (2006), 1–2, 148–49, 227, 231; "PM Olmert's Speech at the Email: Peter Berton to the author, February 7, 2012; "Alexander Menquez," "Growing up Jewish."

25. Shapiro, *Edokku*, 8–9.

26. Moustafine, "Harbin Connection," 81–82.

27. "Largest Far East Synagogue Renovated in Northeast China Province," *Beijing Xinhua in English*, June 13, 2005, n.p.

28. Kaufman, *Jews of Harbin* and *Yahadut Harbin*.

29. Qu Wei and Teddy Kaufman, *Homesick Feeling*. In May 2001 Qu Wei lead a Harbin academic delegation to Israel, and in 2003 he and Li Shuxiao edited a photographic history titled *The Jews in Harbin* (Beijing, China: Social Sciences Documentation Publishing House). Pages 186–87 of that book show photos of Wei, Teddy Kaufman, and Ehud Olmert during the May 2001 visit.

PART IV

Creating New Homelands in Argentina, America, and Israel

The final chapters of this volume discuss migrants who acted, at least in part, out of ideological motives, leaving their birth countries and remaking their lives in a new homeland in pursuit of a dream. Many transnationals portrayed in this section sought to hold firm to ideas, practices, and customs they carried with them; their relationship with their adopted homeland was often ambivalent and sometimes strained. Instead of remaking themselves to fit into a host culture, some believed that the surrounding culture should recognize their own ideals and practices. Together these chapters demonstrate how sensitive the expression of transnational ideas and identities are to the environmental factors. Even immigrants who identify strongly with their new homelands are obliged to work within the constraints of a new social and political context.

Ellen Eisenberg's pathbreaking chapter uses transnational and comparative analysis to examine the origins and settlement patterns of Jewish farmers from the southern Pale of Russia who established agricultural colonies in the United States and Argentina. Rather than stressing the success or failure of colonies, Eisenberg "emphasizes the common ideological ties and transnational connections" of the sponsors and settlers. Using this approach she teases out distinctive patterns in immigration as well as the similarities and differences between those individuals and groups that opted for America and Argentina. She argues that the outcomes of settlement experience in two very different settings can be best understood when the colonists are viewed as transnationals who carried certain skills obtained in Russia with them to the United States and Argentina. Although from the same homeland, once they moved to the United States and Argentina their fates became tied to the expectations of their hosts and the surrounding physical and cultural contexts.

Like Eisenberg, Ava F. Kahn focuses on people who wanted to live together in self-governed rural communities; however, instead of Russians from the southern Pale, she describes young Jewish Americans who founded kibbutzim in Israel. In Israel these ideological immigrants faced challenges establishing their cherished American practices and ideals, particularly those that diverged from the mores of their adoptive homeland. In this way they encountered a problem analogous to that of Eisenberg's Pale farmers. In both chapters transnationals arrived in their new homeland with an ideology that was at odds in several ways with that of their new compatriots. Kahn reveals how Americans in two different eras incorporated American Jewish values into these new communities. She demonstrates that the timing played a paramount role in producing the confluence of conditions necessary for Americans to band together to found kibbutzim and then to employ ideas learned in one nation to contribute to another's evolution. In the United States, these young Jewish Americans rooted their identities in a sense of Jewishness. Once they disembarked in Israel, however, they were identified as Americans. Even though many resented not being fully accepted by their Israeli neighbors, this did not keep them from sustaining a relationship with the customs of their former homeland.

Joan Roland uncovers a similar dilemma for Jewish Indians. The Bene Israel were labeled "Jews" in India but were regarded first and foremost as Indians once they reached Israel and the United States. They also left their homes freely and sought to maintain close contact with the land of their birth. As in Eisenberg's and Kahn's chapters, the importance of context dominates Roland's chapter. Roland demonstrates that ascribed identities—labels and expectations imposed on immigrants by others—can play a determinative role. In both countries Indian Jews needed to "negotiate their identities" in order to adapt to new settings; however, because of differences in their surroundings and their origins, Indian Jews formed distinct communities in Israel and the United States. Although Indian Jews may have emigrated from the same areas of India, their new environment shaped the expression of their identities. In India, the Bene Israel were part of a small Jewish minority. In Israel, they joined the large Jewish majority, but were identified, in the eyes of their fellow citizens, as members of a small Indian minority. In the United States, on the other hand, Jewish Indians have had more latitude. They can choose to be seen as part of the ever-growing Indian diaspora or seek to join the American Jewish community. Either way, however, they must navigate within larger communities with whom they share commonalities but also important differences.

Roland's chapter alludes to how the internet and ubiquitous airplane travel affect the experience of Jewish immigrants and how American Jews view world Jewry. Even though only a century separates migrants from the Russian Pale and those from India who made their way to America, advances in transportation and communication have transformed what it means to be a transnational. Trips between an adopted homeland and a country of origin that once might happen only a few times in a lifetime, if at all, are now possible routinely. Even in the 1970s and 1980s, as Kahn's chapter described, regular visits by Young Judea members and Hadassah Women kept Americans in Israel in close contact with those in the United States. Now communication, once delayed, is instantaneous. Emigrants have access to the same media, with only a minimum of delay, as kin who never left. In this way, travel, and virtual communication, can reinforce transnational identities. As historians, we can only guess what the implications will be for immigrants, the immigration process, and transnational identities. These chapters, however, may offer some indication of what we might expect to find in the future.

9

CULTIVATING JEWISH FARMERS IN THE UNITED STATES AND ARGENTINA

Ellen Eisenberg

Many immigrants to the Americas in the nineteenth century were drawn across the Atlantic by the promise of plentiful and fertile farmland. Although the vast majority of Eastern European Jewish immigrants became city dwellers, their ranks included a contingent of aspiring farmers destined to settle agricultural colonies in the Americas. Those bound for Argentina became part of an extensive agrarian experiment that, despite being largely abandoned by the mid–twentieth century, was central to the formation of Argentine Jewry. Those heading for the United States established scattered settlements that were mostly short lived and quickly forgotten. Studies of Jewish agricultural colonization in both countries long emphasized the failure of the agrarian experiment, variously attributed to the colonists' lack of farming experience and aptitude or to factors beyond their control, including poor crop prices and a general decline in the farm sectors of both countries.

Although the issue of colony failure has been widely discussed and debated, this exploration took place largely within the separate contexts of Argentine and American Jewish history. More recent comparative work on Jewish agricultural experiments emphasizes the common ideological ties and transnational connections of the sponsors of various Jewish agricultural projects, not only in Argentina and the United States but also in Palestine, the

Soviet Union, Canada, and elsewhere.[1] In addition to illuminating these ties, a transnational approach can help bring into sharper relief the patterns of migration that shaped the colonies and explain group and individual variations in settler outcomes.

Clearly, the larger colonization project in Argentina shaped the migration stream of Jews to that country—at their peak in the 1920s, over 30,000 Jews, or more than a fifth of the country's total Jewish population resided in the colonies.[2] Examination of the characteristics of colonists settling in Argentina and the United States demonstrates that individuals who shared certain regional origins and occupational backgrounds were more likely to persist in the colonies and find success as farmers. Even when colonies were short lived, they opened new areas to settlement and settlers' distinctive origins shaped emerging Jewish communities.

Colony Origins

Beginning in the 1880s, agrarian ideologies began to spread rapidly among East European Jews, a group that more often acted as intermediaries between peasants and larger markets than engaged in commercial farming. Shaken by pogroms early in the decade, and influenced by both the haskalah's emphasis on the importance of productive labor and the agrarianism of Russian populism, many began to articulate a belief that the Jewish "problem" could be solved through a return of Jews to the soil. While groups like the BILU and Hibbat Zion advocated the establishment of kibbutzim in Palestine, others saw a potential for Jewish regeneration through agricultural labor and communal life in the free societies of the Western Hemisphere.[3] One such group, the Am Olam, inspired at least half a dozen groups to organize themselves as settlers and depart for the United States in the early 1880s. These Am Olam groups had a direct role in the organization of at least five of the approximately forty Jewish colonies established on US soil in this period and influenced a number of the others.[4]

Sympathy for the dire plight of Russian Jews in the wake of the 1882 pogroms and panic at the thought of huge numbers of migrants arriving in the West led Western Jewish sponsors to aid these Am Olam groups and consider the benefits of agricultural colonization more broadly. Jewish authorities in France, Germany, and England worked to discourage settlement in their countries and to facilitate transmigration to the Americas. American Jewish philanthropists, reluctantly conceding that the United States was the best option for the refugees but fearing that the crowding of impoverished and unacculturated migrants in cities would lead to an anti-Semitic backlash, supported colony experiments as part of an effort to encourage settlement in the hinterland. Further, many believed that the experience of farming and living in rural settings would hasten the Americanization of the newcomers. A variety of organizations, including the Hebrew Emigrant Aid Society (HEAS) and the United Hebrew Charities embraced the idea of colonization, although the extent of the settlement program was limited because the condition of the refugees necessitated a focus on immediate relief.[5] Unlike the Am Olam colonists, who emphasized farming and, in many cases, commitment to communal living, the American sponsors focused on the dispersal of immigrants and the creed of self-help.

Baron Maurice de Hirsch, a German Jewish banker who lived in Paris, quickly emerged as the chief sponsor of colonization projects in the West. Hirsch had first become involved through the French Alliance Israelite Universelle (AIU), serving on that organization's central committee beginning in 1873. Although the AIU played a key role in aiding the early Am Olam groups to reach the United States, it did not play a continuing part in the colonization projects in the West, focusing more on defense and educational efforts. Hirsch himself continued until the mid-1880s to believe that it was preferable to aid Russian Jews with educational programs in their homeland, in the hope that they would gain acceptance and win rights there, just as Western Jews had in their countries. By the late 1880s, however, Hirsch abandoned this hope and embraced an emigration plan that included extensive organization of colonies.[6] Like the Am Olam pioneers, Hirsch believed that agricultural labor would "normalize" Jews by placing them in productive occupations from which they had historically been excluded. Further, Jewish farming would help solve the "Jewish problem" by countering the negative stereotype of the parasitic Jew. As his administrators instructed a group of colonists en route to Argentina, "You are going in order to open a path for your brothers in captivity, accused of depreciating honest agricultural labor. Baron de Hirsch wishes to demonstrate to the world through your mediation that the accusation is false, and that Hebrews also can be good workers when they have the means to be so."[7] In 1891, he came to the aid of several struggling colonies in the United States by establishing the Baron de Hirsch Fund. The Jewish Colonization Association (JCA), which he founded in the same year and to which he donated ten million dollars in the first five years, focused its efforts on Argentina, a country that was actively encouraging European immigration. Although these organizations funded agricultural projects in both countries,

Hirsch's plans for Argentina dwarfed anything proposed in the United States: he purchased large tracts of land, hoping to settle 25,000 colonists in the first year, and as many as 3,250,000 over a quarter century.[8]

The extent of the Baron's colonization project in Argentina never matched these lofty goals, and the flow of settlers was just a trickle in comparison to the larger flood of Italians and Spaniards destined for Buenos Aires. Still, colonization was substantial. By the time of the Baron's death in 1896, about three-quarters of a million acres had been purchased and 6,757 individuals settled in the colonies. Ultimately, the JCA acquired a million and a half acres in a series of clusters in several provinces. Within each colony, farms were divided into individual family holdings. During the first several years, colonists paid taxes and rent. After five years, contracts could be renewed and, subsequently, the colonists could gain the deed and complete payment under a mortgage, enabling them to gain full ownership of the land. The colonies reached their maximum population in 1925, with approximately 33,000 families, about two-thirds of them farming, mostly raising wheat in land more suitable for cattle. Those not farming worked in colony villages and towns as merchants, artisans, or professionals.[9]

Although the aspirations for the colony project in the United States were considerably more modest, the goals were quite similar. Colonists saw their experiments as a means of demonstrating to the world both the revitalization of the Jewish people and a model of cooperative settlement. As one wrote, "Our motto is a return to agriculture, and our aim, the physical and spiritual rehabilitation of our people."[10] One South Dakota colony called in its constitution for the creation of a network of Russian Jewish colonies in America, stating, "The colony Bethlehem Judea is founded . . . to help the Jewish people in its emancipation from slavery and in its rehabilitation to a new truth, freedom, and peace. The colony shall demonstrate to the enemies of our people the world over that Jews are capable of farming."[11]

Bethlehem Judea, notable as the first identifiable Am Olam colony, was founded in 1882 by twelve members of a single chapter.[12] This chapter was one of a dozen or so founded by Russian Jews in 1881–1882—and concentrated in the southern Pale. Both Russian agrarianism and the haskalah movement inspired them. Like their Palestine-bound counterparts in the BILU movement, they believed that agrarianism would solve the Jewish problem by demonstrating the productive capacity of Jews. In contrast to the Zionist pioneers, they placed their faith in America as the most fertile ground for this agrarian experiment. By 1882, chapters from Odessa, Kiev, Balta, Vilna, and Kremenchug made the journey to America with the goal of establishing colonies. The Odessa chapter established New Odessa in southern Oregon by the end of that year.

Along with the Am Olam colonies like New Odessa and Bethlehem Judea, a number of similarly motivated groups of colonists, who may or may not have been formally linked to the Am Olam, arrived in the United States at approximately the same time. Thus, in December of 1881, a group of families from Elizavetgrad and Kiev established a colony at Sicily Island, Louisiana with the help of French and American philanthropists. Although surviving documents provide no clear connection to the Am Olam organization, colonies like Sicily Island and Painted Woods in North Dakota were clearly influenced by the same ideological currents and espoused the same commitment to Jewish regeneration through agricultural settlement. As Herman Rosenthal, leader of colonization attempts in both Louisiana and South Dakota, explained,

> Long ago I had come to the conclusion that so long as we have no toiling class that produces its own bread there will be no end to our tribulations. A people that lives at the expense of the labor of others cannot continue to exist indefinitely. Similarly the Jewish problem will not be solved by the non-Jewish world. . . . In my opinion, one of the best means of averting this danger would be to establish a class of half a million farmers and workers living by the sweat of their brows.[13]

A number of these colonies (but not all) were committed to communalism as well as to agrarianism.[14] The New Odessa colonists in Oregon, for example, renounced any claim to private property and dedicated themselves to communal living, agricultural pursuits, and "mutual assistance in perfecting and development of physical, mental, and moral capacities of [their] members."[15] Bethlehem Judea colonists also held all property communally, an arrangement intended to be lasting and thorough, and had communal housing and dining.

In other cases, members intended to farm together initially and to later separate the land into individual holdings. In states including the Dakotas, Kansas, and Colorado, where land was obtained under the Homestead Act, legal requirements forced settlers to file for titles to individual claims. Such requirements led to conflict between settlers at Painted Woods, North Dakota and their American neighbors when the colonists built a "village" on a tract of land designated for the community school. A set of drawings of the Painted Woods Colony (also known as Wechsler Colony after Saint Paul, Minnesota sponsor Rabbi Judah Wechsler) shows this tight settlement of houses along the Missouri River, suggesting the collective mission of the immigrants and, possibly, shtetl influences. Several images show the settlers traveling together by wagon back and forth from Bismarck and working together to build houses and make hay. A centerpiece, listing the names of all of the settlers, reinforces the clear message that this was a colony—a group endeavor—not simply a collection of individuals (Figure 9.1). Only after their neighbors petitioned did the colonists move their homes to their individual homesteads.[16]

Reflecting some of the same concerns that motivated Baron Hirsch, much colony activity was aimed at improving the reputation of Jews. The New Odessa Colony's efforts to attain moral and mental development and perfection included daily study of topics ranging from mathematics to philosophy and English.[17] Likewise, Bethlehem Judea's constitution declared that the colony was dedicated "to the improvement of the moral and intellectual condition of its members and their families, to promote their welfare by united and harmonious action on their part and to afford mutual assistance to themselves."[18] This emphasis on morality was, in a number of cases, severed from

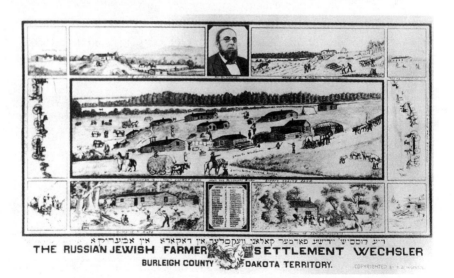

THE RUSSIAN JEWISH FARMER SETTLEMENT WECHSLER
BURLEIGH COUNTY DAKOTA TERRITORY.

FIGURE 9.1. Drawings of Painted Woods Colony in North Dakota (also known as Wechsler) convey the collective mission of the settlers. Courtesy of the Jacob Rader Marcus Center of the American Jewish Archives, Cincinnati, Ohio.

religion. Visiting rabbis bemoaned the lack of religious observance in several colonies, and in some cases colonists flouted Jewish law by raising (and presumably eating) pigs.

Gaps in expectations—between the visiting rabbis and the colonists over religion, between sponsors and settlers over issues like individual versus communal landownership, and even among groups of colonists with different economic and cultural priorities—reflected the ideological diversity of those drawn to the colonization movement. Where settlers sometimes saw the agrarian project as an experiment in cooperative living, elite sponsors instead imagined it would produce Jeffersonian yeoman farmers. Sponsors' belief that colonies should breed self-sufficiency (and loan repayment) was continually foiled by settlers' misunderstandings of the terms and by the real difficulties of farming during turbulent economic times. Such differences and misunderstandings would be a constant theme in both the American and the Argentine colonies.

Migration Patterns and Settler Persistence

Despite the commonalities behind the projects in the United States and Argentina, there were important differences—even aside from the vast differences between the host countries. Although the self-organized groups that dominated the American colonization project shared with sponsors a desire to acculturate and "normalize" in their new host society, the same was not necessarily true for the sponsor-organized Argentine settlers. While the JCA pushed to "Argentinize" the settlers, the colonists "resisted the effort as an attempt to deprive them of their culture, which was all that remained to them of their former lives."[19] Initially, sponsors settled the new farmers in villages, an arrangement that allowed the development of community life. Villages helped nurture emerging institutions like schools and synagogues and housed Jewish merchants and artisans—roughly a third of colony families. However, the distance between homes and fields led the JCA to move away from village settlement and to instead settle families on their land—a move that considerably hampered community life.[20]

Struggles between sponsors and colonists in Argentina were constant. Historian Judith Laikin Elkin argues, "The dominant theme of most memoirs of life in the JCA colonies is the struggle between settlers and administrators." For example, because of its emphasis on the importance of teaching self-sufficiency, the JCA reserved—and often exercised—the right to expel those who fell behind on mortgage payments, a prerogative much resented by colonists. Even in terms of personal relationships, the mostly French, assimilationist-oriented sponsors saw themselves as "culturally superior" to the colonists. The colonists characterized the sponsors as "anti-Semites."[21] Although the tensions were not quite as pervasive in the American colonies, neither were they uncommon. Cincinnati-based sponsors of Beersheba Colony in Kansas, for example, were patronizing to the colonists. Struggles over control soon resulted in open hostilities, with the sponsors confiscating settlers' stock and tools and the colony disintegrating.[22]

Despite the idealistic enthusiasm of many colonists and sponsors, their expectations for the colonies fell short. In the United States, colony after colony dissolved, few lasting more than a couple of years. Those that did survive the first decade—the colonies in the Vineland region of New Jersey—did so only with extensive help from urban Jewish philanthropists. Under the guidance of these sponsors, the southern New Jersey colonies quickly shifted their focus away from agrarian and communal philosophies. New, nonideological settlers were recruited, and the settlements were transformed into mixed agricultural–industrial villages based on private ownership of property.[23] In Argentina, although settlements endured into the 1940s and 1950s, turnover was high and the Baron's loftier population goals were never reached. By the post-WWII period, the experiment was generally considered a failure.[24]

While the issue of *colony* failure has been widely discussed and debated, there has been little effort by historians to analyze the experience at the *individual* level. Although many of the colonies in the United States were short lived, some of their settlers persisted longer than others, and some continued their efforts at farming even after the demise of their colonies. In Argentina, although the colony experiment lasted longer, the length of residence for individual settlers varied greatly. Examination of the persistence of individual settlers in both countries reveals patterns in regional and occupational background that shaped these individual experiences and suggests that transnational recruitment and migration patterns were closely linked to settler success in the colonies.

It has been amply demonstrated by Judith Elkin and others that the common ascription of colony failure to the inadequacy of the Jewish migrants as farmers is misleading. Colonies in the United States and Argentina were plagued with numerous problems that contributed to their demise, including poor site selection and climate, autocratic sponsor policies, unrealistic planning, and poor land distribution policies. Such problems led to high attrition and could even wipe out a colony in a single blow, as happened with the flooded Sicily Island Colony in Louisiana.[25] In addition, the colonies were subject to the more universal difficulties plaguing the agricultural sector in these countries during a period of industrialization and urbanization. This was magnified in Argentina, where colonists found that their children could not pursue higher education in the countryside and that no provision had been made for children desiring to farm to obtain land in the colonies. Many settlers rapidly concluded that life in the city was easier and offered more opportunities for their children.[26] Ironically, in societies where the center was shifting from rural to urban, the movement from colony to city might be considered a sign of successful adjustment—or normalization. As one Argentine colonist explained, "We planted wheat and harvested doctors."[27] Likewise, a colony leader in New Jersey who had once scorned "careers" and had dedicated four decades to farming, came to regard his children's urban, professional careers as the success for which "we have slaved."[28] What is remarkable is not that the colonies in both countries were ultimately abandoned for the city but that some of the colonies' inhabitants persisted as long as they did.

Although difficulties inherent in the location, organization, and economic context of the colonization do explain their demise, variations in the experiences of *individual* colonists suggest that their suitability for the projects should not be ignored. Indeed, if we shift our focus from the survival of specific colonies to the persistence of individuals *within* those colonies, it becomes clear that some settlers were able to succeed, or at least persist, as farmers longer than others. Comparison between those individuals who remained on the farm longer and those who left the projects earlier can add to our understanding of the broader factors that affected colony success and colony failure. The emergence of similar patterns of settler persistence in both the United States and Argentina suggests that transnational migration streams played a key role.

Studies of Jewish colonization—and broader works on Jewish immigration in this period—have tended to speak in very general terms about the migrants' background.[29] Thus, it is assumed that would-be colonists shared the same regional and occupational background that characterized the mass of East European Jewish migrants of the period. Since the majority of Jewish migrants in the post-1880 period were craft workers from the northwest region of the Pale,[30] it is generally assumed that the colonists shared this background. This has been one basis for the assumption that settlers were unprepared for agricultural labor and that this was a key factor in colony failure.

Yet there is considerable evidence to demonstrate that many of the colonists hailed from the South Pale, where some Jews farmed. While farming was not widespread among Jewish residents, it was far more common than in the North. The South Pale, including Podolia, Bessarabia, Kherson, and Ekaterinoslav, had a tradition of Jewish agriculture dating from the mid–nineteenth-century establishment of Jewish colonies in these regions. Bessarabia alone was home to seventeen such settlements, with over 12 percent of Jews in the region working as farmers at midcentury.[31] In addition, Jews from these regions were more likely to be merchants than craft workers,[32] many dealing in agricultural goods, connecting them with agrarian life and products. Together with the Jewish farmers, they created a potential pool of settlers for the colonies in the West.

The presence of farm colonies in the South Pale in the mid–nineteenth century suggests additional distinctions between this area and the more northern and central areas of the Pale. The colonies had been established as part of a larger effort to encourage migration of Jews and others to the region, which was relatively undeveloped. Although poverty was widespread throughout the Pale, the worst conditions were in the north, where traditional trades were flooded as the Jewish population increased rapidly and faced competition from factories. The south offered relatively better opportunities, spurring internal migration from north to south. Because settlement was less dense and relatively recent, communities were somewhat less insular. Odessa, the leading city of the region, was relatively cosmopolitan, and Jews attracted to Western-style reforms were able to participate in Russian life, including educational institutions and revolutionary movements, to a degree not possible elsewhere.[33]

That migrants from the south dominated the colonization movement in both countries is clear. Jews from this region were far more active in organizing themselves for colonization in the West than were their counterparts elsewhere in the Pale. Thus, the Am Olam was founded in Odessa, and nearly all of the chapters founded subsequently were located in the south. Similarly, several of the first groups of Jews organizing themselves to settle colonies in Argentina—like the self-organized group that arrived to settle Moisesville in Argentina on the ship *Weser*—originated in Kamenetz-Podolsk in Podolia.[34] When the Baron de Hirsch and his Jewish Colonization Association took over sponsorship of the Argentine colonies, he saw this region as the most promising recruiting ground because his agent David Feinberg "brought back [from the region] enthusiastic reports about [the residents'] character in general and their adaptability to agriculture in particular."[35] Feinberg's account details several visits to the agricultural colonies in Kherson, Ekaterinoslav, and Bessarabia and the organization of colony groups there.[36]

Recruiters acted on these assessments. For example, when the Wood-bine, New Jersey colony was founded in 1891 by the Baron de Hirsch Fund, the directors favored South Russians "for it was believed they would make the best farmers."[37] Interestingly, twelve settlers who had left the Argentine colonies were also selected. Although the JCA-sponsored migration was not limited to the South Pale, the preference for migrants from that region led to their greater representation in the colonies and, because of the key role of the colonies in the larger Jewish migration, in the Argentine Jewish community as a whole. Within the complex of colonies surrounding Lucienville in Entre Rios were sections named for South Pale shtetls, such as Novobuco 1 and 2, named for Novi Bug in Kherson, and Aquerman, which reflected its settlers' origins in Akkerman, Bessarabia, a center of Jewish agriculture.[38]

In addition to those who were recruited directly or who self-organized for colonization while still in Russia, other migrants—not always sharing the backgrounds or goals of their predecessors—joined the colonies. For example, in New Jersey, as the Am Olam dissolved and sponsoring orga-nizations advocating industrial development took control after 1885, they recruited nonidealistic settlers from New York, with backgrounds more similar to the mass of Jewish migrants. The percentage of new arrivals from the South Pale dropped from nearly 60 percent during the first three years of settlement to only 20 percent during the next five years.[39] In Argentina, where the focus remained on agriculture, settlers from the South Pale who arrived in groups throughout the 1890s and after the turn of the century were joined later by groups from other regions. However, as is often the case with chain migrations, regional patterns established early were replicated by later arrivals, keeping the South Pale an important source for subsequent migrants.[40]

It would seem logical that settlers from the South Pale would be more likely than those from other parts of the Pale to have the skills and attitudes that would allow them to succeed in the colonies. Whether or not they were actually farmers, migrants from these regions were more likely to have some exposure to farming, often as merchants trading in agricultural products. More broadly, migrants from these regions had more familiarity with rural life and were accustomed to interacting with non-Jews—factors that may have smoothed the transition to rural Argentina or America. Thus, it is not surprising that, although the data on settlers' regional origins and premigra-tion occupations are far from complete, they do suggest that these factors did affect individual outcomes on the farm.

Within the rather dismal context of colony hardship and attrition, colonists sharing a South Pale background were more likely than others to remain on the farm, whereas those from other backgrounds—like the more urban Bialystok contingent, who settled in Entre Rios—were quick to abandon the agricultural experiment for a more familiar urban setting like Buenos Aires. As Rebecca Kobrin explains, "The failure of the Bialystok colony became infamous throughout the Argentine Jewish community.... The consensus in the Argentine Jewish community, according to Moyshe Yakhnuk, was that 'when a Bialystoker says 'I want to become a colonist,' everyone must answer him, 'A Bialystoker can never make himself into a colonist.'"[41]

In the New Jersey colonies of the Vineland region, where the establishment of factories in the mid-1880s led to an influx of industrial workers, migrants from the South Pale continued to dominate the farming sector of the colonies even after they became outnumbered by settlers from other regions in the settlement as a whole. For the entire period, 1882–1920, while migrants from the South Pale only represented 40 percent of the total population, they comprised nearly 50 (48.3) percent of the colonies' farmers. While just over half (52.9 percent) of colonists from other regions worked in the colonies' agricultural sector, 75 percent of South Pale colonists did so.[42] These South Pale farmers also appeared to have more success in farming than their counterparts from other regions. Among the early settlers still in the area in 1901, the average landholding and the average acreage under cultivation for those from the South Pale were more than double those of settlers from other regions.[43]

Similarly, in the Argentine colonies, regional origin correlated with colony persistence and farming success. The Lucienville Colony census of 1938 shows that, by that late date, the overwhelming majority of colony residents, 90.4 percent, were from the South Pale.[44] The value of the farms of those from that region indicates the greater success that these individuals found in the colonies: the farms of settlers from Bessarabia and Kherson had an average value of $8,757 and $8,078, respectively, while those of settlers from other regions averaged under $8,000 ($7,978). The disparities in farm values between those from the South Pale provinces and those from elsewhere are apparent even when controlling for the longevity of the colonists in the settlement—indeed, the average farm value for those settlers arriving prior to 1900 was actually *lower* than for those arriving during the first decade of the twentieth century.

That, among colonists from the South Pale, Bessarabian settlers tended to be most successful may reflect the greater presence of Jewish farming in that region. While the percentage of Jewish farmers in all of the provinces of the South Pale was higher than elsewhere in the Pale, *within* that area Bessarabia had the highest concentration of Jewish farmers and agricultural colonies. Bessarabia later became a center of the Jewish agricultural cooperative movement.[45] Indeed, two of the organized groups of settlers that arrived in Clara Colony in 1894 came from Soroki and Kiliya, Bessarabia, both of which were sites of agricultural cooperatives during the first decades of the twentieth century.[46] Not surprisingly, the Jewish colonists pioneered the development of economic cooperatives that were later replicated by farmers in other parts of Argentina.[47]

Since the 1938 census of the Lucienville Colony listed settlers' premigration occupations, it is possible to look directly at the effect of the Argentine settlers' prior experience on their success in the colony.[48] The average farm value in 1938 for those colonists who claimed farming as their premigration occupation was $8,896, compared to $7,589 for those who had been merchants and $7,305 for craft workers. The advantage of farmers over nonfarmers is consistent within regional categories: the farms of those immigrants who claimed agricultural experience, whether from Bessarabia, Kherson, or other regions, had values that were consistently higher than those of their counterparts who listed other prior occupations. In the case of colonists from Bessarabia, those claiming prior experience as farmers had farms valued at over 30 percent more than the farms of those who did not claim farm experience.[49]

Historians have tended to overlook the distinct profile of immigrants who joined the agricultural colonies in the United States and Argentina. The few who do recognize the efforts of the JCA to recruit colonists from the South Pale tend to emphasize the mismatch between the farming techniques used in Russia and Argentina and, on that basis, dismiss the significance of these origins.[50] The data presented here suggest that premigration experiences influenced not only the decision of immigrants to settle in the colonies but also their degree of success once there. In both the New Jersey and the Entre Rios cases, settlers from the South Pale comprised the majority of colony farmers and made their farms more prosperous than those of their neighbors from other regions. In Argentina, where the regional data can be supplemented with occupational data, those claiming agricultural experience found more success as farmers than the other settlers.

Colony Legacies

In addition to shaping the outcomes for individual settlers in the colonies, the transnational migration patterns that were established by the early arrivals had longer term impacts on Jewish communities in these regions. Even when colony projects unraveled quickly, it was not unusual for some colony veterans to remain in the area, either as farmers or as merchants in nearby towns. Not surprisingly, they were often followed in chain migration by relatives and friends from their hometowns, reinforcing regional patterns. For example, a cluster of Jewish colonies triggered chain migration to North Dakota from the South Pale that shaped the Jewish community even after the colonies' demise. Jewish settlers continued to arrive as independent farmers, filing homestead claims in the area.[51] When Rabbi Benjamin Papermaster arrived in nearby Grand Forks in 1891, "he found that most of the families were from the Ukraine section of Russia."[52]

In addition, even after sponsors had gone out of the business of supporting group endeavors, they often continued to see areas opened up by the projects as potential sites for aspiring individual Jewish farmers. As late as the 1930s, the JCA and the JAS, respectively, brought Jewish refugees from German and Austria to the dwindling colonies in Argentina and New Jersey.[53] Thus, both sponsored settlement and chain migration fostered continued settlement in these remote and often unlikely areas. Most significant among these areas was Argentina; it is not an exaggeration to claim that it was largely because of the colonization project that Argentina became a major destination for Jewish migrants. During the period of mass migration up to 1930, Argentina was second only to the United States for Jewish migrants—yet this migration stream began only after the first colony project in 1889. In other words, "Baron de Hirsch's project placed Argentina on the eastern European Jewry's map," as a possible destination.[54] As Rebecca Kobrin notes, "In the history of turn-of-the-century Jewish migration, the JCA stands out: in contrast to other Jewish organizations that provided aid to Jewish immigrants only after they arrived at their destination of choice, the JCA actually shaped the migratory path by recruiting tens of thousands of East European Jews to consider settling in rural Argentina and Brazil."[55]

The legacy of the colonies also shaped settlement patterns *within* Argentina, opening up areas that otherwise likely would not have attracted Jewish migrants. Although some of those Jews who left the colonies in the provinces of Entre Rios and Santa Fe moved to Buenos Aires, many others relocated to the provincial capitals. The result, according to Elkin, is that "Argentina is the only country in Latin America where considerable numbers of Jews settled elsewhere than in the national capital."[56]

A similar example can be found in North Dakota, where the early colony activity "popularized the idea of coming to the midwestern free-land areas," both through word of mouth and through Jewish press reports.[57] Thus, though the population of the former Painted Woods colony dwindled to only three families by the turn of the century, it rebounded with an influx of forty more by 1906. Six years later, there were 250, reflecting a broader migration of Jews to the state.[58] By the end of the 1910s, North Dakota was fourth in the nation (and first in the trans-Mississippi West) in numbers of Jewish farmers, with many concentrated in the area of the former colonies in the western part of the state.[59]

Likewise, even after the dissolution of the New Jersey settlements as colonies, aspiring Jewish farmers continued to arrive in the region, and the nearby town of Vineland saw growth in its Jewish community as former colonists and their descendants purchased property there. The history of Jewish farming in the region led the Jewish Agricultural Society to assist refugee German and Polish Jews to settle there in the 1930s, 1940s, and 1950s. Although the organization was, by this point, no longer in the business of supporting colonies, it did believe that independent immigrant Jewish farmers were more likely to adjust when they were less isolated. Jewish agricultural districts such as those in North Dakota and New Jersey thus became logical sites for settlement. In 1941 alone, JAS aided the settlement of 140 farming families in the area of the former New Jersey colonies; a decade later, approximately 1,000 Jewish families had been so assisted.[60] Such settlers—and their sponsors—had no illusions by the 1940s about grand colonization experiments. Rather, they saw this as a practical solution to a refugee crisis.

Focusing on the experience of colonization illuminates transnational patterns that can be obscured in broader studies of the mass migration of East European Jews. Shifting focus from the mass migration to the particular stream that carried settlers to agricultural colonies provides insight into characteristics that shaped both the colonies and their broader regional—and, in the case of Argentina, national—legacies for emerging Jewish communities. In addition, understanding the impact of regional and occupational origins on settlers' ability to persist in the colonies furthers our understanding of the factors influencing community survival and suggests the need to look more closely at the impact of South Pale origins on the economic, social, and cultural development of the colonies.

Notes

1. Of particular note is the special issue devoted to Jewish agricultural settlement in *Jewish History* 21, no. 3/4 (2007), edited by Jonathan Dekel-Chen and Israel Bartal. This

issue grew out of the international conference "To the Land!: 200 Years of Jewish Agricultural Settlement" held in Tel Aviv and Jerusalem in June 2005.

2. Judith Laikin Elkin, "Goodnight, Sweet Gaucho: A Revisionist View of the Jewish Agricultural Experiment in Argentina," *American Jewish Historical Quarterly* 67, no. 3 (1978): 209; Robert Weisbrot, *The Jews of Argentina* (Philadelphia: Jewish Publication Society, 1979), 70.

3. Efforts at sponsored Jewish agrarian settlement expanded to the Soviet Union as well during the interwar years, as documented by Jonathan Dekel-Chen. Efforts in Argentina, North America, Palestine, and the USSR shared common ideologies of normalization and were supported by overlapping networks of Western sponsors. See Jonathan Dekel-Chen, "JCA-ORT-JAS-JDC: One Big Agrarianizing Family," *Jewish History* 21, no. 3/4 (2007): 263–78.

4. Groups from Kiev, Balta, Kremenchug, Vilna, and at least two different groups from Odessa journeyed to the United States. They established, or helped to establish, New Odessa (Oregon), Bethlehem Judea (South Dakota), Alliance and Carmel (New Jersey), and an unnamed colony in Arkansas. See Abraham Menes, "The Am Oylom Movement," *YIVO Annual* 4 (New York: YIVO Institute for Jewish Research, 1949) and Ellen Eisenberg, *Jewish Agricultural Colonies in New Jersey, 1882–1920* (Syracuse, NY: Syracuse University Press, 1995), ch. 2.

5. Eisenberg, *Jewish Agricultural Colonies*, ch. 2.

6. Samuel Joseph, *History of the Baron de Hirsch Fund: The Americanization of the Jewish Immigrant* (Fairfield, NJ: Augustus M. Kelley, 1978), 11. Note that in 1900, the Baron de Hirsch Fund was reorganized as the Jewish Agricultural and Industrial Aid Society (JAIAS), later the Jewish Agricultural Society (JAS).

7. Qtd. in Judith Laikin Elkin, *The Jews of Latin America*, rev. ed. (New York: Holmes & Meier, 1998), 109. For more on the Argentine colonies, see also Weisbrot, *Jews of Argentina* and Haim Avni, *Argentina and the Jews* (Tuscaloosa: University of Alabama Press, 1991).

8. Elkin, *Jews of Latin America*, 109. See also Haim Avni, "El proyecto del Baron de Hirsch: La gran vision y sus resultados," *Indice* (Buenos Aires), special edition to commemorate the 100th anniversary of the Weser (July 1990): 34–35.

9. Elkin, *Jews of Latin America*, 111.

10. B. Dubnow, qtd. in Menes, "Am Oylom Movement," 16.

11. Menes, "Am Oylom Movement," 26.

12. Eisenberg, *Jewish Agricultural Colonies*, 43.

13. Menes, "Am Oylom Movement," 24.

14. Eisenberg, *Jewish Agricultural Colonies*, 33.

15. New Odessa Community, incorporation papers, Douglas County Courthouse, Roseburg, Oregon.

16. Mary Ann Barnes Williams, *Pioneer Days of Washburn, North Dakota and Vicinity* (1936), repr., McLean County Historical Society (1995), 20. See also Ellen Eisenberg, "From Cooperative Farming to Urban Leadership," in *Jewish Life in the American West*, ed. Ava F. Kahn (Seattle: University of Washington Press, 2002), 113–32.

17. Menes, "Am Oylom Movement," 29–30.

18. Ibid., 26–27.

19. Elkin, *Jews of Latin America*, 119–20.

20. Ibid., 113.

21. Ibid., 112.

22. Eisenberg, *Jewish Agricultural Colonies*, 56.

23. Ibid., chs. 4–6.

24. Elkin, "Goodnight, Sweet Gaucho," 208–9.

25. The colony was located on an island in the Mississippi River and was destroyed by a flood.

26. On the problems of the Argentine colonies, see Elkin, "Goodnight, Sweet Gaucho" and *Jews of Latin America*, 114–20. On the American colonies, see Eisenberg, *Jewish Agricultural Colonies*, ch. 2.

27. Elkin, *Jews of Latin America*, 105.

28. Sidney Baily, qtd. in Elizabeth Frazer, "Our Foreign Farmers," *Saturday Evening Post*, October 13, 1923, 23. See also Eisenberg, *Jewish Agricultural Colonies*, 163–64.

29. See, e.g., Elkin, *Jews of Latin America*, 215; Eugene Sofer, *From Pale to Pampa* (New York: Holmes and Meier, 1982), 129.

30. Simon Kuznets, *Immigration of Russian Jews to the United States: Background and Structure* (Cambridge, MA: Charles Warren Center for Studies in American History, 1975), 35–126.

31. Only 2.3 percent of all Jews in the entire Pale were farmers. The figure for Kherson was 7 percent and for Bessarabia was 12.5 percent. See "Agricultural Colonies" and "Bessarabia," in *The Jewish Encyclopedia*, Isidore Singer, ed. (New York: Funk and Wagnalls, 1901), 1: 252–56 and 3: 111, respectively.

32. Isaac Rubinow, *Economic Condition of the Jews in Russia* (New York: Arno, [1907] 1975), 502, 522ff, 555.

33. For a discussion of these regional differences and their impact on colonization, see Eisenberg, *Jewish Agricultural Colonies*, ch. 1; Eisenberg, "Argentine and American Jewry: A Case for Contrasting Origins," *American Jewish Archives* 47, no. (1995): 1–16.

34. Jose Mendelson, "Genesis de la colonia Judia en la Argentina," in *50 anos de colonizacion judia en la Argentina*, ed. Jose Mendelson (Buenos Aires: Delegacion de Asociaciones Israelitas Argentinas, 1939), 100–103.

35. Theodore Norman, *An Outstretched Arm* (Boston: Routledge and K. Paul, 1985), 20.

36. Leo Shpall, "David Feinberg's Historical Survey of the Colonization of the Russian Jews in Argentina" (Translated from the Russian with an Introduction), *Publications of the American Jewish Historical Society* 43, no. 1–4 (1953): 13, 18–19.

37. Joseph, *Baron de Hirsch*, 50.

38. Moshe Ussoskin, *Struggle for Survival: A History of Jewish Credit Co-operatives in Bessarabia, Old Rumania, Bukovina, and Transylvania* (Jerusalem: Jerusalem Academic Press, 1975), 15–16. For additional evidence of South Pale origins, see Eisenberg, "Argentine and American Jewry," 6–9.

39. These figures are for those colonists for whom a regional origin could be determined. See Eisenberg, *Jewish Agricultural Colonies*, 115, 121.

40. Simon Weil, "Las colonias agricolas de la JCA," in *50 Anos de Colonizacion Judia*, 172–77. Weil names groups from six locations in the south and two in the north. Avni discusses a group from Kherson and one from Bessarabia, organized in 1904. Avni, *Argentina and the Jews*, 59.

41. Rebecca Kobrin, *Jewish Bialystok and Its Diaspora* (Bloomington: Indiana University Press, 2010), 99–101.

42. Eisenberg, *Jewish Agricultural Colonies*, 119.

43. 1901 New Jersey state census of the Alliance Colony, JAIAS papers, American Jewish Historical Society, Waltham, MA: Box 44, "Alliance, New Jersey." These figures are based on 20 of the 145 individuals listed on the census (14 percent) for whom a region of origin could be determined.

44. JCA census of Lucienville Colony, 1938. Lucienville Cooperative, Basavilbaso, Argentina. All of the premigration data on Lucienville settlers that follows is based on this census, which includes data on 168 families. Note that Kherson is recorded as "Jerson" (the Spanish spelling) on this document.

45. See Ussoskin, *Struggle for Survival*.

46. Weil, "Las colonias agricolas," 172–74; Ussoskin, *Struggle for Survival*, 15, 38.

47. Morton D. Winsberg, "Jewish Agricultural Colonization in Entre Rios, Argentina: III," *The American Journal of Economics and Sociology* 28, no. 2 (1969), 189.

48. These figures should be regarded with caution, as many settlers believed that their admission to Argentina was dependent on their identifying themselves as farmers. It is not clear, however, why the settlers would continue to misrepresent their occupational background as much as forty years later. In any case, such possible misrepresentations would not explain the consistent differences between farmers and nonfarmers noted here.

49. The exact figures are Bessarabian farmers—$10,524, nonfarmers—$7,999; Kherson farmers—$8,392, nonfarmers—$7,921; other farmers—$8,345, nonfarmers—$7,652.

50. Avni, "El proyecto," 44–45. For an examination of the evidence of the predominance of Jews from the South Pale among migrants to the colonies, see Eisenberg, "Argentine and American Jewry."

51. Linda Mack Schloff, *"And Prairie Dogs Weren't Kosher": Jewish Women in the Upper Midwest Since 1855* (Saint Paul: Minnesota Historical Society, 1996), 116.

52. Isadore Papermaster, "A History of North Dakota Jewry and their Pioneer Rabbi (part 1)," *Western States Jewish Historical Quarterly* 10, no. 1 (1977): 80.

53. Elkin, *Jews of Latin America*, 111; Eisenberg, *Jewish Agricultural Colonies*, 168–69.

54. Edgardo Zablotsky, "The Project of the Baron de Hirsch, Success or Failure" (working paper, University of CEMA, Buenos Aires, 2005), accessed May 31, 2012, www.ucema.edu.ar/u/eez/Baron_Maurice_de_Hirsch/Exito_o_Fracaso/Working_Paper_289_english.pdf.

55. Kobrin, *Jewish Bialystok*, 96.

56. Elkin, *Jews of Latin America*, 119.

57. William C. Sherman et al., *Plains Folk: North Dakota's Ethnic History* (Fargo: North Dakota Institute for Regional Studies, 1986), 391.

58. W. Gunther Plaut, "Jewish Colonies at Painted Woods and Devils Lake," *North Dakota History* 32 (1965): 101.

59. Sherman, *Plains Folk*, 390.

60. Eisenberg, *Jewish Agricultural Colonies*, 168–69.

10

TRANSFORMING IDENTITIES

Bene Israel Immigrants in Israel and the United States

Joan G. Roland

Numbering perhaps thirty thousand at their peak in the early 1950s, the Jews of India were historically divided into three distinct groups: the Cochin Jews of the Malabar coast in southern India; the Bene Israel of Maharashtra (including Bombay, the Konkan, and Pune) and Gujarat in the west; and the Baghdadi or Iraqi Jews of Calcutta and Bombay. Having never experienced anti-Semitism or discrimination at the hands of their Indian hosts, the first two groups have maintained their identity as Jews over many centuries. (The Baghdadis arrived later.) In the last twenty years a fourth group, the Bnei Menashe, a Burmo-Tibetan ethnic group in northeast India, have been accepted as being Jews.[1] Following the Partition of India in 1947, and the declaration of the independent State of Israel a year later, the majority of Indian Jews voluntarily left their homeland behind. Most, especially the Cochinis and Bene Israel, went to Israel, where there are now, at best estimate, perhaps 80,000 Jews of Indian origin, the majority of whom are Bene Israel. Others went to the United Kingdom, Australia, Canada, and the United States. There are now fewer than 5,000 Jews left in India. This chapter explores how the Bene Israel, the largest of the three traditional Indian Jewish communities, whose origins are shrouded in legend, have negotiated their identity in both Israel and the United States. In Israel, Jewish immigrants from the subcontinent formed the only Indian community and were challenged to assimilate to the larger Israeli culture. In the United States, where there was a large Indian immigrant community, the Bene Israel had the option of being integrated into that reference group and replicating its acculturation or of assimilating to the American Jewish community. Complicating these choices was the issue of transnationalism. To what extent have they developed a transnational identity that embraces India, Israel, and the United States?

"Jews in India, Indians in Israel"

Although they constitute less than 1 percent of the total Jewish population of Israel, the Indian communities of 80,000 there are still larger in absolute numbers and in proportion to the overall population than they ever were in India, where they were truly microscopic. The largest concentrations are in Ashdod, Beersheva, and Dimona in the south; in Lod and Ramle in the center; and in the north, near Haifa. Accepted and respected in India, the Jews maintain a deep attachment to their "motherland" (they call Israel their "fatherland") and appreciate its culture. This section is based on in-depth interviewing of approximately 200 Bene Israel in Israel, about half of whom had previously responded to extensive surveys in the late 1990s and early 2000s.[2]

Immigration History and Early Absorption in Israel

The Bene Israel did well under the British, who preferred them and other small minorities for employment in the lower echelons of the civil services. Although some Bene Israel observers have claimed that it was the attachment to Judaism and the attraction of Israel more than the economic conditions in India that motivated their community to emigrate, others believe that apprehension about competing for jobs in an independent India and the prospects of a higher standard of living in Israel were the main determinants of their departure.[3] The Bene Israel aliyah (immigration) consisted of several waves, the largest ones in the 1960s and 1970s followed by a steady trickle, and continues today, albeit much more slowly.

Because Indians were not refugees, the Jewish Agency of Israel, which facilitated their immigration, had to hold out the offer of attractive economic prospects in Israel. It paid the passage for the Bene Israel and helped absorb them by providing housing, jobs, and other facilities. Mizrachi Jews (those from Middle Eastern and North African countries) as well as Indians were sent to undesirable locations and many of the first generation were never able to afford relocation to more prosperous areas. Thus there was a disconnect between what the potential immigrants heard or imagined about Israel, "the Land of Milk and Honey," and what they actually encountered. Indian Jews from Bombay and Calcutta were shocked at the consumer shortages and minimal infrastructure that they found in the transit camps and remote development towns of the new state.[4]

Bene Israel, with a few exceptions, were not part of the professional elite in Israel, as they have been in other parts of the world, including the United States. A key aspect of the early Indian experience in Israel was the discrimination they encountered, although this was true of many immigrants, especially those from the Middle East and North Africa. Although British colonial attitudes had left many Indians with a sense of racial inferiority, they had not expected the racism and marginalization they found in the Jewish homeland. The fact that India at that time was considered to be poor and backward led other Israelis to look down on the Bene Israel because of their Indianness.[5]

Despite the hardships, some Indian Jews had a substantial advantage over other immigrants because of their proficiency in English. Skilled immigrants, for example, joined El-Al, the Israeli airline, and the Israel Aircraft Industry, in which the accounts and most of the correspondence were in English. The children of these skilled immigrants have done very well. Nevertheless, during the first two decades, certain (although not all) Bene Israel professionals with British-affiliated degrees, high qualifications, and experience in India found that in Israel, where Western-educated professionals seemed to be preferred, they were looked down upon as "Indians" and given subordinate posts or asked to take additional training; many did not want to do so. Thus their standard of living dropped.[6] The experience of immigrants from rural or urban working-class backgrounds, who comprised the majority of the first generation in the 1950s and 1960s, was decidedly different. They were placed immediately in blue-collar and manual jobs, generally in development towns in the Negev Desert or the north. Israel in this period needed experienced craftsmen and tradesmen and some of these workers soon enjoyed a higher living standard than they had in India.[7] The second generation in these towns ended up predominantly in vocational tracks in school and many dropped out of high school to join the workforce to supplement family incomes as tradesmen, clerks, or low-level government employees. High school graduates rarely pursued higher education after the army. They had lower rates of graduation from college than their parents had in India, to the latters' dismay. More recently, however, a great many Indians have been able to move to more prosperous, industrialized areas, where they have found work.[8] Bene Israel who immigrated to Israel in the 1970s often found career opportunities more easily. Highly educated and with more self-confidence, they had a better understanding of how they could fit into a rapidly developing Israel and of how to get ahead by negotiating with employers. They knew that if Israel did not work out for them they could return to Bombay or move on to Western nations.[9] Thus, a sense of transnationalism was growing.

The Religious Crisis

Problems of a different sort emerged in the 1960s, when a dispute over marriage eligibility became a cause celebre. Fearing that the Bene Israel's past ignorance of Orthodox Jewish marriage and divorce laws (because there were no rabbis or Jewish religious courts in India) made them unacceptable for marriage with other Jews unless they underwent ritual conversion, the Sephardic chief rabbi of Israel issued a directive in 1961 requiring officiating rabbis to investigate the female lineage and all divorces that might have taken place among the ancestors of the Bene Israel party applying to marry a non-Bene Israel Jew "as far back as is possible." This slur on the Bene Israel community's Orthodoxy—or, as they saw it, "Jewishness" and "purity"—made them feel like "tainted" outsiders.[10] To Bene Israel, viewing the issue through an Indian lens, the crisis seemed to revolve around matters of race, caste, and purity, rather than Jewish law. Three years later, government intervention finally led to the affirmation that the Bene Israel were Jews in all respects and had the same rights as all other Jews, including in matters of personal status. References to the Bene Israel in the rabbinate's directives were deleted.[11] The long struggle to be recognized as full Jews and to be allowed to marry members of other communities without undergoing ritual conversion prevented the Bene Israel from jumping on the bandwagon of cultural pluralism and ethnic pride that was emerging in Israel in the 1960s. The Bene Israel, who in certain ways were profoundly Indian, were reluctant to stress their Indian ethnicity and particular cultural heritage in various festivals and associational activities, as Mizrachi Jews were doing: it might jeopardize their "Jewishness" even more. It was better to maintain a low ethnic profile. Sociologist Shalva Weil has pointed out that the Bene Israel felt particular pressure to conform to Israeli norms to establish their equality.[12] Their experience of discrimination had indeed mobilized them to strengthen their ethnic organizations, but it was to demand their rights as Jews, not to affirm Indian traditions.

The Construction of Bene Israel Ethnic Identity

The persistence of other Indian cultural markers among these Jews has impeded at times their full integration and absorption into Israeli society. The Bene Israel saw their lack of assertiveness, or what they call their "shyness"—their reserved, quiet nature, deferential attitudes, and respectful, polite behavior—as real disadvantages in Israel, where aggressiveness counts, especially when fighting for rights and benefits with the Israeli bureaucracy. It has been argued that this lack of fight, seen as "lack of ambition," was responsible for Indian Jews being poorly represented in Israel even in those professions in which Indian origin communities (including Jews) have excelled in the Western world.[13]

Although their proud expression of Indianness was delayed, the Bene Israel community since the late 1980s has been making deliberate, self-conscious efforts to affirm their ethnicity publicly in order to preserve and promote Indian as well as typically Bene Israel Jewish customs and culture. They no longer fear that such activities will throw their Jewishness into question. One way of doing this is by performing the music and dance of the "motherland," especially that of Bollywood. Popular culture is the most appealing part of Indian culture to youngsters, who are less familiar with the broader civilization and history of India than the immigrant generation.[14] Since 1987, the Central Organization of Indian Jews has sponsored an annual, now three-day Festival of Indian Music and Dance, held for the last eleven years in Eilat called *Hodu Yada* (Gathering of Indians). Thousands of Indians travel from all over Israel to attend. At the *Hodu Yada* of 2007, marking fifteen years of diplomatic ties between India and Israel, Arun Kumar, India's ambassador to Israel at the time, said, "You [Indian Jews in Israel] are a very important link between India and Israel. This event clearly shows the strong sentimental attachment you have for India even after getting completely integrated into the Israeli society."[15] Indian Israelis invite Indian diplomats to cultural programs and other events across the country and attend the celebration of Indian Independence Day and Republic Day at the ambassador's residence in large numbers.[16] In 2013, the first Indian Jewish National Convention in Israel was held in Ramle and reportedly attended by 5,000 people. It was addressed by Jaideep Sarkar, the Indian ambassador to Israel, who said, "Your Indian blood gives you the capacity to bring together and to build bridges between people of different faiths and creed. . . . I look forward to the day when I can go to the house of the Israeli ambassador to India and have home cooked Indian food in his house."[17] Factors such as class, education, and place of residence have to some extent affected the degree of assimilation and acculturation among the Bene Israel. Working-class members of the community, concentrated in the south of Israel, may have retained a greater degree of Indiannesss than the educated middle-class people in the center and north. Yet it is the latter who have taken the lead in the conscious preservation and transmission of the Bene Israel Indian heritage and values. Women's groups have collaborated with foreign researchers in projects to record traditional Bene Israel folksongs in Marathi as well as with curators of Israeli museums on arranging exhibitions and relevant programs about Indian Jews. India's image has also been bolstered by its popularity as a tourist destination, particularly among young men and women venturing abroad after completing their military service. As many as forty thousand non-Indian Israelis visit the country annually. This has contributed to the enhanced image of Jews of Indian origin in Israel. Bene Israel are proud to discuss their country and its culture with these returning tourists.[18] The establishment of full diplomatic relations between India and Israel in 1992 led to cultural exchanges that emphasize the achievements of India. Sociologist Maina Chawla Singh points out that developments in bilateral trade and collaborations between India and Israel in science, technology, agriculture, and especially the military have "shaped and given a significant boost to collective self-perceptions of the Indian Jewish community in Israel" and have promoted new levels of ethnic pride and a greater willingness to express their particularistic ethnic identity.[19]

When Bene Israel were asked to indicate those aspects of Indian customs and culture they still participate in, unsurprisingly most informants of all ages identified food.[20] Because immigrants who have been in Israel more than forty years still eat primarily Indian-style meals and snacks, young people have grown up with this cuisine. Stores selling the necessary ingredients and cooking utensils—imported from India if necessary—exist in most towns where Indians live. A number of Indian restaurants have also opened in Israel.

Looking Ahead in Israel

Having been Jews in India, their "motherland," where they fared well, the Bene Israel became Indians in Israel, their "fatherland." In some ways they experienced more prejudice and marginality in their new home than they ever did in India because of their "Indian" characteristics. Whether the resolution will be the proud assertion of an Indian Israeli identity by the younger generations within the context of an Israel that has grown more tolerant of ethnicity, multiculturalism, and pluralism or the shedding of Indian identity is still an open question. Ultimately, the preservation and redefinition of Bene Israel Indian culture in Israel will depend upon the second and third generations, most of whom are fully integrating into Israeli society. Some may wish to retain their "subcultures" but are not interested in perpetuating their separateness. They hope to achieve socioeconomic equality and acceptance on equal terms in Israeli society.[21] Indian parents are eager for their children to become Israelis, to assimilate to the normative culture, no longer to be part of a closed community. Friendship networks of the second and third generations naturally tend to be broader than those of their parents. The young people themselves want to shed whatever Indian attributes have kept their parents apart, especially what they see as mentalities or attitudes that prevented them from getting ahead. Those born or raised in Israel from an early age are able to express Indian values and behaviors in an Indian setting and to deal sensitively with a large family. Yet a noticeable mark of their acculturation is their ability to be more assertive among other Israelis and in general to handle the broader Israeli spectrum much better than their elders.[22] If major hindrances to the preservation of Indian culture in Israel include the relatively tiny size of the Bene Israel population and pressures to assimilate, intermarriage may prove a further challenge. Today, with fewer than 5,000 Jews remaining in India, the preservation of the unique Indian Jewish heritage may rest mainly with those Jews of Indian descent residing in Israel. Hopefully, for many second- and third-generation Bene Israel, the increasing legitimacy of ethnicity and cultural pluralism in Israel will result in an intensified appreciation of their heritage as they redefine it and pride in their Indian Israeli identity as they transform it.

Bene Israel in America: An Ethnoreligious Identity

After the Partition of India, many Bene Israel may have wanted to emigrate to the United States, but foreign exchange restrictions imposed by the Indian government and the US national origins quota system, which effectively banned Asian migration, made it difficult. In 1965 the United States passed the Immigration and Naturalization Act, which enabled many more migrants, especially professional or highly skilled technical workers, from the so-called third world to enter. Bene Israel who were now able to migrate to America were more likely to come from cities and large towns in India, while those from the villages, with few skills and resources, generally went to Israel. A subset of Indian Jewish immigrants in the United States consists of those who originally went to Israel or were born there. In the United States, as in India, the Indian Jews constitute a tiny percentage of the Indian population, which, in 2012, reached 3.2 million. It is all but impossible to reliably estimate the number of Indian Jews that are in the United States, but it is probably fewer than 1,000 persons of at least partial Indian Jewish origin, including the second and third generations. They are mainly Bene Israel. Although they are spread out all over the United States, there is a concentration in the greater New York area, including New Jersey and Connecticut. The material in this section is based on responses to survey questionnaires, in-depth interviews, and the community and general press. My informants range in age from twenty-seven to eighty-seven and have resided in the United States from seven to sixty-two years.

In Israel the Bene Israel are an ethnic minority. In the United States they are also a religious minority. As a "double diaspora or minority" they have faced a complex set of challenges: not only to become American but often also to be accepted as Jews by the American Jewish community, which is primarily Ashkenazi. This is similar to, but not the same as, the struggle the Bene Israel faced in Israel in the 1960s. Psychologist Sunil Bhatia maintains that having "Indian ethnicity" affects the social networks, choice of spouses, and the way Indians organize their life in the diaspora.[23] Religion, however, important in India, is also a powerful force and marker of identity for immigrants in the formation and preservation of group identity in the United States. Their Jewish identity is particularly important for the Bene Israel and has added an additional layer to their integration. Have they faced religious or racial discrimination? Has their Judaism supplanted their Indian ethnicity as their primary source of identification? And finally, with community members in India, Israel, and a number of other countries with whom they maintain close contact, to what extent have they developed a transnational identity?

Early Immigrants

The first immigrant generation, those who arrived in the United States from the 1950s through the early 1970s, formed a small community, especially in the greater New York area. In America, places of worship serve as social and cultural centers as well as offering religious services. In Israel, where different ethnic groups typically form their own congregations, there are approximately fifty-five Indian synagogues. In the United States, synagogues, most of which are Ashkenazi, are usually divided according to degree of observance: Orthodox, Conservative, Reconstructionist, and Reform rather than by ethnic origin. In the 1960s and 1970s, few Bene Israel in the New York area tried to integrate into American Jewish congregations. They practiced Indian

Jewish culture in their homes. Even today, although a few older Bene Israel attend Sephardic synagogues, many have never stepped inside an Ashkenazi synagogue because they feel that the liturgy and service are so different that they would not understand anything or be able to follow the prayers. Some of this cohort are even reluctant to attend general American Jewish events; they think they will feel like outsiders. It is possible that the earliest Indian Jewish arrivals came to the United States, as they did to Israel, with attitudes of the colonized: deferential toward "whites," perhaps feeling inferior and expecting inequality and to not be fully accepted as Jews. As in Israel, they encountered negative stereotypes of India as poor and backward in America. The marriage controversy in Israel in the 1960s, where Orthodox American rabbis weighed in on the side of the Israel Chief Rabbinate, affected some Bene Israel in the United States. As in Israel, the older members of the community still retain the Indian Jewish culture and the traditions they grew up with, of which they are increasingly proud. Some of the early immigrants, however, feeling more comfortable in their own group, kept within an almost ghetto-like structure, as was the case with Bene Israel immigrants in the south of Israel.[24]

Just as Indian Jews in Israel have formed ethnic associations, so did the small community in the United States. The first one, Congregation Bina, started in the greater New York area in 1981 with about twenty-five to thirty families, primarily Bene Israel, and a lot of American well-wishers. The goal was to preserve their special culture, traditions, and music.[25] They put out a quarterly to biannual newsletter, *Kol Bina,* off and on for about fifteen years and were quite active in the 1980s and early 1990s, with a mailing list of about 1,000, not all of whom were Jews from India.[26] Congregation Bina organized prayers (they follow a Sephardic liturgy) and a variety of holiday functions in homes and in rented halls, temples, or vegetarian Indian restaurants in New York and New Jersey. Bene Israel who were active in religious worship frequently became spokespersons to explain their traditions to Americans.[27] American newspapers often published long illustrated articles on the community's history, customs, celebrations of holidays, and special recipes.[28] Ten years before the Israel Museum presented its special exhibition on the Jews of India with the help of the Israeli Indian communities, the Jewish Museum in New York mounted, in 1985–1986, as part of a citywide Festival of India, an exhibition of Indian Jewish religious items, artifacts, and photographs. The local Bene Israel participated in several days of programming on their history, customs, and culture.[29]

Unfortunately Congregation Bina succumbed to factionalism (as have Indian organizations in Israel) by the mid-1990s and sporadic efforts to resuscitate it were not very successful. For a couple of years, starting in 1983, the Bene Israel held High Holy Day prayers in their traditional manner in a rented Reform temple in Manhattan's Greenwich Village. After a hiatus of almost a decade, they resumed the prayers, which have been continuing now for the past nineteen years. Somewhere between forty and eighty persons attend, the larger number for the Yom Kippur services. (Unlike in Israel, where many can walk to a Bene Israel synagogue, some very observant Bene Israel do not attend the Manhattan services because of the Orthodox prohibition against traveling on Yom Kippur.) As in India and Israel, the prayers are entirely in Hebrew, with additional sheets supplementing the Sephardic prayer book, but many are recited and chanted according to Indian customs, melodies, and intonation. When the Bene Israel prayer leader, Romiel Daniel, an ordained rabbi and a Yeshiva University–trained cantor, tried to introduce some Ashkenazi melodies for variation, the congregation objected.[30] They came all the way into Manhattan for the unique Indian liturgy and melodies, they said; otherwise, they could have gone to Ashkenazi synagogues in their own communities. Some Bene Israel in the New York area, especially those who have come via Israel, tend not to go to Bene Israel High Holy Day services. They might attend a Sephardic synagogue in Queens with a very mixed Jewish congregation or go to Chabad/Lubavitcher centers, which, although Orthodox, welcome all Jews irrespective of background. The issue of acceptance (are they "really Jews?") is an ongoing one.[31] Nevertheless, those Bene Israel who settled in American cities and towns where there were no other Bene Israel went to local Ashkenazi synagogues, mainly Reform or Conservative, and learned the prayers and melodies, and most found they were soon accepted. A few younger members became very active in these synagogues, becoming officers and board members. One Bene Israel became the president of an Ashkenazi synagogue in New York City as well as its sometimes cantor and rabbi.[32] Some women joined Hadassah. One young woman, a biologist who is quite religiously observant, ended up first in Fort Collins, Colorado, where she linked up with a local synagogue and taught at its Hebrew school. She then moved to Alamogordo, New Mexico, where there was a military base. The few Jews who lived in the region were scattered all over farming areas and this young woman and her husband—having scoured the phone directory for Jewish-sounding names!—invited them and a few military men together for services in their own home and also held a Passover seder.

The Community Today

In 2006 a new organization, the Indian Jewish Congregation of the USA, formed in New York. It puts out a ten- to fifteen–page well-illustrated electronic newsletter periodically, with news from India and Israel and occasionally from other Bene Israel communities as well. Readers appreciate its religious homilies, announcements, and accounts of community events, including life cycle rituals, historical reminiscences and maps, biographic articles about well-known Indian Jewish personalities, and Indian Jewish recipes. The new organization has partnered a few times with the well-known Jewish Community Center in Manhattan, which has agreed to help the community promote and integrate Indian Jewish culture, while at the same time retaining its identity and avoiding assimilation by hosting events and holiday celebrations, including one for Indian Independence Day, a mock Bene Israel wedding, and film screenings.[33] The community has held Simhat Torah services and Hanukkah celebrations in various venues—the latter sometimes at the Indian Consulate General in New York, where Indian and Israeli dances are performed, and twice at city hall.

As in Israel, older Bene Israel often feel that many of the more recent, younger immigrants seem less familiar with and attached to their Indian Jewish heritage because the community in India itself had dwindled and they were not brought up in it as intensely as the earlier generation was. They were not exposed to the same traditions, values, and ways; did not appreciate the effort that was put in by their forebears to retain the Jewish culture in India, where even kosher meat was hard to obtain; and did not have a deep-rooted feeling about the value of retaining their heritage and the same desire to pass it on to the next generation. Now they come to the United States, meet American Jews, and find their knowledge of their own culture and tradition is limited. The older community—not strong and numerous enough, as in Israel, to revitalize it—observes sadly and for the most part, accurately, that younger immigrants may not assert very strongly that India had a vibrant Jewish culture and that they would like to continue practicing it here. They feel it is just easier to fit into the American Ashkenazi Reform and Conservative synagogues. They understand the English services better than the Orthodox Hebrew ones and prefer them to what they had.[34]

In Israel, although the community is large enough for some marriages between second-generation Bene Israel to take place, many Bene Israel marry Jews from other ethnic groups, and some try to maintain some Indian traditions. In the United States, however, in contrast to Israel, many recent immigrants or second-generation Bene Israel have married non-Jews and this intermarriage leads to a number of variations. Some play down the Jewish background; others, especially those who have married Hindus, will celebrate festivals of both religions, particularly with their children. In some cases, especially where the mother is Jewish, the children have been raised Jewish, whether or not the spouse converts to Judaism. Most Bene Israel say they would like to pass down at least some of their religious customs to their children, but this is not always easy to do. If they attend local synagogues, Jewish life cycle rituals are generally held there. Many younger Bene Israel who are practicing Judaism want everything to be American, not Indian. They want their children to adjust and accept what American Jewish religious and day schools offer.

Nevertheless, they may retain a few practices and traditions at home. In both Israel and the United States, the Bene Israel have retained their distinctive ceremony, called *malida* or *Eliahu ha-Navi,* where participants give thanks to mark a special occasion, such as a life cycle ritual, recovery from illness, moving into a new home, return from the army (in Israel), educational success of a child, and so forth (Figure 10.1). They recite specific prayers invoking the prophet Elijah and blessings, accompanied by the *malida* ritual, an offering to God of particular foods, including a special mixture of parched rice, coconut, fruits, nuts, rose water, sugar, and cardamom, which is then eaten. Although the second generation generally does not perform this ritual, they may go to their parents' homes for it, seeing it as more of a cultural than a religious custom.[35] In both countries, Bene Israel have also retained the practice of wearing white for mourning.

Just as in Israel, where the emphasis on cultural pluralism in the past half century has made people familiar with other Jewish traditions, most American Jews have become quite interested in "exotic" Jewish communities. Synagogues, Jewish community centers, and women's organizations often offer lecture series on different communities: Ethiopian, Yemenite,

FIGURE 10.1. Bene Israel at a Malida ceremony in Or Yehuda, Israel. Courtesy of Nissim Moses.

Moroccan, Indian, and so on. When Bene Israel are asked to give a talk about the Jews of India and their customs (sometimes followed by an Indian meal!) younger ones who may not know the heritage and the history typically email the president of the Indian Jewish Congregation of the USA, asking what they can read in order to prepare for the talk.[36] A few Indian Jews have used their unusual backgrounds and talents to write, speak, make art, or perform music professionally. Some have authored cookbooks.[37] Sociologist Bandana Purkaysastha argues, "Ethnicity is not about the transmission of cultural templates through the generations. Instead ethnicity is actively constructed within situated contexts."[38] Siona Benjamin, a very successful Bene Israel artist who immigrated in 1986, has done just this. Her paintings center on the theme of "finding home," in which she blends imagery and symbolism from Judaism, Hinduism, Buddhism, and Islam as well as pop culture. Another Bene Israel artist, who immigrated first to Israel and then to Houston in the United States, Ben Tzion Ben Yosef Yakov, has also combined Hindu symbols and Jewish religious iconography. In the 1990s, a Hanukkah program that he helped sponsor drew many Hindu families and priests.[39] Other Bene Israel artists have exhibited work that does not necessarily draw on their Indian or Jewish experiences.

Socioeconomic Factors

Because their economic status was partially determined by US immigration regulations that privileged educated and skilled migrants, Bene Israel in America reflect the overall middle- to upper middle-class position of most Indian immigrants. In this respect they are better off than their counterparts in Israel. Ninety percent of Bene Israel in America see themselves as middle class (not including lower middle) or above.[40] This, of course, is self-perception and partly depends on whether individuals are comparing their standard of living to that in India, Israel, or the United States. On average far more possess masters, doctorates, medical, and legal degrees than their counterparts in Israel. This mirrors the profile of all Indian immigrants in New York, most of whom value higher education as a route to social mobility. Like immigrants everywhere, the older generation often took jobs that were below what they had had in India but ended up with a better lifestyle. As their counterparts in Israel, younger people who came to attend universities or already had degrees found good jobs quickly. They have confidence in themselves, are proud to be Indians, and feel that they're equal to other Americans and will succeed. In contrast to Israel, the vast majority of Bene Israel, especially those raised in the United States, say that they have encountered no ethnic or racial discrimination or prejudice, although a few do recount specific incidents. Those who have not succeeded as well as they would have liked will occasionally cite Indian ethnicity rather than religious belief as a factor. The fact that they report so little prejudice is somewhat surprising, as many Indian immigrants in the United States attest to having experienced discrimination of one sort or another, especially at work, because of skin color, foreignness, or accent (Figure 10.2).[41]

Identity: "We Are Jewish but Still Indian!"

When a sample of Bene Israel were presented with seven categories—Jewish, Indian Jewish, Indian, Indian American, American, American Jewish, and "other"—and asked to rank them in order of priority of how they saw themselves, the options were perceived as ethnoreligious categories, rather than racial. Not factoring in variables of age or length of stay, half selected Indian Jewish if categories that were selected as either first or second choice are combined. More than a third selected Jewish and a quarter American. Bhatia has pointed out that some Indians see "American" as "white Anglo-Saxon" and feel that they will never really be seen as one even if they have citizenship.[42] One of the few Bene Israel who considers himself Indian first and Indian Jewish second, even though he has been in the United States seventeen years

FIGURE 10.2. Bene Israel dancing at Simhat Torah in New York City, 2009. Courtesy of Evelina Samson.

and is a citizen, remarked, "Wherever I go, people say, 'oh, you're Indian' not 'oh, you're a Jew.'" One young woman expressed it well: "If people are talking about religion, I say I'm a Jew. If they're talking about issues of ethnicity, I say I'm from India." Thus the Bene Israel negotiate a multilayered ethnicity. In almost all cases, Bene Israel children who were born in the United States or who came before adolescence consider themselves Americans, as their counterparts in Israel would consider themselves Israelis.

Although Bene Israel all over share a nostalgia for home and miss the warmth of India, a major difference between Bene Israel in Israel and the United States is that the latter are part of a large non-Jewish Indian immigrant community and seem to experience some affinity with other Indians.[43] Those in business and computer industries are especially likely to socialize with compatriots. The same is true for those who live in small communities where there are few other Indians and so they may seek each other out. Bene Israel have marched as a community, along with other Indian religious communities, in India Independence Day parades. On the other hand, because the popular holiday of Diwali has Hindu religious significance, they have participated individually, but not collectively, in the annual Diwali festival held in Manhattan. Some Bene Israel in the United States seem to want to retain aspects of Indian culture, but many seek inclusion into the American Jewish community more than with the broader Indian community. Interestingly, none of my respondents belonged to the major Indian immigrant organizations, the Association of Indians in America and the Federation of Indian Associations in America. There is a feeling that the former group tends to link Indian culture with Hinduism.[44]

Consumption plays an important role in the retention of culture. Today, "being ethnic makes one a good American."[45] As in Israel, food laboriously prepared at home by Bene Israel women, especially for Jewish holidays, continues the tradition of Indian Jewish cuisine. As in Israel, many Bene Israel enjoy Bollywood films and rent or purchase videotapes and DVDs. Similarly, the older generation watches Indian television programming on weekends. They read the Indian immigrant weekly newspapers as well as the American press.[46] Those who have come from Israel may keep up with the Israeli press online. Again as in Israel, a few, especially the first generation, attend classical Indian music or dance concerts.[47] The latter are occasionally performed at special Bene Israel functions. Indian Jewish teenagers in the United States also enjoy the latest Indian pop and fusion music, such as bhangra.

Many Bene Israel in the United States still speak Marathi, Gujarati, and Hindi with others and have more opportunity than their counterparts in Israel to enjoy theatrical performances in these languages, especially in Marathi, which take place in areas of dense Indian population. As in Israel, Bene Israel in the greater New York area retain close ties with the Indian Consulate, those in the greater Washington area with the Indian Embassy. They attend cultural events at both of these venues, where special Indian Jewish-focused programs have been presented. The diplomats also attend Indian Jewish functions held elsewhere.

Bene Israel as a Transnational Diaspora

Sociologist Peggy Levitt argues, "The term 'transnational' recognizes that religious people, practices, and institutions are 'rooted in particular places but also transcend their borders.'"[48] Migration deeply affects Indians' perspectives, personally and as a group, on issues of national, ethnic, and religious identity. Among Indian Jews there appears to be an ethnoreligious transnational solidarity.[49]

In Israel, Bene Israel have the luxury of being transnationals in a way that many other ethnic Israeli communities do not: unlike those from Middle Eastern countries, they are free to visit, or even return to, their country of origin. They have warm feelings toward their homeland and travel there independently or organize tours that enable the participants to travel around the country as well as to visit their families. This contact, as well as frequent visits to Israel by Indian relatives—facilitated by the establishment of full diplomatic relations between the two countries in 1992—as well as family from the West, provides opportunities to renew social and cultural ties.[50] Furthermore, there is a constant trickle of Israeli Bene Israel migrating to the United States. Bhatia has discussed how the experiences of the second-generation and the more recent first-generation immigrants in the United States "are shaped by the back-and-forth movement between multiple homes and societies, communication between the home and host cultures via media and technology, commercial linkages . . . the presence of a social network across borders, and the immigrant communities' emphasis on preserving their home culture."[51] Many Bene Israel in the United States retain an active involvement with India and Israel and regularly exchange phone calls, internet and social media communication, and actual visits among extended family and friends' networks in all three countries as well as in Canada, the United Kingdom, and Australia. They may seek work enabling them to travel to and reside in these countries where they have close connections. Occasionally marriages are arranged transnationally. Accounts of trips to India are reported in the community newsletter.[52] Some US-based Bene

Israel send substantial charitable contributions to Indian Jewish institutions in both Israel and India and donate books, CDs, DVDs, videos, and other materials to libraries in their home country. Both American and Israeli Bene Israel are greatly concerned about the maintenance of Jewish cemeteries and schools in India.[53] The Indian Jewish Congregation of the USA newsletter reports frequently on Jewish events in India (and occasionally on Bene Israel events in Canada) such as holiday celebrations, synagogue anniversaries, performances, and lectures.[54] Bene Israel respond quickly to speeches and articles from all over the world that they feel misrepresent or insult their community. They are particularly sensitive to references to the Bene Israel community in India as being "black." They also joined their coreligionists in Mumbai and Ahmedabad in vigorous protest campaigns when stores and a restaurant used Nazi insignia and the name of Hitler. The Bene Israel communities in Israel and the United States were horrified by the attacks on Mumbai in November 2008 and participated in several memorial services, evenings of remembrance, and reflection forums. The fact that one of the places attacked was Chabad House, a (non-Indian) Jewish institution and that several of the victims were Jews who happened to be there, made the massacres particularly poignant and frightening for them.[55] Emerging intelligence warnings of possible terrorist attacks against Jewish institutions in India at the time of the 2013 Jewish holidays, necessitating increased security, have disturbed Bene Israel in Israel and the United States.[56]

With so many relatives and friends in Israel, and the constant trickle of Bene Israel migrating from there to the United States, the American Bene Israel community is also very interested in Israel and Indo–Israeli relations and will occasionally sponsor a program on some aspect of this topic. Israeli diplomats have addressed the US community on efforts to promote a knowledge of and sympathy for Israel among non-Jewish intellectuals and media personalities in India. Israeli-based Indian authors are invited to give readings. Bene Israel in the New York area have participated as a community in the annual Salute to Israel parades. In 2007, a celebration of India's Independence Day featured a program in New York and was attended by representatives from the Israeli and Indian consulates, which included Indian and Israeli music and dance.[57] The Indian Jewish Congregation of USA newsletter, to which Bene Israel residents in Israel and India contribute, publishes many articles from the Hebrew press, often translated by the Israeli-raised editor, about Indian Jews in Israel and their activities. Festivals, cricket matches, youth activities, dance performances, and events sponsored by the Indian Mission in Israel and synagogue celebrations in India and Israel are reported. It also has links to relevant websites in these countries and occasionally to those in the United Kingdom, Canada, and Australia.[58] At the first Indian Jewish National Convention in Israel in 2013, Jaideep Sarkar, the Indian ambassador to Israel, said to the attendees, "Eventually you must play the role that the Indian and Jewish diaspora has played in the United States of bringing India and Israel closer to America." Clearly he was thinking of the advantages of transnationalism.[59]

Conclusion

There are substantial differences between the Bene Israel communities in Israel and the United States, partly due to contrasting size but also because of the structural differences between the immigrant cohort of the two societies. Being so much larger, with significant concentrations in a number of locales and with numerous synagogues of their own, the Israeli community has been able to preserve much more of its heritage, tradition, customs, practices, and liturgy than the tiny, scattered Bene Israel community in the United States has been able to do. Further, although both countries have large immigrant populations, in Israel the Bene Israel comprise the entirety of the Indian population, whereas in the United States the Bene Israel community is a tiny part of a much larger Indian immigrant population. This distinction has affected the nature of assimilation. By the early 1970s, Americans were accustomed to seeing professional and highly skilled (non-Jewish) Indians in various walks of life and the Bene Israel fit right into this context. Indian ethnicity was not a problem. In Israel, there was no broader segment of Indians that the Bene Israel could identify with or be compared to. They had to deal with their Indianness and eventually their pride in their origins and heritage on their own.

Most of the early immigrants who went to Israel were from lower- to lower middle-class backgrounds, either urban workers or small craftsmen or tradesmen from villages, and were assigned housing and jobs by the government. The professional Bene Israel—doctors, teachers, engineers, accountants, government officials, and so on—who emigrated constituted a small percentage. The majority of those who went to the United States in the early years, on the other hand, were, because of American immigration laws, either urban professionals, highly skilled technical workers, or advanced students and could choose where they would live and work. The overall socioeconomic status, and sense of satisfaction, of the Bene Israel in the United States, therefore, was considerably higher than those of their Israeli counterparts.

Both communities have had to deal with the question of acceptance by other Jews, many of whom were not even aware that there were Jews in India. This was exceedingly important for the Bene Israel in Israel, the Jewish state. They ultimately won the battle for halachic equality vis-à-vis marriage with the rabbinate and this facilitated their integration. Bene Israel in the United States grappled with the challenge to be recognized as "real" Jews by American, especially Ashkenazi, Jews and in most cases succeeded. Those for whom affiliation with synagogues was not so important had other constituencies to which they could assimilate.

In Israel, where Jews constitute 80 percent of the population and Judaism, however practiced, is the dominant religion, Bene Israel are most likely to marry Jews, either from their own community or from other ethnic backgrounds. In the United States, where Jews are a small minority, some Bene Israel do marry Jews, but a great many (as is true for American Jews in general) marry non-Jews. Marriage with non-Bene Israel affects both groups in that Bene Israel customs and practices will be diluted, but in Israel, the family will almost always still be Jewish, whereas in the United States, marriage with non-Jews may make it even more difficult for the Bene Israel partner to maintain Indian Jewish traditions.

Bene Israel immigrants have long negotiated their identities as Jews, Indians, Americans, and Israelis. They have not, however, long been the subject of scholarly attention as transnationals. The extent to which the second and future generations in both Israel and the United States consider themselves Indian, Israeli, or American (or some combination thereof) remains to be explored. How will assimilation to Israeli or American Jewish norms and intermarriage affect preservation of Indian Jewish culture and traditions? How will increasing globalization and close economic ties between India, Israel, and the United States affect the transnational identities of the Bene Israel? To what extent have Bene Israel in Israel and America returned to India to participate in the economic growth there? These and other questions remain to be studied.

Notes

1. The Bnei Menashe are composed of members of the Mizo, Kuki, and Chin peoples. Converted to Christianity by missionaries in the nineteenth century, some of them, in the mid-twentieth century, came to believe that they were originally Jewish, descendants of the tribe of Menashe. They began to study normative Judaism. In 2005 the Sephardic Chief Rabbi of Israel accepted them as a lost tribe but said they would have

to undergo formal conversion to Judaism if they wished to immigrate to Israel. A total of 8,000 people are expected to do so.

2. See Joan G. Roland, "Adaptation and Identity among Second-Generation Indian Jews in Israel," *Jewish Journal of Sociology* 37, no. 1 (1995): 5–37; Roland, "The Transformation of Indian Identity among Bene Israel in Israel," in *Israel in the Nineties*, ed. Frederick Lazin and Gregory Mahler (Gainesville: University of Florida Press, 1996), 169–93; Roland, "Religious Observance of the Bene Israel in Israel: Persistence and Refashioning of Tradition," *Journal of Indo-Judaic Studies* 3 (spring, 2000): 22–47.

3. Interviews with informants in Israel, 1990s and early twenty-first century; See also Shirley Isenberg, *India's Bene Israel: A Comprehensive Inquiry and Sourcebook* (Berkeley, CA: Judah L. Magnes Museum, 1988), ch. 30.

4. Maina Chawla Singh, *Being Indian, Being Israeli: Migration, Ethnicity, and Gender in the Jewish Homeland* (New Delhi: Manohar, 2009), 95, 98–99. See Joseph Hodes, "Bene Israel Aliyah and Absorption in Israel, 1948–1960," *Journal of Indo-Judaic Studies* 12 (2012): 60–62, 66. Because large groups of new immigrants had to be accommodated and dispersed, and because it wished to secure and populate its more remote areas, the government created "development towns" with few amenities and low-level work as well as agricultural cooperatives in northern and southern Israel.

5. Interviews with informants in Israel, 1990s and early twenty-first century. See also Singh, *Being Indian*, 110–11, 211 and Hodes, "Bene Israel Aliyah," 62.

6. Interviews with informants in Israel, 1990s and early twenty-first century; Weil estimated that in the early 1970s, 75 percent of the Bene Israel in Lod spoke English with varying degrees of fluency. Shalva Weil, "Verbal Interaction among the Bene Israel," *Linguistics* 193, no. 13 (1977): 78.

7. Responses to questionnaires from and interviews with informants in Israel in the 1990s and early twenty-first century. See also Singh, *Being Indian*, 138. Singh has pointed to long-term implications of the politics of spatial location in the 1960s in the areas of work allocation, family income levels, social class, and opportunities for upward mobility.

8. Roland, "Adaptation and Identity"; Singh, *Being Indian*, 149, ch. 4.

9. Singh, *Being Indian*, 150.

10. See B. J. Israel, "The Bene Israel Struggle for Religious Equality in Israel," in *The Bene Israel of India* by Israel (New York: APT Books, 1984), 89–90; *Hindustan Times*, May 12, 1961; *Indian Express*, May 13, 1961; Roland, "Transformation of Indian Identity," 172–74.

11. "Statement of the Government on the 'Bene Israel' Problem," special session of the Knesset, August 17, 1964; *Times of India*, September 2, 1964, 13. See Roland, "Religious Observance," 23–24.

12. Shlomo Deshen, "Political Ethnicity and Cultural Ethnicity in Israel during the 1960s," in *Urban Ethnicity*, ed. Abner Cohen (London: Tavistock, 1974), 281–309; Shalva Weil, "Names and Identity among the Bene Israel," *Ethnic Groups* 1, no. 3 (1977): 210–11.

13. Interviews with informants in Israel, 1990s and early twenty-first century; Roland, "Transformation of Indian Identity," 174–76. And see Singh, *Being Indian*, 211.

14. Goldberg has commented on the fact that certain features of the non-Jewish environment that were not practiced by Jews in their homeland became prominent in Israel. See Harvey E. Goldberg, "Historical and Cultural Dimensions of Ethnic Phenomena in Israel," in *Studies in Israeli Ethnicity*, ed. Alex Weingrod (New York: Gordon & Bareach, 1985), 188.

15. *Indian Jewish Congregation of USA Newsletter* (hereafter *IJCUSA Newsletter*) 2, no. 1 (2008): 6.

16. *IJCUSA Newsletter* 4, no. 1 (2010): 10; 4, no. 2 (2010): 6.

17. "Indian Jews Must Play a Role Akin to Diaspora in US," accessed October 7, 2013, http://zeenews.india.com/news/nation/indian-jews-must-play-a-role-akin-to-diaspora-in-us_881348.html.

18. Interviews with informants in Israel, 1990s and early twenty-first century.

19. Singh, *Being Indian*, 215, 221.

20. Questionnaires and interviews with informants in Israel, 1990s and early twenty-first century.

21. See Ernest Krausz, "Edah and 'Ethnic Groups' in Israel," *Jewish Journal of Sociology* 28, no. 1 (1986): 5–18.

22. Interviews with informants in Israel, 1990s and early twenty-first century.

23. See Sunil Bhatia, *American Karma: Race, Culture, and Identity in the Indian Diaspora* (New York: New York University Press, 2002), 204.

24. Romiel Daniel, interview, January 2011.

25. *Kol Bina* 1, no. 1 (1981): 3; 1, no. 3 (1982); 3, no. 2 (1984).

26. *Kol Bina* 3, no. 1 (1983); 4, no. 1 (1984).

27. *Kol Bina* 1, no. 2 (1981); 1, no. 3 (1982); 2, no. 2 (1983); 3, no. 1 (1983); 3, no. 2 (1984).

28. See Joshua Hammerman, "Indian Traditions Spice up Chanukah," *Daily News*, December 5, 1982; "Robert M. Shubov, "Israel Is in the Hearts, but India Is Still in Their blood," *India West*, December 24, 1982; Cara De Silva, "Kofta Curry and Kiddush Cups," *NY Newsday*, September 8, 1993; Steve Lipman, "Jews from India," *Jewish Week*, January 13, 1984.

29. See *Kol Bina* 5, no. 1 (1985).

30. *IJCUSA Newsletter* 1, no. 5, July 3, 2007, 12.; Romiel Daniel, interview, January 2011.

31. Of my total sample of eighty-five individuals, including more recent arrivals, 57 percent felt accepted by American Jews, 26 percent did not, and 17 percent responded, "Sometimes." In 2008, however, Romiel Daniel said, "The acceptance here has been more than what we all dreamed for. We want to integrate within mainstream Judaism, not assimilate."

32. Altogether, 44 percent of my sample attended Bene Israel services and 53 percent attended American synagogues—often the same people. Some 28 percent did not attend at all.

33. *IJCUSA Newsletter* 2, no. 2 (2008): 2.

34. When asked how their practices have changed, 31 percent of my sample said they had become more religious, 22 percent less, and 47 percent remained the same, so it is difficult to draw conclusions here.

35. Roland, "Religious Observance," 28–31.

36. Khandelwal has pointed out that a number of Hindu immigrants have made an effort to learn more about their religion to be able to explain it to Americans, and even to their own children. See Madulika S. Khandelwal, *Becoming American, Being Indian* (Ithaca, NY: Cornell University Press, 2002), 78–79.

37. When asked if they think Americans have respect for Indian culture, 68 percent said yes, 22 percent said no, 11 percent said educated Americans do.

38. Bandana Purkayastha, *Negotiating Ethnicity: Second-Generation South Asian Americans Traverse a Transnational World* (New Brunswick, NJ: Rutgers University Press, 2005), 14.

39. *Houston Post,* December 11, 1993.

40. Eight percent see themselves as upper class and 46 percent as upper middle. Only 10 percent reported they were lower middle or working class.

41. Bhatia, *American Karma,* chs. 5 and 6, 193; Bandana Purkayastha, *Negotiating Ethnicity: Second Generation South Asian Americans Traverse a Transnational World* (New Brunswick, NJ: Rutgers University Press, 2005), chs. 2 and 4.

42. Combining first and second choices, 50 percent selected Indian Jewish, 37 percent Jewish, and 26 percent American. Interestingly, very few (15 percent) put down Indian, Indian American, or American Jewish as first or second choice. Thirty-three percent of the Bene Israel saw themselves first as Indian Jewish, 17 percent as Jewish, and 22 percent as American. "American" could have signified citizenship or culture. A number of respondents who have been in the United States for quite a while but are not American citizens were less likely to choose an "American" category. See Bhatia, *American Karma,* 176, 212. No one wrote "Israeli Indian" or "Israeli American" in the "other" category, although quite a few had been born or lived in Israel before coming to America.

43. Approximately 70 percent of my informants speak of a special connection with non-Jewish Indians in the United States; about 15 percent say, "Somewhat."

44. The Association of Indians in America sponsored a Goddess Festival at the American Museum of Natural History in New York in conjunction with Diwali. Progressive South Asians have objected to the sectarian focus of this event presented to American audiences. Khandelwal, *Becoming American,* 60–64.

45. Rudrappa argues that retention of ethnic cultures and networks "is now seen to potentially facilitate the social mobility of new post-1965 immigrants." Sharmila Rudrappa, *Ethnic Routes to Becoming American: Indian Immigrants and the Culture of Citizenship* (New Brunswick, NJ: Rutgers University Press, 2004), 168–69; See also Khandelwal, *Becoming American,* 37

46. It is worth mentioning that John Perry, for many years the editor–owner of *News India-Times,* which strongly supported Indian nationalism and the conservative Bharat Janata Party (BJP), is a Bene Israel who had also worked for ten years as a journalist in Israel. He probably supported the BJP because of its pro-Israel, anti-Muslim stance. Perry was instrumental in restarting the Bene Israel High Holy Day prayers and renting the Village Temple in the early 1990s. See Sandhya Shukla, *India Abroad: Diasporic Cultures of Postwar America and England* (Princeton, NJ: Princeton University Press, 2003), ch.4.

47. *IJCUSA Newsletter* 1, no. 5 (2007): 4.

48. Peggy Levitt, *God Needs No Passport: Immigrants and the Changing American Religious Landscape* (New York: New Press, 2007), 22.

49. Bhatia, *American Karma,* 185.

50. Interviews with informants in Israel, 1990s and early twenty-first century.

51. Bhatia, *American Karma,* 22.

52. *IJCUSA Newsletter* 4, no. 1 (2010): 6–7.

53. *Kol Bina* 4, no. 1 (1984); *IJCUSA Newsletter* 1, no. 8 (2007): 2–4.

54. *IJCUSA Newsletter* 1, no. 3 (2007): 4; 1 no. 4 (2007): 8.

55. In 2006, a restaurant calling itself Hitler's Cross and displaying Nazi insignia opened in Navi Mumbai. The restaurant withdrew the name and insignia. A similar objection was raised when a new line of bedspreads called the "NAZI Collection," using the swastika

on a brochure (the promoters said that NAZI stood for "New Arrival Zone of India) appeared in stores. After receiving letters from India and abroad, the dealer apologized profusely and withdrew the line. See *IJCUSA Newsletter* 2, no. 4 (2008): 2.

56. "Mumbai Ups Security at Jewish Institutions Following alert," accessed October 3, 2013, www.israelhayom.com/site/newsletter_article.php?id=12243; accessed September 28, 2013, hindustantimes.com/India-news/Mumbai/Synagogues-in-city-on-alert-after-Bhatkal-s-disclosure/Article1—1126784.aspx.

57. *IJCUSA Newsletter* 1, no. 5 (2007): 4.

58. These websites may include explanations of holidays in Marathi, Indian Jewish cuisine, recordings of Indian Jewish liturgy, Indian classical dance and music, photographs and YouTube videos, articles on Indo–Israeli economic relations, and articles and books about the community written by Indian Jews or non-Indian scholars. *IJCUSA Newsletter* 5, no. 2 (2011): 4–5, 10.

59. "Indian Jews Must Play a Role Akin to Diaspora in US," accessed October 6, 2013, http://zeenews.india.com/news/nation/indian-jews-must-play-a-role-akin-to-diaspora-in-us_881348.html.

11

TRANSNATIONAL ASPIRATIONS

The Founding of American Kibbutzim, 1940s, 1970s

Ava F. Kahn

"The reality of the American dream emboldened [Golda Meir's] Zionist dream."

Marie Syrkin, "Golda Meir and Other Americans,"
in *Like All the Nations*?

"There is more than one way to be Jewish, even in Israel."

American-born Reform Rabbi Miri Gold of Kibbutz Gezer
(Gold is the first non-Orthodox rabbi to be paid by the State
of Israel), "Historic Decision in Israel: Rabbi Miri Gold
Recognized by State," press release, May 29, 2012,
http://urj.org/about/union.

"Goodbye, America, / Goodbye Yankee fashion, / I'm going to Palestine, / To hell with the Depression!"[1] These song lyrics reflect the aspirations of many Zionist youth who grew up in the 1930s. The most intrepid founded kibbutzim in Israel in the 1940s. Thirty years later, a new generation of American pioneers shipped their record collections to Israel. This time they proclaimed, "The Times They Are a-Changin.'" Drawn to Israel during periods of great optimism, American youth of the 1940s and 1970s created kibbutzim that mirrored their values, emphasizing independent thinking, gender equality, and American religious practices.

This chapter illuminates these two narrow windows of time, periods of confluence for American Jews. Buoyed by Israel's victories in the 1948 War of Independence and the 1967 Six Day War, groups of idealistic and adventurous Americans chose kibbutz life. The United States and Mandatory Palestine both faced turmoil in the 1930s and 1940s. The United States combated a depression and world war, while Palestine struggled with riots, revolts, and the 1948 war to defend a sovereign Israel. American Jews also struggled during these decades. Anti-Semitism peaked in the 1920s and 1930s; by the late 1940s the realities of World War II forced American Jews to come to terms with the devastation of the Holocaust and the need for a Jewish state. American Jews raised during these turbulent decades sought out alternatives including Marxism, socialism, and Zionism.[2] Some Jews believed that they were "at an impasse with American society."[3] These factors led Zionists to consider emigration to Israel. This set of push-and-pull factors would not be replicated until the 1970s.

While the turbulent 1930s and 1940s produced risk takers, full of idealism, who wanted to emigrate and create a new Jewish society in Palestine, in the years that followed young American Jews were less inclined to follow in their footsteps. By the mid-1950s, the realities of both Israel and the United States had changed. From the vantage point of Jews in the United States, Israel looked less inviting because of food rationing, border attacks, and the omnipresent fear of open war with the Arab states. The founding of the new American settlements in significant numbers did not start again until after the Six Day War in 1967, when the Israeli victory, combined with American domestic unrest and a newfound sense of utopianism, created a new generation willing to risk the hardships of building a kibbutz.[4]

Five American kibbutzim—Sasa and Gesher Haziv, founded in the late 1940s, and Ketura, Gezer, and Adamit, founded in the 1970s—provide the focus for this chapter. These kibbutzim built transnational communities that would fuse what the founders perceived as the best values of the United States with those of Israel.

In the United States, the future founders of these kibbutzim identified as Jews; in Israel they were identified as Americans. After they made the decision to join an "American" kibbutz they gained an in-between status in Israel. As a Ketura member explained, "Once you've made the jump you don't fit in any place really."[5] To properly understand these American kibbutzniks, it is necessary to view them as products of both the United States and Israel. When such a transnational approach is taken, circumscribed national histories become less significant, and some important connections between American Jewish and Israeli history become evident. Ideas and people emigrate and immigrate, taking with them valued religious and social practices and concepts. American Jews shaped their Israeli kibbutzim in their own image. Often, historians have noted the influence of American funds and politics in Israel, but as we will see, people and ideology also played a role.[6]

American Dreams Transplanted: The Role of American Zionist Youth Movements

Zionist youth movement members in the 1930s and 1940s believed that they had the power to influence Jewish history while at the same time creating an alternative choice for American Jews. As one youth group member explained it, "So we had a dream. Why shouldn't we solve several problems at one shot, build a new society, and really take the world by the scruff of its neck and lift it up?"[7] These American-educated youth viewed their desire to settle in the new State of Israel in American terms. They equated themselves with nineteenth-century American settlers, who, as their schoolbooks taught, established a nation by trial and error. In the words of one of Sasa's founders, "We see ourselves as American pioneers going West."[8] Kibbutz life, they theorized, would be similar to the pioneers' experiences in which people in new settlements had to rely on each other for survival. Their juxtaposition of American and Israeli ideologies was reinforced by none other than Louis D. Brandeis, the first Jew to sit on the US Supreme Court. Expressing his support of American Zionists, Brandeis wrote in 1934, "In their self-governing colonies . . . [kibbutz members] have pure democracy."[9] This support, the reframing of kibbutz settlements in the spirit of America's founding fathers, helped the American kibbutzniks view their choices squarely in the context of US history.

The American Jewish youth movements Hashomer Hatzair (the Young Guard) and Habonim (the Builders) created the catalyst for much of American emigration before 1967. Conceived as a synthesis between Zionism, socialism, and Marxism, Hashomer Hatzair, a Jewish scout movement, began in Eastern Europe, where it trained members for settlement in prestate Israel. The movement aimed to turn the members of the new Jewish working class into pioneers who would help "normalize" the Jewish people by farming instead of joining the merchant class.[10] Organization of the first US branches began in the 1920s.[11] The American branches of Hashomer Hatzair enforced a strict moral code, supported the establishment of a binational state in what was then called Palestine, and emphasized its members' physical and mental development, all with the goal of pioneering new settlements, kibbutzim, where its members would live in socialist societies.[12] With their rejection of established values and rebellion against social norms, members had more in common with the youth of the 1960s than with their peers who adhered to 1940s social standards. In hindsight, a member reflected, "We were the hippies of our time."[13] Many moved out of their parents' homes while in their teens and became fiercely antimaterialistic.[14] The movement's ideology excited some young Americans who grew up in the Depression. Explaining why she belonged to Hashomer Hatzair, Batya Ariel reasoned, "I knew what it meant for a father to be out of work, I knew what social injustice was. The Movement offered an explanation short of Marxism; it offered answers."[15] The Depression and the rise of anti-Semitism "made the American dream less attractive"[16] and the idea of starting a new society in an expected Jewish state more exciting. By 1936, the movement had approximately 3,000 members throughout the United States and Canada.[17]

At the same time, the Labor Zionist movement attracted members; American Habonim, founded by Labor Zionist in the 1930s, included adults as well as youth. Its principles stressed Jewish education, tradition, and training for kibbutz life. While Hashomer Hatzair emphasized discipline and ideology, it was often said, "Habonim's motto was the right to be confused" as it was less ideological than other Zionist movements.[18] Although Hashomer Hatzair and Habonim both affirmed Zionism, socialism, and pioneering, Habonim's policies provided more flexibility. Emigration to an Israeli kibbutz became a goal, not an absolute.[19]

For those who chose kibbutz life, the two movements supported separate and jointly operated training farms in the United States and Canada that sought to imitate life on Israeli kibbutzim. On these farms, run by movement members who were usually under the age of twenty-five, the curriculum included agriculture, Hebrew, Jewish culture, and the challenges of group living. By 1948, Hashomer Hatzair, Habonim, or a combination of the two operated four farms.[20]

Fascinated by the spirit of the young Zionist and Israeli pioneering in general, the American press of the late 1940s characterized these farms in romantic, often noble, terms. Donald E. Craig of the *New Republic* began a 1947 article with, "In the windswept barnyard of Cream Ridge, New Jersey farm Audrey Grossman, a 21-year-old filing clerk from Saint Paul, Minnesota, was trying to scrape a five years' accumulation of dirt from an old haybaler. As she dug into the messy machinery's gears and corners, she hummed a tune from 'Oklahoma.'"[21] Craig went on to compare the training farms favorably to the failed American utopian Brook Farm started by transcendentalist Unitarians in mid–nineteenth-century New England that emphasized equality with the aim of creating a "new Jerusalem."[22] For observers, the young future kibbutzniks forged links between America's idyllic agrarian past and the land of the Bible.

If the kibbutz movement seemed out of step with youth culture in the 1940s, it was very much in line with the counterculture movement of the 1970s. By the 1960s, communal farms had lost their nobility in the eyes of many conservative middle-aged Americans, not least because of the taint that collective enterprise assumed during the Cold War. A generation earlier, the idea of a kibbutz had seemed idyllic; now kibbutz life fit American concerns about troubling antiestablishment rebellion, not the heroic American past. For some young Jews, joining a kibbutz in Israel became parallel to what their counterculture peers were doing in America. Noted a founder of Young Judea's Kibbutz Ketura, "Our ideology was not such that we wanted to go build a commune out in Wyoming or something. . . . We obviously had Zionist ideology that went along with what we were doing, but with a definite understanding of Americans that wanted to get together and go live on a commune. And [most parents thought] that wasn't a nice thing to do."[23] As one kibbutznik put it, "Today communes in the United States belonged to the world of the eccentrics, while in Israel the kibbutz was mainstream. Israel's mothers and fathers belonged to kibbutzim."[24] A Gezer founder expressed his goals in the language of the 1960s, "Kibbutz for me [was] an attempt to live an unsold-out life."[25] It was the place where questioning young American Jews could create something relevant in American antiestablishment terms and authentic in Israeli terms.

Instead of growing up with memories of the Depression, anti-Semitism, and America at war, the founders of 1970s kibbutzim came of age in a prosperous United States. While not all kibbutz founders joined in 1960s activism, the antiwar, counterculture, and Civil Rights movements influenced their decisions. Some belonged to American Zionist youth groups, especially Young Judea and Habonim. "It was 'in' to be ideological, to belong to a movement, and to have goals and causes. So, belonging to Young Judea was more attractive," commented one kibbutznik.[26] For some, Jewish groups

or the social justice movements of the 1960s and 1970s were their voluntary associations, much like their parents' Hadassah, religious, or political
involvements. Whether they were active in civil rights, peace movements,
the Radical Zionist Alliance, or more moderate groups such as Young Judea,
then sponsored by Hadassah, all learned the arts of organizing, writing, and
following democratic procedure.[27] These skills were extremely useful when
they organized the kibbutz and later in the day-to-day running of a collective farm. Members of these youth groups often participated at the forefront
of 1960s activism. Young Judeans marched in the 1963 Freedom March on
Washington; Habonim members started the first high school SDS chapters
in 1965.[28] Although some joined the antiwar movement, many became dis-
gruntled with the New Left after it equated the US role in Cambodia with
Israel's raids on terrorist bases on its borders.[29] As the counterculture frag-
mented along ethnic lines, some became perplexed, questioning where they
fit. A founder of Kibbutz Adamit saw it this way: "The primary emphasis in
the 1960s [was] national self-determination whether for the Vietnamese or
the American Indians or Blacks or Chicanos. . . . I found myself . . . supporting
one liberation movement after another—never feeling at home."[30] When he
joined a Jewish caucus, he realized that he had a specially tailored alternative.
He could join a Zionist–socialist community in Israel, the kibbutz. Although
there were often differences in ideology and practice between American Jews
affiliated with Jewish youth groups and those who discovered the Israeli kibbutz on their own, all saw the kibbutz as a way to actualize their 60s values.
Israel was young, successful, Jewish, and very far from the American Jewish
establishment.

The American Israeli Kibbutz

Just thirty years before, the first American kibbutz received the assistance
of one of the most influential American Zionists, Justice Louis D. Brandeis.
On July 5, 1937, fifty-three American Hashomer Hatzair members from New
York, Boston, Detroit, Chicago, and Canada along with a group of Polish immigrants established Ein Hashofet (Spring of the Judge) twenty mile southeast
of Haifa, named in honor of Brandeis, who supported their goals and helped
with their finances.[31] Not only did Ein Hashofet founders connect with elite
contemporaries, but they also identified with the American history. This identification is made explicit in the following comment by one of the founders:
"When at the end of the first year of our settlement at Ein Hashofet, we gathered to survey our trials and accomplishments thus far, recollections of that

first winter in New England three hundred years ago arise, in spite of the vast differences in conditions and objectives that characterized the two undertakings."[32] Similar comparisons would be made by Americans who followed. Their identities became transnational, with roots in the United States, the Zionist movement, and a new Jewish country.

Members of Kibbutz Sasa exemplified these identities. In 1949, one hundred men and women in their early twenties established the first all-American kibbutz, Sasa, the fifth Hashomer Hatzair kibbutz. (Americans had settled on others kibbutzim, including Ein Hashofet, that had been established jointly by several nationalities.) Ninety percent of the founders had been members of the Hashomer Hatzair youth movement; 30 percent had joined the movement before age thirteen.[33] Although many of their parents most likely were immigrants to the United States, the members of Sasa significantly described themselves as "'pure' Yankee."[34] A "homogeneous group and pretty idealistic, enthusiastic, adventuresome and innovative"[35] who wanted "to find a better way of life,"[36] for them, founding a kibbutz meant creating a society in which there was complete equality for all people and a liberal and open way of life.[37] While in the United States, the youth movement had a strict code of sexual prohibitions, even banning its members from pairing off, and forbade smoking; when they reached the kibbutz in Israel, attitudes changed. According to one member, "In the states there was abstinence. . . . On the kibbutz—there you could smoke like a fiend or be a sex maniac."[38] The movement opposed religious and civil marriages, but 70 percent of Sasa's founders married by its fifth birthday. Members of Sasa were willing to challenge movement ideology on this point to make their more traditional parents "feel better."[39] However, as members of a left-wing movement, they remained more socially radical than those who belonged to the Labor Zionist Habonim.

Habonim's first postwar kibbutz, Gesher Haziv, also reached its new site in 1949.[40] Its eighty founders trained on farms in Canada and the United States before emigration to Israel. Once in Israel, they continued their training on an established kibbutz before settling with forty kibbutzniks of European background. When settled on their kibbutz, north of town of Nahariya near the Mediterranean Sea, the spectacular views excited all, but primitive living conditions challenged the community. Water was brought in by truck, showers at hosting kibbutzim were allowed once a week, and kerosene provided fuel for cooking and lighting. Mothers and children had to remain at the training sites, as the kibbutzim's primitive conditions were unsafe for children. The land needed to be cleared before farming could commence. However, for the

Americans, just having their own land in Israel accomplished many of their long-sought goals.[41]

Although Americans continued to join other immigrants in founding kibbutzim, they could not sustain their pioneering spirit at 1940s levels.[42] The 1950s saw immigration slow to a low of 187 Americans in 1956. However, in the late 1960s this rate again began to increase. Immigration grew to over 7,000 a year during the 1970s.[43] The founders of kibbutz Gezer, Adamit, and Ketura joined this wave. Some had college degrees, others little or no college; most were in their early twenties. All brought their youthful American confidence and energy to Israel: "We can fight to bring to Israeli life such Western notions as civil rights, sexual equality, a little efficiency in vast bureaucracies, Jewish consciousness, political solutions to a war-weary people," an optimistic founder of Gezer proclaimed.[44] Beyond their energetic ideals for Israel, they wanted to establish homes and raise their children in the idyllic environment they envisioned. To achieve their goals, they believed that they needed to create their own communities, not join established kibbutzim.

Because baby boomers wanted to control their own destinies, the process of establishing kibbutzim, in some cases, needed to be reinvented. None of the post-1967 migrants spent time on training farms in the United States; all received their knowledge of kibbutz life from Israelis. While some future kibbutzniks belonged to Habonim, most came to Israel as newly recruited group members, as individuals, or members of the Hadassah-sponsored Young Judea Zionist youth organization.

Prior to the birth of Kibbutz Ketura, neither Hadassah nor Young Judea had played a role in establishing a kibbutz. In fact, Hadassah had helped to create only one other American settlement: Neve Ilan, a moshav, established by young professionals, former Young Judeans in their thirties, and their families near Jerusalem.[45]

Kibbutz Ketura, born in the minds of American Young Judea members, eighteen-year-olds who took part in their movement's 1969–1970 "year-course" in Israel, would make transnational history.[46] Traditionally, Young Judea members spent a structured post–high school year in Israel studying Hebrew and Judaica, traveling, and living on kibbutzim. On completion of the program, students returned to the United States, attended college, and took their places in the leadership of the American Jewish community. However, some of the 1969–70 year-course members decided to follow a different path. By the end of their year in Israel, they agreed that they would not attend college in the United States but return to Israel the following year and create their own kibbutz. One of their program directors observed:

> At this time there was much unrest and confusion in America, especially on the campuses. This was the time of a search for more humane values, and better and more direct relations between people. There was also rebellion against intellectual values (the campus uprisings), and a feeling that the academic world of the university was not relevant to the essential needs of human growth. Members of the Garin [seed or initial group] were, I think, very much influenced by this atmosphere.[47]

In the United States, this group merged with a slightly older Young Judea group, whose members had been on "year-course" two years earlier and had been equally influenced by the turmoil of 1960s America. According to Mike Solouney, a member of the second group, "It was the period of the [Vietnam] war, and all these things in our culture—people were dropping out into communes and people were going off to war or evading the draft. All this had an effect on us."[48]

To the year-course participants, the idea of a Young Judea kibbutz made sense, since young people in Habonim and Hashomer Hatzair had been organizing kibbutzim for more than forty years. For them, it was the natural culmination of their years (some since the fourth grade) of Young Judea training, which taught them a love of Judaism and a love of Israel, although founding a kibbutz of their own had never been presented as an option. They viewed kibbutz formation as a form of rebellion against a conformist American life. The Young Judeans chose to establish their kibbutz in a remote area, forty miles north of Eilat, where they could build a cultural center that would contribute to Israeli life.

The transnational identity of Ketura members was continually reinforced by their ongoing connection to Young Judea and Hadassah. This was reflected in both personal and organizational connections. The sons and daughters of Hadassah members helped found Ketura; a few were children of national or regional Hadassah officers. This close relationship with Ketura led the Hadassah leadership to refer to them as "our kids" and like proud parents they spoke about them in glowing terms: "Ketura is the living example of idealistic youth from Hashachar [another name for Young Judea, literally "the dawn"] who have gone down to the Arava to create a kind of society that is enriching them as Jews and Zionists and which is also contributing greatly to the future of the State of Israel."[49] Furthermore, when new members emigrated in groups, they often received financial assistance from Hadassah in appreciation of their dedication and to make their "transition easier."[50] Over the years the Hadassah leadership provided the kibbutz with used kitchen equipment and a dentist's chair from the Hadassah Medical Center in Jerusalem as well as bedding, a piano, and even a motorcycle.[51] Along with the national organization, regional chapters of Hadassah and parents of kibbutz members also helped them with funds for building a community center with a synagogue, a tennis court, and a swimming pool.[52] Beyond the gifts, Hadassah most importantly used its significant influence with Israeli settlement and kibbutz organizations to push for kibbutz improvements and building funds. Because Ketura was the first kibbutz founded by the Young Judea youth movement, they did not have a track record with Israeli kibbutz associations and governing bodies. However, because Hadassah had an impressive history of dedication to Israel, it was able to pull strings for the kibbutz.[53]

Hadassah supported the kibbutz not only because of its quasiparental ties. As the kibbutz matured it became an important part of Young Judea's year-course and high school programs. The national chairman of the Hadassah Youth Department reflected, "This aliyah by American youth [Ketura members] is based on knowledge of Israel—its strength and its weaknesses. These Hashachar [year-course] graduates made their decision after a living experience in Israel."[54] Because Hadassah wanted Ketura members to share their experiences with other Young Judeans, the organization paid a yearly subvention to Ketura, and in return the kibbutz welcomed Young Judeans to work on the kibbutz and study in its classrooms.[55] This, in addition to visits and other interactions with Hadassah members ensured that a constant connection with the United States was maintained that was, up to that time, unique for an Israeli kibbutz.

Ketura officially received its land on Thanksgiving Day, November 22, 1973. On that day, the Israeli army, which had had a small training camp there, transferred the land to the "blue jeans" brigade, as Ketura founders were dubbed, due to their generational uniform of white shirts and blue jeans.[56] A Hadassah officer noted "how significant it was that a group of young Americans should be in Israel giving thanks for being allowed to move in to begin raising turkeys, to do the kind of pioneering which the first settlers in the United States did—and to be grateful that there is a country to which Jews can go as [a] right."[57] Once again noting the metaphorical parent–child relationship between Hadassah

FIGURE 11.1. Norm Frankel, member Kibbutz Gezer, 1979. Courtesy of Norm Frankel.

and the new kibbutzniks, she continued, "That our having been blessed with such children willing to settle in this 'forsaken spot' augers well for the future."[58] The Hadassah board planned to give the kibbutz a television as housewarming gift, but in keeping with the times the kibbutzniks chose to receive a stereo instead so that they could play their record collections.[59] In 1976 the kibbutz was nominated for the Herzl Award for pioneering Zionism because of the fact that it was Young Judea's first kibbutz.[60]

The founders of Kibbutz Gezer also sought a nonestablishment life. Its site in central Israel between Modi'in, Ramle, and Rehovot had a long history of failure; its evolution in the 1970s mirrored the transformation of 1960s Jewish youth. In the 1940s Gezer had been a viable kibbutz. After it was overrun by Arab armies during the Israeli War of Independence it never recovered; by 1961 it was vacant.

In the early seventies, with Americans again emigrating to Israel, Gezer reemerged as a settlement site. A group of Conservative Union Synagogue Movement youth from Boston settled there in 1972. Although they had high ideals, they failed economically. During the early 1970s Gezer became a way station for young American drifters who would stay from a day to many months. This transient population impeded the settlement process. By the end of 1973 few lived at Gezer. In 1974 another attempt was made. This time Habonim members and others interested in kibbutz life formed an emigrant group in the United States. They held meetings and started a newsletter named *The Carrot and the Shtick*.[61] After six months of training in Israel on Kibbutz Afkim, thirty members, whose average age was twenty-five, began to build their homes at Gezer on July 4, 1974, the birthday of the United States and the same date that the members of Sasa had chosen to found their kibbutz twenty-five years earlier. The members of this new kibbutz had goals beyond settlement. As one of the founders said, "We don't see aliyah to kibbutz as an end in itself. Those of us who have grown up in the Labor Zionist Youth movement, and many of us who haven't, consider aliyah to Gezer as a part of our personal ideology. This means a realization of our commitment to Israel, to a socialist lifestyle, and a creative Jewish existence. These commitments, however, will not end when we reach the kibbutz."[62]

Independent Thinking

The founders of 1970s kibbutzim had role models in the 1940s generation. The 1940s generation had become known for its flexibility and its confrontations with kibbutz movement ideology. The members of Gesher Haziv, for example, were committed to a socialist Zionist lifestyle. But that did not mean that they had lost their American individualism. One month after settlement, Sasa held a two-day seminar on kibbutz equality, democracy, and culture. These transplanted American values led them to approve members' desires to pursue higher education, even when this education would not directly benefit the kibbutz as a whole, contrary to the prevailing kibbutz movement ideology.[63] As opposed to most kibbutzim, which valued the collective, Sasa wanted to create an environment where each individual was important. Besides granting members' requests for higher education,[64] Sasa also gave time off work for members to undertake arts and cultural activities, emphasizing individual personal development.

The desire to honor individual members' requests was just one characteristic of American pioneers; they were also pragmatic and undogmatic. An observer at Gesher Haziv commented, "Americans [as compared to Europeans] take a much more rational and calculating attitude to the kibbutz. . . . No one way of doing things is necessarily sacred. . . . If a new method proves to be more effective, saves time, or labor, or money, the old method is quite cheerfully discarded."[65] Members of Sasa were not satisfied with the education offered their children, so they started their own egalitarian school that educated their children as well as boarded underprivileged urban children.[66]

At Gesher Haziv, the members questioned the ideology of their kibbutz movement as well. They decided that they did not want their children to sleep in separate children's houses, as was then mandated by the kibbutz movement. Instead, they chose to have children live with their parents. As one member, Dvora Schasberg, said, "Having your children live apart from you did not come down from Sinai."[67] A founder believed that the children sleeping at home "molded the character of the kibbutz" by making it more family oriented than more traditional kibbutzim of the time.[68] The members of Gesher Haviz further connected themselves with the United States of the 1950s by adopting Dr. Benjamin Spock's *The Common Sense Book of Baby and Child Care,* which emphasized physical contact with children rather than the established German methods of the day, which were viewed as being more efficient and clean.[69] According to Schasberg, in the early 1950s Americans "were the vanguard of all this kind of education."[70] She concluded, "I think a lot of the American girls would have left" had the American way of raising children not prevailed.[71]

The 1970s generation also wanted to change Israeli society. As confident Americans raised with the idea that anything was possible, it did not occur to them that they could fail or could not make their own rules. Just making aliyah was not enough. They needed to reshape Israeli society in the image of the American 1960s. As a Ketura founder stated, "We came here because we wanted to be able to effect changes in Israeli society and we felt that by effecting changes in our small society we would be able to also include the outside society."[72] To do this they worked to influence their fellow Israelis. Although most of their victories were local, influenced by American activism and the Israeli kibbutz movement, Americans created distinctive patterns of communal life. American kibbutz members along with American immigrants who had settled in Israel's cities helped introduce American-style feminism and pluralism to their native-born Israeli neighbors.

Equality

Americans of the 1940s and 1970s brought with them their own interpretation of gender equality. The kibbutz, like many American communes, allowed members to live in socialist communities that emphasized gender equality.

However, on the kibbutzim of the 1940s and 1950s, women who, in their youth movements, had seen themselves as equals of men, were pushed into cooking, cleaning, and doing all of the childcare, while men were working in building and agriculture. For the founders of Sasa, founding a kibbutz meant creating a society in which equality was not just a concept but a reality. At Sasa the situation was in part resolved by making men responsible for at least 25 percent of the "service" jobs. This gave women a greater opportunity to work at skilled jobs.[73] However, not all were satisfied.

By the 1960s, the fight for women's rights was no longer just an issue for socialists; it had become an important part of the American culture wars. Sixties kibbutz founders brought a new American understanding of feminism and women's rights with them to Israel. However, in the 1970s, most Israeli kibbutzim still differentiated between men's and women's work. Usually only women were drafted to work with small children and most other domestic jobs. This became an obstacle for American women who contemplated life on an Israeli kibbutz. Giving men and women the ability to choose the type of work they wanted to engage in became an important marker of American kibbutzim. The National Organization for Women (NOW), founded in the United States in 1966, influenced how Americans Jews viewed their roles on the kibbutz.

The youthful American kibbutz founders objected to traditional work assignments and included feminism in their kibbutz platforms. The members of Ketura had the added example of watching the women of Hadassah work side by side with male and female Israelis.[74] A male kibbutz founder explained, "Our work attitudes and our social attitudes [are] that women should be and are for all intents and purposes equal to men. . . . Some of the jobs that might have been considered to be reserved for men or reserved for women are not that way in Ketura."[75] In these American kibbutzim, men as well as women worked in the baby houses and kitchens, and women could chose to work in the fields. On their kibbutzim their feminism was taken for granted. "I grew up with certain socialist and feminist ideas—and I need a particular kind of creative Jewish lifestyle which is in an American tradition. . . . Gezer allows me a full Jewish life without totally giving up important things from my American culture," concluded a male kibbutz member.[76] For many Americans kibbutzniks, feminism was second nature; therefore, it became an important part of their kibbutz identity.

However, off the kibbutz, Americans faced challenges in their efforts to influence gender equality on other kibbutzim and within the kibbutz governing movements. Vivian Silver, the secretary of Gezer, in an attempt to gain gender equality in her kibbutz movement, sought to have the move-ment enforce a rule, first passed in 1930, that ensured that women would hold one-third of the elected offices in kibbutz organizations. But it was not always observed. Silver, an advocate of women's rights in the United States before her aliyah, received limited support from other members of her kib-butz movement's governing body. "I tried to pass this resolution . . . I felt so alone in the fight at the time. We lost. And when I brought it to a meeting of the movement, there was a lot of scorn there too."[77] According to analysis, this was viewed as "too far-reaching a change."[78] Therefore, although gender equal-ity was widely practiced on American kibbutzim it was difficult for Americans to establish the practice in nationwide kibbutzim governance. American kib-butzniks united with others in forming a nationwide committee that worked for equality of work assignments and kibbutz management on all kibbutzim and in their regional and national organization.[79]

The women from Ketura and the other American kibbutzim continued to face difficulty when working with male government officials. A manager of Ketura commented that while her leadership was respected at home, in working with the Ministry of Housing, the Ministry of Absorption, and other officials, she was treated in a pejorative manner. "Among the 'big men' I was related to as a woman rather than as kibbutz secretary."[80] With few female kibbutz mangers at the time, American women felt that they had to prove their ability as women and Americans before they were accepted.

Religion

Influenced by their youth movements, each settlement's members selected a different way to express their Judaism. Secular European immigrants often could not understand why Americans wanted to preserve religious practices. For many Europeans of the postwar era, only two options existed secularism or Orthodoxy. Most American kibbutzniks did not subscribe to Orthodoxy. However, some, following nontraditional American examples, felt comfort-able adapting Jewish traditions, if not religious practices, to fit their needs. Although Kibbutz Sasa's members, following the practices of Hashomer Hat-ziar, celebrated Passover as an agricultural festival, they reimagined and mod-ified the ritual to reflect their American identity. In 1949, just three months after settling on the rural and isolated hills of the Upper Galilee, Kibbutz Sasa's members created a Haggadah for their first Passover that reflected their American and their Jewish identities:

Why are we, Jewish youth from the American *Galut* celebrating *Pesach* in Sasa in the Galil?

How could one possibly explain all that has taken place in these packed years of our lives so that now quite calmly and irrevocably we have prepared to leave our native land and language and move off to a little sliver of a stretch of rock and desert?

What is our Jewishness, the Jewishness grown in the cities of the Galut. I am a Jew because: it is impossible to exist in this world without being attached to some national cultural or mixture of national cultures. Because we do not want to live the hypocritical and hounded existence that would follow in the wake of an attempted escape from Jewishness and because we want to identify ourselves with the millions of Jews who were slaughtered during the Hitlerian era. Today we are culturally mongrels with a blurred internationalist outlook and a great deal of metropolitan Americanism. In spite of this, there is a slim but unbreakable subconscious threat that ties us completely to our Jewishness.[81]

According to one of its authors, the Haggadah, with this introduction written in English, not Hebrew, "integrate[d] or introduce[d] things that would be specific to us."[82] Other American kibbutzim also adapted and personalized Jewish activities. Unlike the secularists at Sasa, the Habonim members at Gesher Haziv wanted a Reform or Conservative type of Judaism. After working out a compromise with the European members of the kibbutz, who wanted no religious practices, they were able to establish progressive religious services in which men and women sat together and both boys and girls could become bat and bar mitzvah. While Gesher Haziv maintained religious options for its members, it had no Orthodox members.[83]

The pioneers of the 1970s reflected a more pluralistic American Judaism, and their youth movements mirrored their mixed practices. Other American Jewish communal organizations, such as Jewish Federations and women's groups, including Hadassah, had members who followed varying religious practices. Most Israeli kibbutzim, on the other hand, characterized their members as religiously Orthodox, or secular, or even non-Jewish.[84] Going against the Israeli norm, Americans established kibbutzim that were inclusive. Ketura's founders, products of Hadassah's Young Judea youth movement, wanted a settlement where all their members would feel at home. This meant that for the first time in Israel a kibbutz would have both members who adhered to Jewish traditional practices such as a kosher kitchen and Shabbat observance and members who chose to observe only the practices that they deemed relevant. Reflecting Young Judea practices, Ketura adhered to Shabbat and kosher laws in public, while members were free to ignore them in private.[85] Soon after their founding, when a community center for the kibbutz was envisioned with a library, classrooms, and a synagogue, it would be named in honor of a Hadassah president who had worked tirelessly for their support. This decision again reinforced their connections with Hadassah as well as their commitment to religious observance.[86]

For their first foray to instill pluralism beyond the kibbutz, they requested that regional interkibbutz activities be moved from Friday to Saturday nights so that their observant members could attend. They were victorious, and these events were among the few in which observant and secular Jews could socialize together. In 1987 Ketura received the Speaker of the Knesset Award that honored their "excellent activity in advancing mutual respect, toleration and good neighborliness in education and deed" and a year later the Presidents' Tolerance Award from the Israeli government.[87]

Kibbutz Gezer also observed a form of Jewish pluralism drawn from the United States. One member commented, "Only at Gezer, . . . can I live without being embarrassed about my American background—and my American style of Jewishness."[88] They lit candles on Friday nights and "like good American Jews went to the synagogue on the High Holidays."[89] Gezer attracted Jewish Americans who came from Reform and Conservative backgrounds. One such American was Detroit-born Miri Gold, who arrived at Gezer in the mid-1970s. Her determination would push Gezer to the forefront of the pluralism fight. With no one to prepare children for bat and bar mitzvah and lead the community spiritually, Gold enrolled in Hebrew Union College in Jerusalem to become a Reform rabbi. In 2005, she became the test case for the movement for non-Orthodox rabbis to be paid by the Israeli government for their work.[90] After a landmark Supreme Court decision in 2012, Gezer will be home to the county's first paid non-Orthodox rabbi. This decision will have long-term effects for all Israelis.[91]

The members of the secular Adamit took a very different approach; they founded a kibbutz that admitted non-Jewish as well as Jewish members. Their common ground lay in their American background, not in their adherence to Jewish practices. All American kibbutzim, whether leaning toward

traditional or secular practices, demonstrated a high level of religious tolerance that is not evident in most Israeli communities.

Conclusion

The most influential characters in this narrative are time and context; events
in both the United States and Israel came together to motivate young American Jews in both eras to create kibbutzim that were distinctly American. In
the 1940s, soon after World War II and Israel's War of Independence, American transnationals joined others in seeking to enhance the image of Jews in
the world by helping to create a strong, independent Jewish state. By the
1970s, after the Six Day War, that mission had been accomplished.

Although the wars of 1948, 1967, and 1973 caused suffering and hardship,
the fact that Israel had become a prosperous state gave the 1970s generation
advantages. Many saw 1967 as "the height of the American Jewish romance
with Israel."[92] It was a euphoric time to be settling in Israel; however, it was
laden with many political and social decisions. American kibbutzniks chose
to build inside the "green line," not in the territories captured in the 1967 war.

Each group entered a different Israel. By 1970, Israel was a thriving, established country that attracted Americans: it had reached the age of twenty-
two years old and had weathered many battles. Newcomers no longer lived
in unsafe tents and struggled along with little food and water. The concept of
pioneering now reflected decades of Israeli settlement.[93] Unlike the 1940s pioneers, many 1970s youth had spent time in Israel before founding a new kibbutz; they were not the sons and daughters of the immigrant working class,
nor were they products of a depression economy. They belonged to the middle
class or above. The majority were the children of affluence, part of the postwar
baby boom. Having grown up in the optimism and relatively stable economic
conditions of the 1950s, the teens of the 1960s felt that they "were born to be
the best and the brightest."[94] Part of the biggest generation in history, they
were filled with idealism and hope for the future. Confident of their values
and anticipating unlimited opportunities, they saw the slogan "do your own
thing" not as an aberration but an ideal.

This optimism, the number of kibbutzniks with college degrees, and their
commitment to gender issues was noted by the Israeli press, which labeled
the kibbutzniks as "American" well after their settlement. A 1982 article in the
Israeli newspaper *Davar*, titled "From Ein HaShofet to Ketura and Yahel: The
North American Immigration to Israel Celebrating Its Jubilee," emphasized
their openness and tolerance that they brought from the United States as well

as their commitment to education.[95] Noting that most have college degrees and that many created educational programs such as the school at Sasa, which educates its youth along with Youth Aliyah children, and children from the regional area together for elementary through high school. This integrated concept was perceived as unique, as immigrant youth without parents were usually educated separately. A high level education is noted by the Americans as well, as text books from the 1960s line the library of Kibbutz Gezer.[96]

The 1970s generation left the United States at the height of the women's movement. This colored their relationship with the Israelis they worked with, as their expectations of gender interactions were dramatically different from many of their new compatriots. Most of the women had been fighting sexism in the United States, and when they reached Israel members of their kibbutzim federation called them "cute" rather than respecting them as elected officers of their kibbutzim. They had to refight battles that had been to some degree won in the United States.

Unlike many of their European, Middle Eastern, and African counterparts among new immigrants in Israel, Americans freely chose to leave their homes in the United States.[97] They intended to keep strong ties with the United States and their families. This created a paradox for the immigrants. On the one hand, other Israelis respected them for leaving their families to immigrate to Israel, but, on the other hand, they were not always trusted, because they could easily return to the United States (and often did).[98] Batya Ariel, a Sasa founder, believed that they were taken less seriously than Europeans because "Americans never burned their bridges, so that they always have this possibility of going back."[99] Ariel recalled that one of the ideological leaders of Hashomer Hatzair said on a visit to Sasa, "The next time I come, there will probably be half of you here."[100] Without the full support of the kibbutz movement, Hashomer Hatzair members at Sasa had a difficult time maintaining morale and group cohesion.

The later kibbutzim also had morale problems. In their first decades, the three kibbutzim achieved much just by sustaining their existence, but they also faced disappointments. As members left for a variety of reasons, kibbutzim found it difficult to thrive. Without a continuous stream of new American activists and financial support, idealistic goals often became out of reach. However, most felt that with their American experiences they had a sense of purpose and had something to offer to Israel.

In both the 1940s and 1970s, the young Americans founded kibbutzim at a time in their lives when exploring different lifestyle options was often expected and possible. Many kibbutzniks of the 1940s had grown up in the kibbutz movement and moved from their families' homes to communal living, never having had a chance to think of themselves as individuals. With hindsight, Batya Ariel views her comrades as "a group of people who were unsettled in many respects. They were evolving as people . . . first learning . . . what they might be interested in, what they might want to do with their lives."[101] She wrote in 1985, "How idealistic and innocent we were and young! . . . We were quite ignorant of any real knowledge of the country we were going to and the one we were leaving behind."[102] Seventies-era kibbutzniks' lives were also in flux, but many had the advantage of a greater knowledge of Israel before their immigration.

Most of these migrants thought that they were not unusual and that in time others would follow in their footsteps. This for the most part did not happen. Kibbutz Lotan, founded in 1983 and affiliated with the Reform movement, was the last all-American kibbutz to be established in Israel.[103]

All kibbutzim discussed here still exist, but due to changes in the Israeli economy, kibbutz structures have changed to varying extents. Kibbutzim in Israel were founded as socialist institutions with all working "according to [their] abilities" and all being supported "according to their needs." Among the kibbutzim chronicled, Sasa and Ketura completely rejected privatization, although their industries have changed. Both have deemphasized agriculture in favor of industrial projects at Sasa and business projects at Ketura. All retain an American entrepreneurial character. Ketura is recognized as a leader in the environmental movement and water conservation, Sasa in education.[104] Gesher Haziv has privatized but retained some of its mutual assistance practices for veteran members while founding new community organization structures. Adamit, on the other hand, faced dire economic problems and had to sell land and attract a tourist business; today it is trying to reclaim some kibbutz structure.[105]

When Marie Syrkin insightfully concluded, "The reality of the American dream emboldened her Zionist dream,"[106] her subject was Golda Meir. However, the same could be said for most American kibbutz founders in Israel. In the 1940s and 1970s, idealistic American Zionists committed to use their American experiences to transform Israel. Today several kibbutzim still reflect the origins of their founders. Whether it be education at Sasa, the tolerance and environmental endeavors of Ketura, the cry of "play ball" on the baseball diamond of Gezer, or Rabbi Gold's victory for religious pluralism, all demonstrate the effects of American kibbutzim in shaping the Israeli landscape.

Notes

1. Abraham Karp, *Haven and Home* (New York: Schocken, 1985), 278.
2. Yosef Criden and Saadia Gelb, *The Kibbutz Experience* (New York: Schocken, 1974), 30. For further discussion, see Ava F. Kahn, "Pragmatists in the Promised Land: American Immigrant Voluntary Associations in Israel 1948–1978" (PhD diss., University of California, Santa Barbara, 1989).
3. Criden and Gelb, *The Kibbutz Experience*, 31.
4. Only two kibbutzim were started in the 1950s and early 1960s that had a significant number of American members; neither settlement was founded solely by emigrants from the United States.
5. Leah Kayman, oral history transcript, Ava F. Kahn, interviewer, January 7, 1984 (New York: American Jewish Committee, Oral History Library, New York Public Library), 9.
6. E.g., see Peter Grose, *Israel in the Mind of America* (New York: Knopf, 1983).
7. Criden and Gelb, *The Kibbutz Experience*, 31.
8. Sasa founder, taped interview with author, February 1983.
9. Louis D. Brandeis, "Palestine and Jewish Democracy," in *The Curse of Bigness: Miscellaneous Papers of Louis D. Brandeis,* ed. Louis Dembitz Brandeis, Osmond K. Fraenkel, and Clarence M. Lewis (New York: Viking, 1934), 241.
10. John R. Snarey, "Becoming a Kibbutz Founder: An Ethnographic Study of the First All-American Kibbutz in Israel," *Jewish Social Studies* 46, no. 2 (1984): 106.
11. Dov Vardi, "Beginnings" (typescript), 15. This is ch. 1 of an unpublished manuscript on the history of Hashomer Hatzair in America. Vardi, who found a letter dated October 22, 1922, from an American group of HaShomer Hatzair, gave permission; however, this is the only known reference to their existence before 1923. Yaakov Morris believes that Hashomer Hatzair was not started in the United States until 1928. See Yaakov Morris, *Pioneers from the West* (Westport, CT: Greenwood, 1972), 20. According to John R. Snarey ("Becoming a Kibbutz Founder," 106), the Young Guard set up a branch in New York in 1923, and by 1927 there were branches in four cities that were administered by the New York office.
12. Batya Ariel, interview with author, transcript, 111.
13. Author interview with a founder of Sasa, February 1983.
14. Snarey, "Becoming a Kibbutz Founder," 122.
15. Batya Ariel, interview with author, transcript, 110.
16. Snarey, "Becoming a Kibbutz Founder," 107.
17. Ibid.
18. Dvora Schasberg (also spelled Davora Schusberg or Shusberg), oral history transcript, Ava F. Kahn, interviewer, February 12, 1984 transcript (New York: American Jewish Committee, Oral History Library, New York Public Library), 24. The "right to be confused" motto was attributed to Berl Katznelson (1887–1944), a Labor Zionist leader and educator.
19. Criden and Gelb, *The Kibbutz Experience*, 31.
20. David Breslau, ed., *Arise and Build: The Story of American Habonim* (New York: Ichud Habonim Labor Zionist Youth, 1961), 58. Supported by Habonim and Hashomer Hatzair, the Histradrut, and donations, the farms received no major funds from the organized Jewish establishment in the United States, since many American Jewish leaders

felt that there was little need for Americans to emigrate to Israel. Melvin I. Urofsky, *We Are One!* (Garden City, NY: Anchor/Doubleday, 1978), 265.

21. Donald W. Craig, "To Build a Nation," *The New Republic,* December 1, 1947, 16.

22. "Brook Farm," accessed March 12, 2014, www25.uua.org/uuhs/duub/articles/brook-farm.html.

23. Peggy Ginsberg, oral history transcript, Ava F. Kahn, interviewer, January 7, 1984 (New York: American Jewish Committee, Oral History Library, New York Public Library), 12.

24. "A Strong Wind and Good Music at Adamit" (Kibbutz document, Adamit archive).

25. David Twersky, "Have You Sold Out?" *Response: A Contemporary Jewish Review No. 29* 10, no. 1 (1976): 46, 47.

26. Debby Weisman, oral history transcript, Zvi Fraser, interviewer, November 24, 1980 (Institute of Contemporary Jewry, Oral History division, Hebrew University of Jerusalem), 14.

27. Young Judea was founded in 1909 and affiliated with the Zionist Organization of America; in 1941 Hadassah became a cosponsor, by 1967 Hadassah assumed full sponsorship of the organization.

28. Debby Weisman, oral history transcript, 9; Jack Nusan Porter and Peter Dreier eds., *Jewish Radicalism: A Selected Anthology* (New York: Grove, 1973), xxii.

29. Aliza Samuel, "I Listen Again to Joan Baez," *Midstream,* May 1975, 35.

30. Richard Bamberger, oral history transcript, Ava F. Kahn, interviewer, February 12, 1984 (New York: American Jewish Committee, Oral History Library, New York Public Library), 1.

31. Joseph B. Glass, *From New Zion to Old Zion: American Jewish Immigrants and Settlement in Palestine 1917–1939* (Detroit: Wayne State University Press, 2002), 266–67.

32. S.B.Z. "Ein Hashofet after One Year," *Pioneers From America—75 Years of Hehalutz,* ed. David Breslau (Tel Aviv: Bogrei Hehalutz America, 1981), 170.

33. Snarey, "Becoming a Kibbutz Founder," 111, 109.

34. Kibbutz Sasa, *The Launching: Sasa's First Year* (Israel: Haaretz Press-Zionist Organization/Youth and Hechulutz Department, 1951), 16.

35. Kibbutz Sasa, "Founders' Gathering" (1984), 24.

36. Kibbutz Sasa member, interview with author, February 1983.

37. Ibid.

38. Snarey, "Becoming a Kibbutz Founder," 123.

39. Ibid., 122.

40. Americans helped found the Anglo-Baltic Kfar Blum in 1943.

41. Menucha Kraine, "The First Year Gesher Haziv: Yesterday and Today," *Arise and Build,* accessed March 12, 2014, www.habonimdror.org/resources/arise%20and%20build/The%20First%20Year%20Gesher%20Haziv%20Yesterday%20and%20Today.htm.

42. Barkai (1950), Kissufim (1951), and Lahav (1952) were among them.

43. Kevin Avruch, *American Immigrants in Israel* (Chicago: University of Chicago Press, 1981), 37.

44. Vivian Silver, "From New York to Kibbutz Gezer," *Response: A Contemporary Jewish Review No. 29* (summer 1976), 119.

45. The members of Neve Ilan, who were older on average than most kibbutz founders and who included families with children, were also influenced by US political and social trends of 1960s. Their goals were similar to the founders of Ketura, who wanted to

live in a Jewish pluralistic community that valued cooperative economic, cultural, and social life. See Kahn, "Pragmatists in the Promised Land," 145–48.

46. Young Judea's year-course in Israel started in 1956.

47. "An Interview with Joe Wernik, Momo Forman, and Asaf Carmi about Kibbutz K'tura," *Hamagshim Journal* 5, no. 3 (1974): 10.

48. Mike Solouney, oral history transcript, Ava F. Kahn, interviewer, January 7, 1984 (New York: American Jewish Committee, Oral History Library, New York Public Library), 3. Although it was possible to evade the draft by emigrating to Israel, this was not an answer for these who were pacifists, for in Israel they would be required to join the Israeli army.

49. Young Judea Minutes, Hadassah Zionist Youth Commissioner, July 10, 1974, box 18, folder "Young Judea Minutes Kibbutz Ketura 1968–1991," Hadassah Collection (RG8), American Jewish Historical Society, New York; Pre-Convention Hadassah National Board Minutes, August 8, 1975, Young Judea Minutes Legal Size Box 2, folder "Minutes Hadassah National Board 1967–1980." Hadassah Collection (RG8), American Jewish Historical Society, New York.

50. In 1986, Hadassah gave each of the ten immigrants to Ketura two hundred dollars when they left the United States. An accompanying letter stated, "In making aliyah you are fulfilling the highest ideal of the movement." See letter from Ruth Popkin, National President of Hadassah to Julie Baretz, September 4, 1986, Box 15, "Young Judea, Kibbutz Ketura Financial Contributions from Hadassah 1980–1994." Hadassah Collection (RG8), American Jewish Historical Society, New York.

51. E.g., see "Letter from Marcel Dubois, Kibbutz Ketura to Mr. Y. Dekel, Head of Supplies Division Hadassah, Jerusalem," September 15, 1980; "Letter from K. J. Mann, M.D., Director General, Hadassah Medical Organization, Jerusalem to Mrs. Bernice S. Tannenbaum, HMO Chairman, Hadassah, New York," November 26, 1980; "Letter from Elaine Glenn, Fundraising Chairman, National Youth Activities Department to Leah Kayman, Kibbutz Ketura," February 2, 1982. Box 14, "Kibbutz Ketura Correspondence 1973–1984 (two folders), Hadassah Collection (RG8), American Jewish Historical Society, New York.

52. In addition to Hadassah, kibbutz and settlement associations and the Jewish Agency sent support to Ketura. For examples of support from Hadassah and other sources, see "Letter from Sam Roth, Mazkir Ketura, to Charlotte Jacobson, Chairman, World Zionist Organization, American Section," December 10, 1976; "Letter from Marcel Debowy, Mazkir, Ketura to Bernice Tannenbaum, National President, Hadassah," November 4, 1979. This letter states in part, "Kibbutz Ketura is most appreciative of the interest and care that Hadassah has given it, both on the large scale of the Rose Halpern Center and on the smaller scale of the surplus supplies made available through Bea Usdan's work." Box 14, "Kibbutz Ketura Correspondence 1973–1982"; Letter from Charlotte Jacobson, Chairman to Leah Kayman, Mazkira, Ketura, January 19, 1983. This letter notes member support: "I was informed by one of our Hadassah leaders that her husband is willing to contribute $7,500 toward the tennis courts for Ketura." Box 14, "Kibbutz Ketura Correspondence 1982–1984. Hadassah Collection (RG8), American Jewish Historical Society, New York.

53. Much of this work was done by Charlotte Jacobson in her capacity as a long-time Hadassah National Board member and president as well as chair of the American

Section of the World Zionist Organization. E.g., see letters about furnishing the kibbutz community room and obtaining an upgraded ambulance. "Letter from Charlotte Jacobson, chairman, The Jewish Agency-American Section, Inc. to Mr. Raanan Weitz, Chairman, Settlement Department, W.Z.O.," April 26, 1974. Box 14, "Kibbutz Ketura Correspondence 1973–1982;" Letter from Charlotte Jacobson, Chairman, to Mr. Mordechai Degani, Chairman, Magen David Adom Headquarters, January 3, 1983. Box 14, "Kibbutz Ketura Correspondence 1982–1984." Hadassah Collection (RG8), American Jewish Historical Society, New York.

    Kibbutz Ketura members considered Jacobson a mentor. See "Hadassah Mourns the Passing of Charlotte Jacobson, Former Hadassah President," accessed March 12, 2014, www.hadassah.org/site/apps/nlnet/content2.aspx?c=keJNIWOvElH&b=5771079&ct=8399585.

54. "37 American Youth Pioneer in Negev," press release, Hadassah News (ca. December 1973), Ketura Archive.

55. "Letter from Richie Goldenstein, Mazkir, to Frieda Lewis, National President, Hadassah," December 18, 1983. National Board Minutes. Box 15, "Young Judea, Kibbutz Ketura financial contributions from Hadassah 1980–1994." Hadassah Collection (RG8), American Jewish Historical Society, New York.

56. "Mrs. Matzkin Report," December 6, 1973, Hadassah National Board Minutes, Box 18, "Young Judea Minutes, Kibbutz Ketura." Hadassah Collection (RG8), American Jewish Historical Society, New York.

57. Ibid.

58. Ibid.

59. Ibid.; "Mrs. Matzkin Reports on Her Recent Trip to Israel," Executive Committee Minutes, July 10, 1974, Box 18 "Young Judea Minutes, Kibbutz Ketura." Hadassah Collection (RG8), American Jewish Historical Society, New York.

60. In 1976 Ketura was nominated for the Herzl Award for a Zionist act in Israel. The nomination in part reads, "The members of Kibbutz Keturah were raised in the Jewish youth movement 'Young Judaea' [sic] in the United States. This youth movement is attached to Hadassah. In the past, this movement had no tradition of Hagashamah [settlement in Israel]. A group of young people, graduates of this youth movement, decided to change this tradition and to establish a kibbutz in the Arava. Three years passed since they arrived in the Arava, established a beautiful settlement and made things grow and flourish there. They are the real Chalutzim [pioneers]. And additional young people, from Jewish communities and youth movements in the United States, who were very far from Zionist Hagshamah, follow in their steps and come to Israel (Yahal—the first kibbutz of the Reform movement). These young people deserve the Herzl Award—the Award will assume a national pioneer meaning if it is granted to this group." The nomination was signed by Guri Mir, general secretary of the General Organization of working and studying youth. Dated November 21, 1976. Box 14, "Kibbutz Ketura Awards," Hadassah Collection (RG8), American Jewish Historical Society, New York.

61. *Gezer* is the Hebrew word for "carrot."

62. Kenneth Bob and Susan Geit, "A Few Words from Gezer" (Kibbutz Gezer, Ihud Habonim, Labor Zionist Youth, spring 1975, 1).

63. Esty Kofsky, oral history transcript, Ava F. Kahn, interviewer. February 12, 1984 (New York: American Jewish Committee, Oral History Library, New York Public Library), 9.

Kofsky, a member of American Habonim in Detroit, came to Israel in 1950 at the age of twenty-seven.

64. Sam Israel (pseudonym), interview with author, February 1983.

65. Ira Eisenstein, "Americans in Israel," *The Reconstructionist* 16 (January 1951), 9.

66. There often was a large educational gap between Westerners and Jews who arrived from African, Asian, and Middle Eastern countries.

67. Dvora Schasberg, oral history, 9.

68. Ibid., 8.

69. Ibid., 11; Esty Kofsky, oral history, 13. The members from European backgrounds, accustomed to caring for babies in an extremely sterile environment, believed in having little physical contact with their children. They restricted play on the floor and wore white smocks when they were with their children.

70. Dvora Schasberg, oral history, 12.

71. Ibid., 11–12. Some of the European members of the kibbutz wanted to retain the German childrearing methods.

72. Leah Kayman, oral history transcript, 11.

73. Snarey, "Becoming a Kibbutz Founder," 118.

74. Women such as Charlotte Jacobson were extremely supportive of Ketura. A former Hadassah president wrote on Jacobson's death, "Ask anyone at Kibbutz Ketura in the Arava, where she was a mentor, for the name of one person who gave them unconditional strength, encouragement and inspiration and you will hear hers. Charlotte loved young people and they loved her." Bonnie Lipton, *Jerusalem Post*, May 23, 2010, accessed March 12, 2014. www.jpost.com/Opinion/Op-EdContributors/Article.aspx?id=176227.

75. Mike Solouney, oral history, 12.

76. Matthew Nesvisky, "Getting Together at Gezer," *Jerusalem Post*, September 16, 1977.

77. Sylvie Fogiel-Bijaoui, "Co-optation and Change: The Women's Sections of the Kibbutz," in *One Hundred Years of Kibbutz Life: A Century of Crises and Reinvention*, ed., Michal Palgi and Shulamit Reinhart (New Brunswick, NJ: Transaction, 2011), 75. Silver immigrated to Israel in the mid-1970s. As a leader of the Jewish Women's Movement she addressed the National Jewish Women's Conference in 1973. The title of her talk was "Sexism in the Jewish Student Community." The talk was published in *Response*. Vivian Silver Salowitz, "Sexism in the Jewish Student Community," *Response: The Jewish Woman—An Anthology* (summer 1973), 55–58.

78. Sylvie Fogiel-Bijaoui, "Co-optation and Change," 75.

79. Members of Ketura and Gezer founded this interkibbutz committee.

80. Judie Oren, "Women and the Kibbutz," *The Jerusalem Post*, July 15, 1983, 9.

81. Batya Ariel et al., eds., "Sasa Haggadah," ca. spring 1949, 17 (Sasa archives).

82. Batya Ariel, oral history, 15.

83. Esty Kofsky, oral history, 23.

84. One example is the Christian Kibbutz Nes Ammin in the Western Galilee.

85. Mike Solouney, oral history, 26.

86. Letter from Leah Kayman to Charlotte Jacobson, April 4, 1982, Box 14, "Kibbutz Ketura Correspondence 1973–1984 (two folders)," Hadassah Collection (RG8), American Jewish Historical Society, New York.

87. Letter from Shlomo Hillel, speaker of the Kenneset, to Kibbutz Ketura members, Box 14, "Kibbutz Ketura Awards," Hadassah Collection (RG8), American Jewish Historical Society, New York.

88. Matthew Nesvisky, "Getting Together at Gezer," *Jerusalem Post*, September 16, 1977.

89. Miri Gold, talk at congregation Beth-El, Berkeley, California, March 13, 2013.

90. "Rabbi Miri Gold, the 'Poster Girl' of the Battle to Recognize Non-Orthodox Rabbis," accessed March 12, 2014, www.haaretz.com/jewish-world/jewish-world-news/rabbi-miri-gold-the-poster-girl-of-the-battle-to-recognize-non-orthodox-rabbis.premium-1.433204.

91. This is a very complex issue. Gold will be paid by the Culture Ministry by the Religious Council, which pays the Orthodox. The court decision is to be enforced in only rural not urban districts. See "Historic Decision in Israel: Rabbi Miri Gold Recognized by State," accessed March 12, 2014, http://urj.org/about/union/pr/2012/?syspage=article&item_id=89826. See Amada Borscel-Dan, "A Landmark Baby Step to Religious Pluralism," accessed March 12, 2014, www.timesofisrael.com/a-landmark-baby-step-to-religious-pluralism; accessed March 12, 2014, http://urj.org/about/union/pr/2012/?syspage=article&item_id=89826; accessed March 12, 2014, www.haaretz.com/jewish-world/jewish-world-news/rabbi-miri-gold-the-poster-girl-of-the-battle-to-recognize-non-orthodox-rabbis.premium-1.433204.

92. Yossi Klein Halevi as qtd. in Sue Fishkoff, "The '67 Paradigm Plays Out Differently in Israel, U.S.," *J. The Jewish News Weekly of Northern California*, May 3, 2013, accessed March 12, 2014, www.jweekly.com/article/full/68479/the-column-the-67-paradigm-plays-out-differently-in-israel-u.s.

93. Because future kibbutzniks moved into completed buildings, not tents as had earlier generations, and were given more institutional support, there was some jealousy between new immigrants and veteran kibbutzniks. At Ketura, the buildings were left by the army. Part of the normal process of kibbutz building had become the conversion of army settlements into kibbutzim.

94. Landon Y. Jones, *Great Expectations* (New York: Ballantine, 1980), 1.

95. Arnon Magen, "From Ein HaShofet to Ketura and Yahel: The North American Immigration to Israel Celebrating Its Jubilee," *Davar*, June 6, 1982. Translated from Hebrew.

96. Comment made by Miri Gold, talk at congregation Beth-El, Berkeley, California, March 13, 2013.

97. Other exceptions include Jews from India, Mexico, Canada, Great Britain, South Africa, and Australia.

98. Batya Ariel, oral history, 21. Ariel elaborated, "Americans were admired . . . because they left their families . . . because [to] people who had lost their families, the family was exceeding important."

99. Ibid.

100. Ibid., 22.

101. Bayta Ariel, transcript, 13–14.

102. Bayta Ariel, "Sasa—July 1984," *Hei Newsletter* (February 1985), n.p.

103. Founded in 1985, Har Halutz was established by American Reform Jews in the central Galilee.

104. Michael Livni, "Ecology, Eco-Zionism, and the Kibbutz," in *One Hundred Years of Kibbutz Life: a Century of Crises and Reinvention* ed. Michael Palgi and Shulamit Reinharz (New Brunswick, NJ: Transaction, 2011), 310.

105. Dan Cohen, "The Good Life, on a Kibbutz," *Haaretz*, September 22, 2010, accessed March 12, 2014, www.haaretz.com/print-edition/features/the-good-life-on-a-kibbutz-1.315085.

106. Marie Syrkin, "Golda Meir and Other Americans," in Brinner and Rischin, *Like All the Nations?*, 115.

CONTRIBUTORS

TOBIAS BRINKMANN is the Malvin and Lea Bank Associate Professor of Jewish Studies and History at Penn State University, University Park. Between 2004 and 2008 he taught in the Department of History and the Parkes Institute for the Study of Jewish/non-Jewish Relations at the University of Southampton, UK. He is currently working on a study about Jewish migration from Eastern Europe between 1860 and 1960. Recent publications: *Sundays at Sinai: A Jewish Congregation in Chicago* (University of Chicago Press, 2012); Editor, *Points of Passage: Jewish Transmigrants from Eastern Europe in Scandinavia, Germany, and Britain 1880–1914* (Berghahn, 2013).

ELLEN EISENBERG is the Dwight and Margaret Lear Professor of American History at Willamette University in Salem, Oregon, where she has taught since 1990. She is the author of *Jewish Agricultural Colonies in New Jersey, 1882–1920* (1995), *The First to Cry Down Injustice? Western Jews and Japanese Removal during WWII* (a 2008 National Jewish Book Award finalist), and *Jews of the Pacific Coast: Reinventing Community on America's Edge* (2010), coauthored with Ava F. Kahn and William Toll. She is currently working on two books on Jews in Oregon. The first, a collection of essays spanning the pioneer period to the mid-twentieth century, is being published by Oregon State University Press. The second, which she will be researching and writing in 2014–2015, is sponsored by the Oregon Jewish Museum and will focus on the period from 1950 to 2010.

ERIC L. GOLDSTEIN is the Judith London Evans Director of the Tam Institute for Jewish Studies at Emory University, where he is also Associate Professor of History and Jewish Studies. He is the author of *The Price of Whiteness:*

Jews, Race, and American Identity (Princeton University Press, 2006) and is currently completing a history of the reading culture of Eastern European Jewish immigrants to America.

JONATHAN GOLDSTEIN, PhD in history, University of Pennsylvania, 1973, has been a research associate of Harvard University's John K. Fairbank Center for Chinese Studies since 1985 and a professor of East Asian History at the University of West Georgia, Carrollton, since 1981. His books include *Philadelphia and the China Trade* (1978), *Georgia's East Asian Connection* (1982; rev. ed. 1990), *America Views China* (1991), *China and Israel* (English ed. 1999, rev. Chinese ed. 2006, rev. Hebrew ed. forthcoming 2014), *The Jews of China* (2 vols., 1999 and 2000), and Stephen Girard's *Trade with China* (2011).

AVA F. KAHN is a former research associate at the Western Jewish History Center, Magnes Museum and fellow at the California Studies Center, Berkeley. Her publications include *Jewish Voices of the California Gold Rush: A Documentary History 1849–1880* (Wayne State University Press, 2002); *Jewish Life in the American West* (Autry Museum of Western Heritage, 2002, 2004); *California Jews* coedited with Marc Dollinger (Brandeis University Press, 2003, 2011) and *Jews of the Pacific Coast: Reinventing Community on America's Edge*, coauthored with Ellen Eisenberg and William Toll (University of Washington Press, 2010). She is working on a documentary film on Jewish reinvention in the post-1960s and researching the role of American Jews in the military and on the home front during WWI.

REBECCA KOBRIN is the Russell and Bettina Knapp Associate Professor of American Jewish History at Columbia University. Her book *Jewish Bialystok and Its Diaspora* (Indiana, 2010)—a transnational study of East European Jewish migration—was awarded the Jordan Schnitzer prize and was a National Jewish Book Award finalist. She is also the editor of *Chosen Capital: The Jewish Encounter with American Capitalism* (Rutgers, 2012) and is currently completing a book on failed Jewish immigrant bankers and American finance.

ADAM D. MENDELSOHN is an associate professor of Jewish Studies and the Director of the Pearlstine/Lipov Center for Southern Jewish Culture at the College of Charleston. He specializes in the history of Anglophone Jewish communities in the period prior to eastern European mass migration. He is the author of *The Rag Race* (NYU Press, 2014), about Jewish involvement in the clothing trade in the United States and the British Empire in the nineteenth century. He co-edited *Jews and the Civil War: A Reader* (2010) with Jonathan D. Sarna.

LARA RABINOVITCH received her PhD from New York University in 2012. She is the coeditor of *Choosing Yiddish: New Frontiers of Language and Culture* (2012) and is now working on a book about pastrami and Little Rumania on New York's Lower East Side.

JOAN G. ROLAND is a professor of history at Pace University in New York City. Her book *Jews in British India: Identity in a Colonial Era* (University Press of New England/Brandeis, 1989) appeared in a second edition, with an epilogue, as *The Jewish Communities of India: Identity in a Colonial Era* (Transaction, 1998). She has published numerous articles and book chapters on Indian Jews in India and Israel and is now focusing on the Indian Jewish community in the United States.

SUZANNE D. RUTLAND, MA (Hons), PhD, Dip Ed, OAM, is professor in the Department of Hebrew, Biblical and Jewish Studies, University of Sydney. She has published widely on Australian Jewish history, including Jewish migration and Jewish women in Australia, as well as writing on the Holocaust, Israel, and Jewish education. Her latest books are *The Jews in Australia* (Cambridge University Press, 2005) and *Nationality Stateless: Destination Australia* (Jewish Museum of Australia and JDC, 2008) coauthored with Sarah Rood. She received a government grant from the Australian Prime Ministers Centre for research on Australia and the campaign for Soviet Jewry and is writing a book on this topic with Australian Jewish journalist Sam Lipski. In 2008 she received the Medal of the Order of Australia for services to Higher Jewish Education and interfaith dialogue.

INDEX

Bold locators reference images in the text.